God Reveals

God Reveals

An Introduction to the Bible

Ave Maria Press AVE Notre Dame, Indiana

The Subcommittee on the Catechism, United States Conference of Catholic Bishops, has found this catechetical text, copyright 2025, to be in conformity with the *Catechism of the Catholic Church* and that it fulfills the requirements of Core Course I of the *Doctrinal Elements of a Curriculum Framework for the Development of Catechetical Materials for Young People of High School Age*.

Nihil Obstat: Reverend Monsignor Michael Heintz, PhD
Censor Librorum

Imprimatur: Most Reverend Kevin C. Rhoades
Bishop of Fort Wayne–South Bend
Given at Fort Wayne, Indiana, on 16 January 2024

The *Nihil Obstat* and *Imprimatur* are official declarations that a book or pamphlet is free of doctrinal or moral error. No implication is contained therein that those who have granted the *Nihil Obstat* or *Imprimatur* agree with its contents, opinions, or statements expressed.

Textbook Writers
Michael Amodei
Michael Pennock

Educational Consultant
Sara Burmeister, PhD
Assistant Clinical Professor
College of Education
Marquette University

Founded in 1865, Ave Maria Press is a ministry of the United States Province of Holy Cross.

Engaging Minds, Hearts, and Hands for Faith® is a trademark of Ave Maria Press, Inc.

www.avemariapress.com

Paperback: ISBN-13 978-1-64680-324-8

E-book: ISBN-13 978-1-64680-325-5

Cover image "Abraham and Melchizedech" by Pierre Paul Rubens. Photo by Leemage / Corbis via Getty Images.

Cover design by Christopher D. Tobin.

Text design by Andy Wagoner.

Printed and bound in the United States of America.

> *Sacred art* is true and beautiful when its form corresponds to its particular vocation: evoking and glorifying, in faith and adoration, the transcendent mystery of God—the surpassing invisible beauty of truth and love visible in Christ, who "reflects the glory of God and bears the very stamp of his nature," in whom "the whole fullness of deity dwells bodily." This spiritual beauty of God is reflected in the most holy Virgin Mother of God, the angels, and saints. Genuine sacred art draws man to adoration, to prayer, and to the love of God, Creator and Savior, the Holy One and Sanctifier.
>
> *Catechism of the Catholic Church*, 2502

We will begin each chapter with a short study and reflection on a piece of sacred art in order to visually portray an important aspect of our faith and to pass on this wonderful tradition of our Catholic faith.

CONTENTS

God Wants to Be Known

Saint Matthew and the Angel and *The Inspiration of Saint Matthew*

Caravaggio

You may wonder how some of the most classic and well-known paintings and sculptures are found in Catholic churches, especially in the many churches in Rome. The answer is the Church recruited and commissioned artists to fill their churches with beautiful pieces that would tell the story of the history of God's People, focusing on ultimately Jesus Christ, God's Son who came into the world. Wealthy benefactors would pay artists handsomely to decorate churches, often suggesting the subject of the art and an overall theme.

This was the case in the early seventeenth century when San Luigi dei Francesi, a parish of French-speaking Catholics in Rome, hired Michele Angelo Merisi (1571–1610), known simply by the name of his hometown "Caravaggio," to paint three canvases detailing aspects of the life of St. Matthew, the author of the first Gospel.

Caravaggio was an interesting person. He had first arrived in Rome homeless, barely wearing any clothes. He had a violent temper and often carried a sword. He was charged with killing a man in a dispute, resulting in a death-penalty conviction that he appealed and finally had overturned. Nevertheless, his career as an artist prospered. He specialized in realism, which was important to the Church at the time, as the Church had just experienced a split due to the Protestant Reformation. Protestants preferred a bare sanctuary and little artwork.

Caravaggio completed his first two pieces, *The Martyrdom of Saint Matthew* and *The Calling of Saint Matthew*. Both were well received. He ran into some problems with the benefactor and the parish over his third canvas. The subject was meant to show how Matthew received divine inspiration as he composed his Gospel. Caravaggio's first attempt, called *Saint Matthew and the Angel* (left), was rejected. They did not want Matthew portrayed as if desolate with bare legs and sitting on a wobbly chair. Also the closeness of the angel interlocking his body with Matthew's was considered too risqué to be placed in the church.

In his second take, *The Inspiration of Saint Matthew* (right), Caravaggio portrays Matthew in a more scholarly pose. Also, the angel is separated from Matthew at a more acceptable distance. Matthew's stool is firmly planted, and his legs are covered. This painting still hangs in a side chapel at San Luigi dei Francesi. (The first painting was destroyed by fire in a Berlin aircraft bunker in 1945 and is known today only from black-and-white photographs.)

Focus Question

How can I know God?

Chapter Overview

Introduction
Discovering God

Section 1
Our Built-In Desire for God

Section 2
God Is Revealed through Human Reason

Section 3
God Reveals More of Himself

Section 4
God Records His Revelation

Introduction

DISCOVERING GOD

While an increasing number of teenagers count themselves as disaffiliated from organized religion, "the vast majority (85 percent) of US adolescents say they believe in God or a universal spirit, including 40 percent who are absolutely certain about this belief and 34 percent who are fairly certain."[1]

Drilling down a bit, one of the central beliefs that most people have about God is that "God is good." This makes sense. It is likely that if we thought of God as evil and vindictive, we would probably spend our time cowering from God's presence, and trying to appease him to keep us from his wrath.

People who believe in God also associate God with creation, not only creation of the planet that we live on, but also of our own personal lives as human beings. Even people who accept that the universe began from a random combustion of particles devoid of a Creator, usually do not hold that their own life and uniqueness was a similar confluence of chance. Instead, people who acknowledge a Creator God understand God to be personal and loving, creating each of us with knowledge of us and out of love for us.

Also, and different from many people who lived in earlier generations, most people today who acknowledge God believe there is but one God. This seems natural to us now, but it wasn't always so. Monotheism did not originate with the Israelites, but the self-Revelation of One God to the Chosen People of the Old Testament was developed in their history. Monotheism contradicts not only *atheism* (belief in no God), but also *polytheism* (belief in many gods) and *pantheism* (belief that God and nature are the same). Accurately, of the major religions, only Judaism, Christianity, and Islam are purely monotheistic.

Pope Francis receives in audience the members of the International Theological Commission at the Vatican. This commission is made up of thirty theologians who advise the pope and the Magisterium.

The Study of God

You know the suffix "-logy" means "study of" (e.g., biology is the "study of life"). Theology is the name for the study of God. *Theo* as a prefix derives from the ancient Greek word *theos*, for God. Theology is different from other fields of study because it is not a field where data can be used to prove a hypothesis. Rather, theology presumes faith. St. Anselm of Canterbury (1033–1109) described theology as *fides quaerens intellectum*—that is, "faith seeking understanding." For Catholic theology, this requires beginning with a personal adherence to a definite set of beliefs. Catholic theology focuses on three aspects of faith: first, it is attentive to the Bible, the Word of God; second, it remains consciously faithful to the Church; and third, it is ordered to communicating the divine truth to all men and women in ways they can understand.

Listening to God's Word from the Bible is the primary principle of Catholic theology. Pope Benedict XVI wrote that "where theology is not essentially the interpretation of the Church's Scripture, such theology no longer has a foundation" (*Verbum Domini*, 35, cf. 31). The Bible was written and formed by members of the Judeo-Christian community, under God's inspiration. Jesus Christ, himself, is the one Word of Scripture; it is his life that is previewed in the Old Testament, shared in the Gospels, and witnessed to among the early Christians who composed and listened to the New Testament epistles. In the Scriptures, God speaks particularly in creation, through the prophets, and especially in the life, Death, and Resurrection of Jesus Christ.

However, it is accurate to say that Catholics understand the Bible differently than many other Christians. The Church's International Theological Commission pointed out that the Christian faith is not a "religion of the book." Rather, it is a "religion of the Word of God," not of "a written and mute word, but of the incarnate and living Word."[2] Catholics believe that **Sacred Scripture** is "the speech of God as it is put down in writing under the breath of the Holy Spirit."[3] One of the things this means is that the Bible cannot be interpreted only according to the way it was intended for its original audience. The Word of God is alive and its message applied anew in each generation.

It was the Church herself, in the first century, that determined which writings were to be in included in the Bible. The complete list is called the canon of the Bible. God continues to guide the Church's **Magisterium** in every generation to preserve, expound on, and spread God's Word to all. This action is associated with **Sacred Tradition**. As means for sharing God's Revelation, both Sacred Scripture and Sacred Tradition "must be accepted and honored with equal sentiments of devotion and reverence."[4]

Regarding other Christians who consider themselves to belong to a "church of the book," they do not assign equal weight to Sacred Scripture and Sacred Tradition. For them, every human concern can be answered in the pages of the Scripture, with the interpretation of passages often being taken literally and according to whatever way individuals choose to understand them.

Sacred Scripture The written transmission of the Church's Gospel message found in the Church's teaching, life, and worship. It is faithfully preserved, handed down, and interpreted by the Church's Magisterium.

Magisterium The official teaching authority of the Church. Christ bestowed the right and power to teach in his name on St. Peter and the Apostles and their successors. The Magisterium is the bishops in communion with the successor of Peter, the bishop of Rome (the pope).

Sacred Tradition The living transmission of the Church's Gospel message found in the Church's teaching, life, and worship. It is faithfully preserved, handed down, and interpreted by the Church's Magisterium.

Jesus is the Aplha and the Omega, the beginning and the end.

Given the criteria mentioned here, the intention of this course is to study how the one, good, Creator God reveals himself to human beings through **natural revelation** and **Divine Revelation**. One of the two sources of Divine Revelation is Sacred Scripture, the Bible; the other is Sacred Tradition. Both flow from the same source (God) and have the same goal (human salvation through Christ). Together they comprise what is called the **Deposit of Faith**.

This course will particularly focus on how God the Father fully revealed himself in the Divine Second Person of the Holy Trinity as told in the Bible. To come to a deeper understanding of how this is true, it is important to understand how the Bible is the inspired Word of God. Along with this, we must understand how the Bible was formed, how it should be read, and how it accompanies the Sacred Tradition of the Church. These are among the main topics you will explore in this course.

---

natural revelation The knowledge of the existence of God and his basic attributes that can be derived by human reason while reflecting on created order.

Divine Revelation The way God communicates knowledge of himself to humankind, a self-communication realized by his actions and words over time and most fully realized by the sending of his divine Son, Jesus Christ.

Deposit of Faith "The heritage of faith contained in Sacred Scripture and Sacred Tradition, handed down in the Church from the time of the Apostles, from which the Magisterium draws all that it proposes for belief as being divinely revealed" (*CCC*, glossary).

SECTION *Assessment*

Comprehension

1. What do most US teenagers believe about God?
2. Differentiate between monotheism, polytheism, and pantheism.
3. How is theology different from other fields of study?
4. Explain the difference between belonging to a "church of the book" and a "religion of the Word of God."

Vocabulary

5. Define *Magisterium*.
6. Explain *natural revelation* in comparison with *Divine Revelation*.

Reflection

7. How do you understand the Bible to be "divinely inspired"?

Section 1

OUR BUILT-IN DESIRE FOR GOD

How much of your life is ordered to the future? Do you imagine your life being better or more fulfilling when you:

- ☑ pass your driver's test?
- ☑ finish high school?
- ☑ get accepted to college?
- ☑ make enough money to live independently?
- ☑ fall in love?
- ☑ have your own family?
- ☑ retire?

Modern psychology presents the issue in a similar way, claiming that you will not be happy until a certain number of your basic needs—such as food, health, safety, love, and **self-esteem**—are met. American psychologist Abraham Maslow (1908–1970) developed a pyramid to represent a human's hierarchy of needs. In the pyramid, the most basic needs come first. According to Maslow, we

---

self-esteem A sense of happiness and contentment about who you are as a human being. People with self-esteem consciously appreciate their own worth and importance.

must first meet the basic needs before we even can become aware of the other needs. Maslow's pyramid looks like this:

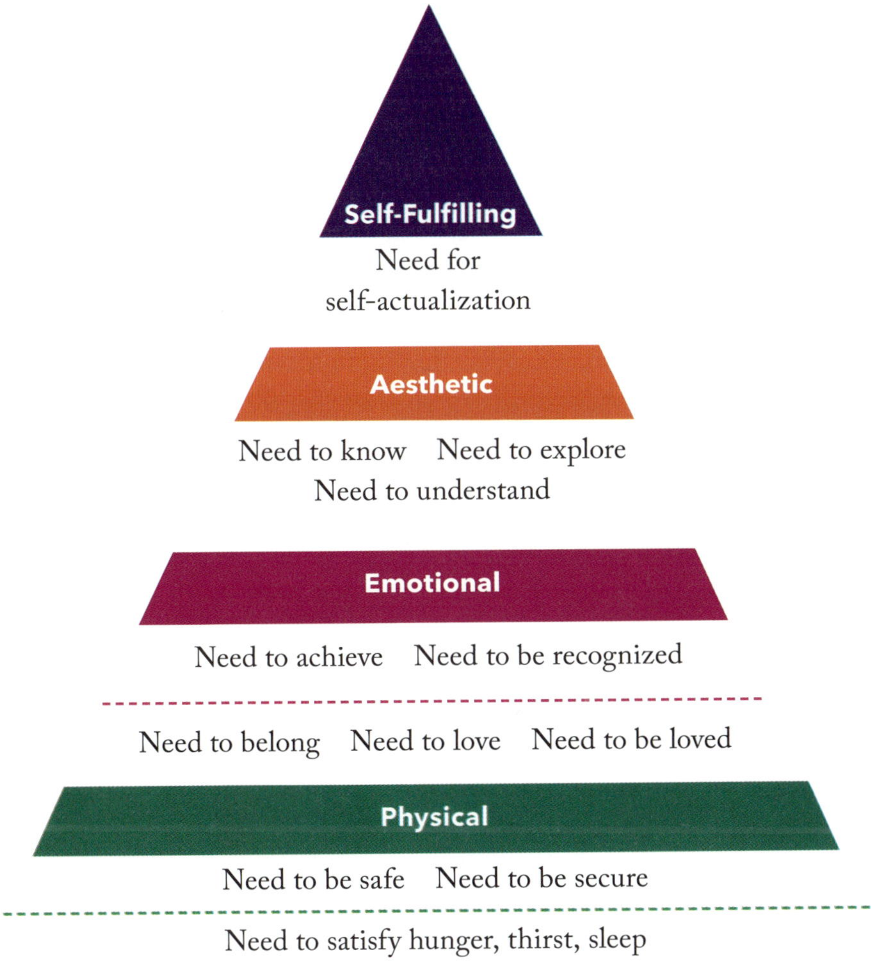

Maslow contended that once we are able to satisfy our physical needs, including our need for security, we are able to move to addressing our emotional needs. The emotional needs are related to the fact that human beings are social beings. We need to feel part of a group. We need to be loved and to be able to offer love. We need to have someone believe in us and to know we are competent. Emotional needs have a great effect on our self-esteem. Maslow also includes two higher levels in his hierarchy of needs. Aesthetic needs include an appreciation of beauty in many forms, as well as the need for order and balance in our lives. Finally, we have a desire, according to Maslow, to strive for our full potential as a person. This is a lifelong process and one that occurs the more we challenge ourselves.

Is happiness and fulfillment really only future-oriented? Is happiness and fulfillment something to be achieved by working through a series of steps or completing a set of goals? More importantly, is happiness and fulfillment even possible using Maslow's hierarchy of goals or completing a set of goals as referenced in the questions that opened this section?

Part I of the *Catechism of the Catholic Church* begins by clearly stating that only in God will we find happiness and truth and that "the desire for God is written in the human heart" (*CCC*, 27). Because we are created by and for God, the *Catechism* goes on to say that, similar to Maslow's hierarchy of needs, our quest is never over. We can never stop searching for God.

Pope Benedict XVI recognized that today there are many people who do not claim they have a desire for God. Rather than searching for something spiritual, they reach for things like concrete goods, career achievements, or human companionship in order to achieve satisfaction and happiness.

A Journey of Faith

Even when people will not acknowledge their desire for God, Pope Benedict pointed out that the very presence of the desire remains. The key, he said, is to recast our inauthentic desires into authentic ones and to show the satisfaction that comes with a search for God. He suggested two aspects.

The first, he said, was to "discover or rediscover the taste of the authentic joy of life." True joy, he pointed out, involves things that are *lasting* in several areas of life: family, friendship, solidarity with those who suffer, self-denial for the sake of the other, love of knowledge, art, and the beauty of nature. These are enduring things because you can imagine them carrying on past your life on earth and into eternity. For example, can you imagine building on relationships with family and friends in eternity? Can you imagine growing in greater appreciation of beauty in eternity? And can you imagine growing in knowledge—especially of God—in eternity? The very nature of eternity is that it has no end. These are lasting and productive things that will keep us very busy as we live forever.

The second aspect in a search for God, according to Pope Benedict, is "never to be content with what you have achieved." The path of incomplete desire is always open to God. Pope Benedict termed it a "healthy restlessness" that leads us to search for a deeper good while at the same time recognizing that restlessness directed to earthly things will not bring lasting satisfaction.[5] St. Augustine of Hippo (354–430) famously wrote that "our hearts are restless until they rest in God."

Five Desires that Point to God

Different from Maslow's hierarchy of needs and different from the consciousness of animals, human consciousness also desires spiritual experiences. Five typical spiritual experiences are desired often:

1. Perfect knowledge and truth
2. Perfect love
3. Perfect justice and goodness
4. Perfect beauty
5. Perfect home and being

Notice the word *perfect* before each of these experiences. We seek perfect representations of these things, something that is spiritual and beyond our earthly experiences. Our desire for perfection in these areas is what is spiritual about them. The desire for perfection is really a desire for God who is perfect.

Fr. Robert J. Spitzer, SJ, a philosopher and theologian, has written about how our unfulfilled satisfaction for these desires in this world is evidence for God. Think about how this works. Our desire for perfect knowledge and truth is evidenced from the time we are young. Have you ever been around a child who can't take an answer at face value? "Why?" and "Why is that?" are incessant questions children ask. We wonder why, even to adulthood, a person needs to ask "Why?" even though the answer has been given. The reason is that we know intuitively that all answers are in some way incomplete. There is always more to know. Our conscious and

Fr. Robert J. Spitzer, SJ

continual questioning is a sign that it is perfect knowledge and truth that we seek, answers that can be provided only by God.

We also desire perfect love, and we expect that in our human relationships. Does that ever happen? Have you ever witnessed a spouse in a marriage who is perfectly forgiving, self-giving, and honest at all times? Probably not. Yet, we have an idealized desire for this type of perfect love in our human relationships, including friendships. (You have probably been let down at one time or another by a close friend. And you have probably let down your close friend too.) Yet this desire for perfect and unconditional love does not leave us. It is not the desire that is in error; it's that we are looking in the wrong place. Only God can fulfill this desire for perfect and unconditional love.

Just as the young child screams, "Why?" he or she also can be heard saying, "That's not fair!" Adults, too, have a built-in sense for justice. We all wonder why people suffer, why there are wars, why some people have more than others. Again, this is a longing for perfect justice and goodness that cannot be ultimately achieved on earth. Perfect justice and goodness is a gift reserved to God and to be granted in his time.

Perfect beauty is also left to God. In this world, we find many beautiful things—sunsets, water views, music—but we eventually get bored with them or try to perfect them ourselves. Have you ever used filters on your phone camera to make a natural scene look "better"? Additionally, while we are attracted to "perfect beauty" we wonder what its origins are. This wonderment also leads us to God.

The fifth spiritual desire is for the perfect home and being. This equates to the desire—spoken of by politicians, religious leaders, and in Christmas cards—for peace, joy, love, and unity in our world. Not ever attained in the history of our world, these desires likewise translate to our desire for the perfect home, a home that is with and made by God.[6]

Even though we may go through times in life when we ignore or reject God, "he never ceases to call every person to seek him, so as to find life and happiness" (*CCC*, 30). This search for God requires the effort of our mind and will, as well as the help of others. Some of the ways to know God can be accomplished by our own human reason.

SECTION *Assessment*

Comprehension

1. According to Maslow, what is necessary in order to be aware of higher-level human needs?
2. Is happiness only future-oriented? Explain your response.
3. According to Pope Benedict XVI, what are two aspects of desire?
4. How does the word *perfect* before our earthly desires make them spiritual desires?

Vocabulary

5. Define *self-esteem*.

Reflection

6. Why do you think people from childhood to adulthood ask "Why?" or "Why is that?" even if they have been given the answer?
7. What is something you imagine bringing fulfillment to your life in the future?

Section 2

GOD IS REVEALED THROUGH HUMAN REASON

This book is about how God is made known through Sacred Scripture, the Bible. But before moving on to that primary topic, let's consider people who may never once have the opportunity to read the Bible. Would these people be deprived of ever knowing about God? The Catholic Church answers clearly, "No, they would not."

The Church recognizes that knowing God is connected with faith, *and* it is also a matter of knowledge. A person can know that God exists by deducing evidence observed in nature; that is what is known as natural revelation. Many philosophers and great thinkers throughout history have come to believe in God based solely on their ability to think and reason. These include ancient pre-Christian philosophers such as Plato and Aristotle, and United States founding fathers Thomas Jefferson and Benjamin Franklin. Those who recognize the existence of God by human reason but reject Divine Revelation (see Section 3, "God Reveals More of Himself") are called **deists**.

More recently, the most renowned atheist philosopher of the late twentieth century, Dr. Antony Flew (1923–2010), came to acknowledge God at the end of his life. Flew was influenced by Aristotelian arguments of a god who has super characteristics of power and intelligence (though Aristotle never used the term *god*). This is commonly called the "teleological argument," which states that the intricacies of the design in nature require an Intelligent Designer (God).

The teleological argument has grown in acceptance with advances in the understanding of DNA. Formerly, it was possible to think of microscopic forms of life as simply blobs of protoplasm that were generated randomly by natural forces. Research showed that even the simplest single-celled creature studied

---

deist One who believes in God based only on natural reason, not on any specific Divine Revelation or teachings of a religion.

Dr. Antony Flew

has DNA with 482 genes comprising 580,000 amino base pairs. Antony Flew came to the conclusion that there is mathematically virtually no chance of such complexity of a living organism arising naturally. In a 2004 symposium, Flew said: "What I think DNA material has done is to show that intelligence must have been involved in getting these extraordinarily diverse elements together. . . . The enormous complexity by which the results were achieved look to me like the work of intelligence."[7]

Discovering God by human reason is often the first step in accepting Revelation that can come only from God (e.g., the existence of an afterlife∞). Understanding natural revelation is an important tool as you make your way in a world where your contemporaries use science as the ultimate arbiter of what is true. Just make sure to be aware of incorrect premises about God (and creation) that can come from using our human reason. For example, *Scientific American* published a piece by Dr. Avi Loeb, former chair of the astronomy department at Harvard University and a member of the President's Council of Advisors on Science and Technology. Loeb proposed that it was possible that our universe was created in a laboratory by beings from a civilization more advanced than ours who used quantum mechanics to do so. Loeb said these other-worldly creators of what he called our "baby universe" would study the advancements in our universe to perpetuate knowledge and to create other baby universes moving forward. Loeb's interesting premise was meant to dissuade the acknowledgment of a sole Intelligent Designer, or God. Catholic scientist Dr. Stacy Trasancos called it really "a throwback to ancient myths, with a modern-day quantum twist." She added that "it still runs into the old question, 'Who created the laboratory and designer?'"[8] This question about

∞ Note

Antony Flew never accepted belief in an afterlife as it was something that could not be revealed to him through reason. He did say, however, that while he did not "believe in the God of any revelatory system, I am open to that."

life's origins was answered years ago by Aristotle and his deduction of a "prime mover and first cause" and later incorporated by St. Thomas Aquinas (1223–1274), a **Doctor of the Church**, and one of the greatest scholars in Church history, who offered five proofs of God's existence based on human reason.

Aquinas's Five Ways for God's Existence

Note that the "five ways" for God's existence offered by St. Thomas Aquinas in his classic work *Summa Theologiae* (*Summary of Theology*) are not proofs in the sense that science would define the term today.[9] Rather, they are "converging and convincing arguments" (*CCC,* 310) for the existence of God. His arguments are based on (1) motion, (2) causality, (3) contingency, (4) degrees of perfection, and (5) design. The first three arguments are "cosmological arguments"—that is, based on the understanding that the cosmos or universe requires a first cause, which is God. Note also that the fifth way, design, is based on the teleological argument that convinced Antony Flew that there is a God.

Aquinas's first three ways, the cosmological arguments, are these:

1. God is the Prime Mover.

Our senses can observe that many things are in motion. The earth itself is in motion. The scientific definition of *motion* is "the reduction of something from potentiality to actuality." For example, fire, which is *actually* hot, makes wood, which is *potentially* hot, to be *actually* hot. Similarly, something that is potentially in motion cannot be actually in motion unless it is moved by another force. Think about a boulder that plunges down a hill after an earthquake or after being pushed by a tractor. The earthquake and the tractor are examples of the force or the mover. Taking this example back a step, the force that caused the movement would also have needed something to move it.

The world is in motion in both time and space. For there to be motion there must have been a "prime mover" or "first mover" who started everything. That "unmoved mover" is God.

Doctor of the Church A Church writer of great learning and holiness whose works the Church has highly recommended for studying and living the faith.

2. God is the First Cause.

Consider how Johannes Kepler (1571–1630), a German astronomer, used the cosmological argument of the "first cause" to convince his friend of God's existence.

Kepler discovered that the earth and planets traveled around the sun in elliptical orbits. One of his closest friends insisted that God did not exist and that the universe began and operates by its own means. Kepler made a model of the sun with the planets circling around it. When the friend saw the ingenious model, he commented, "How beautiful! Who made it?"

Tongue in cheek, Kepler answered, "No one made it; it made itself."

His friend rejected the answer and insisted that Kepler tell him who made the model.

The famous astronomer then answered, "Friend, you say that this toy could not make itself. But listen to yourself. This model is but a very weak imitation of the vast universe, which I think you said made itself."

Nothing causes itself. Even a model, like the one made by Kepler, requires a creator. Everything that exists results from something or someone that came before it. Logically, there has to be a first cause or "uncaused cause" that is eternal and started the universe off.

3. God is the Necessary Being.

Contingency, a main premise of Aquinas's third way, is connected with the Big Bang Theory. Contingency refers to something that depends on something else in order to happen. The Big Bang Theory is the name for the most-cited current explanation and cosmological model of how the universe began. It states that the universe began with one small particle (atom) that then inflated over millions of years to form the present cosmos while continuing its expansion.

Yet, the "one small particle" that began the expansion must have always existed and had no beginning. "Nothing" cannot create "something." For anything to exist, there must be a necessary, eternal being (God) who always existed and brought other beings into existence.

Cosmologist and atheist Stephen Hawking admitted that the Big Bang Theory constitutes an argument for God. "If the rate of expansion of the universe one second after the Big Bang had been smaller by even one part in a hundred thousand million million, the universe would have already recollapsed before it reached its present size." Without the intervention of a necessary being, human life would have been impossible.

The fourth way is based on the procession of degrees from less to more—for example, "more true" or "less true."

4. God is the Absolute Being.

It is possible to recognize different degrees of not only truth, but also goodness, justice, beauty, and so on in the world. Think of the words "good, better, best" or qualifying something as "most beautiful." You can only speak of such different degrees of qualities by comparing them to a supreme model or absolute being as a reference point: God.

In other words, things cannot be more perfect or less perfect unless there is a wholly perfect being. Whatever is perfect is the cause of the less than perfect—that is, the higher is the cause of the lower. The grades of a student with the 3.8 GPA, a very good average, are nonetheless "less perfect" when compared to someone who has a perfect 4.0 GPA. This means that there must be a perfect being, which is the cause of perfections of the less-than-perfect beings. This is the perfect or absolute being, God.

Finally, the fifth way, based on the teleological argument, is this:

5. God is the Grand Designer.

The world contains beauty, symmetry, and power that only a grand designer could create. The earth's environment is a marvel in itself. As far as we know there are no other planets in our solar system able to sustain life.

Prominent scientists have a difficult time imagining the possibility of human life forming in the universe out of chance alone. Other scientists who remain skeptical that God created the universe and life in it have

> not been able to prove that the universe created itself or evolved from matter.
>
> Someone must have put the laws into nature that make human life in a well-ordered universe possible. There is more evidence that God is the Creator than there is that he is not.

In summary, St. Thomas Aquinas's arguments for the existence of God point out that dependent beings exist and that all dependent beings must have a cause for their dependent existence. The "first cause" cannot also be a dependent being, which means that there must be a first "uncaused cause" of the existence of every dependent being. Aquinas's five ways do have limits. For example, they are all based on the experiences of our senses, which are not infallible. However, if his arguments were determined to be valid, they would prove the existence of God in an established scientific method.

Contemplating Creation and the Human Person

Using your senses and reason, you can uncover that God exists and identify some of his attributes as did St. Thomas Aquinas. The bishops of the First Vatican Council (1869–1870) captured this truth: "The same Holy Mother Church holds and teaches that God, the source and end of all things, can be known with certainty from the consideration of created things, by the natural power of human reason" (*Dei Filius*, chapter 2, quoted in *CCC*, 36). The *Catechism* also reminds us that the way of approaching God by using human reason has a "twofold point of departure" (*CCC*, 32). These two ways are through our contemplation of creation and our contemplation of the human person.

In fact, the first verse of the first book in the Bible (Gn 1:1) states that God is the Creator of the universe. The writer of the Book of Wisdom in the Old Testament suggests that those who cannot determine God from his creation are fools:

> Foolish by nature were all who were in
> ignorance of God.
> and who from the good things seen did not
> succeed in knowing the one who is,
> and from studying the works did not
> discern the artisan. (Ws 13:1)

And St. Paul emphasizes in the Letter to the Romans that human beings can discover the existence of God by studying his creation: "Ever since the creation of the world, his invisible attributes of eternal power and divinity have been able to be understood and perceived in what he has made" (Rom 1:29).

Human reason and intelligence will lead most people to ask, regarding the created world, "Where do these beautiful things come from?" St. Augustine suggested this path of inquiry:

> Question the beauty of the earth, question the beauty of the sea, question the beauty of the air distending and diffusing itself, question the beauty of the sky, . . . question all these realities. All respond: "See, we are beautiful." Their beauty is a profession. These beauties are subject to change. Who made them if not the Beautiful One who is not subject to change? (*Sermo* 241, 2, in PL, 38, 1134, quoted in *CCC*, 32)

An examination of human behaviors and tendencies in general or an honest reflection on your own thoughts as a human person can also help you to gain an understanding of God and how to approach him. Is it an accident that human beings possess a longing that the material world cannot satisfy? You probably sense that life has meaning because *your* life has meaning. Your study, hard work, self-discipline, and desire to develop your skills mean something because they all help you to become the person God intended you to be.

Though honest thinking can help you discover God's existence, the human reason and senses that can help you learn about God can also confuse you. Your mind is hampered from discovering naturally knowable truths by passion, imagination, and sin. Sin can lead you to persuade yourself that one of God's revealed truths is false. In order to avoid these dangers and enter into an intimate relationship with God, you need the help of God's **grace**. Building on what you discover through human reason, with God's grace, you can freely accept God's Revelation of himself by faith.

SECTION *Assessment*

Comprehension

1. How did DNA expand the acceptance of the "teleological argument" proving God's existence?
2. What is meant by the term "cosmological argument" in terms of proofs for God's existence?
3. On what are St. Thomas Aquinas's five arguments for God's existence based?
4. Explain how the existence of dependent beings points to a first "uncaused cause."
5. What is the twofold point of departure for contemplating God's existence?
6. How can sin hamper human reason?

Vocabulary

7. How did Antony Flew become a *deist*?
8. Define *grace*.

Reflection

9. Which of Aquinas's arguments for God's existence did you find most convincing? Least convincing? Explain.

---

grace The name for God's gifts to us that are free and undeserved and that assist us in responding to his call to be his adopted children.

Section 3

GOD REVEALS MORE OF HIMSELF

What do you associate with the word *reveal*? Do you think of the climactic scene in the *Wizard of Oz* when Toto the dog discovers a man behind the curtain, not the hoped-for wizard? Recently "reveal parties" have been popular, in which a man and a pregnant woman will smash a piñata or cut into a cake to reveal a color of confetti or frosting. If the color is blue, the couple is expecting a boy. If it is pink, they are expecting a girl.

The word *reveal* means "making previously unknown or secret information known to others." How can you connect this definition with God? How does God reveal previously unknown information about himself to human beings?

The Church speaks of two categories of Divine Revelation: private and public. Since private revelations are often the ones imagined when a person thinks of a revelation of God, let's address those types first. Have you ever believed that God is speaking directly to you? Some people think God (maybe through a deceased friend or relative) communicates to them through a dream, while at prayer, or even through a special song on the radio or a bird that perches on a window ledge! God *could* be speaking directly to a person in examples like these. Private revelations of this sort may help people connect with God and even live out their faith more fully. But it is extremely unlikely that these types of private revelations would be recognized by the Church as something in which others should believe.

There have been countless private revelations to saints and other Catholics over time. All of the **apparitions** of the Blessed Virgin Mary are considered private revelations. St. Hildegard of Bingen, St. Bridget of Sweden, and St. Teresa of Avila are among the many saints who received private revelations.

---

apparition An appearance of a heavenly being—Christ, Mary, an angel, or a saint.

The Basilica of the Sacred Heart in Paray-le-Monial, France, is the location of Alacoque's revelations.

Another example is St. Margaret Mary Alacoque (1647–1690), who began receiving private revelations just before her profession into the Order of Visitation as a sister. The visions continued over a number of months. On December 27, 1673, while praying before the Blessed Sacrament, she experienced a vision of Jesus's Sacred Heart as a symbol of his love for all people and this message from the Lord: "My divine Heart is so inflamed with love for mankind . . . that it can no longer contain within itself the flames of its burning charity and must spread them abroad by your means." Jesus also revealed to St. Margaret Mary twelve promises he would bestow on those who practiced devotion to his Sacred Heart (see Chapter 1 Review, Chapter Project 3).

The Church has established criteria to judge private revelations as well. The first is that private revelations do not add to or complete the Deposit of Faith. Second, the Magisterium must carefully analyze private revelations. Human beings are prone to forgetting facts and distorting memories. Also, there is always a possibility that Satan influences some private revelations. Third, a private revelation must not contradict the Deposit of Faith. Finally, even if the Church does approve a private revelation, the faithful are not obligated to believe in it. A faithful Catholic is only required to believe in the Deposit of Faith found in Sacred Scripture and Sacred Tradition.

Public revelation is the other type of Divine Revelation. Public revelation is what is included in the Church's Deposit of Faith—that is, Sacred Scripture and Sacred Tradition together. Remember, the Church does not derive the revealed truths of God from Sacred Scripture alone. Sacred Tradition hands

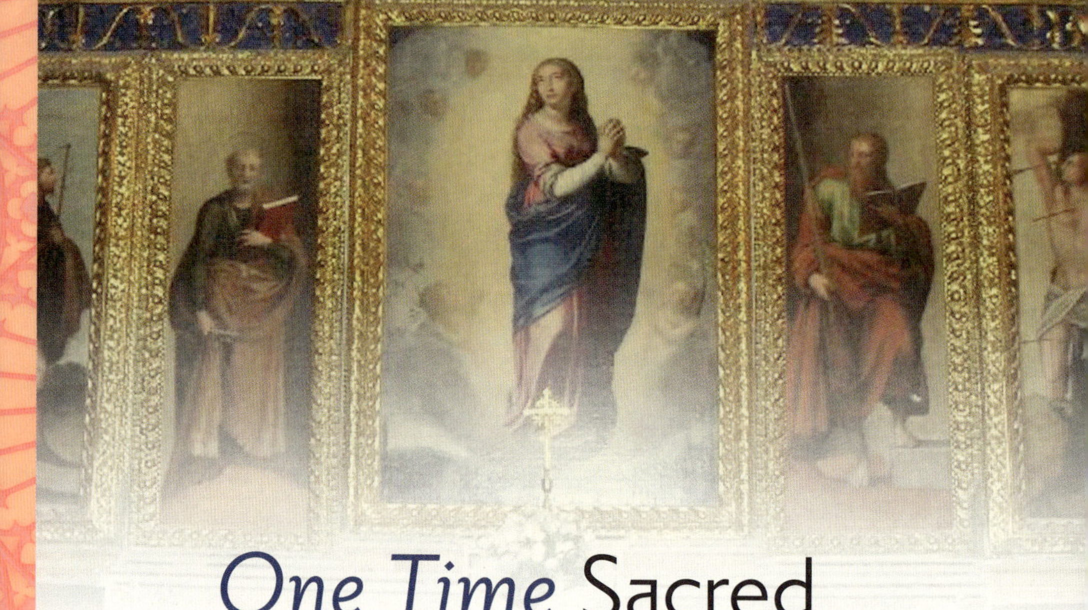

One Time Sacred Scripture *and* Sacred Tradition *Worked Together*

Focus Question: How can I know God?

In the mid-nineteenth century there were several revolutions in Europe, one of which caused the end of the Papal States in which the Catholic Church had politically controlled most of the land that is today Italy. In 1849, during the uproar, Pope Pius IX was forced to flee the Vatican. He took up residence for nine months at Gaeta, a city on the Mediterranean Sea south of Rome. While he was in Gaeta, the pope had several things on his mind in connection with the revolution. For one, he pondered the growing influence of modernism, which seemed to reject all supernatural truth. He considered ways the Church might respond.

Pope Pius also spent quite a bit of time at prayer during these months of exile, often before a painting of the Immaculate Conception by Scipione Pulzone, which was kept in what is called the Chapel of Gold. It was during this time that he felt God was speaking to him in prayer to proclaim a *dogma* on the Immaculate Conception—that is, that Mary, the Mother of God, was preserved from sin from the moment of her conception throughout her entire life. A *dogma* is a truth which the Church teaches that has been specifically revealed by God. Acceptance of dogma is essential for complete faith and the deepest possible relationship with God. Dogma is a function of Sacred Tradition as determined by the Church's Magisterium.

The belief that Mary was always pure and preserved from sin was already believed by many in the Church from at least the sixth century when Mary's birthday on September 8 was marked with a feast. That meant something special because the Church typically celebrated only the death of a saint, the day the person enters heaven and is forever free from sin. By celebrating Mary's *birth*, the Church was saying that Mary was sinless from the moment she was conceived.

Pope Pius IX had studied the history of belief in the Immaculate Conception before his time in Gaeta. Years before his proclamation, the pope had sent a letter to the bishops of the world to ask what they, their priests, and their people believed about the Immaculate Conception. An incredible 90 percent supported the belief and wanted the pope to proclaim it a dogma. In some way, this dogma about Mary was a clear reflection of the general belief of Catholics, both at that time and in preceding generations.

Something else Pope Pius had to consider was this: All dogma must have roots in Sacred Scripture. Did the Immaculate Conception qualify on that criterion? Several Scripture passages apply. In Genesis 3:15, God speaks directly to the devil, saying, "I will put enmity between you and the woman, and between your offspring and hers." This woman is revealed in the Letter to the Galatians to be Mary: "But when the fullness of time had come, God sent his Son, born of a woman, born under the law, to ransom those under the law, so that we might receive adoption" (Gal 4:4). Most prominently, when the Angel Gabriel comes to Mary to announce the birth of Jesus, he calls her "favored one"—that is, "full of grace" (Lk 1:28).

This famous early fifteenth-century work of Russian artist Andrei Rublev is called Trinity. *It depicts three angels who visited Abraham at the Oak of Mamre (Gn 18:1–8) and is considered an icon of the Blessed Trinity.*

Pope Pius IX defined the dogma of the Immaculate Conception with his encyclical *Ineffabilis Deus* (*Ineffable God*). In it he noted the history of devotion to Mary under that title and the testimonies he received from other bishops. He officially declared the dogma in these words:

> The most Blessed Virgin Mary was, from the first moment of her conception, by a singular grace and privilege of almighty God and by virtue of the merits of Jesus Christ, Savior of the human race, preserved immune from all stain of original sin. (*Ineffable God*, 2803, quoted in *CCC*, 491)

But the story of this dogma does not end there. Four years after his proclamation, on February 11, 1858, the miracle at Lourdes, France, occurred. There, the Blessed Virgin Mary appeared for the first time to a fourteen-year-old girl, Bernadette Soubirous. In one of the apparitions, Mary told St. Bernadette, "I am the Immaculate Conception." When the young girl announced the Lady's name to the local pastor, he was amazed. There was no way she could have known that title for Mary as it had not been told to her. It was a stunning revelation to the Church that Mary herself had confirmed the dogma. Never in the history of the Church had a teaching of faith received such obvious support from the spiritual realm.

Further Study and Reflection

- Tradition identifies the parents of Mary as Sts. Joachim and Anne. Write a short report that details the origins of that tradition. Also answer: "How did the Church determine September 8 to be the birthday of Mary?"
- Read the *Catechism of the Catholic Church*, 492. Quoting the Second Vatican Council document *Lumen Gentium*, it describes Mary as the "splendor of an entirely unique holiness" by which she is "enriched from the first instant of her conception." What do these descriptions of Mary mean? How are they connected to Christ's work of salvation?

Sculpture of the Virgin Mary in the sanctuary of Lourdes, France.

on God's Word, first given to the Apostles by Christ and the Holy Spirit, to the successors of the Apostles (the pope and bishops). Also enlightened by the Holy Spirit, they spread God's Word to the ends of the earth. The Church teaches that there is no further public Divine Revelation after Jesus's Passion, Death, and Resurrection. This does not mean that God stepped out of human history after Jesus ascended to heaven, but rather that Jesus has fulfilled the goal of salvation by redeeming all human beings from the power of sin. It is now the task of the Church to connect people with God through prayerful study of Sacred Scripture and Sacred Tradition. For this reason, the Church calls on Catholics to accept the divinely and publicly revealed Deposit of Faith.

What Is It God Wants to Reveal?

A synonym for Divine Revelation might be "Supernatural Revelation," not in a paranormal sense, but rather indicating that God shares with us his mysterious self at a level that we could never discover through nature or natural reason. Amazingly, the all-powerful and infinite God *wants* to make himself known to us and invite us into a relationship with him.

The one, true God is different from the imagined ancient gods, including the gods of the Romans and Greeks who only demanded that people worship and serve them. The one, true God is not a God of retribution who imposes

Giant images of the Holy Trinity are displayed on Good Friday in San Miguel, Philippines.

punishment on those who disobey or ignore him. Rather, he is a God of love. Mysteriously, God is also the Holy Trinity: Father, Son, and Holy Spirit. There are Three Divine Persons in one God. This is a mystery of the highest order, but try thinking of it this way: since God is love, does it make sense that he would be just one and all alone? The Holy Trinity is an active sharing of love between Three Divine Persons. The Father, the Son, and the Holy Spirit are equal and have existed for all eternity, meaning the Holy Trinity has no beginning or end.

People did not come to know about the Holy Trinity overnight. We know this because of the written record of Sacred Scripture. Although the Three Persons of the Holy Trinity always act together, Sacred Scripture associates creation and much of the Old Testament with the work of God the Father. Sacred Scripture records all of **salvation history** from the preparation for the coming of God the Son into the world, through the life, Death, and Resurrection of Christ on earth, to the coming of the Holy Spirit to the Apostles at Pentecost. The New Testament Letter to the Hebrews opens with a reflection that acknowledges the long preparation it took to reach this stage:

> In times past, God spoke in partial and various ways to our ancestors through the prophets; in these last days he spoke to us through a son, whom he made heir of all things and through whom he created the universe. (Heb 1:1)

Both our Jewish ancestors who lived prior to Christ and the first Christians passed on the events of salvation history orally before recording them in writing. The Old Testament records the steps in salvation history that prepare the way for the coming of Christ. The New Testament records the climax of salvation history, the coming of the preexisting Son of God into the world (see John 1:1–16).

---

salvation history The term used to describe God's presence and work throughout all of human history.

covenant A binding and solemn agreement between human beings or between God and people, holding each other to a particular course of action.

Chosen People A name to describe the descendants of Abraham who made a series of covenants with the one, true God. The Sinai Covenant made through Moses solidified them as God's chosen ones. Other names used for the Chosen People in the Old Testament are Israelites, Hebrews, and Jews.

The Stages of Divine Revelation

God's Revelation to humanity began with the creation of the world and the first human beings whom "he invited into intimate communion with himself and clothed them with resplendent grace and justice" (*CCC*, 54). This relationship was not ended when our first parents sinned. Beginning immediately afterward, God sought to save humanity "part by part" (*CCC*, 56) by establishing **covenants**, forming a **Chosen People**, calling prophets, and sharing his wisdom. All of these stages occurred before the birth of Christ:

With relationships damaged by sin, people kept hiding from God out of fear, as did Adam and Eve, and fleeing his call. Noah was a righteous man whom God saved from a flood along with his family and other creatures. God made a covenant with Noah in which he promised to never destroy the world again. This covenant was an early sign that God wanted to save *all* people (nations) from the punishment of sin.

Later, God called Abram from his homeland, promising that Abram would be the father of a great nation, and renamed him "Abraham." Abraham would have descendants who would be stewards of God's promises to him. God later reaffirmed the promise he made to Abraham with Abraham's son, Isaac, and grandson, Jacob, who was renamed "Israel." The People of Israel were the priestly Chosen People, the first to hear God's Word.

When the Israelites became slaves in Egypt, God freed them, created a covenant with them through the great prophet Moses on Mount Sinai, and gave them his Law so that they could serve him faithfully and prepare for the arrival of his Son.

Anytime the Israelites fell into sin, God sent prophets to further form his people for a New Covenant that would not be made up of written laws, but rather would be written on their hearts. The prophets called the Chosen People to purification and redemption. They spoke of Jesus's coming centuries ahead of his birth.

Throughout the history of the Chosen People, God inspired authors to create **wisdom literature** in the form of psalms, proverbs, and poems that would support the people in prayer and contemplation of the mystery of his plan.

The last prophet to prepare the way for Jesus was his relative, John the Baptist. Jesus even called him "more than a prophet" (Lk 7:26), explaining that John was the messenger that Scripture predicted would come immediately before him. "The fire of the Holy Spirit dwells in him and makes him a forerunner of the coming of the Lord" (*CCC*, 718).

Like the mystery of the Holy Trinity, the **Incarnation** is a mystery of faith that cannot be grasped with a limited human mind. The Son of God assumed human nature in order to accomplish salvation for all. Jesus was born into the world of the Virgin Mary through the power of the Holy Spirit. His Passion, Death, and Resurrection, known as the **Paschal Mystery**, is the key to our salvation.

The *Catechism of the Catholic Church* teaches: "Christ, the Son of God made man, is the Father's one, perfect, and unsurpassable Word. In him he has said everything; there will be no other word than this one" (*CCC*, 65). The Church's Sacred Tradition works with Sacred Scripture to help us understand mysteries of faith such as the ones introduced in this section. For example, teachings from Church councils in the first centuries of Christianity defined the theology of the Holy Trinity and Incarnation. Although much of Sacred

---

wisdom literature Collections of wise sayings, proverbs, and short stories that offer insights into the proper way to live. Hebrew wisdom literature began to be collected during the Babylonian Exile and the post-exilic periods.

Incarnation The assuming of a human nature by Jesus Christ, God's eternal Son, who became man in order to save humankind from sin. The term literally means "being made flesh."

Paschal Mystery Christ's work of redemption, accomplished principally by his Passion, Death, Resurrection, and glorious Ascension. This mystery is commemorated and made present in the sacraments, especially the Eucharist.

Tradition is based in Sacred Scripture, Sacred Tradition is a body of written literature that grows over time as times change. Its major teachings do not change, but the application of those truths evolves and expands. This textbook has a strong focus on helping you to understand Sacred Scripture, including how it is inspired by God and formulated by human authors. Within that study, a prominent objective will be learning about the Divine Person of Jesus Christ—the "unsurpassable Word"—and how to know him better.

SECTION *Assessment*

Comprehension

1. What are two categories of Divine Revelation? Explain a major difference between the two.
2. What are three criteria the Church uses to judge private revelations?

Vocabulary

3. Why are *apparitions* examples of private revelations, not public revelations?
4. Name the seven stages of *salvation history* discussed in this section using one word only for each stage.
5. Define *Paschal Mystery.*

Reflection

6. How do you imagine the Three Divine Persons of the Holy Trinity?
7. Share how you understand Jesus as the "Father's one, perfect, and unsurpassable Word."

Section 4

GOD RECORDS HIS REVELATION

If you were sitting in a classroom of your peers at any school in your nation—if not the world—and your teacher held up a copy of the Bible, it's likely that just about every person in the room would recognize it and know that it is a significant book and a holy book. As a reference point for this claim, the Bible is the best-selling book of all time. It is listed in a recent Guinness World Record as having five billion copies sold. By contrast the Qur'an, Islam's sacred book, had sold 800 million copies and *Harry Potter* by J. K. Rowling had 500 million in sales.

The Bible is actually a library of books (more information in Chapter 2) that span the breadth of salvation history. Each of the books of the Bible and the Bible itself has one author: God is the author of Sacred Scripture (*CCC*, 105). The previous statement and how it is understood has led to differences among Christians and their view of the Bible.

Some Christians believe that, though God is the author of the Bible, he worked through a single human secretary of sorts to record his words; for example, some hold that Moses transcribed all of the books of the Old Testament (even though he lived in a very particular time, the fourteenth to thirteenth century BC). This notion of God using one person to transcribe his words is not a completely farfetched concept in other religious traditions. The Mormon religion (Church of Jesus Christ of Latter Day Saints) believes one of its earliest writings was etched on gold plates in an ancient Egyptian language and found in upstate New York in 1827. According to Mormon beliefs, through a supernatural event, God himself placed the sacred Mormon writings on earth, and the founder of the religion, Joseph Smith, translated the writings into what became the Book of Mormon. Very few Christians would go to the extreme of believing that God delivered a physical copy of the Bible from heaven to earth for someone to find and then share. Also, this erroneous belief is in contradiction to the Church's teaching that "no new public revelation is to be expected before the glorious manifestation of our Lord Jesus Christ."[10]

Even those who acknowledge that God cooperated with several human beings to author the books of the Bible sometimes have a fantastical image of how God did it. You probably know that many of the epistles (letters) of St. Paul are included in the New Testament. You might not know that Paul's main occupation was a tentmaker. Can you imagine Paul out in his workshop weaving camel hair to make a tent when God suddenly calls him to come transcribe a letter? Can you picture Paul racing into the house, picking up his scribe's pen, dipping it in black soot, before shouting: "Okay, God. I'm ready. Dictate away." Presumably in this scenario God would also correct the punctuation and spelling!

Neither of these examples reflects what the Church believes about the statement "God is the author of the Bible." The clouds did not open up, and angels did not descend from the sky presenting the believers with a completed text of Sacred Scripture, handwritten by God himself. Nor did God dictate the contents of the Bible word for word. To comprehend the statement "God is the author of Sacred Scripture" requires us to understand the meaning of inspiration and how God inspired the human authors who cooperated with him when writing the sacred books. Once the meaning of *inspiration* is understood, the question of the **inerrancy** or truthfulness of the Bible must also be addressed.

Inspiration and Sacred Scripture

You are familiar with the words *inspired* and *inspirational* in everyday speech. You may have had a coach or teacher who *inspired* you with encouragement

St. Paul, like other inspired authors, was free to use his own words and sentences to communicate what God desired.

---

inerrancy Refers to the belief that the Bible is infallible or without error.

or an example to better yourself in a certain area. You may find a song lyric or the words of a poem *inspirational.* Some people believe that the reason the Bible is inspired is because of examples like these. The words of the Bible have inspired many people to better themselves. And the Bible contains prayers, wisdom, songs, and poems that definitely fit the definition of inspirational. But these are not reasons why Sacred Scripture is inspired.

Rather, while God is the true author of the Bible, he worked with many different human authors to reveal himself. God inspired these human authors to write those truths that are necessary for salvation, and to do so without error. While human authors may not have always been conscious of the deeper implications of what God wanted to communicate, God "made full use of their faculties and powers so that, though he acted in them and by them, it was as true authors they consigned to writing whatever he wanted written, and no more" (*CCC*, 106).

The human authors were free to use their own words and sentence construction to write what God wanted to communicate. They also had the freedom and discretion to include stories, references, and incidents that would be especially understood by the audiences for whom they were writing. For example, the Gospel of Matthew is the only Gospel to include the story of Joseph taking Mary and Jesus to Egypt after Jesus was born. Why? Probably because he wanted to associate Jesus with Moses, since by the time of the writing some years after Jesus had ascended into heaven, Jesus was being referred to as the "New Moses." Additionally, he wanted especially to connect Jesus with Moses, who was also called from Egypt, as he was writing for Jewish converts to Christianity who would have been in tune with the reference. The

The angel told Joseph in a dream, "Rise, take the child and his mother, flee to Egypt, and stay there until I tell you" (Mt 2:13).

Moses led the Hebrews from slavery in Egypt to freedom in the desert; Jesus leads us from the slavery of sin to salvation.

connection between Jesus and Moses is what God wanted communicated and what he inspired Matthew to write.

How the two main parts of the Bible (Old Testament and New Testament) and various books were developed and written will be explored in more detail in later chapters. For now, understand that the ancient Israelites (called "Jews" after the Babylonian Exile) and the earliest Christians believed certain writings clearly indicated that God's Spirit had guided the human authors in the truth. The writings themselves were then understood to be inspired.

There is something else to consider regarding God's inspiration of Sacred Scripture. The particular books of the Bible had to be officially recognized as God's inspired word. The task to approve or disapprove of which writings were inspired fell to the Church. Many religious writings of the Jews and early Christians were not accepted as inspired. The inclusion of the books of the Old Testament (most of which are in the Hebrew Scriptures) meant that the Church did appreciate that the Jews were God's Chosen People and that their inspired books told of the part of salvation history that was the preparation for the coming of Jesus Christ. (The title *Christ* means "Anointed One" or "Messiah.") The Apostles and their successors who received their positions through the inspiration of the Holy Spirit determined which writings were suitable to include in a *canon*, or official collection of biblical books. The four main criteria for inclusion in the New Testament were:

1. ***Inspiration of the Holy Spirit.*** The Church determined which books were inspired.
2. ***Apostolic origin.*** The author of the book needed to be an Apostle or someone closely associated with the Apostles.
3. ***Liturgical use.*** St. Paul's letters, for example, were often read as part of the liturgy. The liturgical context was an important factor for inclusion in the canon.
4. ***Universality.*** For a writing to be considered part of Sacred Scripture, its audience had to be outside a local community or region. St. Paul's Letters to the Corinthians, for example, were read beyond Corinth and throughout the Roman Empire.

After a number of years, the Church-approved canon of the Bible included forty-six Old Testament books and twenty-seven New Testament books.

Truth and Sacred Scripture

The truth of Sacred Scripture is linked to its inspiration by the Holy Spirit and the fact that God is its author. God who is good and perfect cannot lie and cannot make mistakes. For this reason, we can be guaranteed of the Bible's truth or inerrancy.

Inerrancy of Sacred Scripture has been studied by Church Fathers, popes, and Church councils for centuries. The Second Vatican Council (1962–1965) confirmed again that the inspired books of the Bible teach the truth, leading the Council Fathers to release the document *Dei Verbum* (Word of God). Notably:

> Since therefore all that the inspired authors or sacred writers affirm should be regarded as affirmed by the Holy Spirit, we must acknowledge that the books of Scripture firmly, faithfully, and without error teach that truth which God, for the sake of our salvation, wished to see confided in the Sacred Scriptures. (*Dei Verbum*, 11)

Truth is defined as "conformity to fact or actuality." This definition works well when speaking of mathematical truth or scientific truth, as when a hypothesis is drawn, then proven or disproven through experiments and observation, and then verified by others through many occasions of testing. There is very little mathematics in the Bible. There are some discussions of weight, measurements, and currency, but the examples are limited. It is the same for science. The biblical authors' understanding of science was primitive to their time and culture. The Bible does not contain examples of modern science.

However, there are several other kinds of truth besides mathematical and scientific truth. For example, you may be able to say to yourself, "It is true that my mother (or grandmother, sister, etc.) loves me." This type of statement is an example of relational truth. It cannot be verified by experiments or calculation. Rather, you know it is true from your experience. The Bible has some examples of relational truth. There are mothers, fathers, brothers, sisters, husbands, and wives mentioned in Sacred Scripture. Jesus had relationships with family, followers, enemies, religious leaders, and political leaders. Within all of these examples of relationships are lessons that communicate truths about human life. Sacred Scripture also contains a great deal of moral truth. There are many laws and standards for living, such as the Ten Commandments and the Beatitudes.

Most of all, the Bible is a book of religious truth. This type of truth describes God's relationship with people throughout salvation history, both in the Old Covenant between God and the Chosen People and in the New Covenant established by Jesus between all who come to believe in him and the Father who sent him. Truth "for the sake of salvation" is the best way to understand how Sacred Scripture is perfectly true. With the help of the Holy Spirit, all faithful Catholics support the Church's Magisterium in passing on the revealed truth of both Sacred Scripture and Sacred Tradition. By virtue of the Holy Spirit dwelling in us, we are able to grasp the meaning of God's Revelation and pass it on to others without error. This *sensus fidei* (sense of faith)

is the truth that the Church faithful as a whole—laypeople to bishops—are able to understand, live, and proclaim the truths of Divine Revelation. This applies to reading, studying, and praying with the Bible accompanied by our faith. The next chapters of this textbook are intended to encourage and assist you in that goal.

SECTION *Assessment*

Comprehension

1. Share one example of how some Christians have misinterpreted the statement "God is the author of Sacred Scripture."
2. Explain how God worked with human authors to communicate the truth he wished to reveal.
3. How are we guaranteed that the Bible is truthful?
4. How did Matthew connect Jesus to Moses in his Gospel?
5. In what way is the Church's determination of the biblical canon also inspired?
6. What were the four criteria used by the Church to determine if a writing would be included in the biblical canon?

Vocabulary

7. How does biblical *inerrancy* differ from a dictionary definition of truth?

Reflection

8. On a scale of 1 to 10 with 10 being "expert," rate your level of knowledge of the Bible. Explain your rating.
9. Share your own example of relational truth.

Section Reviews

Focus Question

How can I know God?

Complete one of the following:

- Write down five ways that you can know God or better know God. After you have your list, look up twelve ways that philosopher and author Dr. Peter Kreeft offered for knowing God. How many of your ways are on Dr. Kreeft's list?
- *Meditation* is a process of carefully examining your innermost thoughts while removing yourself from noises and distractions. How might meditation help you to know God? What are three steps you can take to focus yourself on the process of getting to know him?
- Write a short profile of a person you know who, through some twists and turns in life, has come to know and believe in God. What is a lesson from this person that you can use to further your own search for God?

Introduction

Discovering God

Review Points

- In spite of a drop in participation in organized religion, most people still believe in God. They hold that God is good and that he is the Creator of the universe. By contemplating the world—its origins and movement—we can come to know God (see *CCC*, 32). The human person is also a source of knowledge and discovery about God (see *CCC*, 33).
- The Christian faith is not a "religion of the book." The Church's Magisterium, through its continuing inspiration by the Holy Spirit, keeps the Bible from becoming a dead source of writings. Rather, Sacred Scripture and Sacred Tradition have the same divine source; they flow out "from the same divine well-spring" (*Dei Verbum*, 9). They accompany each other with the same goal, which is to make the Divine Word present until the end of time.

Assignment

What percentage of your classmates would you estimate believe in God? What percentage of your classmates would you estimate practice their religion (e.g., worshipping on Sunday, being active in their parish)? Share your opinion of any discrepancy between the two percentages.

Section 1
Our Built-In Desire for God

Review Points

- Our desire for God is part of a lifelong journey. It is a desire that is "written in the human heart" (*CCC*, 27). Pope Benedict XVI suggested two aspects as we search for God. The first is to "discover or rediscover . . . an authentic joy of life." The second is to keep searching and to "never be content with what you have achieved."
- One of the reasons we never are completely satisfied while on earth is that we have desires for that which is *perfect*—in other words, God. Instead of basing our search in him, we often limit it to human solutions and goals in such areas as knowledge and truth, love, justice and goodness, beauty, and home and being.

Assignment

People will often consult an owner's manual for a vacuum or a car, yet rely on themselves or the latest psychology to figure out how best to live their lives. Why do you think so many people do not seek the help of God to figure out the best course for their lives?

Section 2
God Is Revealed through Human Reason

Review Points

- It is possible to determine that God exists using your reason and your senses. St. Thomas Aquinas offered his "five ways" for God's existence based on human reason.

- Approaching God using human reason has a "twofold point of departure" (*CCC*, 32)—that is, through contemplating creation and contemplating the human person. These approaches are written about in Sacred Scripture. Human reason leads most people to question the origins of the world and its beauty. Human reason also helps us to understand that our own lives have meaning and that there must be a God who implanted this meaning within us.
- Human reason has its limits. Sin can pollute our understanding of ourselves and the world around us. We can only enter into an intimate relationship with God with the help of God's grace.

Assignment

Look up the encyclical *Humani Generis* by Pope Pius XII. Read paragraph 2. What does this paragraph say about why human reason is limited?

Section 3
God Reveals More of Himself

Review Points

- Divine Revelation means that God breaks into the human world to make himself known. The subject of his self-Revelation is that he is one God in Three Divine Persons: Father, Son, and Holy Spirit. Divine Revelation that is public is part of the Church's Deposit of Faith and must be accepted by Catholics.
- Divine Revelation took place gradually over time. Sacred Scripture records salvation history, which began at the creation of the world and reached its culmination in the Paschal Mystery of Jesus Christ.

Assignment

Rewrite John 1:1, replacing "Word" with "Jesus." Does this adjustment change the meaning of the passage or not? Explain.

Section 4

God Records His Revelation

Review Points

- It is accurate to say that "God is the author of Sacred Scripture." He worked with human authors to reveal himself and the truths that are necessary for salvation. The Magisterium of the Church through the Apostles and their successors determined which writings were to be included in the *canon*, or official collection of biblical books.
- Related to inspiration from God, the Bible is inerrant. Sacred Scripture is truth for the sake of our salvation. By virtue of the Holy Spirit dwelling in each person, we are able to understand the meaning of Divine Revelation and pass it on to others without error. This is called *sensus fidei* (sense of faith).

Assignment

If human authors drew on their own background, education, skills, and talents to assist God in writing Sacred Scripture, what do you think the reader must do to better understand the meaning of the Bible?

Chapter Projects

Choose and complete at least one of the following projects to assess your understanding of the material in this chapter.

1. Compare Caravaggio's Paintings with Rembrandt's Saint Matthew and the Angel

The Dutch artist Rembrandt Harmenszoon van Rijn (1606–1669) was born just four years after Caravaggio painted his two works portraying God's inspiration to St. Matthew. In 1661, Rembrandt painted the same subject, an oil painting titled *Saint Matthew and the Angel.*

Compare Rembrandt's painting with the two Caravaggio paintings at the beginning of this chapter. Also, include a comparative background on the lives of the two artists. Write an essay that includes the following information:

- who commissioned the works
- the mediums used
- your own description of each painting
- where the paintings were originally housed
- where the paintings are today
- critical reviews of the paintings
- brief biographies of the artists, including information on their religion

Add a concluding section to your essay that addresses your impressions of the paintings and your preference.

2. Create a 3-D Model That Helps to Explain the Existence of God

In order to help his friend understand that God exists, astronomer Johannes Kepler made a model of the sun with the planets circling around it (see Section 2, "Aquinas's Five Ways for God's Existence"). Think of a three-dimensional way that you could help someone who does not believe in God to believe. If you know someone who does not believe, try to understand the reasons why. If you do not know of an unbeliever, choose the obstacle(s) to belief you yourself have. In your project, include a reference card that states the doubt(s) you are addressing.

Create your 3-D object, and explain it in detail in a one-page written summary or share a three- to five-minute oral explanation on video with a link that can be shared with your teacher. *Note*: Your model does not have to involve astronomy.

3. Draw an Image of the Sacred Heart of Jesus

Read more about the history of devotion to the Sacred Heart of Jesus, focusing on the visions and devotions of St. Margaret Mary Alacoque. Use her descriptions of the Sacred Heart of Jesus as the starting point for drawing your own image of the Sacred Heart. Use color for your drawing (e.g., paints, colored pencils, fine colored markers, etc.). Around your image or on a separate sheet of paper, list the twelve promises Jesus shared with St. Margaret Mary for those who are devoted to his Sacred Heart.

4. Uncover the Origins of a Church Teaching

Sacred Scripture and Sacred Tradition work together through the inspiration and teaching of the Magisterium to establish the Church's dogma and beliefs. Most of the following questions were debated in Church councils in the fourth and fifth centuries. Choose any four of the questions. Do the following for each: (1) write your own hypothesis (answer) to the question before doing any research, (2) write how the Church answered the question (cite Sacred Scripture when applicable), (3) state the council and/or main **apologist**(s) who debated the question, and (4) write the year the answer to the question became official Church teaching.

Questions

- Is Jesus mostly divine or mostly human?
- Is Jesus God?
- Is Mary the mother of the human Jesus, the divine Jesus, or both?
- How many natures are there in Jesus Christ?
- How many persons are there in Jesus Christ?

---

apologist The name for a "defender of the faith." A Catholic who works to dispel false rumors about Catholicism and Christianity and who makes the faith appear more reasonable and acceptable to non-Christians.

- Is it possible for a person who lives a sinless and holy life to save himself or herself?
- Were the Seven Sacraments instituted by Christ himself?

Include references from your research parenthetically where they apply.

5. Hold a Debate between a Believer and an Atheist

You can choose to play both roles (believer and atheist) in a question-and-answer debate or pair up with a classmate for this project.

Use questions like the following for your debate. Choose three of the questions an atheist would ask a believer and three of the questions a believer would ask an atheist. You can also come up with questions of your own.

Questions from an atheist to a believer

- If God is real, why is there so much evil in the world?
- How can the Bible be real if it's full of contradictions?
- Why do I have to be responsible for the sin of Adam and Eve?
- How can Christianity be credible when there are so many Christians who are not credible?
- Why are there so many different religions and Christian denominations?

Questions from a believer to an atheist

- Isn't atheism just another religion?
- How did our DNA get programmed with such uniqueness and complexities without a programmer?
- Are you certain God does not exist, or would you admit that there is a possibility that there is a God?
- How do you determine the morality of an action?
- What evidence would you need to be convinced of God's existence?

Research and prepare your responses to each question from both points of view. Then set up a video camera and record a back-and-forth debate. If you are working with a partner, it's best not to practice your debate before recording so that responses will be more of a free-flow discussion rather than just a citation of researched responses.

Faithful Disciple
St. Hildegard of Bingen

St. Hildegard of Bingen

St. Hildegard (1098–1179), from Bingen, a town in present-day Germany, was known for many things. She was a Benedictine abbess, a musical composer, a philosopher, and a scientist. But it was her mystical visions from God that have helped her remain one of the most influential saints. After her eventual canonization by Pope Benedict XVI in 2012, St. Hildegard was also named a Doctor of the Church, only the fourth woman of thirty-five saints to receive that title.

Hildegard was a sickly child and suffered from various illnesses throughout her life. Around the age of three, she began to have visions, which she would eventually call "*umbra viventis Lucis*"—that is, "the reflection of the living Light." As an adult, she would sometimes share her visions with others while wondering if they had the same kind of experiences. Instead, she said, they "would inquire with astonishment whence such things might come. I also wondered."[11] At the end of her life, she described her visions:

> [The vision] rises up high into the vault of heaven and into the changing sky and spreads itself out among different peoples, although they are far away from me in distant lands and places. . . . I have never fallen prey to ecstasy in visions, but I see them wide awake, day and night. . . . The light which I see thus is not spatial, but it is far, far brighter than a cloud which carries the sun. I can measure neither height, nor length, nor breadth in it; and I call it "the reflection of the living Light." As the sun, the moon, and the stars appear in water, so writings, sermons, virtues, and certain human actions take form for me and glow.[12]

At age eight, Hildegard's parents placed her in the care of Jutta, the daughter of a count, and only six years older than her. The two girls were cloistered near a Benedictine monastery and both eventually professed in the Order of St. Benedict. Hildegard succeeded Jutta as prioress. Regarding Hildegard's visions, Jutta had noticed them and shared them with a monk at a nearby community, but nothing was done about publicizing them. Not until around the age of forty did Hildegard receive a command in one of the visions to have the messages published, but she was hesitant. Though she was convinced these revelations were from God, she was afraid of what people might think of her. When an inner voice continued to strongly urge her to make her visions known, she finally told a spiritual director. Through him she was assigned a monk who, from then on, recorded all of her visions. Hildegard had never learned to write.

Hildegard continued to dictate her visions for the rest of her life. Twenty-six of her visions are recorded in her principal collection known as *Scivias* (from the Latin *Sci vas Domini*, "Know the Ways of the Lord"). She is credited with three other books of visions. Additionally, she wrote on other topics such as the Rule of St. Benedict, the lives of saints, and commentaries on the Gospels. And she was an accomplished musical composer; many of her chant compositions survive to this day.

St. Hildegard lived to age eighty-one. She died on September 17, 1179. Regional calendars listed her as a saint many years before she was officially canonized by Pope Benedict XVI.

Comprehension

1. Name two things with which St. Hildegard is associated. For what is she most known?
2. How did St. Hildegard describe the light she sees in her visions?
3. What happened to Hildegard when she was eight years old?
4. Why didn't Hildegard want her visions to be published?
5. Name one other topic Hildegard wrote on besides her visions.

Reflection

Explain St. Hildegard's visions in terms of public or private revelations. Why might someone be uncertain about accepting Hildegard's visions? Why might someone easily accept their authenticity?

Prayer

Catholic Relief Services (CRS), founded in 1943 to help World War II refugees, is the official agency of the United States Conference of Catholic Bishops to provide international aid to poor people in need. This prayer composition of CRS encourages us all to reach out to Jesus, the Good Shepherd, to come to the aid of those in need.

Prayer to the Good Shepherd

Lord of the 23rd Psalm,
I have known death,
and you have refreshed my soul.
I have known fear,
and you have comforted me.
I have known hunger,
and you have set a feast before me.
In the darkest valley
no calamity of humankind or nature has separated us.
Teach me to walk as you walk
Beside those in mourning
so that they will know joy,
Beside those in fear
that they will know comfort,
Beside those in hunger
that they will feast until their cup overflows.
As your goodness and love follow me,
May mine follow my neighbor
That the threat of the worst terrors
May turn to the knowledge of the comforts of
the house of the Lord,
Where you have invited us to dwell forever.
And so let me strive to help build on earth
What you have promised us in heaven.
In the face of all calamity, present and yet to come,
Let me lead my neighbor beside quiet waters,
The quiet waters of the Good Shepherd.
Amen.

How the Bible Came to Be

Saint Jerome in the Wilderness

Leonardo da Vinci

St. Jerome (AD 342–420), an irascible scholar and hermit, is depicted in a famous painting by Caravaggio in his well-known occupation as translator of the Bible (see inset). Leonardo da Vinci (1452–1519), the scientist, sculptor, and painter who lived more than one thousand years after Jerome in the High Renaissance period, focused on a different age and aspect of Jerome's life.

In his oil painting on a wood panel, *Saint Jerome in the Wilderness*, dated between 1480 and 1490, da Vinci shows a rocky terrain where an older St. Jerome is seated on a rock near what looks like a cave. Unsurprisingly given da Vinci's scientific understanding of human anatomy, the muscles and bones of Jerome's torso are visible beneath the flesh. Jerome is known to have spent his last years fasting in the desert around Jerusalem, which would have withered his body.

There are other parts of the painting to consider. Jerome is holding a rock, as if he is about to use it to strike his chest. This was a common form of penance for sinners. The lion near the feet of Jerome seems tame. There was a legend that after Jerome pulled a thorn from the paw of a lion it became his companion for the rest of his life. Another interpretation connects the lion to St. Mark, the author of one of the Gospels Jerome translated, who is often accompanied by a winged lion.

On the right of the painting is a faint drawing of a church. As some have speculated, given Jerome's older age and his residence in the desert near Jerusalem, he could perhaps be gazing at the "New Jerusalem" that he will experience at death. In the upper corner at the left is a botanical scene, reflecting again da Vinci's scientific background.

Understanding the artist's mindset is also helpful. Da Vinci painted *Saint Jerome in the Wilderness* at a time in his life when he himself was depressed. In fact, the painting is unfinished.

The history of what happened to the painting is also fascinating, albeit filled with some legend. It was originally housed as part of the Vatican collection, before it was unknowingly confused as old wood and cut into two pieces. One of the pieces was crafted into a table top while the other wound up with a shoemaker who used it for the top portion of a stool. In 1820, Napoleon Bonaparte's uncle, Cardinal Joseph Fesch, recognized and purchased the painting from a Roman junk dealer. Years later he was able to locate the other section, and the painting was put back together with the cut piece still visible. Cardinal Fesch sold the painting to Pope Pius IX, who returned it to the Vatican museum.

Focus Question

How is God's Word collected and codified in the Bible?

Chapter Overview

Introduction
What Do You Know about the Bible?

Section 1
How God's Word Was First Shared

Section 2
The Development of Written Books

Section 3
Setting the Canon of Scripture

Section 4
Different Biblical Translations

Introduction

WHAT DO YOU KNOW ABOUT THE BIBLE?

The Church's *sensus fidei* (sense of faith) introduced in Chapter 1 has a connection to a Catholic's responsibility to read and share the Bible. Remember, *sensus fidei* refers to any baptized Catholic's possession of the essential truths of the faith. With that possession comes the responsibility to study and know what the Church teaches about that truth and then to share it.

Sacred Scripture is the written record of God's Revelation. In order to actively share and defend the faith, we need to be "up to speed" on the contents of Sacred Scripture, how to study the Bible, and most importantly, how to interpret the Bible. This last detail is where Catholics especially turn to the Magisterium for help. The Church encourages Catholics to be cautious in personal interpretations of the sacred texts, witnessing that personal interpretation by Protestants has led to thousands of splinter communities and divisions. It is common even among uninformed Christians of all kinds to cite random Scripture quotations to back up a belief or behavior without knowing the context and intention of the passage.

Given your enrollment in this course, you likely already have some degree of acquaintance with the Bible. Read and review the questions and answers below to test how much you remember and know.

1. What is the meaning of the word Bible?

The word *Bible* comes from a Greek word, *biblion*, which means "book."

2. How is the Bible different than other books?

The Bible is more accurately a library of books. It is made up of seventy-three books. The Bible is divided into two main parts, the Old Testament and New Testament.

3. What is the meaning of the word Testament?

Testament is another word for "covenant."

4. Why should Catholics bother to read the Old Testament?

The Old Testament tells the history of the Chosen People (the Jews) prior to the birth of Jesus. The books are divinely inspired. They are heard in liturgy and contain many beautiful prayers.

5. Did the Church translate the Bible into Latin so that the Catholic laity could not read it?

No. Pope Damasus I did commission St. Jerome to translate the Bible from Greek and Hebrew to Latin in the fourth century, but the reason was so *more* people could read the Bible. Latin was the common language at the time.

6. Are there differences between Catholic and Protestant Bibles?

Yes, there are differences. Catholics include seven Old Testament books and parts of two others (Daniel and Esther) that Protestants chose to omit when they separated from the Church.

7. Is the Bible read at Mass?

Readings from the Bible are read at Mass. They are gathered in the Lectionary ("book of readings") and arranged around one of three annual cycles, each of which unfolds the whole mystery of Christ from the Incarnation until his Ascension to heaven. While the Lectionary does contain the Gospel readings, sometimes the Gospels are read instead from a separate book of Gospels.

8. Why do Catholics believe some things that are not in the Bible?

Remember, the Bible is not the sole means that God uses to hand on the truths of Revelation. There are things taught through Sacred Tradition that are not explicitly found in Scripture. However, like Sacred Scripture, Sacred Tradition is passed down from the Apostles, and nothing in Tradition can contradict what is in Scripture.

9. How should Catholics read the Bible?

Catholics should read the Bible contextually—that is, paying attention to the broad historical, cultural, and geographical context in which it was written. Catholics should examine its various literary styles. And Catholics rely on the Magisterium for interpretation of the texts.

10. What is the most important message of the Bible?

Christ is the unique Word of the Scriptures. The most important message of the Bible is that Christ—the Word of God—became man and brought salvation to humankind through his life, Death, and Resurrection.

Your study of the Bible will unearth many other questions and considerations. You will also explore in more depth the questions and answers presented here. Realize as you begin that no matter your current level of faith, religious practice, or even whether or not you are Christian, the Bible will be an interesting and even addictive study. The Bible is filled with dramas, characters, conflicts, journeys, and literature that you will likely find match or exceed any of those you have studied in literature or history courses. Begin with an open mind to what you are about to learn.

The Tools for Biblical Study

There are several translations of the Bible. You will learn why this is so in Section 4. This textbook shares references from the *New American Bible, revised edition*. It is also the translation of the Bible you hear in the readings at Mass. Optimally, you should have your own copy of this edition to accompany you

with this course, but, if not, any other Catholic edition of the Bible will suffice. Two other primary Catholic editions are the *New Jerusalem Bible* and the *Revised Standard Version* (see Section 4, "Different Biblical Translations," "Catholic Editions of the Bible Today").

There are other ancillary aids for biblical study that many find helpful. Most of these are available online. For example:

- A *biblical commentary* analyzes, evaluates, and explains the biblical texts. The *New American Bible, revised edition*, and most other editions of the Bible have commentaries right on the pages—for example, in the bottom margin. In this area of the page you can also find cross-references to other related biblical passages.
- A *biblical atlas* provides maps to help you to navigate around the ancient biblical world. Your physical Bible might also contain some good maps, usually in the back. There are many online sites with excellent biblical maps.

- A *biblical dictionary* offers definitions of names, places, and terms used in the Bible.
- A *biblical concordance* lists the occurrences of words in the Bible, from large words to small words. There are large printed versions of concordances, but a word search of an online version of the Bible fulfills the same task.

You should also keep as reference an overview of Sacred Scripture provided in the *Catechism of the Catholic Church,* paragraphs 101–133. Much of this information will be disseminated in this text.

How to Locate and Read Bible References

To read the Bible, you must first know how to locate biblical references. A typical Bible reference looks like this: Jn 1:1–18. Pick up your Bible and follow these steps to locate and read the passage and follow along with the other examples listed here.

1. "Jn" is an abbreviated title for the book, in this case the Gospel of John. Common abbreviations are listed in your own Bible (usually in the front) or in the Appendix to this book, "Canon of the Bible." If you are not familiar with the order of the books, look in the table of contents of the Bible.
2. The first number listed is the chapter number; the verses follow after the colon (:). For this example, look at chapter 1 of the Gospel of John, verses 1 through 18. (The passage begins with "In the beginning was the Word" and ends with "The only son, God, who is at his Father's side, has revealed him.")
3. Whenever there is a dash (–) in a Bible reference, it indicates that you should read several chapters or verses in sequence. In the example from Jn 1:1–18, you are to read the verses (in chapter 1) from 1 through 18. If you find a reference without a colon (e.g., Gn 1–2), this indicates the reading of entire chapters (e.g., Genesis chapters 1 and 2).
4. A semicolon (;) is used to separate two distinct references or verses. For example Lk 6:12–16; 7:18–23, means Luke, chapter 6, verses 12 through 16, and Luke, chapter 7, verses 18 through 23. A comma separates two or more verses in the same chapter. For example, Is 9:1, 3, 8, means Isaiah, chapter 9, verses 1, 3, and 8.

5. Sometimes you will see something like this: Prv 6:6f. The "f" means the following verse. You would read Proverbs, chapter 6, verses 6 and 7. You may also be given a reference like Prv 6:6ff. The "ff" means an indeterminate number of subsequent verses. So, in this example, you would read Proverbs, chapter 6, verse 6, and several verses that follow.

Chapter 1 explained how it is accurate to say that "God is the author of Sacred Scripture" while also acknowledging that God shared through inspired human authors the truth he wanted communicated. This chapter looks in more depth at how that took place, from its beginnings in an oral tradition, to the writing of the sacred text, to how the Church determined which writings are sacred, and to why there are differences in various editions of the Bible today.

SECTION *Assessment*

Comprehension

1. Why should Catholics be cautious in personally interpreting the Bible?
2. Why is a Catholic likely more familiar with the *New American Bible, revised edition*, than any other?
3. What is the difference between a biblical commentary and a biblical concordance?
4. Write out in longhand the meaning (not the passage) of Mk 10:43–45.
5. Write out in longhand the meaning (not the passage) of Ws 4:5ff.

Reflection

6. Rate and explain how important it is to you to be "up to speed" on the contents of Sacred Scripture.
7. Which of the ten review questions and answers in this section would you like to explore in more detail? Explain.

Section 1

HOW GOD'S WORD WAS FIRST SHARED

We have become used to knowing that almost every major event that takes place over the course of a day will be recorded on video and broadcast almost immediately on the internet. You, yourself, are caught on video virtually non-stop throughout each day. Consider all the cameras placed randomly on traffic lights, businesses, and homes. If you were to go missing, law enforcement would be able to search out clues from these sources.

From this experience, you may imagine a similar—albeit ancient-world—version of how the words and events of Sacred Scripture were recorded and remembered before being written down. *Spoiler Alert*: There were no stenographers who wrote down the words of Jesus as he spoke them and then passed on these notes to the **evangelists** who authored the four Gospels. More accurately, it was not the goal of the Apostles to record word for word what Jesus said, but instead to share the significance of his words and his very presence. They came to recognize with the eyes of faith that Jesus is the culmination of God's Revelation in history. He is the very presence of God. He is God himself in the flesh. The importance of who Jesus is and what he was teaching was what they wanted to pass on.

The Gospels are the heart of the New Testament and of the whole Bible because through them we can know Jesus Christ, the Son of God, and learn how to live as his disciples. Catholics stand at Mass when the priest or deacon reads the Gospel but sit for the other readings. This is just one way in which we recognize the Gospels as the most important biblical text. We will use the Gospels as the primary example of how the living Word of God was

---

evangelist The name for one who proclaims in word and deed the Good News of Jesus Christ. The "four evangelists" refers to the authors of the four Gospels: Matthew, Mark, Luke, and John.

shared, first orally, and then in written form. The development of many other sacred books in both the Old Testament and New Testament follows a similar prototype.

Stages in the Formation of the Gospels

Before written texts were produced, there were two other stages in the formation of the Gospels.

The first stage was the time of Jesus's own life. Jesus is the Word of God (reread John 1:14) who lived in a particular time and place in history. Using Roman records of the reign of Herod the Great, who was alive at the time of Jesus's birth, biblical scholars estimate that Jesus was born in 6 BC.[∞] Jesus's public ministry began about AD 28, and he was crucified between AD 30 and 33.[≈] The first stage of the formation of the Gospel was the historical record of Jesus's own life, according to both followers and witnesses who knew him and interacted with him.

∞ Note

The years BC or "before Christ" are numbered in reverse. According to historical research, Herod the Great was appointed king of the region of Judea by the Romans and reigned from 37 to 4 BC. Herod the Great's reign helps us to date the birth of Jesus. In the sixth century, a Roman monk and mathematician, Dionysius Exiguus, attempted to calculate a chronology of the Christian faith on the Roman calendar. He set Jesus's birth in 754 on the Roman calendar. Anno Domini ("year of the Lord"), or AD 1, was 754 years after the city of Rome was thought to be founded. This date was problematic since it was at least four years after Herod the Great died. Because the Gospels mention Jesus's persecution at the hands of Herod, it is safe to assume that Jesus was born at least four years earlier than Dionysius calculated—that is, approximately 6 to 4 BC on the Christian calendar.

≈ Note

Likewise, using historical information from the Gospels and other sources, we can determine that Jesus died at thirty-three years old. This information includes dating the years of the high priesthood of Caiaphas (e.g., Matthew 16:3–4), and the governorship of Pontius Pilate who served from AD 26 to 36 according to Roman records.

The second stage occurred in the years immediately after Jesus's return to heaven. This was a time when the Apostles and other disciples orally preached the Good News. How long this period was in years has been reevaluated recently by Scripture scholars. In past times, the four canonical Gospels were usually dated between AD 65 and 100; however, Brant Pitre (see the feature "The Gospels Are Ancient Biographies" in Chapter 4, Section 3) has made a convincing argument that at least two of the three synoptic Gospels were written prior to AD 62. If so, the second or oral stage is shrunken to a time closer to the life of Jesus, and the Gospels can then be looked at more as "ancient biographies written by the students of Jesus and their followers, written well within the lifetime of the Apostles and eyewitnesses to Jesus."[1] If on the other hand, particular Gospels and other New Testament writings were written at later dates toward the end of the first century, then the second stage, or **oral tradition**, was more prolonged.

The coming of the Holy Spirit at Pentecost began the second stage of the formation of the Gospel: its oral sharing.

The oral tradition can be understood as something like the passing on of a key event from your own life (e.g., the 9/11 attacks on the World Trade Center in New York) by only word of mouth for many years before the event is written down. However, it is wise not to think of the practice of the oral tradition as something like the "telephone game" you may have played at a youth group meeting. In this game, a beginning story is passed by whispering it through a chain of several people. By the end of the game the story has many points that differ from the original. Ancient people had a more precise way of listening

---

oral tradition The process of sharing stories and other important pieces of information by word of mouth.

than people today as the spoken word was their main means of communication. One way was to utilize a "method of loci"—that is, to associate a story with the location where it was told to them. Psychologists today verify that this remains a way to accurately remember and repeat spoken information.∞

Oral tradition and the passing on of religious and family stories have been part of many cultures, including among African American slaves.

The written accounts themselves provide evidence that the Gospel was shared orally in the Church's first years. For example, Peter's message to those gathered in Jerusalem on Pentecost was a preached sermon (see Acts 2:14–26). In Antioch, Jews who had come to accept Christ also shared their message with Gentiles through the spoken word. On both occasions, many came to accept Jesus and request membership in the Church. Acts records several other sermons that both St. Peter and St. Paul preached about Jesus.

What was the exact subject of the preaching? The Apostles established a core or message that "Jesus is Lord and the fulfillment of the promise to God's Chosen People." They presented a basic outline of Jesus's life,

∞ Note

Much of the oral tradition included the use of song lyrics and poetic verse to help people to more easily remember and recite back what they had heard. Rhymes remain an important device in helping children to learn language and develop their imaginations. In order to learn language, we have to be able to hear language. The use of nursery rhymes furthers this development as children memorize the basic patterns and structures of language and develop their imaginations to help them remember what they have been told.

his saving Death, and his glorious Resurrection and Ascension to heaven. This core message is known by a Greek word, *kerygma*, which means "proclamation."

The sharing of the kerygma did not come without several challenges. The Roman Empire was a blending of both language and culture. Jesus primarily spoke Aramaic (though he certainly knew Hebrew from his synagogue studies). Strict Jewish sects, such as the Pharisees, spoke and understood Aramaic. Jesus also spoke a common form of Greek known as *koine Greek*. This would have been understood by Jews who had adopted the Hellenistic customs, including the Sadducees. Coptic Egyptians also spoke primarily koine Greek. The Apostles were likely challenged by having to translate Jesus's words and concepts from one language to another so that each audience could better understand.

Culturally, the Apostles faced many challenges as well. Just imagine the differences between an audience of faithful Jews who worshipped the one, true God and who had read, prayed with, and studied the **Torah** and an audience of **Gentiles** of various experiences of worshipping false gods or no god at all. For the first audience, the Apostles would have been able to refer to clear evidence from the Scriptures that described and prophesied the Messiah. For the Gentiles, they would have to interrupt the preaching of the kerygma to provide background context for how Jesus's words and actions fit in with salvation history and God's plan for their redemption. This effort also was required in the written Gospels where several Jewish rituals had to be explained with extra detail (see, for example, Mark 7:3) to help the Gentiles to better understand.

Other Examples of the Oral Tradition in Forming the Bible

The written Old Testament developed over a much longer period of time than the New Testament, from approximately 950 BC to the first century BC when the last Old Testament books, the Books of Maccabees, were finalized. Throughout this period, most people did not read or write. For centuries legends, myths, and stories were passed on orally.

The Book of Genesis, which tells two different stories about the creation of the world in its first three chapters, was most definitely shared orally for

---

Torah A Hebrew term that, in the broadest sense, reflects the totality of God's Revelation. However, *Torah* most commonly refers to the first five books of the Old Testament, also called the "Law" or, in Greek, the "Pentateuch."

Gentile A term for one who is not Jewish.

thousands of years. From a literary standpoint, these texts may have drawn on other sources, including myths from the ancient Near East. The Israelites, under the inspiration of the Holy Spirit, adapted these lessons to tell how God had been working throughout their history to create and form them as a people. The laws of the Old Testament that mainly occur in the Books of Leviticus, Numbers, and Deuteronomy may have been written in some form earlier than other books to formally preserve them.

Before closing this discussion about the oral tradition, a first-century Apostle must be highlighted. The Acts of the Apostles details three missionary trips of St. Paul who was known as the "Apostle to the Gentiles." Over the course of his ministry, Paul traveled over ten thousand miles. While he did write letters to the communities he visited on his journeys to offer further encouragement and instruction, Paul first evangelized through fiery sermons.∞ For example, several of the kerygmatic elements used by all of the Apostles are contained in a sermon Paul gave in the synagogue at Perga (see Acts 13:16–41).

Paul was truly chosen by God's providence to share the Gospel far and wide throughout the Roman Empire. He had many advantages that helped him in his travels. For example:

- He was born and raised Jewish. His Jewish name was Saul. He studied to be a rabbi under the famous teacher Gamaliel in Jerusalem. These factors gave him a great knowledge of Hebrew Scriptures and how they foretold the coming of Christ. He also studied and spoke Greek.
- Saul was also a Roman citizen, perhaps something he inherited from his father. His Roman name was Paul. With Roman citizenship, Paul was able to travel feely throughout the Empire.
- The Roman Empire was at peace during Paul's life. This was known as *Pax Romana* ("Peace of Rome"). The Roman roads, carefully built to carry Roman armies, were open to everyday citizens, from business people to sightseers. The roads were also well-marked with distance posts and guarded by Roman soldiers to promote safety.

∞ Note

St. Paul has been credited with writing thirteen letters preserved in the New Testament, seven of them by himself, and six others that are also attributed to him.

How Were Early Christians Able to Tell and Retell the Gospel?

Focus Question: How is God's Word collected and codified in the Bible?

In learning that the Gospels (and the whole of the New Testament) were preserved through oral storytelling for upwards of thirty or forty years after Jesus left the world, you might wonder how the first-century Christians were able to keep accurately in their memories Jesus's words and the events surrounding them.

The biggest reason why they were successful is that the oral culture was prevalent and the Church was part of this culture and adopted it as a means of sharing of the Gospel. The early Christians knew how to employ patterns or forms for remembering the stories and words of Jesus. Let's look at the patterns of three types of oral stories that transitioned to the written Gospels.

1. Pronouncements

This type of story highlights a main "pronouncement" of Jesus. In order to make it memorable, the form also includes a setting and an action (often including some dialogue), prior to the significant saying of Jesus.

Mark 2:15–17

Setting vs. 15	While he was at table in his house, many tax collectors and sinners sat with Jesus and his disciples; for there were many who followed him.
Action vs. 16	Some scribes who were Pharisees saw that he was eating with sinners and tax collectors and said to his disciples, "Why does he eat with tax collectors and sinners?"

Pronouncement vs. 17	Jesus heard this and said to them, "Those who are well do not need a physician, but the sick do. I did not come to call the righteous but sinners."

2. Miracles

Miracle accounts do not share something that Jesus *said*, but rather what he *did*. The way the account is presented to help the listener remember also has a threefold pattern. It includes a description of the need, Jesus's miraculous action, and the response of the witnesses to the action.

Mark 1:29–31

Description of Need vss. 29–30	On leaving the synagogue he entered the house of Simon and Andrew with James and John. Simon's mother-in-law lay sick with a fever.
Miraculous Action vs. 31a	He approached, grasped her hand, and helped her up.
Response vs. 31b	Then the fever left her and she waited on them.

3. Parables

Parables are allegorical stories. Jesus used everyday events, natural items, and people to help his audience to understand their meaning. A distinct feature about Jesus's parables is that they typically end with a surprising twist or unexpected ending. Both of these elements helped people to remember them.

Mark 12:41–44

Everyday Event vss. 41–42	He sat down opposite the treasury and observed how the crowd put money into the treasury. Many rich people put in large sums. A poor widow also came and put in two small coins worth a few cents.

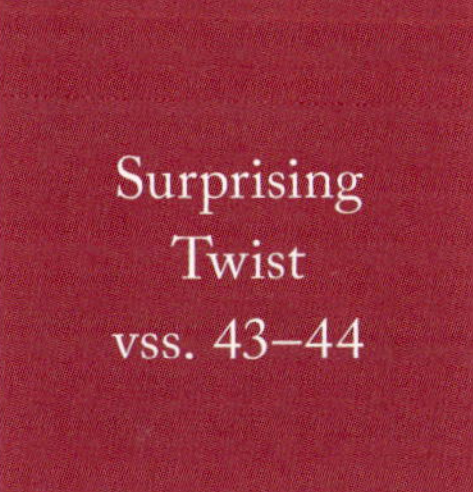

Calling his disciples to himself, he said to them, "Amen, I say to you, this poor widow put in more than all the other contributors to the treasury. For they have all contributed from their surplus wealth, but she, from her poverty, has contributed all she had, her whole livelihood."

These stories of the words and actions of Jesus were told first among those who had converted from the Jewish faith to Christianity. They were probably told in Aramaic. By the time these stories were put in written form, much of the membership of the Church was Greek-speaking Gentiles. The stories had to be translated not only from one language to another, but also from one culture to another.

Further Study and Reflection

- Antithetical parallelism was a common Hebrew style of Jewish writers at the time the New Testament was composed. Research and define its meaning. Explain how Matthew 7:17–18 is an example of antithetical parallelism.
- Read paragraph 76 of the *Catechism of the Catholic Church*. Answer the questions: Who handed on the Gospel orally? Who handed on the Gospel in writing?

Additionally, Paul was a tentmaker by trade, which helped to support his missionary work. Perhaps he shared the kerygma about Jesus Christ with his customers, either as part of an opening conversation starter or after a sale was completed. In any case, St. Paul's influence on the growth of the Church is unsurpassed. He provided a bridge between Judaism and Christianity and between a persecuted religion and a state religion. Finally, he was a bridge between the oral tradition and written tradition. His First Letter to the Thessalonians is the oldest piece of writing in the New Testament.

SECTION Assessment

Comprehension

1. Which books are at the heart of the Bible? Why?
2. What were the first two stages of Gospel formation? Briefly explain each.
3. Summarize the message of the Apostles' kerygma.
4. Name and explain two challenges for sharing the kerygma.
5. What were two advantages that St. Paul had as an evangelizer?

Vocabulary

6. Which two *evangelists* are not also Apostles?
7. Define *oral tradition* as it pertains to the New Testament.

Reflection

8. Why do you think there were four Gospels and not just one?
9. Which group of people would you find easier to convert to Christianity, those who already believed in God or those who did not? Explain.

Section 2
THE DEVELOPMENT OF WRITTEN BOOKS

Many authors wrote the Bible over a period of about a thousand years. As mentioned, the earliest Old Testament books are dated to about 950 BC. The New Testament books were composed in the first century AD. The Gospel of John and the letters of John may have been finalized in the first few years of the second century AD. Since most people could not read or write, and the oral tradition was well established, it's worth asking, Why did they even bother with a written document? Also, as there were no typewriters or printing presses and each copy of a Bible had to be composed by hand, the cost to produce the written form was expensive. Yet, despite the challenges, there were very good reasons for God's Word to be written down.

This section will explore these basic questions:

- Why was the Bible written down?
- Who were the authors of the Bible?
- How did they compose the written copies?

Even though the Old Testament was written over the course of nine hundred years and the details of its composition are less known, the answers to the questions are similar when comparing it to the New Testament, which was mainly composed in the second half of the first century AD.

Why Was the Bible Written Down?

Writing had emerged in the Near East around 3500–3000 BC and in Egypt and Mesopotamia (modern-day Iran and Iraq) at about the same time. Pictograms—that is, pictures that represented words—were the first form of writing. Centuries later the Phoenicians developed symbols for letters of the alphabet. The ancient Egyptian form of **hieroglyphic writing** was more stylized than pictograms but not based on an alphabet. The discovery of the **Rosetta Stone** in Egypt in 1822 was the key to cross-translating hieroglyphics and two other Egyptian languages.

It would almost seem illogical for the Old Testament to have been written down as early as it was. But with other more urban and advanced civilizations taking up writing, Israel began to employ **scribes** to record the oral tradition in the time of King Solomon. Biblical scholars believe that the scribes first wrote down the oral traditions about Israel's history from the creation of the world up to the conquest of Canaan. This material is the first section of the Bible, the **Pentateuch**.

Besides keeping up with other nations, the writing of the biblical text was done for political reasons. It furthered the religious and political authority of priests, and it projected the power of Israel's kings. As time went on, the written text began to supplant the oral tradition in authority. The Book of Deuteronomy, for example, instructed the Israelites to put written prayers on the entrances of their homes. This showcased that written words had become important to the masses, not just to those in power. Jews today continue to post **mezuzahs** containing tiny scrolls on their doorposts.

The period of writing the books that would eventually be the New Testament canon took place over the course of only about seventy years, from AD 50 to 120. Still the question must be answered in this case too: Why the need for a written record? Jesus taught using vivid stories and used short sayings, striking images, and poetic language, making his words easy to remember (see the feature in Section 1, "How Were Early Christians Able to Tell and Retell the Gospel?"). And, even in the first century AD, not many people could

---

hieroglyphic writing An Egyptian term that literally means "sacred carvings." This type of writing was first used exclusively for inscriptions on the walls of tombs or temple walls.

Rosetta Stone An ancient Egyptian stone that contained writings in several different ancient languages and led to the understanding of hieroglyphics. It was discovered in 1799.

scribe Ancient Jewish record keeper who was trained in the earliest forms of writing before literacy was widespread.

A Jewish custom exists to this day of putting readings from the Torah on the doorposts of entrances to homes, hotels, and places of business. They are contained in a mezuzah, a decorative case containing a piece of parchment from the Torah.

write, and the cost of producing copies of a text was expensive. But there were at least four good reasons for the New Testament to be recorded in writing:

1. *The Second Coming of Jesus was delayed.* The first generation of Christians believed that Jesus would return during their lifetime. In that case, they figured there was no need to take the time to write down any of his Gospel. As the years went on and more and more of the Apostles and other eyewitnesses were dying, it became imperative for a written record to be kept.
2. *There were weaknesses in the oral tradition.* Despite the best efforts, distortions were setting in with the oral retelling. For example, one of the

---

Pentateuch In Greek it means "five books." The term refers to the first five books of the Bible: Genesis, Exodus, Leviticus, Numbers, and Deuteronomy.

mezuzah A Hebrew word that means "doorpost." Practically, it consists of a small scroll parchment on which one of two passages is written: Deuteronomy 6:4–9 or Deuteronomy 11:13–21. The parchment is placed on the front and back doorposts of a Jewish home and on every door in the home except for the bathroom. The practice is taken from Deuteronomy 6:9: "Write them on the doorposts of your houses and your gates."

Apostles would preach at a local church, and someone would come along later and distort the message (see, for example, 2 Thessalonians 3:11–15). The Christian message needed consistency. The words and events in the life of Jesus also needed to be arranged in chronological order.

3. *A catechetical aid was needed.* There were so many new Christians being initiated into the faith that a manual of written instruction was needed.
4. *Writings also served as helpful guides in liturgy.* The Church began rather quickly to include readings from Sacred Scripture in Eucharistic celebrations. Additionally, it is important to note that one of the first documents written by Church Fathers in the second century AD was also for **catechesis**. It is called the *Didache* ("The Lord's Teachings through the Twelve Apostles to the Nations"). It quotes the Gospels and provides instruction on how to conduct Baptism and Eucharist; how to treat Apostles, bishops, and prophets; an overview of Jesus's Way of the Cross; and a prophecy of the Second Coming.

In summary, the Gospels and other New Testament epistles were written down and collected because the world did not end as the early Christians expected, heresies were setting in that demanded correction, and Christians needed a constant and objective source for instruction and worship.

Who Were the Authors of the Bible?

We've established that God, working with human authors, is the one author of the Bible. As for the identity of the human authors, again there is a difference in what we know between the Old Testament and New Testament. In the Old Testament, it was the scribes that recorded stories of the kings. While the writing began during the reign of King Solomon, the scribes also recorded stories of his predecessors King Saul and King David. These eventually would be classified as historical books (see Chapter 4, Section 1, "Survey of Old Testament Books"). Some of the prophets, such as Isaiah and Jeremiah, wrote their own books. Their secretaries and disciples, however, were often the ones to collect and record their prophesies, sayings, and teachings. In the case of the Book of Isaiah, there may have been as many as two additional authors or

---

catechesis A term that describes a process of "education in the faith" for young people and adults with the view of making them disciples of Jesus Christ.

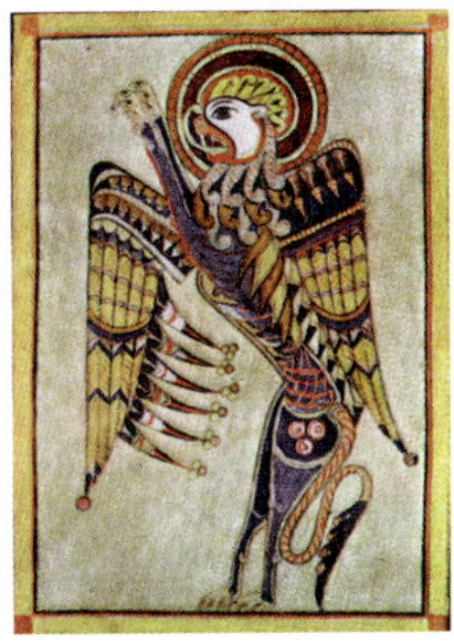

editors besides the prophet who completed the book over many years.

Many of the other Old Testament books are compilations, the work of several writers and editors. In the sixth century BC, editors collected, combined, and improved the texts. When you consider that authors and editors formed the Old Testament over the course of about one thousand years, it is easy to understand why many of the Old Testament books are compilations. The Book of Genesis, for example, has two creation accounts. Some books, such as the Psalms and Proverbs, are really collections of wisdom from many people over the years.

The identity of the New Testament authors in many ways is easier to gauge, because the Gospels are titled by names (Matthew, Mark, Luke, and John) and the epistles are letters that mostly identify the writers in the salutations. The Church has never deviated from teaching that the Gospels were authored by evangelists Matthew, Mark, Luke, and John, though they may have been assisted by other writers and editors in the process. For example, John 3:23 mentions the "disciple whom Jesus loved" but does not name the disciple. In approximately AD 180, Church Father St. Irenaeus attributed the fourth Gospel to John, and Church Tradition identifies John, an Apostle whose father was Zebedee, as the beloved disciple.

The Gospels of Matthew, Mark, and Luke are very alike, so much so that they are known as the *synoptic Gospels*. *Synoptic* is Greek for "one eye." Regarding the authorship of the first three Gospels, the view of the Church by the second century was that the Gospel of Matthew was written by the former tax

In the left column are traditional symbols of the four evangelists. The winged man represents St. Matthew; the winged lion, St. Mark; the winged ox, St. Luke; and the eagle, St. John.

collector, Matthew (also known as Levi), who became an Apostle. The Gospel of Mark was attributed to John Mark, who, after being associated with Paul, became an assistant to Peter (see Acts 12:12; 12:25; 13:5, 13; and 15:37–40). Luke, a Gentile Christian, who might have been attracted first to Judaism, is named the author of the third Gospel as well as the Acts of the Apostles. Evidence for this is that both the Gospel and Acts are addressed to the same person, Theophilus, which means "friend of God" (see Luke 1:1–4 and Acts 1:1–2). Like the Gospel of John, biblical scholarship has discovered clues to why these Gospels were identified with the evangelists Matthew, Mark, and Luke. You will read more about the synoptic Gospels in Chapter 5.

Thirteen of twenty-seven New Testament books are attributed to St. Paul. These are known as the Pauline epistles (letters). According to the latest biblical scholarship, however, St. Paul probably personally wrote only seven of them: Romans, 1 and 2 Corinthians, 1 Thessalonians, Galatians, Philippians, and Philemon. Six other letters—Ephesians, Colossians, 2 Thessalonians and the **pastoral letters** 1 and 2 Timothy and Titus—likely were written by close disciples of Paul or by admirers who wanted to keep his apostolic legacy alive.

Other letters in the New Testament that don't have a specific audience are called *catholic* or *universal* letters. They were credited in tradition to various Apostles such as John, Peter, and Jude.

How Did They Compose the Written Copies?

Biblical authors wrote in the languages of Hebrew, Aramaic, or Greek on papyrus pages or on parchment (pages made from animal skins). The pages were either pasted together, end to end into long strands, and rolled around wooden rods as scrolls or folded and sewn together into a **codex**, which resembles more closely a modern book. Eventually the scrolls went out of use.

The scribes and copiers were well-paid professionals. Their job was made more difficult because the written form of Hebrew and Aramaic uses no vowels, capital letters, or punctuation. By copying by hand, transcription mistakes crept into their works. Scribes were more than just copiers. They also edited the material. A scribe of an Old Testament text might take several different

---

pastoral letters Three epistles of the New Testament–the First and Second Letters to Timothy and the Letter to Titus–that are specifically addressed to individual pastors in the Church.

Egyptians also crafted papyrus for writing in biblical times.

scrolls with something in common in them and form an entire book out of them. For example, if a Jewish scribe from Egypt had several scrolls associated with the prophet Jeremiah, this information might have been blended in with material from a Jewish scribe living in Jerusalem. Also, the Jerusalem scribe may have edited the material so that his community might better understand the cultural references and overall message. Don't forget that as the author of the Bible, God made full use of the authors' faculties and powers so that they communicated exactly what he wanted written and no more. This includes God's inspiration of the scribes as editors.

As you might imagine, producing a Bible before there was a printing press was expensive. *Papyrus* is the name for the plant from which pages were made. The papyrus plant has tall, three-sided reeds. When the outer skin of the reed is shaved, the underlying layer is very fibrous and durable. After this layer is

---

codex The name for an ancient book that used papyrus or parchment stacked together and bound rather than strung together on a scroll. The term comes from a Latin word that means "trunk of a tree" or "block of wood."

A rabbi and master craftsman makes parchment in his basement workshop to be used for religious articles.

stripped off each of the three sides of the stalk, the strips are laid horizontally on a flat surface parallel to one another. Then a second layer is laid perpendicularly on top of the first layer and glued together. The layers are pressed and dried. Once dried, they could be burnished into smooth writing surfaces. Papyrus plants were plentiful, but as writing surfaces they were not long-lasting in very moist or very dry weather.

Parchment was more durable and more expensive. It was made from the skins of goats, sheep, or cows. The highest quality of parchment, called *vellum*, came from the skin of calves. An even more exclusive form of parchment came from unborn calves and is called *uterine vellum*. In whatever form, the parchment was prepared by soaking the skins for a few days in both water and chemicals, allowing all of the remaining animal hair to be scraped off. After it was dried, the parchment would be stretched and made suitable for writing. The total cost for the parchment needed for producing an ancient Bible was calculated by the number of lines of text. In Roman currency, the cost was about 30,000 *denari* or about forty years of wages for an average worker.

Remember, there was no easy way to make additional copies of a Bible. Each edition had to be copied over by hand so that the Word of God could be shared with more people. Sometimes words were omitted or added to the new copies by scribes. This is one reason archaeologists search for and study the earliest copies possible. For the most part, biblical scholars and translators today work with Scripture copies found hundreds of years after the original texts were written. For some Old Testament books, translators use versions from AD 1000, and for the New Testament they use copies dating from AD 300. Fortunately, the Dead Sea Scrolls∞ (discovered in Israel in the late 1940s) reproduced some Old Testament books that predate the birth of Christ.

∞ Note

The Dead Sea Scrolls were discovered by two teenage Bedouin boys as they chased a young goat in one of the many caves by the shore of the Dead Sea in Palestine. When the boys threw a rock into the cave to scare the young goat, they heard the sound of shattering pottery. When they checked, the boys found eight earthenware jars containing parchment scrolls. The scrolls contained manuscripts from Hebrew Scriptures written in Hebrew and Aramaic. The scrolls were sold at auction several times before they finally came to the attention of the patriarch of Jerusalem. Almost all of the Dead Sea Scrolls have now been translated into English.

SECTION Assessment

Comprehension

1. When were the books of the Old Testament written?
2. When were the books of the New Testament written?
3. What were the original reasons that the books of the Old Testament were written down?
4. Name the three reasons the New Testament was written down.
5. What was the role of scribes in the Old Testament?
6. What do some biblical scholars claim about the authorship of the Gospel of John?
7. What were the advantages and disadvantages of using papyrus as a writing surface?

Vocabulary

8. How did the discovery of the *Dead Sea Scrolls* improve the accuracy of biblical translations?
9. Define *Pentateuch*.

Reflection

10. What are your thoughts on the sacredness of the Bible after reading how, when, and why it was composed?

Section 3

SETTING THE CANON OF SCRIPTURE

It is interesting to consider that the Church was up and running before there was a New Testament. Internal structures were established by the Apostles and the leaders they commissioned. Baptisms were taking place, the Eucharist was being celebrated, and the sick were being cared for. All of this and more happened without the written New Testament. There was a Church before the New Testament.

This section explains more about how the biblical canon was determined and approved by the Church. *Canon* derives from a Greek word, *kanon*, which means "a measuring rod." When the term is used with the Bible, it is meant to describe the standard necessary for books to be considered inspired by God. For the Old Testament books, the Church, as descended from the Jewish people based on Jesus's own family ancestry, accepted the totality of Hebrew Scriptures as inspired. For the New Testament, the writings that would eventually make up the canon were tested for inspiration based mostly on their connection with the Apostles or, secondarily, their use in liturgy.

The Old Testament Canon

From the beginning, the Church did accept the books of the Old Testament as inspired because they were part of the Hebrew Scriptures. In the first century AD, however, the Jews had more than one edition of the Hebrew Scriptures. An older edition was written in Hebrew. But as most Jews in the centuries before and during the time of Jesus spoke Greek, there was also an edition of Hebrew Scriptures written in Greek.

The Greek translation was referred to as the *Septuagint*, which means "seventy." The name arises from a Jewish legend in which seventy (more accurately, in spite of the Septuagint moniker, seventy-two) elders assembled in

Ptolemy Philadelphus, king of Egypt, summons seventy-two men from Judea to translate the Hebrew Scriptures into Greek.

Alexandria, Egypt, to translate the Bible from Hebrew into Greek. The translators divided into six teams, and when they were finished, a legend holds that each of their translations was exactly the same. In actuality, *many* translations were created in Alexandria, and they had to be combined into one version and translated into *koine* (common) Greek, likely around the fourth century BC.

Something else happened with the translation from Hebrew to Greek: a number of new texts were added that did not appear in the Hebrew version. The Hebrew version had a total of thirty-nine books. The Septuagint had forty-six books with the addition of the books of Tobit, Judith, 1 and 2 Maccabees, Wisdom, Sirach (sometimes called Ecclesiasticus), and Baruch (including the Letter of Jeremiah), along with additional material in Esther and Daniel.

The early Christians, both Gentiles and Christians with Jewish roots, generally preferred the longer Greek Septuagint for prayer and use in liturgy, probably because most of them spoke Greek themselves. The apostolic leadership, as a result, followed their example and used the fuller Septuagint version. Meanwhile, sometime in the first century AD, most Jews began to use only the Hebrew version of Scripture. Also, the Hebrew translation was translated orally into Aramaic around this time, a process known as *targums*. As the Church was already independent of Judaism at this point, Church leaders were neither consulted nor persuaded by that decision, and they continued to use the longer Greek Septuagint as the Old Testament. As result, the Catholic Church had forty-six books in the Old Testament from its earliest days. The additional books that are unique to the Greek versions of the Old Testament are known as the **deuterocanonical** books.

The Bible's canon (both Old Testament and New Testament) proceeded on without much controversy. Several local Church councils—including Hippo in 393 and Carthage in 397—approved the canon as it is in the Bible today. The Council of Hippo approved the use of the additional deuterocanonical books, and the Council of Carthage confirmed the decision. The canon was unchallenged until Martin Luther and the sixteenth-century Protestant Reformation. The Protestants decided to use the shorter list of books in the Hebrew version of Scriptures—still being used by Jews at that time—rather than the Septuagint. They relegated the additional books from the Greek version to an extra section of the Bible called the *Apocrypha*, a word that means "hidden." At the Council of Trent (1546) the Church accepted its traditional version of the Old Testament as divinely inspired with little debate. The decision to use the Septuagint is valid based on scholarship; for example, the Jews of Jesus's time used several different versions of Scripture, and some Jews used the Septuagint. Thus, the canon of the Old Testament remains the same as it was from the Church's earliest years.

The New Testament Canon

It took a few centuries before the Church was able to state with certainty which of the many books that were written after the time of Jesus should be considered suitable for proclamation and, hence, for being part of the New Testament. The apostolic tradition of the Church determined which books were to be included in the canon and which were not under the inspiration of the Holy Spirit. By AD 200, the current canon of the New Testament was generally accepted.

---

deuterocanonical The term for the writings that are in the Catholic Old Testament but not in the Hebrew Scriptures. It means "second canon."

Both Protestants and Catholics are in agreement on the twenty-seven books of the New Testament canon. The Council of Trent also clarified that three specific passages in Gospels that had periodically been under question were indeed inspired and their authenticity should never be questioned again. These are:

Mark 16:9–20. This so-called longer ending of Mark's Gospel may have been added in the second century and written by someone other than Mark. It describes appearances of the risen Jesus, drawing on traditions found in later Gospels (e.g., Luke 24 and John 20).

Luke 23:43–44. These verses that describe Jesus's sweat at the Agony in the Garden "like drops of blood falling on the ground" were probably not part of the original text of Luke as they are absent from the oldest papyrus manuscripts and other manuscripts that had wide geographical distribution.

John 7:53–8:11. The story of the woman caught in adultery was missing from early Greek manuscripts. It may have been placed originally in other sections of John or in the Gospel of Luke.

Other books that were written in the first two centuries and that contain much of the same information about Jesus as found in the Gospels were unacceptable for other reasons. Some of these books, including the Gospel of Thomas and the Gospel of Judas, were deemed heretical because of claims that they possess a "secret knowledge" (*gnosis* in Greek) that guarantees a person's immortality.

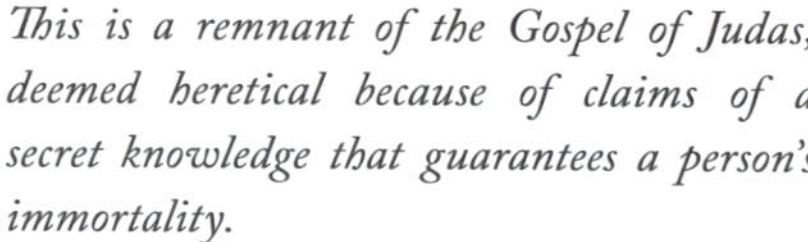

This is a remnant of the Gospel of Judas, deemed heretical because of claims of a secret knowledge that guarantees a person's immortality.

These Gospels take a dim view of material reality, including the human body, and contradict Jesus's teaching on the Kingdom of God. The Gospel of Thomas also teaches that a woman cannot enter heaven without becoming a male. Thirteen bound codices of gnostic material were discovered by a farmer near the Egyptian town of Nag Hammadi in 1945.

A papyrus copy of the Gospel of Judas, in more than one thousand scattered pieces, surfaced in the Egyptian desert in the 1970s. Scholars believe it was written sometime between AD 130 and 180. The novelty of this writing is that it portrays Judas Iscariot in a favorable light as the only Apostle to whom Jesus revealed the "true" knowledge of the Kingdom—namely, strange and bizarre gnostic secrets about creation and humanity. One of its teachings says that the God of the Old Testament was evil. St. Irenaeus mentioned the Gospel of Judas in his *Against Heresies* (ca. AD 180), calling it fictitious history. Biblical scholars in every age since have agreed.

Other gnostic gospels were rejected because they downplayed the suffering and Death of Jesus.

SECTION *Assessment*

Comprehension

1. What is the meaning of the term *canon* when used in connection with the Bible?
2. How did the Septuagint differ from the Hebrew version of the Old Testament?
3. Why did the early Church prefer the Septuagint to the Hebrew translation of the Old Testament?
4. Why were three Gospel passages (see the subsection "The New Testament Canon" in this section) disputed as inspired texts?

5. How are the Gospels of Thomas and Judas examples of gnostic gospels?
6. What are two reasons why it is valid for the Church to continue to use the canon of the Septuagint?

Vocabulary

7. What is meant by *deuterocanonical* books of the Old Testament?

Reflection

8. State in your own words, as if talking to a Protestant friend, why Catholic and Protestant versions of the Bible are different.

Section 4

DIFFERENT BIBLICAL TRANSLATIONS

The Christian Bibles in the first four centuries were primarily written in koine Greek for the Greek-speaking population of the Roman Empire. However, there were plenty of Latin translations in existence as well. Among many local Latin editions two were more widely circulated: one that originated in Europe and the other from Africa. The Old Testaments of both versions were translated to Latin from the Septuagint. However, when a division in the Roman Empire occurred between the East and West in AD 395, more people in the West began to speak Latin as their everyday language; and a new consolidated and more precise Latin edition of the Bible was needed.

A young man from current northeast Italy named Jerome had come to Rome after his elementary studies and become proficient in both Greek and Latin literature. At age eighteen, he was baptized and entered a strict monastic community at Aquileia, a Roman colony on the Adriatic Sea. While there, he continued his studies of Greek and tried to master Hebrew. When the monastic community broke up, Jerome went first to Antioch, where he was ordained a priest, and then back to Rome. He spent three years in Rome working under Pope Damasus, who requested that he revise the existing Latin translations of the Gospels and, perhaps, other books of the New Testament.

Jerome used a combination of the existing Latin versions and some of the Greek editions of the New Testament to revise and provide a new translation of the four Gospels. It is also likely he was able to complete the revision of the other New Testament books during his three years in Rome. After the death of Pope Damasus in 384, Jerome traveled in the Holy Land visiting the shrines before permanently settling at a monastery in Bethlehem. There, in 387, he began to translate the Old Testament to Latin from an ancient form of the Septuagint. In 390 he expanded his project and took on translating the Old Testament from the original Hebrew source.

Jerome's translation of the majority of the Bible is known as the Vulgate, from the Latin *versio vulgata*, which means "the version commonly used." Besides Jerome's attention to the original sources, his translation reflected the way that people spoke the language; and it soon became the most commonly used edition in the Church. St. Augustine, who lived in the same period as Jerome, preferred Jerome's New Testament translation and came to appreciate his translation of the Hebrew Old Testament to Latin as well. In his *The City of God*, Augustine wrote: "In our own day the priest Jerome, a great scholar and master of all three tongues, has made a translation into Latin, not from Greek, but directly from the original Hebrew" (bk. 8, chap. 43). His translations are known for their clarity, fidelity to the original translation, and elegance of diction. For example, long Hebrew sentences that contained no breaks between words and no punctuation were broken up and properly punctuated by Jerome.∞ Jerome is both a saint and a Church Father.

The first volume of the first edition Latin Vulgate translation of the Bible. This copy is one of the three existing copies printed, illuminated, and bound, circa 1455, by Johannes Gutenberg.

The Vulgate was the first Bible printed on the **Gutenberg Printing Press** in about 1455, and it was confirmed as the official Latin edition of the Bible at the Council of Trent in 1546. This was the time of the Protestant Reformation when many new English versions of the Bible came

∞ Note

The Hebrews did not put space between words or punctuation to save space on a page. Also, ancient Hebrew (like modern Israeli Hebrew) had no vowels. Jews read the text as if the words had vowels, but the lack of written vowels made the translation of the text even more difficult.

into circulation. The Council of Trent stated that the Vulgate was worthy of belief, reliable, truthful, trustworthy, and authoritative. It remained the official Latin edition of the Bible until 1979, when the *Nova Vulgata* (a new translation from the original Hebrew texts) took its place. The original Vulgate, however, continues to hold a revered place in the Church.

It's important to be clear that neither the Vulgate nor the *Nova Vulgata* was ever the "official *Bible* of the Catholic Church." Their status is only as "official *Latin* version of the Bible." Today, the Church has many approved Bible options. The next section looks at some of the English-language approved Catholic Bibles.

Catholic Editions of the Bible Today

Today, there are editions of the Bible in every language. There are many translations into English, some under Catholic sponsorship, others under Protestant sponsorship. Until the twentieth century, English-speaking Catholics mostly used the *Douay-Rheims Version*, translated between 1582 and 1609 from the Vulgate and its revision done by Bishop Richard Challoner (1749–1763), an English Catholic bishop. Challoner mainly revised the wording of the *Douay-Rheims* to make it less antiquated and more readable. Then, in 1943, Pope Pius XII encouraged the translation of the Bible using the original languages (i.e., the Old Testament from Hebrew; the New Testament from Greek). Several translations have been published since the latter half of the twentieth century.

There are two types of modern biblical translations to consider. The first type is the *formal* or *literal translation*, which tries to stick as close as possible to the wording in the original text. Literal translations of the Bible are almost always used for serious biblical studies. They are important because sometimes what the original authors meant depends on subtle clues used in the writing that are best preserved in literal translations. The disadvantage of this style is that the translations are harder to read because the Hebrew or Greek syntax interferes with the smooth flow of English text.

Gutenberg Printing Press The name for the first printing press to use movable type. It was created by goldsmith Johannes Gutenberg in Germany in 1440. It produced up to 3,600 pages per day in comparison to about forty hand-copied pages per day.

The second type of biblical translation is called *dynamic equivalence.* This method does not focus on keeping the exact Hebrew or Greek wording, but rather on forming an easy-to-read translation with proper English grammar and syntax. A way to think of this style is that rather than "word for word," the translation is "thought for thought." As long as the meaning of the original text is preserved, this approach is satisfied. An advantage of dynamic equivalence translations is that they are easy to understand, read, and pray with. A disadvantage is that they often miss clues to intended meanings from the original translations and incorporate some of the translator's personal doctrinal views into the biblical text.

There are approved Catholic versions of the Bible that utilize both types of translations. (Remember, a Catholic Bible has forty-six books in the Old Testament while a Protestant Bible has thirty-nine.) The *Revised Standard Version Catholic Edition* (RSVCE) is similar to the older *Douay-Rheims* and has sound biblical scholarship. It is used for Mass readings in Canada. The RSVCE language has a poetic tone and fits in the category of formal translation. Biblical scholar Brant Pitre explains: "No translation is perfect, but the RSVCE strives to be as literal as possible (i.e., close to the original Hebrew and Greek) and yet also uses beautiful English."[2]

The *New Jerusalem Bible,* borrowing heavily from the French *La Sainte Bible*, is a dynamic equivalence translation. Its use of inclusive language and attention to poetic sections makes it a very readable edition. The introductions and notes to guide the reader are also substantial and helpful. In Ireland, either the *New Jerusalem Bible* or its earlier edition,

the *Jerusalem Bible*, has been used in liturgy. In keeping with other modern biblical translations, some editions have replaced the name for God in the Old Testament (YHWH) with "Lord" out of respect for the Jewish people, who hold God's name unpronounceable due to his majesty and greatness.

For a clearer understanding of differences between the formal and dynamic equivalence translations, it's helpful to compare how each translates the same passages. Here are three examples:

REVISED STANDARD VERSION CATHOLIC SECOND EDITION	PASSAGE	NEW JERUSALEM BIBLE
Thus the heavens and earth were finished, and all the host of them. And on the seventh day God finished his work which he had done, and he rested on the seventh day from all his work which he had done.	Genesis 2:1–2	Thus heaven and earth were completed with all their array. On the seventh day God had completed the work he had been doing. He rested on the seventh day after all the work he had been doing.
The Lord is my shepherd, I shall not want; he makes me lie down in green pastures. He leads me besides still waters; he restores my soul. He leads me in paths of righteousness for his name's sake.	Psalm 23:1–3	YHWH is my shepherd, I lack nothing. In grassy meadows he lets me lie. By tranquil streams he leads me to restore my spirit. He guides me in paths of saving justice as befits his name.
"Therefore do not be anxious about tomorrow, for tomorrow will be anxious for itself. Let the day's own trouble be sufficient for the day."	Matthew 6:34	"So do not worry about tomorrow: tomorrow will take care of itself. Each day has enough trouble of its own."

In these examples you may be able to tell that the *New Jerusalem Bible* has translated the text in more readable English syntax; however, some of the literal biblical language has been altered (most prominently Psalm 23). Remember that both biblical versions are approved for use by the Church. The RSVCE—the literal translation—may be chosen for biblical studies and the *New Jerusalem Bible*—a dynamic equivalence translation—for personal prayer. Many teachers, scholars, bishops, and priests recommend having more than one edition of the Bible to use for different situations.

There are Catholic Bibles that combine both a literal and dynamic equivalence approach. One of these is the *New American Bible, revised edition* (NABRE). The Old Testament of this edition was revised in 2011, the culmination of nearly twenty years of work by scholars and theologians, including bishops, revisers, and editors. The New Testament remains unchanged from the 1986 edition of this Bible. The Church in the United States uses the NABRE for the readings at Mass and other liturgies. The NABRE is also the translation used in this textbook.

The Inclusion of Biblical Chapters and Verses

You learned previously how to locate and read Bible references (see the introduction to this chapter, "How to Locate and Read Bible References"). But why and when did the chapter and verse references become part of the Bible? The clearest answer is to aid the ease of use. Imagine if someone asked for the

Codex Sinaticus is a fourth-century Greek manuscript of the Bible that contains the oldest complete copy of the New Testament.

location of a quotation from the Book of Isaiah. It wouldn't be very easy to tell the person to "turn to the nineteenth page of Isaiah" or "page 1270 of the Bible" to find the quote because there would always be variations between the pagination of different editions of the Bible.

The division of the Bible occurred as early as the fourth century AD. Each book of the Greek version of the Bible (Septuagint) was divided into smaller parts that resembled chapters. On first inspection, it seems as if some of the translations were organized around the Church's liturgy cycle so that readers for each Mass might know when to begin and when to stop. The problem with that explanation is that the divisions differed from version to version, meaning that the divisions were not universally accepted in the Church at that time. By the sixth century, Jewish leaders had divided the Hebrew Scriptures into small sections that looked like verses. These divisions occurred within larger sections organized by subjects or themes. Some of the divisions of the larger sections were designated as part of a three-year lectionary cycle for daily synagogue readings.

By the tenth century, smaller subdivisions of verses were added to the Hebrew Scriptures. These markings were, again, intended to help indicate synagogue readings as well as provide places for readers to pause. At first the numbered verses were placed in hand-copied editions of the Hebrew Scriptures. After the invention of the printing press around 1450, the Church kept the Hebrew verses for its Old Testament. In 1555, verses were added to the New Testament by a French printer named Robert Estienne. This version of the Vulgate with verses was soon widely distributed in the thousands.

Issues around how the Bible was translated, differences in Catholic editions, and how and why the Bible is divided are all interesting and important in biblical studies. But the most important consideration for selecting a Bible is to choose one with which you will read, study, and pray to the point that it actually wears out and you will have to get another.

SECTION Assessment

Comprehension

1. Why was St. Jerome a good candidate to translate the Bible to Latin?
2. Name one thing that was different about the Vulgate from other Latin translations of the Bible.
3. Explain the difference between formal or literal and dynamic equivalence translations of the Bible.
4. Why is it inaccurate to say that the Vulgate was "the official Bible of the Catholic Church"?
5. Why were chapters and verses added to the Bible?

Vocabulary

6. What connections can you make between the Protestant Reformation, the translation of the Bible to Latin, and the *Gutenberg Printing Press*?

Reflection

7. Do you think it would be more difficult to be a translator of a language that was not your native language? Explain your answer.

Section Reviews

Focus Question

How is God's Word collected and codified in the Bible?

Complete one of the following:

- Research the Divine Office or Liturgy of the Hours and write a short explanation. Explain its importance in the Church. Also, tell how Sacred Scripture is essential to this practice.
- Use two different biblical commentaries (e.g., *Collegeville Bible Commentary* and *New Jerome Biblical Commentary*) and compare the story of the Great Flood from Genesis 7–9. Summarize something different that each commentary has to say about the flood.
- Use a biblical concordance to look up each of the following, and complete each verse or apply the correct Scripture reference:
  - "My God, my God ________________." (Ps 22:___)
  - God blessed them saying, "Be fertile and multiply; fill the earth and subdue it." (____)
  - "____________________, let this cup pass from me." (Mt ____)
  - _________________________, who is good, whose love endures forever. (Ps ____)

Introduction

What Do You Know about the Bible?

Review Points

- God reveals himself through Sacred Scripture. Catholics have the twofold duty to be knowledgeable about the formation and contents of the Bible while at the same time being careful to avoid personal interpretations of the sacred texts without the help of the Magisterium.
- The Bible is an addictive form of study. Several basic tools help the student to better understand its place and purpose.

Assignment

Read and summarize the *Catechism of the Catholic Church*, 131–133, in one or two sentences.

Section 1
How God's Word Was First Shared

Review Points

- From a base of oral traditions, eventually both the Israelites and early Christians began to record their sacred stories in written form. The Old Testament was composed over the course of about nine hundred years. The books of the New Testament were composed from the latter half of the first century into the early second century AD.
- The Gospels are at the heart of the New Testament. They were formed in three stages: (1) the historical life of Jesus, (2) the oral sharing of the kerygma, and (3) the writing of the four Gospels and other New Testament books.
- Saul, known by his Roman name, Paul, bridged the oral and written traditions of the New Testament. His First Letter to the Thessalonians is the oldest piece of writing in the New Testament.

Assignment

Create a simple Venn diagram to highlight some of the similarities and differences between the formation of the Old Testament and the formation of the New Testament.

Section 2
The Development of Written Books

Review Points

- Understanding the development of the written books of the Bible involves asking questions about why it was written, who wrote it, and how the authors composed written copies.

- The Bible was recorded in order to preserve a permanent record of God's Word, to ensure consistency and unity, to be able to use it more easily for prayer and worship, and to prepare others for entrance into the faith.
- Producing written copies of the Bible was expensive. Each copy was written by hand on either papyrus or parchment.

Assignment

The papyrus plant was called "bulrush" in old translations of the Bible. Where does Isaiah 19:7 say this plant could be found?

Section 3
Setting the Canon of Scripture

Review Points

- *Canon* refers to the official lists of inspired books of the Bible. Two North African Church councils at Hippo in 393 and Carthage in 397 approved of the Old Testament and New Testament canons. The Council of Trent later affirmed the canon.
- Catholics have forty-six Old Testament books and twenty-seven New Testament books in their canon. Protestants removed seven books from the Greek translation of the Old Testament, calling these books *deutero-canonical*, which means "second canon."
- The primary criterion for whether or not a book was to be in the New Testament canon was its connection with the Apostles.

Assignment

Look up and read the statements from Session 4 of the Council of Trent on Sacred Scripture. Summarize in two or three sentences something you found interesting.

Section 4
Different Biblical Translations

Review Points

- Koine Greek was the common spoken language in the Roman Empire of the first century. When the common language changed to Latin, St. Jerome took on the task to translate the Old Testament and New Testament to a universally accepted Latin version. It became known as the "Vulgate."
- Today, there are several English translations of the Bible that are approved by the Catholic Church for use. Some utilize a *formal* or *literal style* of translation, paying special attention to the original sources. Others are translated in a style known as *dynamic equivalence*, which focuses on making the Bible more readable in English.

Assignment

Do you think the difference between Catholic and Protestant Bibles would make it challenging for Catholic and Protestant teens to do a Bible study together? Why or why not?

Chapter Projects

Choose and complete at least one of the following projects to assess your understanding of the material in this chapter.

1. Evaluate the Religious Nature of Leonardo da Vinci's Mona Lisa

Certainly da Vinci's *Mona Lisa*, which he was working on as late as 1507, is one of the world's most famous (and parodied) paintings. It is also one of the most valuable. In 1962 it was valued at $100 million (nearly $900 million in 2022). But is it a religious painting? The easy answer is that *Mona Lisa* was a secular painting, a portrait of the wife of a wealthy silk merchant. Research and evaluate the religious nature of the *Mona Lisa*, and write your findings in a reflective essay. Include all of these elements:

- Your first impressions of the painting.
- Does it have religious themes based on your first impressions?
- What are arguments that the *Mona Lisa* is a religious painting?
- What are arguments that it is a secular painting?
- What is meant by the Italian phrase *"La Gioconda"*? How is the phrase associated with the painting?
- Who was the subject of the painting? Was she religious?
- Was da Vinci religious?
- What is your conclusion about the religious nature of the *Mona Lisa*?

2. Write a Short Story Using Idioms from the Bible

An idiom is a group of words that when placed together have a meaning that is different than if they were separate. Idioms are also particular to a specific culture or language. You are surely familiar with several idioms and their meaning, such as these:

- "He missed the boat." (He missed an opportunity.)
- "I'm feeling under the weather." (I'm feeling sick.)

- "We'll cross that bridge when we come to it." (We'll handle that problem later.)

Many of today's common idioms come from the Bible—for example, "fall from grace" (Gal 5:4), "fight the good fight" (1 Tm 6:12), and "a little birdie told me" (Eccl 10:20).

Write a short story that includes at least ten biblical idioms (you can find more in an internet search). The story can be on any topic but should be constructed with a common subject or theme and an organized beginning, middle, and end. Underline each of the idioms that you use, and include a parenthetical reference of the biblical origins of the idioms that you choose.

3. Create an Illustrated Biblical Passage

Locate one of your favorite Scripture passages. Create a parchment-like, elegant, illustrated manuscript of one passage. Do it this way:

- Use heavy-bond paper.
- Transcribe the verse in ink in your best handwriting, or use an appropriate computer font.
- Decorate the space around the passage with drawings and designs that capture the spirit of your passage.

4. Recite the Our Father in Aramaic

Aramaic is an ancient language of Palestine. It is spoken only rarely today, but in Jesus's time it was likely his everyday language. He would have spoken Hebrew only when visiting Jerusalem and koine Greek when dealing with Gentile foreigners. Latin was spoken in the Roman Empire, but likely not by Jesus. This background is intended to let you know that when Jesus taught his disciples the Our Father (see Matthew 6:9–13) he likely did so using Aramaic. Look up a recording of the Our Father in Aramaic. Play it through twice, and then answer the following question in writing:

- How does hearing the Our Father in the language spoken by Jesus enrich your understanding of Jesus or this prayer?

Next, practice to memorize the prayer. You can do this by listening to the recording several times, printing the Aramaic words phonetically as an aid, or both. When you have mastered the prayer, record it on a video platform that is shareable with your teacher.

5. Research and Report on a Bible Topic

Research one of these topics in greater depth, and develop a creative way (e.g., written or oral report, graph, display) to share the information with your teacher. (If your report is spoken, present it with a video platform that is shareable with your teacher.)

- Report about some of the complexities of translating the Bible.
- Research the Dead Sea Scrolls. Learn more about their history and significance.
- Look into the "Dead Sea Scrolls Digital Project," a partnership between the Israel Museum and Google that allows users to search and read high-resolution images of the scrolls as well as view short videos that explain and provide background about the manuscripts.
- Explore biblical archaeology and learn about how this discipline helps scholars and Bible readers understand more about the Bible.

Faithful Disciple
St. Paula of Rome

St. Paula of Rome

St. Jerome, a Church Father who was also a **Desert Father**, is credited with the difficult translation of the Old Testament from Hebrew to Latin and the New Testament from Greek to Latin. But he didn't work alone. He had help in editing and proofreading his text from a rich aristocratic woman, Paula, who left Rome to travel with Jerome through the Egyptian and Palestinian deserts before settling near Jerome in Bethlehem.

Paula (AD 347–404) was a member of the family Camilli, a distinguished political family in Rome. At age sixteen she married Toxotius, a Roman nobleman, with whom she had four daughters and a son. When her husband died when Paula was thirty-two, she was able to avoid a legal requirement for widows to remarry because of her established wealth. She used this loophole to be able to spend more time studying her Christian faith. She also joined up with Marcella, the leader of a group of widows and young unmarried women who studied Scripture, prayed together, and lived a semi-monastic lifestyle. She met St. Jerome through Marcella and this group.

A year after her husband's death, Paula arranged for care for four of her children, including her infant son, in order to accompany Jerome on a ship

Desert Father The name for Christians of about the fourth century who withdrew to the desert to live an ascetic life of prayer, fasting, and abstinence. Their teachings had a profound impact on the theology and spirituality of the Church and the development of monasticism.

that would take them to northern Africa. Her remaining virgin daughter Eustochium joined her on the pilgrimage. Some viewed this decision negatively as a mother abandoning her children. She understood the sentiment but was also committed to Christ's call to "give up one's life for his sake and the Gospel" (Mk 8:35). "She knew herself no more as a mother that she might approve herself a handmaid of Christ," wrote St. Jerome. "Yet her heart was rent within her, and she wrestled with her grief, as though she were being forcibly separated from parts of herself."[3]

Paula used her aristocratic ties and her family wealth to found and fund three monasteries in Bethlehem: one for women, one for men, and one for tourists. Each of the monasteries housed people from different parts of the world and from different social classes. The only requirement was renunciation of wealth in order to live better an **ascetic** Christian lifestyle.

Both Paula and Eustochium were dedicated scholars. This is where their lives intersected with Jerome's work on the Vulgate. While in Jerusalem, they were tutored under Jerome in the biblical languages. Jerome read to them the entire Old Testament in Hebrew as part of their studies. Jerome later admitted that Paula's knowledge of Hebrew grew to surpass his own. Though Pope Damasus had asked Jerome to translate the Bible, Paula and Eustochium were the ones who prodded him through the entire project. Paula again used her bank account and credit to acquire many of the rare and expensive original biblical texts that Jerome needed for his translation. Both Paula and Eustochium proofread Jerome's work and compared it to the other Latin translations that were available. Mother and daughter were also instrumental in helping with the actual translation of the Book of Psalms that became part of the Vulgate.

Many gossiped that Jerome and Paula were romantically involved, but that was not true. In Chaucer's "Wife of Bath" story in the *Canterbury Tales* (1387–1400), he wrote a parody of the relationship of Jerome and Paula, having the main characters visit the same pilgrimage sites. Rather, Paula was a devoted ascetic and respected scholar. When she died on January 26, 404, her funeral was attended by many whom she had befriended, including several Egyptian monks. When Jerome died in 419 or 420 he was buried

---

ascetic Characterized by the practice of severe discipline and abstinence for religious reasons.

under the Church of the Nativity in Bethlehem near the graves of Paula and Eustochium.

The feast day of St. Paula of Rome, whom some call a "Church Mother," is January 26.

Comprehension

1. Why was St. Paula able to remain unmarried after becoming a widow?
2. Who was Marcella?
3. What was controversial about Paula traveling with St. Jerome?
4. What types of monasteries did Paula found?
5. Who was Eustochium?
6. How did Paula and Eustochium aid St. Jerome in translating the Bible to Latin?

Reflection

Jesus said: "Whoever wishes to save his life will lose it, but whoever loses his life for my sake and that of the gospel will save it" (Mk 8:34). Imagine and share a radical form of discipleship you might consider.

Prayer

The prologue to the Gospel of John (1:1–18) highlights that Jesus is the incarnate *Logos*, Greek for "Word." The prologue was probably an early Christian hymn in which the last word of one phrase connects with the theme of the next phrase. The prologue also states the main overall themes of John's Gospel: life, light, truth, the world, and the preexistence of Jesus Christ before all of creation.

Pray the words of the first five verses by saying aloud or in your heart each of the lines twice and pausing for reflection before moving on.

John 1:1–5

In the beginning was the Word,
and the Word was with God,
and the Word was God.
All things came to be through him,
and without him nothing came to be.
What came to be through him was life
and this life was the light of the human race;
The light shines in the darkness,
and the darkness has not overcome it.

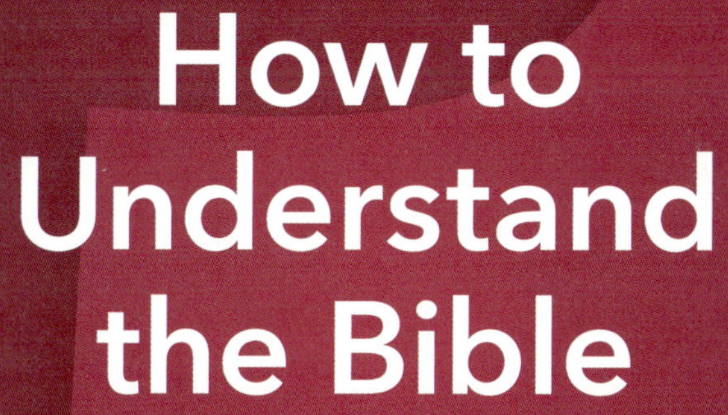
How to
Understand
the Bible

Shroud of Turin

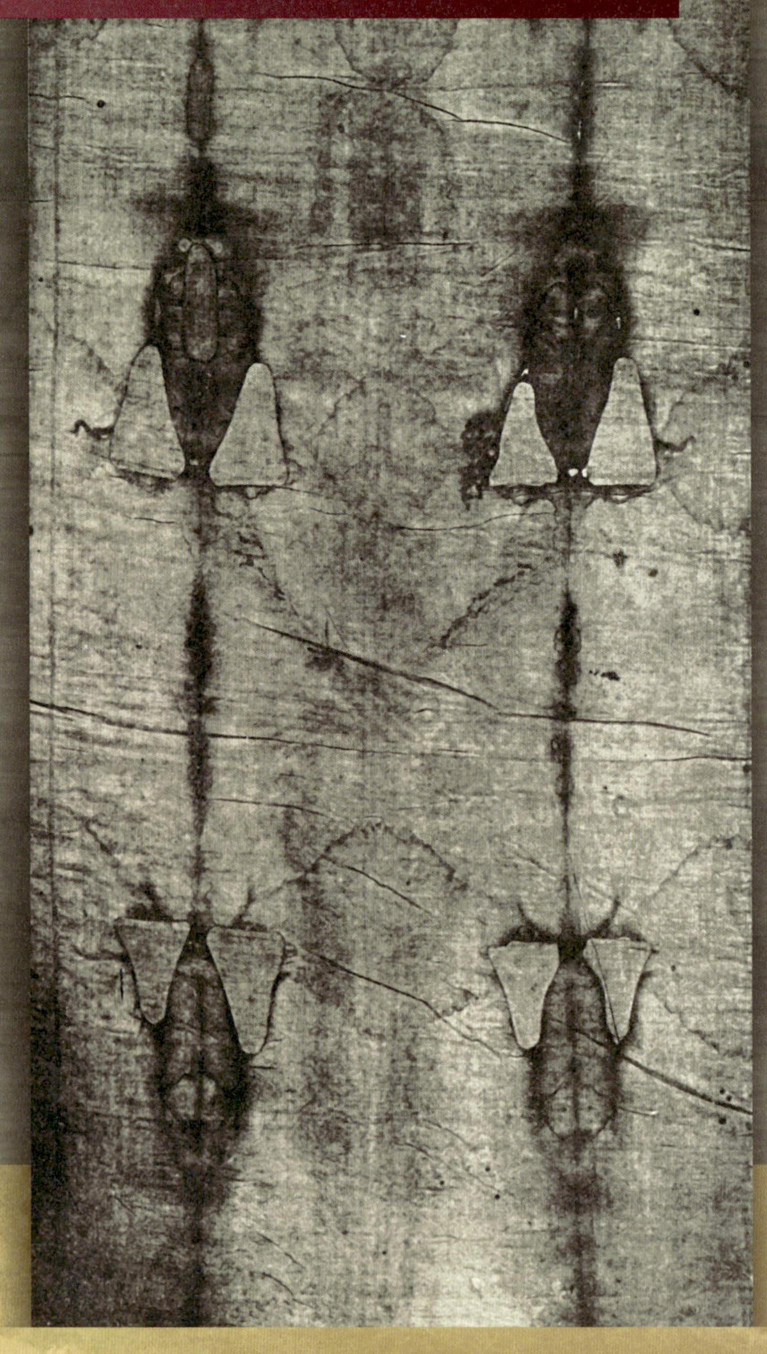

Not a piece of art, but one of the most well-known archaeological items connected with the biblical era, the Shroud of Turin is something that many believe to be the actual burial cloth of Christ. Pope John Paul II on at least three occasions referenced the Shroud of Turin. Twice, in 1978 and then again in 1998, the pope visited the shroud in person. In 1989, when asked by reporters what he thought about the shroud, he said, "It certainly is a relic." Then ten years later in 1998 he was asked if he thought the shroud was the actual burial cloth of Christ. He responded: "I think it is!"

The shroud is a rectangular piece of linen, measuring about 3.5 feet by 14.5 feet. What makes the shroud distinctive is the impression on it of a front and back view of a naked man with his hands folded across his midsection. The impression is believed to be of Jesus, which is why the shroud is believed by some to be the burial cloth used by Joseph of Arimathea to wrap the body of Jesus for burial (see John 19:39–42).

There is documentation of the Shroud of Turin being displayed in Jerusalem as far back as AD 500. Scientific study of the shroud began in earnest in May 1898, when it was photographed by Secundo Pia. When he developed the film he discovered that the negative image was actually positive, and vice versa. This means that when looking at the linen of the shroud with the naked eye, a yellowish-brown image of a man is visible, but when the black-and-white film negative is observed, the image can be seen in much greater detail.

The scientific studies of both the negative of the photograph and of the linen itself have revealed more information about the shroud. First, the image of the man on the shroud is not a stain. It was not painted on the linen. Rather, it is an image seared onto the linen that has not yet been able to be explained. Also, the image can be read by 3D technology whereas paintings cannot. Pollen found on the shroud is consistent with dust from the Near Eastern region and from perfumes Jews used to anoint the body of a person before burial.

There is also blood on the linen. Chemical and biological testing proves that the blood is type AB and antigen group MNS. As there are also no paint pigments of any kind on the shroud, it can be proven that there was no attempt to forge the appearance of blood. DNA testing was also performed on the blood, revealing that the person wrapped in the shroud was a man.

Whereas no physical item will ever offer (especially to atheists and other doubters) proof of God's existence, the Shroud of Turin qualifies as one that comes closer than most.

Focus Question

What are ways I can use the tools of biblical scholarship to grow in a faith-filled understanding of Sacred Scripture?

Chapter Overview

Introduction

How Catholics Read the Bible

Section 1

How the Church Studies the Bible

Section 2

Reading the Bible according to the Holy Spirit

Section 3

Biblical Truth and Scientific Truth Are Compatible

Section 4

Tools of Biblical Scholarship

Introduction

HOW CATHOLICS READ THE BIBLE

In Chapter 2, you learned that a difference between Catholic Bibles and Protestant Bibles is the number of Old Testament books accepted by each. Catholic Bibles affirm forty-six Old Testament books of the original Septuagint. Protestant Bibles use a version of the Old Testament taken from a Hebrew translation that had only thirty-nine books. Besides the differences in the number of biblical books, Catholics and many Protestants also differ on their understandings of how the Bible should be read and understood. Some of these differences involve views on methods of scholarship, science and evolution, the living nature of Scripture, and the role of the Church in interpreting the Bible. These topics will be explored further in this chapter.

To begin, let's consider an even more basic disagreement: the difference between reading the Bible literally and reading it contextually.

Many Protestants are fundamentalists, meaning they interpret each word or phrase in the Bible from a *literalist* point of view. Fundamentalists read the Bible without reference to the culture in which the passage was written or a particular literary form of the passage. On the other hand, Catholics read the Bible *contextually*. From a literary perspective, this means first examining and defining the literary form in its original context, much in the same way you would do in reading a book or an article on the internet. In these cases, you would determine whether you are reading fiction or nonfiction, satire or sarcasm, a news story or an editorial, and so on. Similar types of distinctions must apply when analyzing biblical literature.

Also, a literalist understanding of the Bible often ignores solid scientific evidence on the world's origins, having difficulty reconciling what science teaches with the creation accounts in the Book of Genesis. For example, Catholics understand that the first creation account (Gn 1:1–2:3) was not intended to be a scientific explanation of how creation occurred; rather, it was an account to explain what creation is, who created it, and why. Fundamentalists resist scientific evidence that the cosmos evolved over billions of years and hold instead to the literal words of the Bible that God created the world in six twenty-four-hour periods.

It is important to point out that Protestants are very well-read when it comes to the Bible. Many Protestants can quote Scripture passages and cite references to support their beliefs. Protestant fundamentalists and Catholics agree that Christ is the center of the Bible. There is also agreement that the Bible is inspired and infallible. But there is strong disagreement on the Church's relationship to the Bible. Fundamentalists do not view the Bible as part of the historical Church; that is, they often fail to acknowledge that the divinely inspired texts were handed on to the Church and that the Church determined the biblical canon and now teaches and interprets the Bible's meaning.

When comparing the differences in interpretations between fundamentalist and Catholic views of Scripture in more detail, it is helpful not only to note distinctions, but also to develop a clearer understanding about what Catholics believe about the Bible and how Catholics read and study the Bible.

Seven Beliefs about the Bible

According to theologian Peter Kreeft, Catholics and fundamentalists believe the same seven things about the Bible, but they just believe these things differently.[1] He explained them as follows:

1. The Bible Is Supernatural

Fundamentalists and Catholics agree that the Bible is the Word of God, that God is the author of Scripture. However, fundamentalists tend not to recognize or admit the place of human authors. Fundamentalists often fail to see the great miracle of the almighty God authoring the Bible with the aid of flawed human authors.

Dr. Peter Kreeft is a Catholic convert and the author of more than eighty books on Christian philosophy, theology, and apologetics.

2. The Bible Is Inspired

Catholics and Protestants both accept that the Bible is inspired (see earlier in this introduction). However, fundamentalists and Catholics disagree about how the inspiration took place. Fundamentalists often hold that God dictated the books of the Bible word for word and the human authors were secretaries recording his words. This argument breaks down with the fact that we don't have the original manuscripts of any of the books of the Bible. Any version of the Bible is a reproduction or copy from an earlier version. Yet, even without the original manuscripts, there is 99 percent verbal agreement among the different manuscripts, which is far more than for any other ancient writings. God's inspiration involves his working with human authors and editors.

3. The Bible Is Infallible

Catholics understand that the Bible is infallible (without error), but not necessarily in areas like grammatical, mathematical, or scientific truth (see Chapter 1, Section 4, "God Records His Revelation"). Fundamentalists often disagree with mention of any kind of error in the Bible. Remember, the Bible is primarily a source of symbolic, relational, moral, and religious truth.

4. The Bible and the Church Are Sufficient

This principle has to do with what is perhaps the biggest source of disagreement between fundamentalists and Catholics. Martin Luther taught a theology of *sola scriptura* ("the Bible alone") that rejected the authority of Sacred Tradition, asserting that the Scriptures, especially the New Testament, were the only sources of faith and practice. Luther's argument is easily proven inadequate. Scripture can't interpret itself. To rely on a person's private interpretation is unrealistic and unworkable (e.g., the belief in *sola scriptura* has led to, conservatively, thousands of different Protestant denominations). Most clearly, the infallible Church is needed to guarantee an infallible Bible because it was the Church (the early disciples) who wrote the Bible and the early Church councils that determined the canon of the Bible.

5. The Bible Is Authoritative

Catholics and fundamentalists agree that the Bible's authority is absolute and without fault. The difference is that Catholics understand that the Bible's proper authority can only be preserved and interpreted by the Church.

6. The Bible Is Not Always Literal

Fundamentalists insist on a literal interpretation of almost everything in the Bible. The accounts of creation are an example of this. Also, fundamentalists are known for using biblical passages to predict when the world will end, though Jesus himself said that even he does not know "the day and hour" and that "the Father alone" knows (see Matthew 24:36). Interestingly, one passage fundamentalists do not interpret literally is Jesus's words at the Last Supper: "This is my body" (Mt 26:26). Catholics and most Protestants have a completely different understanding of Jesus's presence in the Eucharist.∞

7. The Bible Is Practical

Here, fundamentalists, at least in the past, have had an advantage over Catholics. Fundamentalists are known for reading, studying, believing, and being devoted to Scripture. Catholics in other generations have been less familiar with using the Bible in these ways. From a negative point of view, fundamentalists, while proficient in using and citing the Bible, have done so in faulty ways as the other six points address.

The primary purpose of the Bible is to present the religious truths that God wishes to reveal through the events of salvation history. Under the guidance of the Magisterium, biblical scholars and individuals work to find the contextual sense of the biblical passages—what the author intended to convey. A fundamentalist approach falls short of this goal because it does not penetrate the biblical text's true meaning. This chapter examines more about the history and methods of biblical scholarship in the Church.

SECTION Assessment

Comprehension

1. Explain the difference between reading the Bible literally versus contextually.
2. How would fundamentalists interpret the Genesis account of God's creation of the world in six days?
3. How would Catholics interpret the same creation account?
4. What is the Catholic response to Luther's theology of *sola scriptura*?
5. What is the primary purpose of the Bible?

Reflection

6. What is ironic about the way fundamentalists often interpret Jesus's words from the Last Supper: "This is my body"?
7. What can Catholics learn from fundamentalists about how to use the Bible?

∞ Note

In the Eucharist, the Body and Blood of Christ, "the whole Christ is truly, really and substantially contained" (Council of Trent, quoted in *CCC*, 1374). The term *transubstantiation* is used to express how the reality (substance) of bread and wine changes into the reality of Jesus—his risen, glorified Body and Blood (namely, the Real Presence of Christ). Many Protestants believe that the bread and wine at their worship services are only symbolic of Christ's presence.

Section 1

HOW THE CHURCH STUDIES THE BIBLE

Discoveries of early biblical manuscripts, a greater understanding of ancient languages, and new archaeological discoveries all contribute to how the Church studies Sacred Scripture. Biblical scholarship, a field that began in the early twentieth century with some hesitancy around the issue of **modernism**, took off in earnest with the release of *Divino afflante Spiritu* (*By the Inspiration of the Spirit*), the 1943 encyclical by Pope Pius XII that encouraged scholars to "go back wholly in spirit to those remote centuries of the East" to determine the particular modes of writing that an author was likely to use (*Divino afflante Spiritu*, 21). The pope called not only for new translations of the Bible (see the introduction to Chapter 2), but also for biblical scholars to use all the tools of **biblical criticism** to help them fully understand the meaning of Scripture passages as intended by the author.

Don't think of the term *criticism* in a negative way. Rather, it means looking *carefully* at the biblical texts in their historical and literary contexts. The four methods of criticism—historical, source, form, and redaction—involve scholarly detective work. The purpose of these methods is to determine (1) what the biblical authors intended to say for the audience for whom they wrote, (2) what traditions of the particular community were in place before

---

modernism A movement of the late nineteenth and early twentieth centuries that attempted to reduce Church teaching to modern advances in history, science, and biblical research.

biblical criticism A general term that describes several ways to understand biblical texts in their original setting, for discovering the intention of the original author, and for examining their literary style. It includes form criticism, historical criticism, source criticism, and redaction criticism.

the biblical author wrote the text, and (3) and how Jesus fit into these events. The third stage is intended to establish as near as possible the exact words and actions of Jesus.

Characterizations of Exegesis

The Church asks you to read Sacred Scripture carefully, prayerfully, and with awareness that the biblical authors wrote passages for different cultural and historical settings. The Second Vatican Council document *Dei Verbum* offers questions and guidelines to aid in the critical interpretation of a biblical text, which is known by its Greek name *exegesis*. Exegesis, or critical interpretation, means studying the passages in depth in order to learn what God is revealing. Exegesis requires that you ask questions such as these:

- What is the type, or literary genre, of writing?
- What occurred historically at the time this was written that might shed light on what this passage means?
- Who first wrote this material?
- How did these texts come to be part of the canon of the Bible?
- How was the material gathered and edited?
- If any changes were made, why were they made?

Exegesis involves detective work. In a sense, the *exegete* (person using exegesis) "interrogates" the biblical passages, gathers additional information, assesses its relevance to the passage, and uncovers material that helps us to understand what God wants to reveal.

You may not personally have the knowledge or skills of a bishop or a scholar, but you too can learn more about God's Revelation through biblical exegesis. Your everyday life prepares you to examine the biblical text because you regularly interpret oral and written communications. Anytime someone communicates with you, you ask yourself questions about what was said. You assess whether the person is reliable and whether he is communicating his own idea or what someone else wants him to say. You might question whether this person is being serious or joking around with you. Questions about the source of a communication, its form, its origin, and whether it has been modified are questions that you usually answer without even having to think about them.

In the 1993 document *The Interpretation of the Bible in the Church*, the Pontifical Biblical Commission wrote, "What characterizes Catholic exegesis is that it deliberately places itself within the living tradition of the Church."[2] Within the life of the Church, using exegesis, the Magisterium and Catholic Scripture scholars search for the literal meaning or *literal sense* of the biblical text while at the same time not excluding the spiritual sense.

Tools for Critical Interpretation

The *Catechism of the Catholic Church* defines the literal sense as "the meaning conveyed by the words of Scripture and discovered by exegesis, following the rules of sound interpretation" (*CCC*, 116). The Church particularly uses four types of the critical interpretation of the Bible: form criticism, historical criticism, source criticism, and redaction criticism. Each is explained as follows.

Form Criticism

Scripture experts use *form criticism* to determine how each biblical book took shape in the period of oral tradition before the authors put it into writing. Form criticism also identifies the literary genres used in the Bible.

The form of the text provides us with clues about what the text means. If you can identify a literary genre of a piece of writing, you can adjust your expectations about what and how you will learn from the content. Think about how you can immediately tell if a series of numbers is a phone number or a social security number. Based on the number of digits and the placement of hyphens, you know whether you can use this information to call a person on the phone or to verify a person's identity. This type of patterning with words, sentences, and style helps scholars and, in fact, any reader of the Bible to determine different literary genres. Several examples follow:

- ***ALLEGORY***
  An extended comparison in which many elements of a story stand for deeper realities like abstract ideas, moral qualities, or spiritual realities (see Proverbs 9:1–6).

- ***CREED***
  A formal statement of religious belief (see Deuteronomy 26:5–10).

- ***ETIOLOGY***
  A story that gives the cause of something (see Genesis 32:22–32).

- ***FABLE***
  A brief story with a moral, often involving animals that act and speak like human beings (see Judges 9:7–15).

- ***HISTORY***
  A chronological narrative or record of events, as in the life or development of a people, country, or institution (see 1 Kings 1–2).

- ***LAW***
  A rule of conduct or standard of behavior established by proper authority, society, or custom (see Exodus 20:1–17).

- ***PROPHECY***
  An inspired utterance made by a prophet that expresses God's will (see Amos 1–2).

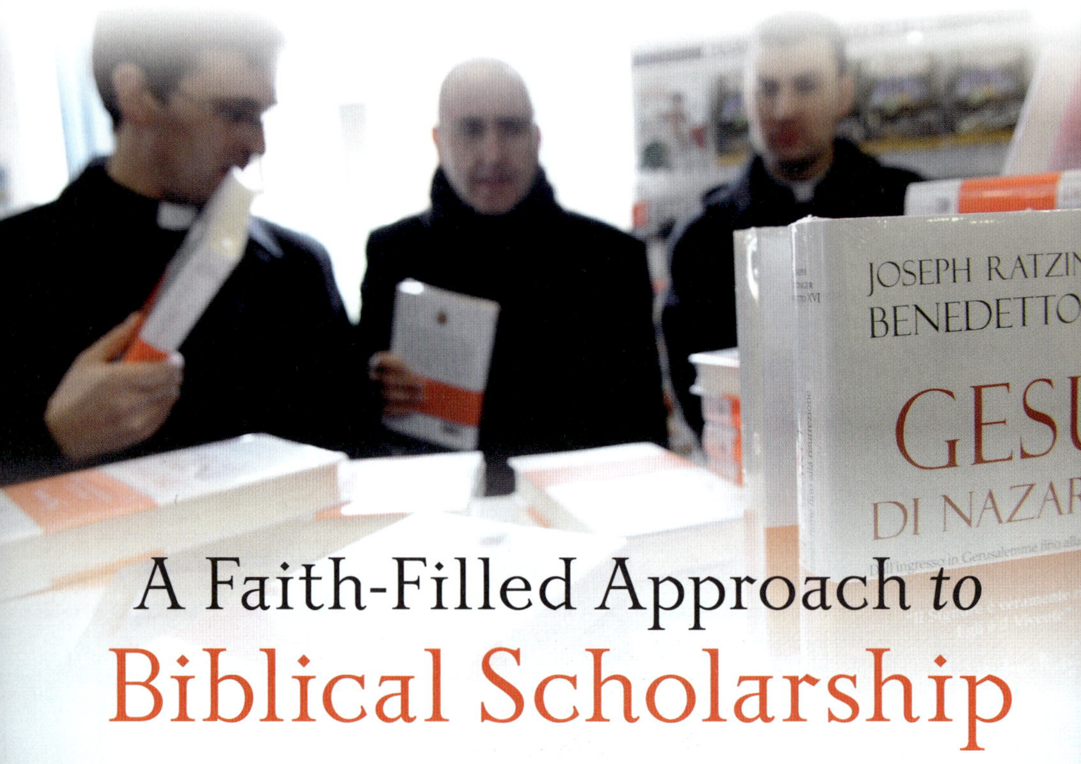

A Faith-Filled Approach *to* Biblical Scholarship

Focus Question: What are ways I can use the tools of biblical scholarship to grow in a faith-filled understanding of Sacred Scripture?

Before he became Pope Benedict XVI, Joseph Ratzinger was already a biblical scholar. As pope, he supported Catholics joining in the efforts of contemporary biblical scholarship. Yet, he was hesitant in allowing biblical scholarship to be in any way separated from a *faith-filled* study of the Bible. For example, he reminded biblical scholars to always acknowledge God as the primary author of the Bible. Because of divine inspiration, he taught, biblical passages can contain more meaning than their human authors could ever have imagined.

Also, Pope Benedict pointed out that in spite of some great results from biblical scholarship since the late nineteenth century in understanding the origins and meaning of biblical texts, there have also been serious errors made. One general error is that biblical scholars tend to ignore the entire coherency of the Bible. They have tended not to look at what God is trying to communicate throughout the unity of all of the books of the Bible, instead focusing on individual texts. Also, Pope Benedict issued a second warning about historical criticism: it tends to examine a biblical text only according to the era in which it was written. Rather, the biblical text should be interpreted for how it speaks through *all* ages into the present and also into the future.

After he became pope, Benedict XVI focused a great deal of effort on encouraging Catholics to read and study the Bible. He also viewed God's Word as a source of ecumenical dialogue and practice with other Christians and interreligious dialogue with practicing Jews from whom much of the Old Testament originates. In 2005, at a conference called "Sacred Scripture in the Life of the Church," Pope Benedict reiterated that the Church venerates the Bible as she venerates the Body of the Lord. He encouraged all people of faith to practice "the diligent reading of Sacred Scripture accompanied by prayer."[3]

In 2008, Pope Benedict participated in an event designed to show by his own actions that he meant what he had said. He was the first reader in a "Bible-reading marathon" that was streamed worldwide. Pope Benedict read the first chapter of the Book of Genesis in Italian. The second reader was Rome's chief rabbi, Riccardo Di Segni, who read more of Genesis in Hebrew. The prologue to the Gospel of John was read in Greek. Other readers included cardinals, politicians, scholars, athletes, students, soldiers, and factory workers, about twelve hundred people in total who read the entire Bible over a six-day period. Muslims, who don't consider the Bible a sacred book, were invited to read passages as well. The event set out to achieve the world record for continuous Bible reading, but its main purpose was to encourage people everywhere to make Bible reading a more constant practice in their lives.

The Bible-reading marathon was only a kick-off for a formal Church synod—*The Word of God in the Life and Mission of the Church*—called by Pope Benedict to further address the balance needed between biblical scholarship that leads to theologically sound biblical reading and study for all Christians. In 2010,

he summarized his comments in a post-synodal apostolic exhortation *Verbum Domini* (*God's Word*). Pope Benedict offered support for the Church's reasoned entrance into the field of biblical scholarship while acknowledging "the benefits that historical-critical exegesis and other recently developed methods of textual analysis have brought the Church" (*Verbum Domini*, 32). The pope added a reminder that the Church's living Magisterium must be the arbiter that rejects in any way a split between human study of the Bible and its divine origins and primacy as God's living Word.[4]

In the course of his entire life as a biblical scholar, Pope Benedict's sound approach to the study of the Bible included these essential points:

- Sacred Scripture is a unity, and individual texts must be understood in light of the entire Bible.
- Sacred Scripture is based in history. The one historical subject that is present in all of the Bible is the People of God.
- Sacred Scripture must be read as part of the Church; the Magisterium ultimately is the interpreter of biblical texts.

According to Pope Benedict, "Tradition does not obstruct access to Scripture but opens it; and conversely the Church has a decisive say in the interpretation of Scripture."[5]

Further Study and Reflection

- Look up and define the word *hermeneutics* related to biblical studies. What did Pope Benedict mean by the phrase "hermeneutics of continuity" in connection with biblical scholarship?
- Read paragraphs 29–30 of Pope Benedict XVI's *Verbum Domini*. From your reading, answer: "What did St. Bonaventure, St. Augustine, and St. Jerome say about biblical studies?"

- ***GENEALOGY***
  A record of one's ancestry (see Matthew 1:1–17).
- ***RIDDLE***
  A question or statement that teases the mind, requiring thought and application (see Matthew 11:11).
- ***PARABLE***
  A vivid story told to convey religious truth, often with a surprise ending (see Matthew 13:33).

Consider the parable of the good Samaritan (see Luke 10:25–37). Because Jesus used the literary form of a parable, you may assume that he was not speaking of actual, *historical* persons when he told the story. Rather, he used the story to make the point that people should be compassionate and loving to all, even enemies. Because Jesus's lesson was so important, the early Christians repeated this parable among themselves. The author Luke then emphasized the story's significance by including the parable in his Gospel.

Historical Criticism

Using *historical criticism*, Scripture experts try to determine the historical and cultural context of the biblical text. Historical criticism uses archaeological and historical research to discover more about the time period in which a text was written.

For example, you may be familiar with the **Ark of the Covenant** from the Old Testament. Why do you think that people do not know where the Ark is today? Historical research reveals that the Ark of the Covenant was a chest made of wood and gold, built by the Chosen People after Moses received the Ten Commandments. (Exodus 25:10–22 describes its design. Exodus 37:1–9 describes its construction.) It would have measured

Ark of the Covenant The most important symbol of the Jewish faith. It served as the only physical manifestation of God on earth. The Ark was built while the Israelites wandered in the desert and was used until the building of the First Temple.

approximately four feet by two-and-a-half feet. The original tablets of the Ten Commandments were in the Ark. The Ark traveled with the Israelites in the desert until King David brought it to Jerusalem around 1000 BC.

The last time the Old Testament mentions the Ark is when the Babylonians demolished the Jerusalem Temple in 587 BC. There was no mention of the Ark when the Jews rebuilt the Temple about seventy years later. The scholarly consensus is that the Babylonians destroyed the Ark and melted it down for its gold.

Source Criticism

If God did not dictate the Bible to its authors, then where did the authors get their material? When scholars and the Magisterium use *source criticism*, they attempt to find out where biblical material came from. For example, some believe that the history in the Books of Kings came from court records written by royal scribes. In the New Testament, source criticism reveals that the author of Luke's Gospel used three main sources in his writing: the Gospel of Mark, a collection of writings also found in Matthew's Gospel, and material unique to Luke.

Redaction Criticism

An expert using *redaction criticism* focuses on the editor or editors who collected and arranged sources in a biblical chapter or book. Redaction criticism also tries to determine how a given biblical author's theology or understanding of God influenced the way that he organized the material.

For example, consider the genealogy of Jesus. When the evangelist Luke recorded Jesus's family tree, he traced his lineage back to Adam, the common ancestor of *all* people, to show that his Gospel was written for Gentile Christians. The author of Matthew's Gospel, on the other hand, traced Jesus's ancestry to Abraham, the father of Judaism, and so displayed a different but not conflicting theology. Because he was writing for a predominantly Jewish-Christian community, Matthew included material showing that Jesus Christ fulfilled the prophecies made to the Chosen People.

Among other reasons, the Bible is complex because it was written for different audiences, its events occurred in different times and cultures, and it was written in different languages. While you should not think that the Bible is too difficult for you to read yourself, you should also realize the value of

Scripture scholarship. The Church's Magisterium, the living, teaching office of the Church, takes great care in guarding with dedication and expounding faithfully on any interpretation of Sacred Scripture. Many bishops have great expertise in the study of Sacred Scripture, and all the bishops of the Church have access to the important work of Scripture scholars.

SECTION *Assessment*

Comprehension

1. What is the intention of the third stage of biblical criticism?
2. Name one question that an exegete might ask in analyzing a biblical text.
3. Which form of biblical criticism is concerned with identifying literary genres?
4. Explain what redaction criticism reveals about the differences in the genealogies of Jesus from Luke's and Matthew's Gospels.

Vocabulary

5. How did *modernism* affect Catholic biblical scholarship?

Reflection

6. How does understanding the literal sense of a biblical text differ from fundamentalism?
7. Name two questions that you think are the most important when studying the Bible critically.

Section 2

READING THE BIBLE ACCORDING TO THE HOLY SPIRIT

When using some of the standards of biblical criticism described in the previous section, it is important not to forget the difference between studying the Bible and studying other historical sources. In the early twentieth century, some (mostly Protestant) Scripture scholars began to call into question the divine origins of the Bible and instead made the Bible out to be a "myth" that was intended to frame the Christian kerygma around a mostly nonhistorical narrative. This premise is false for a number of reasons.

First, Scripture is organized around *salvation history:* real people, real places, and real events. There is a unity of the Old Testament and New Testament based on **typology**. The Old Testament prefigures Christ and illuminates the New Testament. As St. Augustine put it, "The New Testament lies hidden in the Old, and the Old Testament is unveiled in the New" (quoted in *CCC*, 129). Jesus Christ is the center and heart of Sacred Scripture, both the Old Testament and New Testament. Therefore, it would not make sense to read the New Testament without a good knowledge of the Old Testament.

A prominent example of biblical typology is how the story of the prophet Jonah, swallowed by a great fish, remaining in its belly for three days and three nights (see Jonah 2:1), prefigures Jesus's time in the tomb before his Resurrection. Jesus even explicitly connected what would happen to him with what happened to Jonah, predicting that his own experience in the tomb would be "something greater than Jonah" (Mt 13:41). Typology is an indicator of how salvation history progresses "toward the fulfillment of the divine plan when 'God [will] be everything to everyone'" (*CCC*, 129, quoting 1 Corinthians 15:28). Yet, while making the connection between the New Testament and

typology A form of biblical exegesis in which Old Testament people and events (types) are seen as preceding or foreshadowing New Testament people and events.

the Old Testament is important, we should also take the time to appreciate the intrinsic value of the Old Testament texts based on the human authors' intentions and how God used these sacred writings to inspire and teach the Chosen People.

Second, Scripture must be "read within the living Tradition of the whole Church" (*CCC*, 113). Recall that Sacred Scripture is one of two parts of a single Deposit of Faith that also includes Sacred Tradition. God did not give the authority to interpret Sacred Scripture to biblical scholars, but rather to the whole Church, through the Magisterium. Therefore, to interpret the Bible properly, it must be read within the Tradition of the Church. Even after study and research, if you were to interpret a Scripture passage in a way that contradicts Sacred Tradition, your personal interpretation is more than likely to be wrong. Sacred Scripture cannot reveal religious truths that contradict one another. God's revealed truths make sense only when one aligns with the other. This is known as the **analogy of faith**. The Bible must be interpreted in a way that is in harmony with all of God's Revelation, including the teaching of the Magisterium.

Third, and more succinctly, some of the early biblical scholars seemed to forget that God is the Bible's inspired author. Because Sacred Scripture is inspired, it "must be read and interpreted in the light of the same Spirit by whom it was written" (*Dei Verbum*, 12, quoted in *CCC*, 111). In other words, anyone who wants to understand the Bible must ask for the guidance of the

---

analogy of faith The analogy of faith holds that God's Revelation in Sacred Scripture is never contradictory. In other words, truth cannot contradict truth.

Holy Spirit while reading and studying it. And this objective is not only for biblical scholars. All Catholics should learn about Jesus through frequent reading of the Bible. In the words of St. Jerome, "Ignorance of the Scriptures is ignorance of Christ" (quoted in *CCC*, 133). The more we know about the Scriptures, the more we know about Jesus, which helps us to deepen our bond with him.

Tools for Deepening the Meaning of Scripture

The "senses of Scripture" is a way to describe what the words in the Bible are meant to express. Arising from an ancient tradition in the Church, there are two senses of Scripture. One is the *literal sense*, which is aided by the sources of biblical criticism. The literal sense refers to what the words convey and what the biblical author wanted to communicate. The literal sense looks at how the words were understood at the time they were written and how they were used to describe things that really happened. For example, the descriptions of Jesus's arrest, trial, Passion, and Death are written from a literal sense.

The other sense of Scripture is the *spiritual sense*. The spiritual sense depends on the good exegetical work of the literal sense to bring unity to God's plan in salvation history as told in Sacred Scripture. The spiritual sense has three subdivisions:

- *The allegorical sense.* An allegory is a metaphor or a sustained comparison. In an allegorical work of literature, you can see that the storyline conveys more than one level of meaning. The allegorical sense is similar to typology in that it looks at the entire Bible, especially the Old Testament, in

"Repent and turn away from sin."

light of its fulfillment in Christ. Knowing of Christ's victory over sin, for example, it is possible to recognize that the **Exodus** crossing of the Red Sea prefigures this victory. Because the Exodus was an escape from slavery into freedom, an allegorical reading of this event also connects it to the waters of Baptism that free us from our slavery to sin.

- *The moral sense.* The Bible provides instruction on proper ways to live and behave and to act justly on behalf of God and other people. For example, Abraham teaches us to have faith and to trust in God. A common message of the prophets, up to the time of John the Baptist, was to turn away from sin, to repent, and to reform one's life. When we read these biblical examples from a moral sense, we, too, are to respond to the same call.
- *The anagogical sense.* This sense helps us to view earthly events and other realities in the context of our journey to heaven. Your ultimate goal is to get to heaven, and the Bible is a handbook of sorts to lead you on the way. The word *anagogical* comes from a Greek word for "leading." How does the anagogical sense work in the Bible? For example, when you read about a person who finds treasure buried in the field and then goes out and sells everything he has in order to buy that field, you come to understand that to achieve eternal life you, too, must put everything else aside in order to put God first (see Matthew 13:44). The anagogical sense also helps us to recognize the Church as the "heavenly Jerusalem" and the "Body of Christ," which leads us to heaven.

It is possible to take the interpretive lenses of reading Scripture too far. For example, using the various lenses of interpretation, St. Augustine, while preaching on Jesus's second multiplication of loaves (see Mark 8:1–9), concluded that the seven loaves represented the sevenfold gifts of the Holy Spirit, the four thousand people in attendance represented people from all four corners of the earth, and the seven baskets of leftover fragments represented the perfection of the Church. These interpretations are not part of the Church's official teaching. But in a majority of cases, analyzing a Scripture reading, particularly a narrative portion (not one of the epistles in letter form), using a combination of the literal sense and the subsections of the spiritual sense can

---

Exodus A foundational event in the history of the Chosen People that occurred when Moses led the Hebrews out of Egypt and slavery.

be very beneficial. For example, when you read the parable of the tenants in Mark 12:1–12, you can ask yourself several questions:

- Did the story really happen, or is it just a story told by Jesus to teach a lesson?
- Whom do the tenants represent in the time of Jesus? How are you like the tenants?
- Whom do the servants represent in the time of Jesus? How are you like the servants?
- Whom does the landowner represent?
- Whom does his son represent?
- What does the vineyard represent?
- Does the story have any moral implications (e.g., greed, unfaithfulness, being overly self-sufficient)?
- Does the story preview a path for you to get to heaven?

By using this Catholic approach to studying the Bible, we can more easily overcome the distance of time and the differences in culture and language to discover a solidarity with our ancestors in faith and to form a deeper connection with Jesus, who is the Word of God.

SECTION *Assessment*

Comprehension

1. Why can't the contents of the Bible be made out as a myth?
2. How does the spiritual sense of Scripture depend on the literal sense?

3. If someone said the Bible was like a handbook with ways to lead you to heaven, what type of sense of Scripture would he or she be describing?

Vocabulary

4. Explain the meaning of *typology* by using a biblical example.
5. What is the *analogy of faith*?

Reflection

6. How do you read the Bible according to the Holy Spirit?
7. What caution would you give to someone who wants to do a critical study of the Bible?

Section 3

BIBLICAL TRUTH AND SCIENTIFIC TRUTH ARE COMPATIBLE

Keep this in mind: What you learn in your theology course does not contradict what you learn in science class. Even when one side is misinterpreted (e.g., fundamentalism in the case of Scripture) or claims false authority (e.g., **scientism**), truth will settle the differences. "Truth does not contradict truth." This statement, used most recently by Pope John Paul II, means that truth is ultimately one, even if it is known through different means.

St. John Henry Newman (1801–1890), a Catholic convert from Anglicism and a great theologian, lived at the time when Charles Darwin's **theory of evolution** was introduced. In connection with Darwin's teaching, science proposed that the world was between twenty million and four hundred million years old, not the six thousand years that had been associated with the Genesis scriptural passages. Newman was open to the new scientific evidence, with the understanding that theology could learn from these discoveries. He was comfortable knowing that nothing discovered by science should make someone doubt his or her faith. He wrote: "If anything seems to be proved by astronomer, or geologist, or chronologist, or antiquarian, or ethnologist, in contradiction to the dogmas of faith, that point will eventually turn out, first, *not* to be proved, or secondly, not *contradictory* to anything *really revealed*, but to something which has been confused with Revelation." Catholics who believe in God's Revelation from both Sacred Scripture and Sacred Tradition should always be secure in their faith, Newman said,

---

scientism The belief that only knowledge obtained from scientific research is valid.

theory of evolution The belief that in the progression of a series of events living organisms accumulate changes over successive generations due to genetic inheritance and adaptive variation.

adding that we should not be "the nervous creature who startles at every sudden sound, and is fluttered by every strange or novel appearance which meets our eyes."[6]

Pope Leo XIII (1810–1903), a contemporary of Newman, similarly taught that truth cannot contradict truth. He said that if discrepancies remain between biblical truth and scientific truth, the debate should not be abandoned but rather studied some more to see whether a mistake has been made on either side. "If no such mistake can be detected, we must then suspend judgment for the time being" (*Providentissimus Deus*, 23). Some differences between Scripture and science remain beyond our human abilities to settle in the present.

There is nothing to fear about truth, nor is there anything for the Church, in her understanding of the Bible, to fear about science. Pope Leo also wrote, "There can never, indeed, be any real discrepancy between the theologian and the physicist, as long as each confines himself within his own lines" (*Providentissimus Deus*, 18). In his encyclical *Fides et Ratio* (Faith and Reason), Pope John Paul II said of the Catholic view of science: "Faith and reason are like two wings on which the human spirit rises to the contemplation of truth." The image is easy to comprehend. A bird cannot fly with only one wing. Likewise, there is a coordination between faith and science in unpacking the truth. The *Catechism of the Catholic Church* teaches that scientific research, as long as it is properly carried out and not overriding moral laws, "can never conflict with the faith, because the things of the world and the things of faith derive from the same God" (*CCC*, 159).

Good Science Does Not Contradict the Bible

Just as a cookbook cannot teach a person how to play baseball, a scientific work cannot teach about theology, nor can the Bible teach about science. Paraphrasing Pope Leo, it's about theologians and scientists staying in their own lanes. Biblical writers were not writing as scientists, nor are scientists writing as theologians. St. Thomas Aquinas taught that the sacred writers of Scripture "put down what God, speaking to men, signified, in the way they could understand and were accustomed to." St. Pius XII reiterated, "The words of God, expressed in human language, are made like to human speech, except in error." The Bible is not a technical manual designed to solve all of the mysteries of God in scientific terms. Cardinal Caesar Baronius

(1538–1607) said that "the Bible teaches us how we shall go to heaven, not how the heavens go."[7]

The Catholic Church welcomes the words of historians and scientists who have examined the events depicted in Sacred Scripture to see if there is any record of them elsewhere. Nothing is more important than proof of the existence of Jesus himself. Was there really such a person? Or was he just the invention of the early Christians? Historians, including nonbelievers, have looked into this question.[∞] Drawing on records from Roman and Jewish historians, and judging the New Testament to be historically reliable, they have proven the following:

- Jesus of Nazareth did exist.
- The Romans under Pontius Pilate crucified him.
- Jesus established a Church that persists to this very day.

Thus, Catholics and other Christians have nothing to fear about open-minded scientific research. When either side errors, reconciliation with or rejection of the idea are options. An example of reconciliation occurred when Pope John Paul II appointed a commission of historians, scientists, and theologians to reexamine the famous case of Galileo Galilei (1564–1642), who had been censored by the Church for teaching that the earth revolves around the sun as truth, rather than as yet-unproven hypothesis, and as contrary to Scripture. (According to the thinking of the time, if the earth were not the physical center of the universe, then neither the earth nor those who live on it could be central to God's plan of creation.) In 1992, Pope John Paul II expressed

∞ Note

For example, Cornelius Tacitus (ca. AD 56–117), a Roman senator, wrote in his *Annals*, about followers "of Christ, who had been executed in Tiberius's reign by the governor of Judea, Pontius Pilate," being blamed by the Emperor Nero for the Great Fire of Rome in AD 64. A Jewish historian, Josephus, also mentioned Jesus, "a wise man, if he should be called a man," in his *Jewish Antiquities*. Both men were not believers, yet they acknowledged the existence of Jesus.

clarification for the misunderstanding on both sides that faith and science were irreconcilable.∞

The Church Embraces Truth

Simply put, scientific research and the Christian faith do not contradict each other. They neither prove nor disprove each other. When Jesus was before Pontius Pilate on trial, he answered Pilate's question about whether or not he was a king by stating that he had come into the world to testify to the truth. "Everyone who belongs to the truth listens to my voice," Jesus said. Pilate seemed perplexed by Jesus's statement. "What is truth?" he asked Jesus (see John 18:37–38). When Jesus spoke of truth, he was referring to God. Only God can see how all elements of truth come together.

The principle of "truth cannot contradict truth" actually arose from an Islamic internal debate when Muslims were attempting to discern whether or not to accept or reject truths discerned by pre-Islamic philosophers. Islamic leaders ultimately decided that even if the philosophers made mistakes that contradicted the Qu'ran, the mistakes could be corrected and the dialogue with the philosopher's material could be an opportunity for debates and further reflection and understanding of the Qu'ran. Muslims had no trouble

∞ Note

See John Paul II, "Address to the Plenary Session on 'The Emergence of Complexity in Mathematics, Physics, Chemistry and Biology,'" October 31, 1992, https://www.pas.va/en/magisterium/saint-john-paul-ii/1992-31-october.html As point of fact, a majority of Galileo's scientific colleagues disputed his heliocentric (sun-at-the-center) view primarily because Galileo could not show observable shifts in the position of stars as the earth moved around the sun. Measuring equipment was not available at that time. If Galileo had merely proposed his teaching as a theory rather than conclusively, there would have been less original controversy. Also, Galileo claimed that his "new science" was contrary to certain Scripture passages that dealt with a sun that did not move (see Joshua 10:13). The Church, then as now, did not support a fundamentalist and personal interpretation of Scripture. For more information, see "The Galileo Controversy," *Catholic Answers*, August 10, 2004, https://www.catholic.com/tract/the-galileo-controversy.

Pope John Paul II meets with Jewish and Muslim leaders at an interfaith meeting in Jerusalem in 2000.

accepting the pre-Islamic philosophers, because their truths did not conflict with the truth Muslims believe about the Qu'ran.[8]

Pope John Paul II adapted the Muslim approach to bring together the various elements of truth from science and Scripture to interreligious dialogue. The Church holds the foundation of truth in Christ but does not shun other elements of truth, such as those found in other religions and those of science. The Second Vatican Council document *Nostra Aetate* (In Our Time) teaches, "The Catholic Church rejects nothing that is true and holy in these religions," while at the same time proclaiming Jesus Christ, "the way and the truth, and the life (Jn 14:6)" (*Nostra Aetate*, 2). Pilate did not realize that the Incarnate Truth was standing right before him.

The Church brings all the elements of truth together, for truth itself is universal and can be dialogued with. And if there is grave error in any elements claiming truth, they can be rejected. Truth always wins out.

SECTION *Assessment*

Comprehension

1. What did Pope Leo XIII say should happen if discrepancies remain in a debate between science and the faith?
2. What does the *Catechism of the Catholic Church* teach about scientific research?
3. What three things did non-Christian historians confirm about Jesus?
4. What would likely be Cardinal Caesar Baronius's view if the Bible were described as a "handbook of Church rules"?
5. What did Pope John Paul II learn from an Islamic internal debate that applied to the Church's debate with science?
6. What did Pontius Pilate fail to recognize about truth at the trial of Jesus?

Vocabulary

7. What is a danger of *scientism*?

Reflection

8. How do you understand the statement "truth cannot contradict truth"?
9. Pope John Paul II used the image of the two wings of a bird to describe the complementary nature of faith and science. Develop your own image to describe the same relationship.

Section 4

TOOLS OF BIBLICAL SCHOLARSHIP

Given the understanding that the Church approves of historical and scientific research in the area of biblical scholarship, it's wise to take a look at some of the techniques that scholars use to discover primary sources such as ancient biblical manuscripts, and also other physical evidence. One of the main tools for serious study of the Bible is archaeology. Archaeologists dig up the remains of ancient people (literally), as well as their appliances, tools, furnishings, and, when possible, their writings.

Consider what an archaeologist living thousands of years into the future might be able to discover about you from what remains of your household. Remember, the items would have had to survive buried underground for that great amount of time. Perhaps sturdy metal kitchen utensils would remain. Maybe the remnants of a computer (but probably not the contents of its hard drive). Possibly a toothbrush and plastic containers. Not as likely to be found would be printed books or family albums with portraits originally saved on paper. And certainly archaeologists would prefer scouring an old trash dump where a collection of many families' items were disposed of in one place, rather than only the remains of one family's possessions.

Geography is another point of contact between our world today and biblical times. The center for much of the narrative of both the Old Testament and New Testament was a relatively small strip of land—50 miles wide and 125 miles in length—that sits between the Mediterranean Sea and the Jordan River and is known as Canaan or Palestine. Largely because of its proximity to a perpetually stronger nation, Egypt, this Promised Land of the Jews was an important trading crossroad for thousands of years and for several great empires of the world. Information gained from relics from a variety of people and cultures, not just the Jews, who traversed this land provide helpful backdrop and verification for the biblical accounts.

While most of our writing today is preserved on paper or laptops, this is not wholly true. We have many inscriptions saved on concrete pillars and statues that can survive centuries. The same was true of ancient peoples. The writings and inscriptions from stone carvings have been deciphered, revealing much about the languages and cultures of those who inhabited or traveled through Canaan. Some ancient papyrus and vellum copies of biblical and other texts from the period have been preserved as well (see also the subsection "How Did They Compose the Written Copies?" in Chapter 2, Section 2).

All of these aspects of biblical scholarship—archaeology, language and culture, and geography—are scientific methods encouraged by the Church to help us to understand and appreciate more deeply the Bible, the Word of God. They are also tools that help us to dispel those who attempt to misconstrue the Bible as a collection of myths rather than a source with historical facts and historical chronology.

Archaeological Studies

Archaeological evidence shows that human beings have lived in the Canaan region for over one million years, since the Paleolithic era. Most of this evidence is in the form of the discovery of stone tools from that period. By 10,000

Ruins from the ancient city of Caesarea. Today, Caesarea is an affluent town on the coast of the Mediterranean Sea in Israel halfway between Haifa and Tel Aviv.

BC, after the final ice age, people began to live in groups. By 9000 BC they were engaged in agriculture production. Large settlements were established near the Tigris and Euphrates Rivers in Mesopotamia and the Nile River in Egypt. Because these settlements were in concentrated areas, many artifacts have been found there.

The early Israelites seem to have established themselves in the hills of Canaan, rather than on the coastal plains where larger cities were located. On the hillside were terraced villages that had cisterns that kept water available throughout the year. The people built mostly four-pillared houses; typical structures had a second floor built on beams laid across stone or wood pillars. The people lived on the second floor but would cook on the ground floor. They would also keep animals on the ground floor.

The nation of Israel was formed after the Israelites' Exodus from Egypt in approximately 1207 BC. This dating comes from a discovery by Sir Flinders Petrie, a British archaeologist, of an inscription known as the Merneptah Stele. In the writing, an Egyptian pharaoh, Merneptah, brags about successfully defeating a people called Israel and wiping out the "seed of Israel." The second part of his statement proved to be false.

Biblical archaeology also helps with much insight into Jesus and events described in the Gospels. Michael Hesemann is a German historian and author of *Jesus of Nazareth: Archaeologists Retracing the Footsteps of Christ.* In an interview in the *Catholic World Report*, he recalled that Fr. Bargil Pixner, a

Sir Flinders Petrie, known as the father of archeology, discovered the earliest known Egyptian reference to Israel on a stone slab monument of Merneptah, king of ancient Egypt from 1213 to 1204 BC.

Benedictine biblical archaeologist, described biblical archaeology as "the fifth Gospel." Hesemann added, "Archaeology brings the time and world of Christ back to life, helps us to understand this period, and shows us how realistic the Gospels really are."

Archaeology helps the reader of the Bible in two main ways. First, it helps us to gain a deeper understanding of Jesus's parables, of the people's reactions to Jesus's words, and of the personalities mentioned in the Gospels. Second, it helps to verify the accuracy of the Gospels. Hesemann described an experience of visiting the excavation site at Capernaum, in the region of Galilee where Jesus lived, and comparing it to locations mentioned in the Gospel of Mark:

> You will indeed find everything just the way it was described. In Tabgha, a few miles to the west, you will find a cave, the "Eremos" or "solitary place where he prayed." From there you have the most impressive view on the Lake of Genesareth, you have Magdala just in front of you. When you come to Magdala, which we excavated, you find the remains of the oldest synagogue in Galilee. It is from the first century BC, so we can be sure Jesus preached and healed there. You can see and touch the very stones on which he stood.[9]

Archaeology also involves studying and decoding ancient languages of the Bible. We have previously mentioned some of the sources that aided the translation (e.g., the Rosetta Stone, Dead Sea Scrolls, and Merneptah Stele). With these guides, archaeologists and other biblical scholars translate texts from the various biblical languages. In doing so, they gain more understanding about how the people lived and what their cultures were like.

Influence of Culture

The Jewish people did not live as if in a vacuum. Don't think of them as modern-day Amish, a Christian sect that chooses to separate itself from the world. Amish communities forgo modern conveniences like gas-powered cars and tractors, and oftentimes electricity and natural gas to light and heat their homes. They purposely live separate from modern society and avoid modern culture. The Jewish people—from their earliest times—were part of a multicultural society, mostly living under the dominance of a more powerful nation. In fact, Scripture scholar Fr. Felix Just, SJ, devised a simple mnemonic device to help us to remember nations that controlled Israel throughout its history. It goes like this:

Egypt • Assyria • Babylon • Persia • Greece • Rome

This silly phrase translates as follows: "E" (Eat) is for Egypt. "A" (At) is for Assyria. "B" (Bill's) is for Babylon. "P" (Philly's) is for Persia. "G" (Greatest) is for Greece. "R" (Restaurant) is for Rome. Each of these dynasties in chronological order caused many difficulties for Israel. Nevertheless, the Jewish people adapted elements from each culture. Think of the Ancient Greek Empire, which lasted from approximately the eighth century BC until the Roman victory at the Battle of Corinth in 146 BC. During these years, Jews began to speak common Greek as their everyday language. The Jews had the Bible translated into Greek (the Septuagint), and the Christians formulated the Bible with the addition of the New Testament in Greek as well.

There is also evidence of the influence of these other cultures in the biblical texts. For example:

- The captivity and eventual escape from *Egypt* (Eat) launched the central event of Jewish history.
- The backdrop for the prophetic books of the Bible are the dominations of Israel by *Assyria* (At), *Babylon* (Bill's), and *Persia* (Philly's).
- Alexander the Great, the Macedonian king who expanded the *Greek* Empire (Greatest), eventually drove the Persians out of Turkey and Egypt, through old Assyria and ancient Babylon. Alexander the Great was not only a military leader. He populated the territories he captured with his soldiers, who took local wives. This helped to **Hellenize** the culture, distinguishing it from the classical Greek culture of earlier centuries.

Hellenize A term with Greek origins that literally means "to make into Greek" in both form and culture.

- The *Roman* Empire (Restaurant) maintained the Hellenized culture. Jesus was born at the end of the reign of Herod the Great, a Jewish monarch installed by the Roman Senate. Jesus's life took place under the rule of Roman governorship and Roman taxation, and under the rule of puppet Roman leaders such as Herod.[10]

An important lesson to take from Israel's history and the history of the early Christians is that both had to live as mostly occupied peoples. They had to live their faith at the risk of persecution. The biblical texts of both the Old Testament and New Testament reflect some of those tensions. Besides the prophetic books of the Old Testament, Jesus, for the most part, told his followers to be oblivious to outside foreign influence. When a Pharisee asked Jesus if it were lawful to pay a census tax to Rome, Jesus had them show him a coin that contained Caesar's image. "Whose image is this and whose inscription?" Jesus asked of them. When they answered, "Caesar's," Jesus said to them, "Then repay to Caesar what belongs to Caesar and to God what belongs to God" (see Matthew 22:15–22).

The Geography of the Bible

One reason to pay attention to the geography of the Bible is that it studies the location where God chose to live when he became incarnate and came to earth. Jesus grew up in Nazareth, a village of about twelve hundred people, in the Roman province of Galilee. The Sea of Galilee was the prominent site of

"So Jesus said to them, 'Pay to Caesar what belongs to Caesar and to God what belongs to God.' They were utterly amazed at him" (Mk 12:17).

this region. Nazareth was located about two miles off the main road of southern Galilee.

Jesus and most of his Apostles were Galileans. The Sea of Galilee provided a livelihood for many fishermen. There were also farmers and shepherds in the region. The topography of the land was rolling hills with relatively rich soil. Many of the picturesque details of Jesus's parables originated in his keen observation of Galilean life: birds filling the air, flowers brilliantly arraying the fields, barns bursting with grains, farmers planting seeds in the field, and fishing nets straining under heavy loads.

Galilee's population was mainly Jewish, but there were many Gentiles in the region as well. This made the Galilean Jews more worldly than Jews from the predominantly Jewish region of Judah. Judean Jews looked down on Galilean Jews because of their blending with Gentiles, often distinguished by their unique Aramaic dialect. Judean Jews considered themselves more religious, but there were plenty of very zealous Galilean Jews as well.

Herod Antipas (4 BC–AD 39), the son of Herod the Great, was the appointed Roman ruler of the Roman province that included Galilee in Jesus's lifetime. In recent decades, archaeologists have unearthed the Hellenistic city of Sepphoris, the former capital of Galilee where Herod Antipas was stationed, which had been lost in a fire. Sepphoris was about a one-hour walk from Nazareth, and as a larger city, it may have provided work for the carpenters Joseph and Jesus, though the Gospels do not acknowledge this. In fact, during his lifetime, Jesus may have avoided Sepphoris because it was a power center for Herod Antipas and others who opposed Jesus.

Taking a step back, and looking at the geography of the larger Near East region where both the Old Testament and New Testament take place, one piece of information stands out: the importance of Egypt to the history of the region and to God's People in particular. The Nile River, which flows through Egypt south to north, spilled over to form the Nile valley and delta around it. This **Fertile Crescent**—only about 3 percent of Egypt's area—was surrounded by desert sands. Egypt's control of this nutrient-rich soil and a valuable water source made it rich, powerful, and a necessary partner for other nations in the region for centuries. Israel was situated near Egypt, bridging it with the land of Mesopotamia. Hence this small nation of Israel, which functioned for the majority of its history under the rule of a foreign empire, nevertheless provided its people with a front-row seat to key military, political, and cultural events of the day as people from other nations traveled to Egypt.

Military states, conquest, political domination, and commerce between Egypt and Mesopotamia had existed thousands of years before the Israelites settled in Canaan. Some of the earliest documents that have been discovered were royal documents related to military or business issues between Egypt and Mesopotamia. Other spiritual documents began to be written down by these civilizations, and even the creation myths of these empires reflected power and control. Often these myths suggested that the gods once had to do the work of the fields, but they created human beings to work for them. This is very different from the creation accounts of the Book of Genesis told by the Israelites of one God who is loving and compassionate toward his people. Understanding the interplay of the nations that were in close proximity to one another helps us to appreciate the differences in their writings and beliefs.

Fertile Crescent Also known as the "cradle of civilization" because it was the place where farming became prevalent, the Fertile Crescent is a crescent-shaped portion of the Middle East. Today, it is made up of Iraq, Syria, Lebanon, Israel, Jordan, Northern Egypt, the northern region of Kuwait, the southeastern region of Turkey, and the western portion of Iran.

SECTION Assessment

Comprehension

1. Why did the relatively small territory of the Promised Land have important significance in biblical times?
2. Besides papyrus and vellum, how are many ancient writings preserved?
3. How did archaeologists surmise that human beings have lived in the Canaan region for over one million years?
4. What are two ways archaeology helps readers of the Bible?
5. What does it mean to say that the Jewish people of biblical times did not live in a vacuum?
6. Explain the mnemonic device "Eat At Bill's! Philly's Greatest Restaurant!"
7. What were two significant geographic features of the region of Galilee for people of Jesus's time? How so?
8. Why might Jesus have traveled to Sepphoris? On the other hand, why may he have avoided this ancient city?
9. Why was Israel's location near Egypt important?

Vocabulary

10. Who was Merneptah for whom the *Merneptah Stele* is named?
11. Explain one way that Alexander the Great helped to *Hellenize* the culture in and around Canaan.

Reflection

12. Sometimes Catholics today are differentiated as "cultural Catholics" versus "practicing Catholics." What do you think this means?

Section Reviews

Focus Question

What are ways I can use the tools of biblical scholarship to grow in a faith-filled understanding of Sacred Scripture?

Complete one of the following:

- What is one book, story, person, or event in the Bible about which you would like to learn more? Which form of biblical criticism would help you most in this search?
- The preface to the Pontifical Biblical Commission document that promotes the study of the Bible states that our study "is never finished; each age must in its own way newly seek to understand the sacred books." Look up and read more of the context of the statement; then write a brief explanation of what you think the statement means.
- Write a definition of "biblical criticism" as it applies to your own biblical studies. Does biblical criticism help you to understand Jesus and the Bible more clearly? Explain your answer.

Introduction
How Catholics Read the Bible

Review Points

- Besides differences in the number of books in the Old Testament in their editions of the Bible, Catholics and Protestants tend to read and interpret Scripture in different ways. Catholics read the Bible contextually, which means they examine the original context of a passage to determine better its meaning.
- Catholics and fundamentalists (literalists) believe many of the same things about the Bible (e.g., its inspiration, infallibility, etc.), but they understand these things differently.

Assignment

Share an example from your experience where reading in context (other than the Bible) was crucial to your understanding of the material.

Section 1
How the Church Studies the Bible

Review Points

- Biblical scholarship began in the early twentieth century with some hesitancy around modernism. In the mid-century, Pope Pius XII encouraged Catholic biblical scholars to use the modern tools of biblical scholarship.
- Scripture can be interpreted in different ways in accordance with the Holy Spirit. Biblical criticism in several forms helps a reader to fully understand the meaning of Scripture passages as intended by the author.
- Tools for biblical interpretation include form criticism (which includes analysis of literary styles), historical criticism, source criticism, and redaction criticism.
- Pope Benedict XVI, himself a biblical scholar, encouraged a faith-filled study of the Bible that recognizes God as the primary author of Scripture and the Magisterium as the final arbiter.

Assignment

Read Mark 8:15. What do you think the passage means? Next, read a biblical commentary on the passage. How did the commentary help you to better understand the passage? What questions do you still have about the passage? Where might you find answers to those questions?

Section 2
Reading the Bible according to the Holy Spirit

Review Points

- Biblical typology is primarily concerned with determining the relationship between the Old Testament and the New Testament.
- The whole of Scripture is organized around salvation history. The Bible is not a book of myths. Also Scripture, as a source of revealed truths, only makes sense when all of its truths align. This is called the analogy of faith. The Bible is a divinely inspired text and so must be read and interpreted in light of the same Spirit.

- Two senses for helping us to understand the meaning of Scripture are the literal sense and the spiritual sense. The spiritual sense has three separate senses: the allegorical sense, the moral sense, and the anagogical sense.

Assignment

In what way did the parable of the tenants (see Mark 12:1–12) directly challenge the religious leaders? What senses of Scripture study helped you to answer this question?

Section 3
Biblical Truth and Scientific Truth Are Compatible

Review Points

- The same God who is author of the Bible infuses the light of reason and the discoveries of science on the human mind. "God cannot deny himself, nor can truth ever contradict truth" (*CCC*, 159).
- There is nothing to fear about truth itself or scientific truth as being in contradiction to the Bible. Good science does not contradict biblical truth. The debate between the two should never cease.

Assignment

Finish each of the sentences with one of these endings: what to look for; what to believe; what happened; what to do.

- The literal sense teaches __________________.
- The allegorical sense teaches __________________.
- The moral sense teaches __________________.
- The anagogical sense teaches __________________.

Write one additional paragraph that explains your reasons for finishing the sentences as you did.

Section 4
Tools of Biblical Scholarship

Review Points

- Archaeology is a branch of science that assists historical criticism of the Bible. It studies prehistoric or historic people and their cultures. It does so by looking at human remains, monuments, and writings.
- Awareness of the geographical region where the events of the Bible are situated helps us to understand that both the Israelites and the early Christians lived in a prized land between powerful civilizations in Egypt and Mesopotamia.

Assignment

What is one of your possessions that will tell something about who you are if discovered by an archaeologist in one thousand years? What will it tell?

Chapter Projects

Choose and complete at least one of the following projects to assess your understanding of the material in this chapter.

1. Write a Report about the Shroud of Turin and Carbon-14 Dating

The Shroud of Turin is a venerated relic that is believed by many faithful Catholics to be the burial cloth of Christ. However, the authenticity of the shroud as Christ's burial cloth is not a matter of official Church teaching. It has undergone a multitude of scientific tests, including three independent radiocarbon (carbon-14) tests in 1988. Research more about the carbon-14 testing process and its application to the Shroud of Turin by including the following answers in a two- to three-page essay:

- What is radiocarbon dating?
- Why is radiocarbon dating also known as carbon-14 dating?
- Who was Willard Libby?
- Which materials are eligible for carbon-14 dating, and which are not?
- What are some techniques for measuring carbon-14 content?
- What arrangements were made for carbon-14 dating of the Shroud of Turin?
- Who conducted the three 1988 carbon-14 tests of the shroud, and what were the results?
- Why are the results of the tests in doubt?

Add a written or recorded oral epilogue to your essay explaining how a person might become a radiocarbon dater. Share information about volunteer or internship opportunities in carbon dating from the Library of Congress website (under "radiocarbon dating").

2. Print Quotations about Faith and Science

Design a poster with quotations from four different people commenting on the relationship between science and faith. Two of the people should be scientists commenting on faith (e.g., Albert Einstein), and the other two should be Catholics commenting on science (e.g., Pope John Paul II). Creatively draw and display the quotations on your poster.

3. Identify and Research Literary Genres of Scripture Passages

Make and complete a chart like the following. Look up each passage, and write what type of literary genre (e.g., letter, song, prayer, history) is found in each. In the third column, locate and print a second Scripture reference that is an example of the same literary genre.

SCRIPTURE	GENRE	SECOND SCRIPTURE REFERENCE
1 Chronicles 5:11–22		
Song of Songs 4		
Luke 3:22–38		
1 Corinthians 1:1–9		
Luke 15:1–7		
Matthew 6:9–13		
1 Maccabees 1		
Psalm 23		
1 Peter 5:12–14		
Matthew 16:21–25		
Exodus 6:14–27		
Proverbs 2:13		
Luke 22:42		
Sirach 26:1		

4. Map a Biblical Journey

Choose either the travels of the Old Testament patriarchs or the journeys of Jesus in one of the Gospels, and map them from start to finish. You can use a duplicate of a map of the Near East biblical region to trace either journey. Also create a map key to identify significant places and events on the journey and Scripture passages that refer to them.

- For the patriarchs, begin with Abram's call to leave Haran (Genesis 12), and finish with Joseph and his brothers in Egypt (Genesis 50).
- Follow the path of Jesus through an entire Gospel. Whichever Gospel you choose, note that Jesus's life course leads to Jerusalem, specifically to Calvary, the site of his Death that led to the salvation of humankind.

5. Print and Design Jesus's Name in Four Different Languages

On one large poster, print the name of Jesus in four languages that Jesus may have understood or spoken while on earth:

- Biblical Hebrew
- Aramaic
- Greek
- Latin

Colorfully design the poster, and label (in English) each type of language that is represented.

Faithful Disciple
Pope Pius XII

Eugenio Pacelli (1876–1958) lived in one of the most tumultuous periods of world history. He was born into a family that was part of papal or "black" nobility that was devoted in service to the Vatican. His father, Filippo, was the dean of Vatican lawyers. Yet even they would have had trouble imagining that Eugenio would rise in the Church to become the 260th pope after the death of Pope Pius XI on February 10, 1939. Cardinal Pacelli, at the time a diplomat at the Vatican, took the name Pius XII after his predecessor as his pontificate began just months before the start of World War II.∞

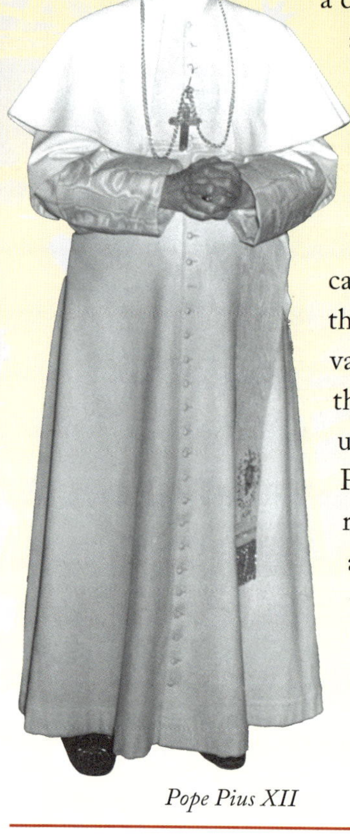

Pope Pius XII

Pope Pius XII was a scholarly pope who, with his writings, planted the seeds of the Second Vatican Council (1962–1965). He issued forty-one encyclicals during his pontificate. In his encyclical *Mystici Corporis Christi* (On the Mystical Body of Christ), he emphasized the value of each member of the Church (including the laity) in the **Mystical Body of Christ** and the universal call to holiness. In a 1952 radio address, Pope Pius's message to Catholics to take a leading role in rebuilding the world led to the creation of a movement known as "Proclamation for a Better World," still active today in many countries. Pope Pius said: "It is a whole world that needs to be rebuilt from the ground up, that needs to be transformed from wild to human, from human to divine, that is, according to the heart

---

Mystical Body of Christ A truth that all of the Church—in heaven, in Purgatory, and on earth—is bound up and directed by Christ the Head. *Mystical* refers to the supernatural life we share with Christ, especially bound up while on earth through the sacraments.

of God."[11] In 2022, Pope Francis praised Pope Pius's words and the movement as he considered his cause for canonization.

Also, in the midst of the war, Pope Pius issued his famous encyclical *Divino afflante Spiritu*, which brought fresh life to modern Catholic biblical scholarship. Previously, the Church had been cautious about employing methods of historical criticism to biblical studies. Pope Leo XIII's 1893 encyclical *Providentissimus Deus* (On the Study of Human Scripture) noted that biblical scholars of the time were dismissive of the truth of Scripture after comparing the biblical texts to the writings of other cultures of the period. Coupled with growing secularization in other areas, Pope Pius X condemned *modernism* (see Chapter 3, Section 1, "How the Church Studies the Bible"), while many Catholic biblical scholars feared being lumped in with his teaching on the subject.

Divino afflante Spiritu began by acknowledging the wisdom of Pope Leo's approach. But fifty years later, in 1943, new discoveries were now in place for understanding biblical languages and uncovering ancient biblical texts. In Pius's encyclical, he exhorted Catholic biblical scholars to study the ancient Hebrew and Greek languages and all branches of philosophy "to explain the original text which, having been written by the inspired author himself, has more authority and greater weight than even the very best translation. . . .

∞ Note

Modern critics have accused Pope Pius XII of timidity for failing to condemn more strongly Hitler's treatment of the Jews during World War II. Pope Pius had good reasons for working behind the scenes. First, he believed that if he spoke out, Hitler would behave even more cruelly than he already was. This happened in Holland in 1942 when the Dutch bishops, at the pope's urging, publicly deplored the Nazi deportation of Jews. In retaliation, the Nazis sped up their roundup of Jews, including all Jewish converts to Catholicism, and shipped them to Auschwitz. Second, by acting in a clandestine manner without arousing the suspicion of the Nazis, Pius was able to help many Jews escape persecution, providing them with shelter and giving them homes. In 1967, Pinchas Lapide, an Israeli diplomat, reported in his book *The Last Three Popes and the Jews* (London: Souvenir Press, 1967) that Pope Pius XII was instrumental in saving as many as 860,000 Jews, a number estimated to be a full 30 percent of Jews who survived Hitler's atrocities.

This can be done all the more easily and fruitfully, if to the knowledge of languages be joined a real skill in literary criticism of the same text" (*Divino afflante Spiritu*, 16). The pope intended that Catholic biblical scholars "discern and define clearly" the literal meaning of the biblical words. His use of *literal* is not associated with a fundamentalist understanding; rather, he meant what the biblical author intended to convey and how the author's original readers understood what the biblical author wrote. This encyclical allowed Catholic biblical scholars to participate more fully in modern biblical scholarship. *Divino afflante Spiritu* is often called the "Magna Carta" of Catholic biblical scholarship.

In other writings, Pope Pius commented on important topics such as medical ethics and peace. He declared 1950, the year he formally defined the Assumption of Mary into heaven, to be a holy year. In his last years, Pope Pius XII suffered from severe stomach pain. He even considered resigning as pope in 1954 because of his illness. Pope Pius XII died in 1958 and was succeeded by Angelo Roncalli, Pope John XXIII, the invoker of the Second Vatican Council.

Comprehension

1. What connections did Pope Pius XII have with the Vatican early in his life?
2. How did Pope Pius XII encourage Catholics to take a leading role in rebuilding the world after World War II?
3. Why is *Divino afflante Spiritu* sometimes referred to as the "Magna Carta" of Catholic biblical scholarship?
4. What did Pope Pius XII mean by telling Catholic biblical scholars to "discern and define clearly" the literal meaning of biblical words?
5. Why did Pope Pius XII consider resigning from the pontificate in 1954?

Reflection

Research some of the accomplishments of the Second Vatican Council. Then answer this question: "Why do you think Pope Pius XII's writings planted the seeds for the Second Vatican Council?"

Prayer

The Bible is a book of prayer. Scripture is filled with many prayers. Jesus, himself, instructed us on how to pray. On one occasion Jesus instructed us to keep our prayers short. Some people think that by heaping on a lot of words, their prayers will be more effective. But Jesus said it is better to keep our prayers short and to the point: "In praying, do not babble like the pagans, who think that they will be heard because of their many words. Do not be like them. Your Father knows what you need before you ask him" (Mt 6:7–8).

The Church has a name for short prayers. They are call *aspirations*. They are one-line prayers that can be memorized easily and recited throughout the day. Read and pray with the following aspirations. Then create your own one-line aspiration, and commit to remembering it and praying it throughout the day.

Aspirations

Jesus, have mercy on me.

Jesus, my Friend and Savior, I love you.

Help me, Lord Jesus.

Praise God!

Mary, Mother of God, pray for me.

Come, Holy Spirit.

Jesus, I trust in you.

What Is in the Bible

Saint Paul Writing His Epistles

➤ *Valentin de Boulogne*

There are more biographical details of the life of St. Paul the Apostle in the Bible than any other saint in the Bible. Paul's conversion—from a strict pharisaical Jew, son of a Roman citizen, who was zealous in his persecution of Christians, to one who transferred the same dedication to converting Gentiles to Christianity after he was confronted by a vision of Christ while on his way to the Syrian city of Damascus—is told in the Acts of the Apostles. Likewise, his extensive three missionary journeys throughout the huge Roman Empire are recounted there.

Though not one of the original Twelve, Paul is called an Apostle because of his outreach to the Gentiles. He was both an *evangelizer* and a *catechist*. The roots of both of these words are Greek in origin. An evangelizer is someone who "preaches the Gospel" or "converts someone to Christ." Both preaching and conversion must be accompanied by instruction in the faith; that is the meaning of catechesis and the task of a catechist.

St. Paul's mission was to do both. He preached the kerygma that Jesus is the Christ, who is raised from the dead and who has brought salvation to the world. He furthered his preaching by instructing his converts through his written epistles in both theology and practical ways to live the faith.

St. Paul, the evangelist writer, is portrayed in this famous piece of art, *Saint Paul Writing His Epistles*, credited to seventeenth-century French artist Valentin de Boulogne (1591–1632). Like other artists of the period, de Boulogne was influenced by the work of Caravaggio (see the sacred art opener at the beginning of Chapter 1) who preceded him. Caravaggio's paintings were known for the use of contrast of light (known as *chiaroscuro*), realism, and drama. This is the case in *Saint Paul Writing His Epistles*, where the light and dark aspects are dramatic. There is also great attention to detail in the painting. Note the wrinkles accented in St. Paul's clothing and also on St. Paul's forehead. The pages with his composition are placed neatly on the table. Some of the pages are curled or flipped rather than just lying flat on the table.

The fine detail of this painting is worthy of the work of St. Paul. He was untiring in his ministry for Jesus. When he founded a local Christian community, he continued to care for it after he moved on. He is the author of about 28 percent of the content of the New Testament. His epistles make up instruction not only to the early Church but to Christians ever since. His writing is one of the earliest examples of evangelizing catechesis.

Focus Question

What are the scope, style, and message of the Old Testament and New Testament?

Chapter Overview

Introduction
The Two Testaments of the Bible

Section 1
Old Testament Categories and Contents

Section 2
Surveying the Old Testament

Section 3
New Testament Categories and Contents

Section 4
Surveying the New Testament

Introduction

THE TWO TESTAMENTS OF THE BIBLE

To be clear, there is only one Bible. Though there are differences in the number and placement of some of the books in the Old Testament between Catholic and Protestant editions of the Bible, the Bible is defined in the *Catechism of the Church* as "the divinely revealed realities, which are contained and presented in the text of Sacred Scripture, [and] have been written down under the inspiration of the Holy Spirit" (*CCC*, 105, quoting *Dei Verbum*, 11).

Sometimes, to distinguish Hebrew Scriptures from the Bible, the term "Jewish Bible" or "Hebrew Bible" is used. This isn't really accurate. There is no standard term for the Bible in Judaism. Hebrew words, such as *miqra* ("scripture") or *kitve haqqodesh* ("sacred texts"), are commonly used. An acronym, TaNaKh, for Hebrew Scriptures appeared in the Middle Ages taken from the first letter of the three main parts of Hebrew Scriptures—Torah (Law), Nebi'im (Prophets), and Kethubim (Writings)—to distinguish the Jewish Scriptures from what Christians had been calling the Old Testament of the Bible.

Recall that the word *testament* means "covenant." The term came into use in connection with the Bible when the Church decided to use the Septuagint translation (Greek version of the Jewish Scriptures). The Greek term *diathéke* was used to translate the Hebrew term *berit*, for covenant. *Diathéke* translates to the Latin as *testamentum*, or testament. The New Testament also used *diathéke* wherever there are passages that refer to the covenants that God made with the Jewish people.

For the New Testament writers, the Old Testament *was* Sacred Scripture. To introduce the story of Jesus, they used the vocabulary and literary forms that already were present in the Jewish world. Except for St. Luke, the New Testament writers were all Jews who had come to believe in Jesus. The New

Testament has roughly four thousand references to the Old Testament. Many of the references include words such as "according to the Scriptures" and "to fulfill what Scripture said." The word *fulfill* is key. The New Testament writers, though valuing God's Revelation in the Old Testament, believed Jesus to be the fulfillment of that Revelation.[1]

The Bible Is a Series of Covenants

Remember, the way that God revealed himself was gradually through a series of covenants (see the subsection "The Stages of Divine Revelation" in Chapter 1, Section 3). The central focus of the Old Testament is the covenant theme of God's love for the Jewish people. The entirety of the Old Testament reveals a loving God who was preparing humanity for the coming of the Savior, Jesus Christ.

Church Father St. Irenaeus was one of the first Christians who strongly connected the unity of the Old Testament with the New Testament. He related the oral preaching of the Apostles that transitioned the written accounts of the New Testament to the messages of the prophets of the Old Testament: "If

At his Transfiguration, the Old Testament prophets Elijah and Moses appeared with Jesus, signifying that he was the fulfillment of their prophecies.

then, the prophets have prophesied that the Son of God was going to appear on earth, and have prophesied also where on earth, and how, and what manner he was going to appear, and the Lord took upon himself all these prophecies, firm is our faith in him and true is the tradition of [apostolic] preaching" (*On the Apostolic Preaching*, 92).

While St. Irenaeus believed that the Old Testament was strongly **Christological** in focus and that Jesus was the fulfillment of Old Testament prophecies, he would also acknowledge that the Old Testament writers were not literally predicting the exact details of the coming of Christ. Rather, what they were expecting was the final fulfillment of the covenants God had established with the Jewish people throughout history. The New Testament writers believed differently. They believed that the fulfillment of the Old Testament covenants was both the coming of "a" Messiah and that "the" Messiah was in fact Jesus Christ.

The New Covenant Compared to the Old Covenant

The New Covenant differs from the Old Covenant in that it was written not on stone tablets (as were the Ten Commandments given to Moses) but onto people's hearts. The prophet Jeremiah was someone who explained this difference, relating God's Word described through "the oracle of the Lord" (see also Chapter 7, Section 2):

> See, days are coming—oracle of the Lord—when I will make a new covenant with the house of Israel and the house of Judah. It will not be like the covenant I made with their ancestors the day I took them by the hand to lead them out of the land of Egypt. They broke my covenant, though I was their master—oracle of the Lord. But this is the covenant I will make with the house of Israel after those days—oracle of the Lord. I will place my law within them, and write it upon their hearts; I will be their God, and they shall be my people. (Jer 31:31–33)

Christological Refers to the study of Jesus Christ; the academic effort to understand who he is.

According to Jeremiah, not only will God's Law (Torah) be written on everyone's hearts, but also the New Covenant is everlasting; there will be no other. The New Covenant gives everyone true knowledge of God.

The New Covenant was initiated at the Last Supper when Jesus pronounced a blessing and instituted the Eucharist; that is, ordinary bread and wine were changed into his Body and Blood. The chalice of blood is especially significant. Jesus said: "This cup is the new covenant in my blood, which will be shed for you" (Lk 22:20). The Old Covenant had been sealed with the blood of an animal (see Exodus 24:8), while the New Covenant is sealed by the Blood of Christ and shared both on the Cross and forevermore in the sacrifice of the Mass.

The treasure of the Bible as a sacred book is that it offers a complete perspective of God's Revelation. The Church did not toss aside the books of the Old Covenant, but included them in the Bible. The *Catechism of the Catholic Church* teaches that "the Old Testament is an indispensable part of Sacred Scripture. Its books are divinely inspired and retain a permanent value, for the Old Covenant has never been revoked" (*CCC*, 121). Also, the Jewish people remain dear to God and the object of his special providence because "the gifts and the call of God are irrevocable" (Rom 11:28). Pope John Paul II said that this passage from Romans acknowledges "the common roots linking Christianity and the Jewish people, who are called by God to a covenant which remains irrevocable" (*Ecclesia in Europa*, 56).

The Old Testament books prepare Christians for the final coming of Christ, even as they prepared the Jewish people for his first coming. The Old Testament books provide us with a vital understanding of God's providence and should be known and studied.

The New Testament is essential because Jesus *is* the New Testament—that is, God's New Covenant with all humanity. As the prophet Jeremiah foretold, Jesus is the New Covenant, signed and sealed in the blood he shed on the Cross. His Resurrection ratified—that is, proved—the truth of this covenant. Jesus initiates a law of love that requires a change of heart. He is the perfect prophet who, through his life and ministry, fulfills all the Old Testament prophecies concerning the Messiah's birth, his teaching and healing, his rejection by the leaders, and his Passion, Death, and Resurrection. The New Testament writings show how his words and actions reveal God's active presence in the world: saving, redeeming, and healing people.

This chapter surveys the categories of books within the Old Testament and New Testament, points to the primacy of the Gospels in the Church, and shares more examples of Christological typology that connect the Old Testament with the New Testament.

SECTION *Assessment*

Comprehension

1. How does the *Catechism of the Catholic Church* define the Bible?
2. Why isn't it accurate to use the terms "Hebrew Bible" or "Jewish Bible"?
3. What does the acronym TaNaKh stand for?
4. How did the term *testament* come into use in connection with the Bible?
5. Why is *fulfill* a key word as it is used in the New Testament in relation to the Old Testament?
6. When was the New Covenant initiated?
7. When was the New Covenant ratified?
8. Why should the books of the Old Testament be read and studied?

Vocabulary

9. What did St. Irenaeus say about the prophets and the Old Testament's *Christological* focus?

Reflection

10. How do you understand the New Covenant to be one that is "written on the heart"?

Section 1

OLD TESTAMENT CATEGORIES AND CONTENTS

Many Christians think that the Old Testament is the exact replication of Hebrew Scriptures. This isn't true. Recall that the books of Tobit, Judith, 1 and 2 Maccabees, Wisdom, Sirach, and Baruch in the Greek translation of Hebrew Scriptures used by Catholics are not included in the translation used by Jews today.

As mentioned in the introduction, Hebrew Scriptures have three main parts: Torah (Law), Nebi'im (Prophets), and Kethubim (Writings). The Old Testament in the *New American Bible, revised edition*, for example, is arranged slightly differently under these classifications:

- Pentateuch (in Greek, "five books")
- Historical Books
- Wisdom Books
- Prophetic Books

Whereas the Old Testament ends with the prophetic books—specifically with Malachi, who predicts the prophet Elijah's return "before the day of the Lord comes" (Mal 3:23)—the TaNaKh places the prophets in its middle section.

Individual books are also arranged differently between the Hebrew Scriptures and Old Testament. For example, the Old Testament places the Book of Ruth between Judges and 1 Samuel in the historical books category because Ruth fits well chronologically in that order. The Hebrew Scriptures place Ruth in the Writings with the Song of Songs, Lamentations, Ecclesiastes, and Esther because all of these texts are read together on certain Jewish holy days. Overall, Jews also read the Scriptures in a different structure and emphasis than

Catholics. Judaism focuses on the Torah, which is read in its entirety in the synagogue every three years. Each Torah reading is accompanied by a reading from the Prophets. In the Catholic Lectionary for Sundays, one Old Testament reading is typically connected with a Gospel reading based on a common theme.

Survey of Old Testament Books

The Hebrew Scriptures have twenty-four books. The Old Testament of the Bible has forty-six books. In considering the arrangement and surveying each of the Old Testament books, the most important thing to keep in mind is that the Bible is not in chronological order. The first books are not necessarily the oldest books, and the final books are not necessarily the most recently written. Nor is it true that events recorded in the earlier books all took place before the events in the later books. For example, Leviticus and Deuteronomy both include details about Moses receiving the Ten Commandments. Many books underwent edits after being first written or were later combined with other books. For example, the Psalms were probably once in shorter collections before coming together to form the larger collection of the Book of Psalms in the current Bible.

The Codex Sassoon *bible is displayed at Sotheby's in New York. It was sold in an auction there in 2023 for $38.1 million. The* Codex Sassoon *is the earliest and most complete Hebrew Bible ever discovered.*

Each of the Old Testament categories is described in the following subsections.

Pentateuch

Genesis, Exodus, Leviticus, Numbers, Deuteronomy

The first five books of the Bible are part of the Pentateuch, which literally means "five books" in Greek. In Hebrew Scriptures, the Pentateuch is called the *Torah*, a word that means "law." Law is the most prominent part of the Pentateuch. Virtually all the religious laws, civil laws, and moral principles of ancient Israel are codified in three collections of laws in the first five books.

The earliest collection of laws is the Covenant Code, contained in the Book of Exodus (the laws are roughly in chapters 19–24). The Deuteronomic Code was created in the second century BC and is in the Book of Deuteronomy. (Deuteronomy means "second law.") The third collection of laws is the Levitical ("Priestly") Code in the Book of Leviticus. It consists mainly of priestly or religious laws that were added by priests when the Jewish people returned to Jerusalem after the Babylonian Exile. Leviticus 17–26 is the source of some of the oldest priestly laws, sometimes called the "holiness laws." Later commentaries on these laws are found in other parts of Leviticus and the Book of Numbers.

Biblical scholarship holds that editors wove four main sources into the Pentateuch. Four sources can be identified because each reads very differently. At times, the editors did not attempt to coordinate the inconsistencies between different accounts of the same story. Consequently, there are places in the Bible where there are two versions of the same event, as in the case of the two creation accounts of Genesis 1:1–2:3 and 2:4–2:25 (see the subsection "Who Were the Authors of the Bible?" in Chapter 2, Section 2).

The four main sources are called the Yahwist (J), Elohist (E), Deuteronomist (D), and Priestly (P) sources.

YAHWIST

The *Yahwist* (J) source is recognized when the Pentateuch uses YHWH for God. (In German, YHWH is *Jahweh*, which is why the abbreviation is a J.) This source uses a vivid, earthy style of writing, often attributing human emotions and physical traits to God. This approach is called **anthropomorphism**. The Yahwist provides the basic outline for the Pentateuch, with accounts of the first human beings, the patriarchs, the Exodus from Egypt, the Israelites' journey in the desert, the covenant at Mount Sinai, and the entry into the Promised Land.

Elohist

The *Elohist* (E) source is identified by its use of *Elohim*, a majestic term for God. Abraham is a central figure. The Elohist retells stories from the northern kingdom's point of view with emphasis on the kings. It is believed that around 750 BC an editor combined the J and E sources. This editor kept some of the repetitions and contradictions between the two sources.

Deuteronomist

Most likely, priests of the northern kingdom composed the *Deuteronomist* (D) material, placing great emphasis on morality. This source portrays Israel's history as a cycle of reward for faithfulness to the covenant and punishment by YHWH for sin. The D source especially highlights Moses's speeches.

Priestly

The *Priestly* source (P) contains census lists, genealogies, numbers, dates, descriptions of proper ways to worship, and the proper use of clean and unclean animals. Like the Elohist, the Priestly source refers to God as Elohim. This is probably the latest of the four sources and likely contributed a coherent framework to the Pentateuch.

The frequent repetitions of laws in the Pentateuch (e.g., the Ten Commandments are listed twice) as they were adapted from different sources allow those who study the Bible to learn in more detail several facets of Jewish life in different eras.

---

anthropomorphism Refers to instances in the Bible when God is described using human characteristics; for example, there are several instances when God "stretches out his hand" over the people (see Exodus 7:5; Isaiah 23:11).

Historical Books

Joshua, Judges, Ruth, First and Second Samuel, First and Second Kings, First and Second Chronicles, Ezra and Nehemiah, Tobit, Judith, Esther, First and Second Maccabees

The historical books narrate the events of salvation history and the formation of Israel as the Chosen People. The Books of Joshua and Judges tell of Israel when it was a collection of tribes; 1 and 2 Samuel, 1 and 2 Kings, and much of what is repeated in 1 and 2 Chronicles detail how Israel gradually became a monarchy ruled by kings.

Later historical books cover the breakup of the kingdom after the disobedience of the kings, sins that preceded the Assyrian and Babylonian exiles, and the period of the exiles themselves. The First and Second Books of Maccabees were written in approximately 100 BC and provide two different views of the Jewish revolt against the Seleucid ruler Antiochus IV and the Hellenistic Greek culture that was imposed on the Jews during his reign.

The Books of Ezra and Nehemiah are often grouped together. Scholars believe that "the Chronicler" wrote Ezra and Nehemiah as well as 1 and 2 Chronicles. The First and Second Books of Chronicles retell many of the stories of 1 and 2 Samuel and 1 and 2 Kings, but focus primarily on the southern

Though there are similarities between the text of Job and Egyptian and Babylonian literature of the time, the Book of Job is unique. The Book of Job rejects the simplistic belief that good is rewarded and evil is punished.

kingdom from the time of King David until the Babylonian conquest of Judah. Ezra and Nehemiah tell the story of the Jews after the Babylonian Exile.

Tobit, Judith, and Esther are inspiring works of historical fiction. Tobit is on a romantic quest. Judith conquers a powerful army. Esther saves her people from genocide. Each of these books was written as encouragement for the Jewish people.

Wisdom Books

Job, Psalms, Proverbs, Ecclesiastes, Song of Songs, Wisdom, Sirach

The spirituality of the wisdom books is very similar to modern science. The wisdom literature of the Old Testament is rational and based on observation. It suggests that faith and an understanding of God can come from rationality as well as through Divine Revelation. This is consistent with what the Church teaches about our ability to discover God through our human reason. Also, interestingly, except in the Book of Sirach, the central themes and characters present in other parts of the Old Testament (e.g., the Exodus, patriarchs, YHWH's presence in history, and the Law) are scarcely included in the wisdom books.

It is likely that most of the wisdom literature was written after the Assyrian and Babylonian exiles, although part of Proverbs might have been written during the time of the kings. Solomon, though known as a wise king, did not write all of the wisdom literature, or even all of the Book of Wisdom, which is sometimes called the "Wisdom of Solomon."

Wisdom literature became very popular in the post-exilic **Diaspora**. It could be shared with people of other cultures. Wise sayings and stories were based in common human experiences. Also, wisdom literature was used to train young people in the Jewish faith. Parents were concerned about their children remaining grounded in their faith and staying out of trouble, especially when physically distant from Jerusalem. It has been suggested that as urban areas formed after the time of Alexander the Great (323 BC), a delinquent element of teens was on the rise (see, for example, Proverbs 1:10–15).

The poetic structure of wisdom literature was influential on New Testament writers. Spiritually deep, these writings have been quoted and paraphrased in secular poems, song lyrics, and all types of literature through to current times.

Prophetic Books

Major Prophets: Isaiah, Jeremiah, (Lamentations, Baruch,) Ezekiel

Minor Prophets: Hosea, Joel, Amos, Obadiah, Jonah, Micah, Nahum, Habakkuk, Zephaniah, Haggai, Zechariah, Malachi

Daniel

The Old Testament lists the writing prophets in its final section, unlike the Hebrew Scriptures, which places the Prophets between the Torah and the Writings. The writing prophets of the Old Testament are so-called because each is named by a book of the Old Testament. The writing prophets are further classified as *major prophets* (Isaiah, Jeremiah, and Ezekiel) and *minor prophets* (the other writing prophets). This does not refer to the importance of the prophet or his message, but to the relative lengths of the books. Lamentations and Baruch are often combined in study with Jeremiah. Lamentations consists of five poems that lament the fall of Jerusalem and may be the work

---

Diaspora A group migration or flight away from the homeland into one or more other countries. The word can also refer to people who have maintained their separate identity (often religious but occasionally ethnic, racial, or cultural) while living in those countries after their migration. The Jewish Diaspora began with the exile of the Jews from the Kingdoms of Israel and Judah and is considered to continue to this day for Jews not living in the State of Israel.

of Jeremiah. Baruch was probably authored by Jeremiah's scribe. The Book of Daniel is classified with the prophets in the Catholic canon of the Bible. The Hebrew Scriptures list Daniel with the Writings.

Keep in mind that prophets are also mentioned in the historical books. Deborah, one of Israel's judges, was called a prophet (see Judges 4:4), as was Samuel, the last of the judges. The Second Book of Samuel mentions the prophet Nathan confronting King David about his infidelity, although no other mention about him is given. Also included among the early prophets are Elijah and Elisha.

Prophecy became a literary movement beginning with the writing of the prophet Amos in approximately 740 BC. After Amos, other books were formed with sayings of different prophets. The written collections of the prophets ceased mysteriously in the last centuries before the coming of Christ.

Note that the biographies of the writing prophets were not typically included in the books named for them. Of the major prophets, some biographical and historical context that is provided helps us to understand the writings:

- The Book of Isaiah was written over the course of three centuries. The book is divided into prophecies concerning Jerusalem, the Babylonian Exile, and the importance of the Temple as the Chosen People return from the Diaspora to Jerusalem. The long span of the writing of the text indicates

In the Hebrew Bible, the Book of Daniel is classified with the Writings, which include wisdom literature with the Psalms. The Christian canon groups Daniel with the prophetic books. The Book of Daniel contains the only pure apocalyptic writings of the Old Testament. However, the prophets Isaiah, Ezekiel, Joel, and Zechariah employ apocalyptic style in certain places.

that there was more than one author. Isaiah of Jerusalem, the prophet for whom the book is named, is said to have served as a prophet during the reign of King Uzziah (see Isaiah 1:1). Uzziah died around 740 BC.

- The prophet Jeremiah began his ministry during the reign of King Josiah in approximately 626 BC. He came from a priestly family and grew up just outside of Jerusalem in the village of Anathoth. Jeremiah remained in Jerusalem during the time of the Exile. His message was one of hope to the people in exile, both in Babylon and in Egypt. In the Book of Jeremiah, he shared the news that God was going to make a New Covenant with his people.
- God called Ezekiel to be a prophet in Babylon while the people were in exile. Ezekiel seems to be the only prophet who served actively as a priest. Priests were charged with maintaining the purity of individuals and of all Israel. The Book of Ezekiel is laid out with a clear division of parts. Ezekiel 1–24 is known as the "Oracles of Judgment," a harsh warning about the people of Israel's impending doom prior to the exile. In Ezekiel 33–48, the prophet takes an encouraging tone while the people are held in captivity. These "Oracles of Hope" speak of the restoration of Jerusalem after the exile and culminate in a grand vision (see Ezekiel 40–48) in which the prophet sees a restoration of a just, new Israel.

The primary literary style of written prophecies in the Old Testament is an oracle. An *oracle*, in its basic form, is a brief, poetic declaration following a formula that establishes it as a message from God. The formula used most often in the prophetic books is "thus says the Lord." Most of the Books of Psalms and Proverbs use oracles, as do the writings of the later prophets. The oracles in the Book of Ezekiel are contained within autobiographical narratives of the prophets. It is important to remember that the prophecies of the writing prophets began as oral speech delivering the oracles in meetings between the prophets and those who heard them. The settings for the speeches varied between places such as the court of the Temple (see Jeremiah 7:1–2), a lesser shrine (see Amos 7:13), or a city gate (see Jeremiah 17:19). These speeches were written down years after they were preached.

SECTION Assessment

Comprehension

1. Name one difference in how the Hebrew Scriptures and Old Testament are divided.
2. What is a difference in how Judaism reads the Hebrew Scriptures and Catholics read the Old Testament at liturgy?
3. *Pentateuch* and *Torah* each refer to the same part of the Old Testament. What does each term mean?
4. Name the three collections of laws found in the Old Testament.
5. Explain how the four sources (J, E, D, and P) found in the Pentateuch are determined.
6. Why is wisdom literature compared to modern science?
7. Explain the meaning of two classifications of writing prophets: major prophets and minor prophets.
8. What formula for oracles is used in most prophetic books?

Vocabulary

9. How does the Yahwist source utilize *anthropomorphism*?

Reflection

10. Which section of Old Testament books do you find most interesting for further study? Why?
11. What is a song lyric, poem, or other contemporary writing you know that draws from one of the wisdom books?

Section 2

SURVEYING THE OLD TESTAMENT

At Eastertime you may have gathered with your family and watched *The Ten Commandments* on television. This 1956 classic directed by Cecil B. DeMille and staring Charlton Heston as Moses is the highest-grossing biblical film ever made. And that is saying something, for there are hundreds of films on just the Old Testament alone, covering themes from creation, to Noah's Ark, to the judges, kings, and prophets. *The Ten Commandments* wasn't even the first Hollywood film made on the Exodus event. The original *The Ten Commandments* was a silent movie from 1923 filmed on the central coast of California with massive Egyptian set pieces, a wild-eyed actor who played Moses, and the crossing of the Red Sea depicted in miniature using gelatin walls of water. Up through today, the Old Testament continues to provide interesting scripts for popular movies because it is filled with everything that is dramatic about the human experience: revenge and reconciliation, sin and repentance, war and peace, and mainly love.

Yet, to really appreciate the Old Testament for what it is, it must be read. Even most public high schools offer units on biblical literature, or at least they did until very recently. As a Catholic looking to deepen your faith by reading the Bible, it's important for you to know and appreciate its main narrative and specific people and events. In that way you can truly become "Bible literate." As Hollywood would attest, the Old Testament is chock-full of exciting storylines, or in the words of a title of a 1965 classic film, it is "the greatest story ever told."

Sampling Key Stories

In this section, you will be presented with reading directions for six different Old Testament passages. Follow this format:

- First, read the opening question.
- Second, read the information in this text for contextual background on the Old Testament passage.
- Third, and more importantly, undertake a thoughtful and careful reading of each passage directly from your Bible. Ask yourself: What does this Scripture passage have to do with my life? What is the Lord trying to tell me in this passage?
- Finally, go back to the opening question and make sure you can answer it.

Jacob's Deception (Genesis 27:1–45)

How did Jacob take his brother's blessing and birthright?

Abraham, the father of the Chosen People, had a son, Isaac. (You likely have heard of Abraham's near sacrifice of Isaac that is recorded in Genesis 22:1–19.) In terms of the Old Testament narrative, Isaac is a transitional character who advances the biblical story between Abraham and Jacob (the son of Isaac). Isaac and his wife Rebekah had two sons, Esau and Jacob. Because he was the firstborn son, Esau was entitled to receive his father's birthright.

Jacob takes his brother's blessing and birthright by tricking Isaac.

The birthright was a privilege that included a ceremonial blessing given by the father. The birthright had several benefits for the firstborn son. He would become the head of the family and be the owner of the family's property. He would be responsible for the care of the younger son(s), his mother, and any unmarried daughters. The blessing was extra significant; it placed him in a special covenant relationship with God. The Hebrews of this period considered the blessing given by the father to be an oral covenant. God would communicate directly with the head of the family. The blessing was also a promise of fertility.

Jacob, the younger son, ultimately received his father's blessing and all the rights and responsibilities that came with it and the birthright. How so? The story is a remarkable one, and a literary masterpiece, in which Rebekah organizes a stunning sequence of events because she preferred Jacob more than she did Esau. Jacob remains passive through the entire operation, worrying only that he might be cursed if the plan fails. He doesn't seem concerned at all with being granted the birthright and blessing.

The incident impacts the entire history of God's Chosen People, the Hebrews. Jacob is eventually given a new name after a struggle with a messenger of God in Genesis 32:23–32. The messenger said: "You shall no longer be named Jacob, but 'Israel,' because you have contended with divine and human beings and have prevailed" (Gn 32:28–29). Likewise the people were called *Israel*, a name related to the Hebrew verb *sara* ("struggle") and the first syllable of Elohim ("God").

Joseph and His Brothers (Genesis 37, 39–50)

How did the family of Jacob wind up in Egypt?

Another dramatic story and great piece of biblical literature revolves around Jacob's twelve sons, especially his favorite son, Joseph. Jacob favored Joseph because he was the only son of his beloved wife Rachel. Polygamy was still practiced in this period.∞ Jacob also had sons with his wife Leah and the handmaids of both Leah and Rachel.

Jacob loved Joseph so much that he had an ornamented tunic made for him. Joseph is also described as a "dreamer." He had elaborate dreams and would often try to explain them to his other brothers. You may have seen or heard of the Broadway musical *Joseph and His Amazing Technicolor Dreamcoat*. It is based on the story of Joseph from the Book of Genesis.

Not surprisingly, Joseph's brothers were jealous of Joseph because their father favored him. They tried to ignore him when he told about his dreams. In fact, "they hated him so much they could not say a kind word to him" (Gn 37:4).

The brothers' hatred and jealousy, Joseph's dreams and his ability to interpret dreams, and his prized ornamental tunic all play a part in how the Israelites (from Jacob's new name Israel) ended up in Egypt as slaves awaiting a return to their homeland and freedom centuries later as led by Moses (see Exodus 1:1–15:21).

∞ Note

Whereas the creation accounts presented the ideal of monogamy, some Jews practiced polygamy during the time of the patriarchs. A theological explanation often refers to Hebrews 1:1 ("In times past, God spoke in partial and various ways"). God's Revelation was gradual and ongoing. Not everyone could follow the dictates of the Torah at that point in history. It is important to note, however, that none of the Old Testament prophets had more than one wife, and they often compared polygamy to idolatry.

Ruth the Moabite (Ruth 1:1–4:16)

How did Gentiles become part of the royal ancestry of King David?

The story of Ruth involves a foreign, Gentile woman's fidelity to the Jewish family of her mother-in-law, Naomi. Ruth was a Moabite—that is, a member of a kingdom that was located in modern-day Jordan along the eastern shore of the Dead Sea. After her Jewish husband died, in Moab, Ruth follows Naomi back to Judah, despite Naomi's protests that she ought to return to her homeland and be married again to one of her own native people.

Instead, once back in Judah, Ruth observes a Jewish law detailed in the Book of Leviticus that required her to marry her nearest male relative. This was called a *levirate marriage*; it would allow her to bear a son that would be her first husband's heir. This law was intended to keep property within the same clan or family by ensuring that there was an heir even if a man died before he had a son. By eventually marrying Boaz, her relative by marriage, Ruth was sealed by covenant to his Jewish family.

The Book of Ruth is a short book, only four chapter in length. It is set in the time of the judges, before King David, around the years 1200–1000 BC, though its final form likely was not completed until about the sixth century BC. The story has a surprising conclusion, revealing how this Gentile woman has a connection, not only to King David, but to Jesus, the Son of God.

David Rises to Power (1 Samuel 16–17)

How did David, who became Israel's greatest king, come to the attention of Saul, Israel's first king?

Late in the eleventh century BC, Israel became like many of its neighboring nations by appointing a king to rule over them. According to the First Book of Samuel, this development was contrary to the warnings given by the prophet Samuel, who counseled that only God himself should be their king. The people did not drop their demand: "Not so! There must be a king over us. We must be like the other nations, with a king to rule us and to lead us in warfare and fight our battles" (1 Sm 8:19–20). Once established, the monarchy itself lasted for just over one hundred years, from about 1047 BC to 930 BC.

The first Israelite king was Saul, who was from the tribe of Benjamin (there were twelve Hebrew tribes). Saul was essentially chosen for his skills as a soldier, though as king he had limited success against Israel's greatest enemy, the Philistines. The Philistines were threats to Israel in two significant ways.

While many positive aspects of Israel's monarch are especially tied to King David, it is equally true that Scriptures also detail his failings—including his ill-fated affair with a married woman, Bathsheba, when he abused his powers and killed her husband to cover his sin (2 Sm 11–12).

First, they had the ability to fashion weapons with iron, which tribal Israel was not yet capable of doing. Israel used bronze, not only for its weaponry but also for its agricultural plows. Iron weapons and plows were much more durable. Second, the Philistines' military strength was partly based on their self-organization. Tribal Israel, however, was poorly organized. King Saul did not have much success at addressing either disadvantage.

A byproduct of the military situation with the Philistines also resulted in an internal threat to Saul and his role as king. The First Book of Samuel shares that Saul was rejected by the people for his sins (see 1 Samuel 15:1–35). But this doesn't explain why his successor would be David, the youngest son of Jesse, who was from the tribe of Judah and not one of Saul's sons. The reading selection from 1 Samuel 16–17 presents two different accounts of how the shepherd boy David came to the attention of King Saul. One of the accounts may be more familiar to you than the other. Can you recognize and name both of the accounts listed in Scripture?

Dramatic Witness of the Prophet Elijah (1 Kings 18:16–43)

How did the prophet Elijah silence the prophets of paganism?

Elijah holds a place among the greatest prophets of the Old Testament. He was not a writing prophet. He was a prophet who symbolized the struggle between the religion of the Chosen People who worshipped the one, true God, YHWH, and the pagan religion of the neighboring Canaanites who worshipped many gods, **Baal** in particular.

The Israelites were susceptible to pagan worship because Ahab, the northern Israelite king (the kingdom had been split in two after the Babylonian exile), married a Canaanite princess, Jezebel. She began to demand that Ahab seize land that did not belong to him. For example, Ahab took the property of a peasant named Naboth. Jezebel then had Naboth executed. Ahab also had over six hundred prophets executed. Elijah was one of the last remaining prophets. The brutality directed to the prophets illustrated to the people what life would be like under a Canaanite ruler who did not heed YHWH and his laws.

Eventually, Elijah was cornered by one of Ahab's assistants, Obadiah, who arranged a meeting between the prophet and the king. Ahab said to him, "Is it you, the disturber of Israel?" Elijah answered, "It is not I who disturb Israel, but you and your father's house, by forsaking the commands of the Lord and you by following the Baals" (1 Kgs 18:17–18).

Elijah and the chariot.

Elijah had a plan to demonstrate that Baal was a false God and YHWH is the one, true God. He summoned the 450 prophets of Baal to Mount Carmel. Elijah would be the only prophet representing YHWH. There would be a duel of sorts to determine whether it was the gods of the Canaanites or the God of Israel who was legitimate and true.

Baal The Canaanite god of fertility, associated with storms and rain. He was the most prominent of the Canaanite gods and the one most often worshipped falsely by the Israelites.

The prominence of Elijah extends past this incident. Though there is no typical miraculous birth story to introduce him as with other prophets, there is a unique miracle story to mark his passing. He is described as being transported into heaven in a whirlwind. While conversing with his successor Elisha, "a fiery chariot and fiery horses came between the two of them, and Elijah went up to heaven in a whirlwind" (2 Kgs 2:11). Elijah is later present at the Transfiguration of Jesus along with Moses. Many Jews in Jesus's time thought Elijah would be the precursor to the Messiah, a role that actually fell to John the Baptist.

The Maccabean Revolt and Final Era of Jewish Independence (2 Maccabees 6:18–7:42)

How did a Jewish scribe and a Jewish mother and her sons protest against the desecration of the Temple?

One of the greatest threats to Judaism occurred very late in the Old Testament timeline, in the second century BC. The Seleucid Empire, a descendant of the old Alexandrian Empire in Babylon, began to rule in Palestine in approximately 200 BC. The Roman Empire was also becoming a powerful force in the region. The Jewish Temple was under threat by the Seleucids. The Temple acted as the most secure "bank" for the Jews in the region, and thus considerable sums of money were stored in Temple treasuries.∞

The Jewish leaders debated among themselves about who would be the high priest and thus be able to negotiate financial and trade deals with the Seleucids. Also, a growing faction of Jews continued to be more Hellenized in attitude, practice, and outlook. Many had become less observant in their religious practice. The Jewish people had been under pagan control since 587 BC. The Temple was at the center of political and religious controversies of both traditional and Hellenized Jews.

The Seleucid ruler, Antiochus IV, perhaps siding with Hellenized Jews in order to squelch the traditional Jews, instituted policies that were met with little resistance among the Hellenized Jews. Among them, he allowed for nudity in Greek gymnasiums. Some of the Jewish males even had surgery to reverse

∞ Note

Temples of most religions throughout the region also served as local banks, so they were nearly always prime targets for outside conquerors who often went to the temple first when they invaded a city.

When Judas Maccabeus, his brothers, and followers had purified the Temple after recapturing it and were ready to rededicate it, they found only enough oil to fuel the lamp for one day. Despite this, the lamp remained lit throughout the celebration until more could be made. Hanukkah is a remembrance of this occasion.

their circumcisions in order to avoid embarrassment when participating in athletics in the nude. Those who went to the gymnasium also had to acknowledge Greek gods who were the gymnasium patrons.

When the Romans advanced in 167 BC to force Antiochus to withdraw his troops from Egypt, he blamed the Jews. He unleashed his army on the Jews in Jerusalem and outlawed the practice of Judaism in all traditional forms. Jews were even forced to eat food forbidden by Jewish law. The final offense came when an altar to Zeus was erected in the Temple and unclean swine's flesh was sacrificed on it. This sacrilege led to a revolt by Mattathias, a local priest, and his sons. Judas, a son of Mattathias, known as "Maccabeus" ("the Hammer"), was a brilliant military strategist. A series of victories by Maccabeus against local military forces of the Seleucids led to revolutionary control of the Temple in December 164 BC, three years from the time the Temple was profaned.∞ The family of Maccabeus, later called the Hasmoneans, was eventually able to become Jewish rulers of Palestine from 141 BC until the Romans conquered them in 63 BC. This was the last Jewish rule of the Holy Land until the establishment of modern Israel in 1948.

This section offers only a sampling of the compelling literature with dramatic plots and characters that make up the Old Testament. Consider undertaking a fuller reading plan of the Old Testament to gain even more depth and breadth of God's Word and action in forming his people (see the subsection "Bible Reading Plans" in the section "Deposit of Faith" in the Appendix for more information).

SECTION Assessment

Comprehension

1. What were the benefits of the birthright that Jacob received?
2. What was Jacob's new name? What did it mean?
3. Why were Joseph's brothers jealous of him?
4. How did Ruth disobey her mother-in-law, Naomi?
5. Why did the Israelites demand a human king?
6. What were the two threats the Philistines posed to Israel?
7. What is the miraculous story associated with Elijah's passing?
8. What was the final offense against the Jews that led to the action by Judas Maccabeus?

Vocabulary

9. What were characteristics of the Canaanite god *Baal*?

Reflection

10. What are your goals to become "Bible literate"? Name three steps in order to accomplish your goals in this area.
11. Which of the Old Testament stories that you read in this section was your favorite? Explain why.

∞ Note

The recapture of the Temple in the Maccabean Revolt under Judas and his brothers is still celebrated today in the eight-day Hanukkah festival. Hanukkah is also called the "Feast of Dedication" or the "Festival of Lights." Jewish tradition holds that even though there was enough olive oil to keep the menorah's candles burning for a single day, they miraculously burned for eight days and eight nights. Today, Hanukkah is celebrated in the month of December.

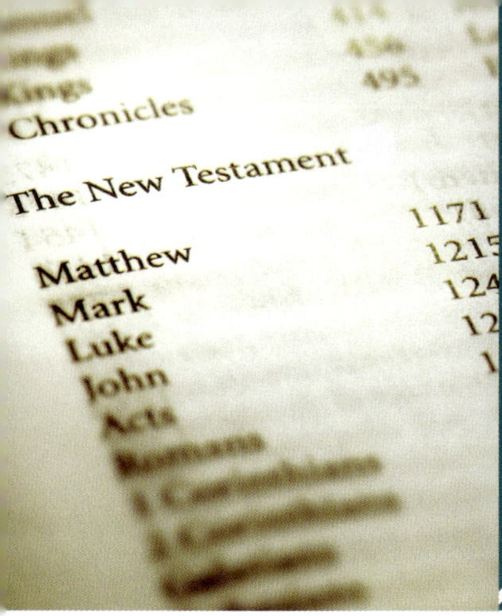

Section 3

NEW TESTAMENT CATEGORIES AND CONTENTS

The New Testament has twenty-seven books. On average, the New Testament books are shorter in length than those in the Old Testament. The books are attributed to eight different authors, including six Apostles: Matthew, John, Paul, James, Peter, and Jude. The other two authors—Mark and Luke—were in close contact with the Apostles. Since all of the books were composed during roughly a fifty-year period over the last half of the first century AD, all of the authors knew and interacted with a number of direct witnesses to the life of Jesus Christ.

The New Testament books include history (Gospels and Acts of the Apostles), books for instruction (epistles), and one prophetic book (Revelation). The Gospels form the heart of the New Testament and of the Bible itself. The Gospels are broken up into two subcategories. The synoptic Gospels (see the subsection "Who Were the Authors of the Bible?" in Chapter 2, Section 2) have a parallel storyline and appear to share different sources. Chapter 5 includes more information on the synoptic Gospels: Matthew, Mark, and Luke. The fourth Gospel, the Gospel of John, was written some decades later than the synoptic Gospels. It is organized around seven "signs" that provide a deep look into the words and actions of Jesus, focusing in great depth on his divinity. The Gospel of John is the subject of Chapter 6.

The Acts of the Apostles follows the Gospels in the canon of the New Testament. Acts, also authored by Luke and in many ways a second part of his Gospel, tells the story of the early Church and the work of the Apostles. The first fifteen chapters are about the foundation of the Church in and around Jerusalem; the final sixteen chapters detail the missionary trips of St. Paul to the Gentiles throughout the entirety of the Roman Empire. Epistles, written in letter form and authored by Paul (in some cases perhaps with the assistance of a close disciple of Paul), make up the majority of the books of the New Testament. The epistles address problems that crept up in the various local churches while at the same time promoting essential teachings of the faith. The oldest text of the institution of the Eucharist is found in an epistle, the First Letter to the Corinthians (11:23–26).

The seven epistles that follow the writings of Paul are called "catholic epistles" because they were written for a universal audience rather than to a local community. The word *catholic* means "universal." Some of these epistles are in letter form, and others are not.

The Four Horsemen of the Apocalypse (often referred to as the Four Horsemen) are figures in Christian mythology, referenced in Revelation 6:1–8.

The Book of Revelation, also called the "Apocalypse" for its **apocalyptic** form of writing, is the final book in the New Testament canon. It is highly symbolic with a vision of John at Patmos, an island off of Greece, in which he addresses seven local churches located in Asia Minor as well as the struggles Christians were facing with the Romans and the Church's final destiny in the **New Jerusalem**.

In considering an overview of the New Testament, it's also important to answer a question

---

apocalyptic From a word meaning "revelation" or "unveiling." Apocalyptic literature is a highly symbolic style of writing in which hidden truths are revealed within a narrative framework. These writings were usually written in time of crisis and used symbolic language to bolster faith by reassuring believers that the current age, subject to the forces of evil, will end when God intervenes and establishes a divine rule of goodness and peace.

New Jerusalem A symbol of the Church that is present both in heaven and on earth through the Communion of Saints. At the Last Judgment, the New Jerusalem will exist in the world transformed by Christ's Resurrection.

The Gospels Are Ancient Biographies

Focus Question: What are the scope, style, and message of the Old Testament and New Testament?

Were the Gospels myths or fairy tales? Perhaps in your Catholic high school theology classroom you have heard fellow students scoff at the Gospel and call it fiction. Perhaps even that person is you!

How can naming and understanding the literary genre of the Gospels as "ancient biographies" further help to dispel arguments that the Gospels are fictional or a myth created by their authors? Biblical scholar Brant Pitre and Catholic apologist Brandon Vogt each provide crucial pieces of evidence.[2]

Biographies from the ancient world (including those by non-Christian authors) had five distinct traits:

1. *Ancient biographies focused on the life and death of one person, not an entire nation or group of people.* The Gospels focus solely on the life of Jesus.

2 *Ancient biographies were short in length, between ten and twenty thousand words.* All four Gospels fit in this range. Mark is the shortest Gospel (11,000 words). Luke is the longest (19,000 words).

3 *Ancient biographies tended to begin with the ancestry of the person.* Two of the Gospels (Matthew and Luke) feature genealogies of Jesus in the opening chapters. Matthew even begins his Gospel with a genealogy.

4 *Ancient biographies did not follow a chronological order.* Whereas modern biographies focus on precise dates, times, and places, ancient biographies focused more on the meaning and message of the person. The Gospels are arranged in this way. Just because events in Jesus's life may be "out of order" when comparing the four Gospels, that doesn't mean they are myth or fiction. It just means each author had a different focus and a different way of organizing the material.

5 *Ancient biographies did not tell everything about the person.* The Gospels were not written to tell everything about Jesus or life in first-century Palestine. The Gospel of John, in fact, points this out in its closing: "There are also many other things, which Jesus did, but if these were to be described individually, I do not think the whole world would contain the books that would be written" (Jn 21:25).

Pitre concludes that "the old idea that the Gospels are not biographies but folklore and fairy stories completely fails to reckon with literary evidence. The Gospels are biographies."[3]

Vogt continues by addressing the credibility of the evangelists. He shares these points:

- *The evangelists had good intentions to write accurate accounts about Jesus.* Luke, in fact, states in his opening that he, like others, had decided "after investigating everything accurately anew, to write down in an orderly sequence for you, most excellent Theophilus, so that you may realize the certainty of the teachings that you received" (Lk 1:3–4).
- *The Gospels make up four independent sources about Jesus.* With four Gospels, there are more independent sources to double-check facts than for any other ancient person.

- *The "criterion of embarrassment" can be applied.* This is a rule that historians use in their studies. If something in the writing embarrasses the author or the subject, that is a sign that it is not made up. The Gospels tell of disciples being weak, cowardly, and misguided. This contradicts how an author bent on fabrication would want to make the subjects the heroes of the story: authors usually don't want their heroes (or themselves) to be embarrassed.
- *The Gospels do not employ the literary style of a myth.* Instead they contain small and often insignificant details. Remember the story of Jesus and the woman caught in adultery (see John 8:1–11). Do you remember what Jesus was doing at the beginning of the story? He was drawing in the sand. A myth would not contain such an insignificant detail.

If you question whether or not the Gospels are myths, Brant Pitre has this advice: "You need to go back and read a few more myths if you think that when you read the Gospels you've seen a myth because you obviously don't know one when you've seen one!"[4]

Further Study and Reflection

- Write a definition of *myth*, and list three reasons why the Gospels do not fit that definition.
- Explain why the following passages might be examples of the criterion of embarrassment: Mark 3:21; John 7:5; Mark 8:22–25.

that an inquisitive person might pose about typology (see Chapter 3, Section 2, "Reading the Bible according to the Holy Spirit"): *Could the New Testament authors have simply constructed the Gospels and other books to match with Old Testament prophecies about Jesus and his preaching?* We can confidently answer "no" because, in fact, many Old Testament predictions of the Messiah are *contradicted* in the New Testament. Others are interpreted differently by Christians than they were by Jews. Consider, for example, how Matthew portrays magi coming from the east, following a star, to visit the infant Jesus (see Matthew 2:1–2). If typology was being employed to connect the visit of the magi with the Old Testament, wouldn't Matthew have referenced Numbers 24:17 ("the star of Jacob") or "caravans . . . bearing gold and frankincense" as found in Isaiah 6:6? Also, the Gospels often portray Jesus as someone who is at conflict with Jewish leaders, who predicts the destruction of Jerusalem and its Temple, and who preaches a transitory, not earthly view of keeping the Mosaic Law. This evidence hardly supports a theory that the New Testament authors created stories to artificially connect the message of the Gospels with the Old Testament.

Survey of New Testament Books

Before the name "New Testament" was used, the Church said the "Gospels and Apostolic Writings" or just the "Gospel and the Apostle," referring to St. Paul, the Apostle of the Gentiles. The New Testament today is often categorized as follows:

- Gospels
- New Testament Letters
- Catholic Letters
- Book of Revelation

The Acts of the Apostles is sometimes included with the Gospels. The Letter to the Hebrews, though not likely authored by St. Paul, is usually grouped with the other Pauline New Testament Letters. An overview of each of these New Testament categories follows.

Gospels

Matthew, Mark, Luke (Acts of the Apostles), John

Symbol of St. Matthew

Symbol of St. Mark

Symbol of St. Luke

Symbol of St. John

The Greek word for "gospel," *euangelion*, is used sixty-six times in the New Testament. It is made up of two words: *eu* ("good") and *angélion* ("news"). Similarly, an *angéliis* or angel is a messenger, and *angélion* is the message or news that the angel brings. The Old English word for "good news" is *gospel.*

Most of the references to "Good News" in the New Testament refer not to the stories of Jesus's life but to the content of what he preached. For example, the first time the word *gospel* appears in the New Testament is in Matthew 4:23 when it is reported that Jesus "went around all of Galilee, teaching in their synagogues, proclaiming the gospel of the kingdom." Jesus wasn't preaching about his life at that moment. Rather, he was teaching the Galileans about how God was entering into the world, what they should believe, and how they should seek repentance so that they could respond correctly to what God was doing in their lives.

That means that the word *gospel* did not originally mean "a narrative of Jesus's life." It only came to be associated with that meaning because of the way it is used in Mark 1:1: "the beginning of the good news [or 'gospel'] of Jesus Christ, the Son of God." The use of *gospel* in that passage sounded so very much like a book title that the term was used to describe the other three narratives about Jesus—Matthew, Luke, and John—because they were written to resemble Mark's "Gospel."

Why were four Gospels written instead of just one? The answer is that each of the evangelists was writing for a different community (e.g., Matthew for Jewish converts to Christianity and Luke primarily to Gentiles).

Even with four Gospels and Luke's second part in the Acts of the Apostles, "God speaks only one single Word" (*CCC*, 102) and that Word is Jesus, the Word of God. The central object of the Gospels "is Jesus Christ, God's Incarnate Son: his acts, teachings, Passion and glorification, and his Church's beginnings under the Spirit's guidance" (*CCC*, 124).

Chapters 5 and 6 are devoted to the organization and content of the synoptic Gospels and the Gospel of John.

New Testament Letters

Romans, First and Second Corinthians, Galatians, Ephesians, Philippians, Colossians, First and Second Thessalonians, First and Second Timothy, Titus, Philemon, Hebrews

In the New Testament, there are twenty-one documents that take the form of letters or epistles. Most of these are standard letters with greetings and salutations, though some are more in the form of a treatise. Fourteen of the twenty-one letters have been traditionally attributed to St. Paul. One of these, the Letter to the Hebrews, does not claim to be written by Paul, but was attached to the group of Pauline letters at the time that it was accepted into the New Testament.

Even among the thirteen letters that in their first verse claim that Paul was their author, there is debate about Paul's role in the authorship of six of those letters. To this point, the practice of dictating letters was common in the first century. It is quite certain that Paul made use of scribes, adding short asides in his own handwriting as he felt it necessary to emphasize some key point (see Philemon 19 and 1

Corinthians 16:21), and allowing at least one scribe, Tertius, to add a personal note of his own (see Romans 16:22). There is a possibility that Paul dictated to others because his eyesight was failing. In Galatians 6:11 he wrote about "what large letters I am writing to you in my own hand!" Perhaps he wrote in "large letters" in order to read his own writing. A second possibility is that Paul hired out the writing to professional scribes because the writing process was so expensive that it made sense to have professionals handle the formalities of the production of the letters.

Paul's letters were organized in a common literary form among Greek-Roman letters of the time. The letters began with the name of the sender. Any co-senders were also named at the beginning of the letter. Letters in the Greek-Roman style also included a formal personal greeting and wishes for good health, or a prayer asking for God's favor. Paul's letters contained these four main sections:

1. *Opening Address.* Since the letters were not placed in envelopes, the opening salutation gives the name of the sender, the receiver, and a short greeting.

2. *Thanksgiving.* A short section of words of thankfulness sets the tone of the letter and what is to follow. Paul's thanksgivings were prayerful and inspiring.

3. *Body.* The bulk of the letter has two parts to it: doctrinal teaching and encouragement. Paul elaborates on Christian truths or corrects errors that have cropped up among the people. He also applies doctrinal teaching to the experiences of the readers' own lives. These sections continue to be applicable to morality today.

4. *Final salutations.* Paul concludes his letters by giving personal news and specific advice to individuals. His final greeting is usually a short blessing—for example, "the grace of our Lord Jesus Christ be with you" (1 Thes 5:28).

St. Paul's letters are not arranged alphabetically in the New Testament, but rather from longest to shortest, beginning with Romans and ending with Philemon. In seven of the letters—Romans, 1 and 2 Corinthians, Galatians,

Philippians, 1 Thessalonians, and Philemon—there is a consistency of literary style and vocabulary. Also, in these letters, Paul emphasizes the imminent end of the world and that Jesus's Second Coming would be soon. This theme influenced other specific points in these letters, especially the urgency of preaching the Gospel throughout the Roman Empire, the necessity of casting off sin (see Romans 13:11–12), and correct ways for married couples to live their marriage (see 1 Corinthians 7:29–31).

In the other six letters attributed to St. Paul, the theme of the end of the world is lessened or even ignored. For example, in 2 Thessalonians 2:16, Paul explains that the coming of the Lord is *not* imminent, and in fact they could expect some clear sign before he returned. Also, 2 Thessalonians, Colossians, and Ephesians use either different vocabulary or assign different meanings to words used in other letters. For example, in these letters Paul uses the Greek word for "Church" (*ekklesia*) to refer to the universal Church as a whole, and not just to a local community (see Ephesians 1:22–23 and Colossians 1:18). However, in other places the use of *ekklesia* does describe local communities—for example, the "church in Corinth" (1 Cor 1:2) or the "churches in Galatia" (Gal 1:2). These types of differences are one of the reasons biblical scholars think that 2 Thessalonians, Colossians, and Ephesians may have been written by disciples of Paul who gave credit to him for what they wrote. A name for this type of writing is **pseudonymous**. Three other letters—1 and 2 Timothy and Titus—may also be pseudonymous works.

The Letter to the Hebrews is a written homily that develops the theme of Christ as High Priest, the model of faith. The letter is associated with St. Paul because of a reference to Timothy (see Hebrews 13:23). However, it is clear that Paul did not write this letter as the vocabulary, style, thought development, use of the Old Testament, and theological themes differ from those letters attributed to Paul. The author of the Letter to the Hebrews is anonymous.

---

pseudonymous A work written under a name that is not the name of the person doing the actual writing. It was a common and accepted practice for disciples and admirers of great teachers to write works under their names to extend their legacies.

Catholic Letters

James, First and Second Peter, First, Second, and Third John, Jude

The catholic letters are called that for three reasons. First, they contain general advice that is helpful to all local churches. Second, they were accepted, even if only gradually, by the churches in both the West and the East.∞ And, third, these letters help us to understand better how the catholic—that is, universal or worldwide—Church developed.

The seven letters were designated as "catholic letters" by Church historian Eusebius in the fourth century. However, the adjective *catholic* was used even earlier when applied by the theologian Origen in AD 230 to the letters 1 John, 1 Peter, and Jude, as well as the noncanonical Letter of Barnabas.

There is a disparity of tone between the three letters of John, which all resemble the tone of the Gospel of John, and the other four catholic letters. Though each of the authors of these letters is identified as an eyewitness of Jesus, like some of the New Testament letters, the catholic letters were written by pseudonymous authors, presenting what the named Apostle might have said in dealing with the situations that developed in the various churches by the end of the first century. All seven letters address some of the moral and ethical issues faced by the early Church. They also refute some of the heresies that were creeping into the Church. The catholic letters are practical too; they offer a path for Christians to deal with difficult decisions, to put Christ above all, and to live in anticipation of the **Parousia**.

Book of Revelation

After the Romans destroyed the Jerusalem Temple in AD 70, Jews and their Christian neighbors likely thought they had seen the worst of the Roman

---

Parousia A Greek word for "presence." It refers to the Second Coming of Christ, which will usher in the presence of God's Kingdom on earth as it is in heaven.

∞ Note

When the Emperor Constantine transferred the capital of the Roman Empire to Constantinople in the fourth century, theological and liturgical disputes, not to mention cultural and political differences, divided some of the segments of the Church in the East. That is why it was remarkable that there was agreement between the West and the East on the use of the catholic letters.

The Second Coming of Christ.

persecutions. They were wrong. By the end of the century, Christians faced imprisonment, beatings, and death. The last book of the Bible, the Book of Revelation, speaks to the Christians about the persecutions using the highly symbolic apocalyptic style of writing in which the author, John of Patmos, was able to disguise the inspired message he intended to share.

John was exiled on the island of Patmos during the reign of the Emperor Domitian (AD 95) where he wrote the Book of Revelation. Whether or not he is the Apostle John has been debated by biblical scholars. Yet, the authenticity of the Apostle's authorship was claimed by early Church leaders Justin,

Irenaeus, Clement of Alexandria, and Tertullian. Much of the literary style of the Book of Revelation is comparable to John's Gospel; in both places he is the only inspired New Testament writer to refer to Jesus as *Logos* (Word). Also both Revelation and the Gospel include pronounced contrasts between things such as light and darkness, life and death, and truth and lies.

The Book of Revelation uses symbols to convey spiritual truths; for example, colors are prominent. White symbolizes victory and purity, red symbolizes violence, and black symbolizes death. Also, the number seven is a sign of fullness or completeness, and six a sign of imperfection.

The Book of Revelation is divided into three parts:

1. Introduction (Rv 1:1–8)
2. Body of Teachings (Rv 1:9–22:5)
3. Conclusion (Rv 22:6–21)

In the body of teachings (Rv 1:9–3:22), John has a vision in which he is charged with writing to seven churches of Asia Minor. This part preaches against heresies and the lack of faith of Christians and opposition that comes from Jews.

There are also a series of visions and symbolic descriptions that are not to be taken literally. Rather, the visions are meant to show both God's anger at the current state of sin in the world and his providential care for the Church in her time of need. The Book of Revelation presents a hopeful perspective of the **eschaton**—that is, the ultimate salvation and victory will take place at the end of the present age when Christ will come in glory. Revelation predicts that Satan's reign will be defeated (see Revelation 11:15; 12:10) and God's plan will take precedence from that time on.

---

eschaton The final age and the end of human history, including the Last Judgment, the defeat of evil, and the creation of a new heaven and earth. *Eschaton* is the Latin form of a Greek word that literally means "last" or "most remote."

SECTION Assessment

Comprehension

1. Which books of the New Testament include historical information?
2. Which book of the New Testament is the second part of the Gospel of Luke?
3. If the Gospels were not a "narrative of Jesus's life," what were they?
4. Why were four Gospels written instead of just one?
5. How did the Letter to the Hebrews get attached to the Pauline letters?
6. What are the two parts that make up the body of Paul's letters?
7. How are Paul's letters organized in the New Testament canon?
8. What are three reasons the catholic letters are called that?
9. What is evidence that the Apostle John also wrote the Book of Revelation?

Vocabulary

10. What is a characteristic of *apocalyptic* writing?
11. What is evidence that six letters attributed to Paul are likely *pseudonymous*?
12. Define *Parousia*.

Reflection

13. How do you understand the relationship between the Old Testament and New Testament? Explain in your own words.
14. Write a one-sentence definition of the Gospels.

Section 4
SURVEYING THE NEW TESTAMENT

When you close the last page of the New Testament, there is no other inspired sacred book to turn to that will enlighten you to any additional truths for what God wants to reveal for your salvation. The New Testament, read in light of the Old Testament, shares the story of the **omnipotent** God who humbled himself, first, to become one of his creations, and then more surprisingly, to suffer death in atonement for our sins. Because of this, the Bible is not only the "greatest story ever told"; it is also the most amazing story of all.

The Second Vatican Council document *Dei Verbum* teaches clearly that the Bible, and New Testament in particular, is Good News that "will never pass away and we now await no further new public revelation before the glorious manifestation of our Lord Jesus Christ" (*Dei Verbum*, 4).

This same message was communicated at least twice in the New Testament itself and recorded by Luke in his Gospel and Acts. The first occasion was on the day Christ rose from the dead. Two of the disciples were walking from Jerusalem to the village of Emmaus, a distance of seven miles. On the way Jesus began to walk with them, though they did not recognize him. The disciples were discussing the events of Jesus's Passion and Death and reports of his Resurrection. But they were unable to connect the dots between Jesus and the Christ who had been prophesied and prepared for in the Old Testament. Jesus provided the interpretation for them: "'Oh, how foolish you are! How slow of heart to believe all that the prophets spoke! Was it not necessary that the Messiah should suffer these things and enter into his glory?' Then beginning with Moses and all the prophets, he interpreted to them what referred to him in all the Scriptures" (Lk 24:25–26).

---

omnipotent An attribute of God that he is everywhere, unlimited, and all-powerful.

Recall, also, a similar speech given by Peter in Jerusalem to Jews who had gathered for the Pentecost feast (see the subsection "Stages in the Formation of the Gospels" in Chapter 2, Section 1) in which he quoted the prophets of the Old Covenant who had foretold the saving events around the life of Jesus. He chastised those who had contributed to Jesus's Death while at the same time convincing three thousand people to be baptized (see Acts 2:14–41). Later, at Solomon's Portico,∞ he again reminded those present that "the God of Abraham, of Isaac, and of Jacob, the God of our ancestors has glorified his servant, Jesus whom you handed over and denied in Pilate's presence, when he decided to release him. . . . The author of life you put to death, but God has raised him from the dead; of this we are witnesses" (Acts 3:13, 15). The New Testament is the culmination of salvation history. It can also be thought of as a love story, not in any superficial sense. *Dei Verbum* explains God's Revelation in Scripture this way: "Through this Revelation, therefore, the invisible God out of the abundance of His love speaks to us as friends and lives among us, so that he may invite and take us into fellowship with himself" (*Dei Verbum*, 2).

Sampling Key Stories

In this section, you will be presented with reading directions for six different New Testament passages. Follow this format:

- First, read the opening question.
- Second, read the information in this text for contextual background on the New Testament passage.
- Third, and more importantly, undertake a thoughtful and careful reading of each passage directly from your Bible. Ask yourself: What does this Scripture passage have to do with my life? What is the Lord trying to tell me in this passage?
- Finally, go back to the opening question and make sure you can answer it.

∞ Note

Solomon's Portico was a porch on the east side of the Temple. (Recall that this was the Second Temple and was constructed by King Herod.) The porch, named for King Solomon, overlooked a deep valley. A *capital* or top part of a column of the porch was found in 2017.

The Incarnation (Luke 2:1–40)

In what ways did the Son of God enter the world in poverty?

The Son of God took on a human nature in order to accomplish our salvation. The Gospel of John, which does not tell of the birth of Jesus in a stable, instead summarizes the nature of the Incarnation:

> And the Word became flesh
> and made his dwelling among us,
> and we saw his glory,
> the glory of the Father's only Son,
> full of grace and truth. (Jn 1:14)

This is really a remarkable statement to think about. Archbishop Fulton J. Sheen, who hosted a popular weekly television program in the 1950s at the advent of commercial television, reflected on what had taken place with the birth of a baby in Bethlehem: "The tiny hands that are not quite long enough to reach the huge heads of cattle are the hands that hold the reins that steer the Sun and Moon and stars in their courses . . . wrapped in swaddling bands, divinity enclosed, wrapped cabin-cribbed, helpless as a babe!"[5] And, yet, though extraordinary that the Eternal God would humble himself to take on human flesh, the process is something that we, as humans, can understand because we, too, are at once made up of both body and soul. Our identity is not based on one or the other, but on both. If God can create humans with two natures in one, he can, too, accomplish the greater miracle of also having two natures in himself: a human nature and a divine nature.

Think more about the humility required for God to become incarnate. Archbishop Sheen used an analogy comparing what God did at the Incarnation to a human being dispossessing himself of his body to become a dog in order to correct the way some dogs behaved for their masters.

Archbishop Fulton J. Sheen

"What a humiliation that would be," said Sheen. "You know that you had a mind that could write poetry, and that could study science. And absorb literature. Yet here you were in the body of a dog . . . knowing all the while that you were better, you were a human."[6]

Magnify the thought of a human being becoming a dog and having to live and associate with dogs with the mind of a human being, and compare it to the all-powerful Creator God becoming a man. God not only had the infinite nature of his divinity contained in a human body, but also had to deal with bodily pain, hunger, and thirst. God also placed an extra limitation on himself by being born into poverty.

The Vine and the Branches (John 15:1–17)

What is the necessity of remaining attached to Jesus and his Church?

Jesus's lesson of a "vine and branches" has at least one common element of a parable. As with the other parables Jesus told, these words describe natural and common things—trees, branches, vines, vine grower—that people who listened to him speak would understand. Yet this passage is different from other parables, such as the parable of the prodigal son where the fatted calf is killed for the derelict younger son, or the parable of the lost sheep where the shepherd leaves ninety-nine sheep to look for one lost one. It is different because this "parable" of the vine and branches does not contain such a surprising ending. Instead, Jesus's lesson makes perfect sense: a branch that is separated from the main vine will die.

This simple lesson of the vine and branches is also a symbol for the Church, especially as defined as Christ's Mystical Body (see the feature "Faithful Disciple: Pope Pius XII" in the Chapter 3 Review). Recall that this image was explained in depth by Pope Pius XII in his 1943 encyclical *Mystici Corporis Christi* (Mystical Body of Christ): "Christ our Lord wills the Church to live His own supernatural life, and by His divine power, permeates His whole Body and nourishes and sustains each of the members according to the place they occupy in the body, in the same way as the vine nourishes and makes fruitful the branches that are joined to it" (55). The image of the vine also gives us a clue as to how we remain attached to Jesus and the Church. We are "implanted" into both Jesus and the Church at Baptism, and we nourish our membership when we celebrate the Eucharist. The water of Baptism, like the waters needed to grow a vine, aids our growth. Jesus himself in the gift of the Eucharist sustains our growth and keeps us alive in him.

Our membership and participation in the Mystical Body of Christ is not passive either. In the second part of the passage (verses 11–17) Jesus summarizes what are to be our actions in one commandment: "love one another" (Jn 15:12). He adds an example of the greatest type of love that he himself will enact shortly after speaking these words: "to lay down one's life for one's friends" (Jn 15:13).

Jesus Questions Simon Peter (John 21:15–19)

How does God love us? How are we to love God?

We are familiar with different types of human love. *Romantic love* is associated with intimate love; in some cases the more intimate knowledge and experience someone has in getting to know another, the more likely it will lead to a love that is bound in strong commitment. Romantic love also is associated with powerful emotions and sexual feelings. But emotions and sexual feelings do not always equate with romantic love. Most times these feelings are connected with infatuation, a fleeting feeling that does not involve commitment. There is also *filial love*—that is, the love we have for a friend or family member. This type of love is long-lasting and loyal, but does not involve sexual feelings. "Filial" comes from a Greek word *phile*, which also means literally the "love one has for a friend." (This is why the city of Philadelphia is known as the "city of brotherly love.")

There is a third type of love, one that is the kind that God has for us. It is known as *agape*, which is also a Greek word. Agape is unconditional, selfless love. It is the type of love that the Three Divine Persons of the Blessed Trinity have for one another. By being unconditional, agape is a love that is not based on what a person does, but rather who the person is. By being selfless, agape does not seek something that will bring you advantage or gain; instead it is only intended to benefit or share with another person. Agape is the type

of love that Jesus instructed his disciples to have for one another (see John 13:34–35).

Something interesting, however, occurs in the conversation between the Risen Jesus and Simon Peter after they had just eaten breakfast along the shores of the Sea of Galilee. Jesus says: "Simon, son of John, do you love me more than these?" Jesus uses the word *agape*, the most intimate form of love. Peter answers Jesus, "Yes, Lord, you know that I love you." He uses the word *phile*, brotherly love. Jesus asks the question a second time, again using the verb *agape*. And again Peter responds, "*Phile*." The third time Jesus asks Peter the same question he uses *phile* instead of *agape*. Jesus has restated the question in Peter's terms. If Peter could not offer Jesus the kind of unconditional, selfless love Jesus was looking for, *phile* would have to do for the moment. This switch of verbs, of meeting Peter where he was, is an important point to consider when critiquing your own love for God and God's love for you.

The Duties of Christians (Romans 12:1–21)

How are we to behave under a New Covenant not made up of written laws?

The Mosaic Law of the Old Testament had directions for all types of behavior. While Jesus said that "until heaven and earth pass away, not the smallest letter or smallest part of a letter will pass away" (Mt 5:18), he was not referring to the end of the world, per se, but rather to the end of the Old Testament age that would come at the time of his Passion, Death, and Resurrection. Christians of the early Church understood that they were liberated from the legal maxims of the Mosaic Law that directed the minutest details of human behavior, yet were still in need of direction and judgment for how to behave and make good choices when confronted with the moral decisions of everyday life.

Instead of maxims to follow, Christians are aided by members of their community who take on God-given roles; for example, prophets assist by helping to decipher the will of God; teachers help Christians to understand themselves in relation to others; and preachers (those who "exhort") offer encouragement to help us do what is pleasing to God. The Letter to the Romans also provides more tailored individual advice for good behavior, drawing on the teachings of Jesus. Some of this advice may be considered more challenging than any of the Mosaic Laws. In any of these directions, the author of Hebrews reminds us to "not be conquered by evil but conquer evil with good" (Rom 12:21).

The Way of Love (1 Corinthians 13:1–13)

Of the three theological virtues, faith, hope, and love, why will only love survive into eternity?

St. Paul describes what were later named and defined as the three **theological virtues** in this poetic and well-known passage. The theological virtues—faith, hope, and love—are different than other virtues that can be gained by our own human efforts and by establishing good habits (e.g., justice, courage, wisdom). The theological virtues come to us directly from God. They raise our human efforts to love to the supernatural perfection of divine love. This is the type of love that binds us together as members of Christ's Mystical Body.

Paul names love as the greatest of the theological virtues (1 Cor 13:13). He also writes that "love never fails" (v. 8), and follows by addressing things that will cease when time comes to an end (e.g., speaking in tongues, prophecy). Love will exist into eternity. As the early Church understood: "God is love, and whoever remains in love remains in God and God in him" (1 Jn 4:16b).

Describing the nature of love, Paul offers a number of positive qualities of love (patience, kindness, celebration of the truth, endurance, fidelity, a positive outlook), but he doesn't describe it as an emotion or a sensual attraction. In fact, he was more inclined to tell of the emotions that did not combine with love (jealousy, selfishness, quick-temperedness, etc.). In particular, note that when Paul taught "love never fails," this is not only an indication that love will

---

theological virtues Three important virtues bestowed on us at Baptism that relate us to God: *faith* (belief in and personal knowledge of God), *hope* (trust in God's salvation and his gift of the graces needed to attain it), and *charity* (love of God and love of neighbor).

survive into eternity, but also a criterion for differentiating between real love and infatuation while on earth. It is only true love that lasts forever.

The End of Evil (Revelation 12:1–18; 20:7–10)

How are evil and Satan ultimately expunged?

Are you familiar with the word *penultimate*? It means the "next-to-last" element in a series of things, such as the next-to-last episode of a television series or the next-to-last scene in a movie. Interestingly, the penultimate element (act, episode, chapter, etc.) is usually the one with the climax of the story. In salvation history, the penultimate action occurs during the events of the Paschal Mystery when Jesus offered his life on the Cross for our salvation. This was the moment when the victory over sin and death was achieved and Satan, "prince of this world is 'cast out'" (*CCC*, 2853).

St. Michael the Archangel

Yet, even after this penultimate scene of Christ's Passion, Death, Resurrection, and Ascension, there is more to the story. The Bible is not complete; there are books of the New Testament that follow the Gospels. The very last book of the Bible, the Book of Revelation, provides a postscript of sorts to what will happen to the evil of the world and to Satan, in particular, after that.

Both Jesus and Mary are central to the symbolic incidents detailed in the Book of Revelation. In Revelation 12:1–6, three characters are mentioned: a woman, a child, and a dragon. It is easy to recognize the child as Jesus and the dragon as Satan, both individual beings. The woman has been interpreted to be a collective representation of both Israel and the Church. However, as the other two characters are definitely individuals, a more accepted interpretation is that the woman, too, is an individual: Mary. Other pieces of evidence detail that the woman comes from heaven and that she wears a crown with twelve stars (representing the twelve tribes of Israel and the Twelve Apostles), making her a queen. Queens in the Old Testament were not *wives* of a king, but *mothers* of a king. As Jesus is the King of the Universe, Mary is the Queen of the Universe.

Satan pursues the woman with the crown before St. Michael the Archangel, whom the Old Testament identified as the guardian and champion of Israel (see Daniel 10:13, 21; 12:1). St. Michael protects her and expels Satan to the desert, where he wages war on Christians. It isn't until Revelation 20 that Satan is released from his bondage and evil's final chapter is written.

The Book of Revelation, and the Bible itself, ends with an Aramaic refrain, *Marana tha*—"Our Lord, come!" It is a prayer for Christ to come in glory at the end of time.

Bible reading plan suggestions are listed in subsection "Bible Reading Plans" in the section "Deposit of Faith" in the Appendix.

SECTION Assessment

Comprehension

1. What are two examples in the New Testament that teach that Christ is the manifestation of what was preached in the Old Testament?
2. How does the identity of a human person help us to understand that God had two natures, human and divine?
3. How does the parable of the vine and branches describe the Mystical Body of Christ?
4. What are we to do to indicate that our membership in the Mystical Body is not passive?
5. What is the difference between *phile* and *agape*?

6. To what time was Jesus referring when he said "until heaven and earth pass away, not the smallest letter or smallest part of a letter will pass away" (Mt 5:18)?
7. What is the penultimate action of salvation history?

Vocabulary

8. What is different about the *theological virtues* compared to virtues that can be gained from human efforts?

Reflection

9. How do you think of the New Testament as a love story?
10. Archbishop Fulton J. Sheen used the analogy of a man becoming a dog to parallel God becoming man. Develop and explain your analogy for the Incarnation.
11. Explain why Jesus used the verb *phile* when asking Peter for the third time, "Do you love me?"

CHAPTER 4 REVIEW

Section Reviews

Focus Question

What are the scope, style, and message of the Old Testament and New Testament?

Complete one of the following:

- Memorize the words of *Sh'ma Israel* ("Listen, Israel") found in Deuteronomy 6:45. This prayer is the heart of the Jewish faith. When you have rehearsed the prayer, recite it for your teacher.
- Read the Beatitudes as they appear in the Gospel of Matthew (6:1–11) and Luke (6:20–26). Note how they are different. Offer your own hypothesis about why they differ.
- Make a set of flash cards for all seventy-three books of the Bible. On one side of the card, list the full name of the biblical book. On the other side of the card, list its abbreviation (see the subsection "Canon of the Bible" in the section "Deposit of Faith" in the Appendix). Quiz yourself and a classmate on matching the biblical books with their abbreviation.

Introduction

The Two Testaments of the Bible

Review Points

- The Bible is a series of covenants. The central theme of the Old Covenant is God's love for the Jewish people. The New Covenant is initiated by Jesus at the Last Supper. It is a covenant written on the hearts of people and sealed by the Blood of Christ.
- The Old Testament remains the true Word of God for Christians. In the Old Testament "the mystery of our salvation is presented in a hidden way" (*CCC*, 122).
- The words of our salvation are contained in the New Testament. The central object of the New Testament is Jesus Christ and his words and actions that bring about our salvation.

Assignment

As our salvation was revealed gradually in the Old Testament before being brought to fulfillment in the New Testament, so too God makes himself known to you personally through the course of your life. Write about three times that you felt God's presence in your life: when you were in elementary school, when you were in middle school, and now in your high school years. If you can write about only one experience, do so in detail. If you cannot recognize God's presence in your life, explain why you think that is so.

Section 1
Old Testament Categories and Contents

Review Points

- The Old Testament is not exactly the same as the Hebrew Scriptures. There are twenty-four books in Hebrew Scriptures and forty-six books in the Old Testament. The books are also grouped differently and are read from different perspectives and focus.
- The Pentateuch is made up of four sources: Yahwist (J), Elohist (E), Deuteronomist (D), and Priestly (P). These four main sources were woven together by editors into the first five books of the Bible.
- Historical books cover the formation of the People of Israel and their eventual breakup after the disobedience of the kings and prior to going into exile.
- Wisdom literature in the Old Testament resembles modern science. It is not "Jewish" (or "Christian") in focus. It suggests an understanding of God through human reason.
- The final section of the Old Testament is the prophetic books. There are classifications of major and minor prophets based on the relative lengths of their books.

Assignment

Use the *Catechism of the Catholic Church* (101–133) to research the meaning of each of the following statements. Write two or three sentences for each that explain their meaning in your own words.

- Christ is the single Word of Sacred Scripture.
- Christians venerate the Old Testament as the true Word of God.
- The Gospels are at the heart of all Scriptures.

Section 2
Surveying the Old Testament

Review Point

Many memorable characters and plot lines mark salvation history as told in the Old Testament. Among these are Jacob's taking of his brother's birthright and blessing, Joseph's role in the Hebrews coming to Egypt, the Gentile woman Ruth's part in the family of Jesus, the rise of King David to the throne, the prophet Elijah's display against paganism, and the remarkable faith witness of a Jewish mother and her seven sons at the time of the Maccabees.

Assignment

Wisdom has several different meanings in the Old Testament. Make a two-column chart. In the first column, print each of the following Scripture references. In the second column, summarize how the passage defines the meaning of *wisdom*.

- Job 12:12
- Proverbs 1:7
- Proverbs 8:12
- Proverbs 24:14
- Ecclesiastes 2:13
- Sirach 39:5

Section 3
New Testament Categories and Contents

Review Points

- The New Testament is made up of twenty-seven books that include history (Gospels and Acts of the Apostles), instruction (epistles), and one prophetic book (Revelation).

- The New Testament fulfills the Old Testament. The typological connections with the Old Testament were not concocted; in fact, many Old Testament predictions of the Messiah are contradicted in the New Testament.
- The Gospels form the heart of the New Testament and Bible itself. Three of the Gospels (Matthew, Mark, and Luke) have common sources. The Gospel of John was written a couple of decades after the three synoptic Gospels.
- Twenty-one documents in the New Testament take the form of letters or epistles. Fourteen of the twenty-one letters are traditionally attributed to St. Paul. The Letter to the Hebrews is the work of an anonymous writer. These letters are grouped in a category called New Testament Letters.
- The seven catholic letters differ from the New Testament letters in that they were not written by Paul and they were intended for the universal Church, not just a local Christian community.
- The Book of Revelation uses an apocalyptic style of writing filled with symbolism to present a hopeful perspective of the eschaton.

Assignment

Compare the incident in which one of the men who came to arrest Jesus has his ear cut off in Mark 14:47–48, Matthew 26:51–54, and Luke 22:50–52. How are these accounts different?

Section 4
Surveying the New Testament

Review Point

The New Testament is the culmination of salvation history. It is a story of love. It begins with the miraculous event of the Incarnation of the Son of God, teaches that our place is to be united with Christ as though a branch to a vine, recognizes that Jesus will come to meet us as we offer our own gift of love to him, reminds us that our behavior is judged on our love of God and neighbor, and points us to love as a theological virtue that comes to us directly from God himself.

Assignment

What are the gifts that Paul lists in the "Body of Christ" passage in 1 Corinthians 12?

Chapter Projects

Choose and complete at least one of the following projects to assess your understanding of the material in this chapter.

1. Draw a Religious Subject Using the Chiaroscuro Technique

The term *chiaroscuro* comes from two Italian words, *chiaro* (meaning "clear" or "bright") and *oscuro* (meaning "obscure" or "dark"). This artistic technique focuses on creating shadows from a single source of light around the subject of a painting This style, connected especially with Caravaggio, and imitated by Valentin de Boulogne in several of his paintings, including *Saint Paul Writing His Epistles*, is also known for its realism.

Use watercolors, colored pencils, or oil paints to draw a religious subject using the chiaroscuro technique. Follow these steps:

- *Pick a religious subject.* For example, find a religious statue of Jesus, Mary, or a saint that you admire. In order to manipulate the single light source, it's preferable that the statue is movable. If you use a statue in a church, chapel, or garden, you will likely not be able to control your lighting.
- *Set up your lighting.* To set up a light source that hits the subject from one side, create a small lightbox from a cardboard box. Paint the inside of the box black, and cut a small hole into one side. Set it next to a window, and allow the daylight to shine through the hole and illuminate your subject inside the box.
- *Take a photo.* Using the camera on your phone, take a photo of the lit statue. Adjust the contrast in your image to see the shadows and highlights.
- *Draw your subject.* Use the photo as a model. Recreate the shadows and outlines in your drawing.

2. Write a Review of a Biblically Based Film

Watch a biblically based, full-length film. There are many to choose from on several streaming platforms, including several options on free sites. Some examples of classic films to consider:

- *The Robe* (1953)

- *Samson and Delilah* (1949)
- *David and Bathsheba* (1951)
- *The Story of Ruth* (1960)
- *The Greatest Story Ever Told* (1965)
- *Jesus of Nazareth* (1977)
- *The Nativity Story* (2006)

Write a review that includes the following elements:

- Introduction (include film title, release date, director's name)
- Plot summary (very brief overview)
- Plot analysis (analyze the rising action, climax)
- Creative elements (acting, writing, cinematography, music)
- Biblical critique (how closely did the film follow the biblical outline)
- Conclusion (your overall opinion of the film, including a rating or recommendation)

Check with your teacher to see if you can do a video or audio recording review of a film in lieu of a written report that includes the same elements as listed above.

⚙ 3. Research and Share Examples of Biblical Typology

Biblical typology has to do with when a person or event in the Old Testament foreshadows a person or event in the New Testament. Most prominently, there are many examples of Jesus hidden in the lives of people from the Old Testament. Write an explanation of how the following are examples of biblical typology. Share at least one Old Testament and one New Testament reference for each.

- Adam and Jesus
- Moses and Jesus
- David and Jesus
- Jonah and Jesus
- Jeremiah and Jesus

4. Compare Two Gospel Infancy Narratives

There is one other Gospel infancy narrative of the birth of Jesus besides the one you read in the Gospel of Luke (see Chapter 5, Section 2, "The Time before Jesus's Public Ministry in the Synoptic Gospels"). Matthew's Gospel is the only other to mention the birth of Jesus. Read Matthew 1:18–2:23 with Luke 2:1–40. Create a chart or table that compares each infancy narrative around the following subjects. In the chart, include which Gospel(s) had a reference to the subject (including the chapter and verse) and why the subject was or was not included. Check a biblical commentary (e.g., the commentary in the NABRE margins) to answer the "why" question.

Subjects

- Dreams
- Shepherds
- Bethlehem
- Magi
- Mary
- Joseph
- Nazareth
- Manger
- Gifts
- Caesar Augustus
- Turtledoves
- Temple
- Simeon
- Anna
- Egypt
- Massacre of infants
- Angels

5. Participate in an Evangelization Project

Religious communities of men and women most often wear distinctive habits or garments that are an outward sign of their commitment to discipleship. Complete a personal "evangelization project" to witness your own Christian discipleship.

Do at least three of the following actions:

- Wear a large religious medal or shirt with a Christian slogan in a public setting.
- Pray before your meal in a fast-food restaurant.
- Ask someone you know if they would like to pray with you in public. (If they say yes, do pray together.)
- Ask a family member if they would like to read the Bible with you. (If they say yes, do read the Bible together.)
- Volunteer to share a personal testimony of your faith in a theology class.
- Do an evangelization action of your own choice.

Write a report on your experiences. Answer the following questions:

- Which experience did you find easiest to do?
- Which did you find most difficult?
- How did people you know react to your action?
- How did those you don't know as well react to your action?
- Which of these actions do you think has the most influence on helping someone else become a more faithful Christian? Explain.
- Which of these actions can you imagine being a regular practice in your life? Explain.

Faithful Disciple
St. Jude the Apostle

According to the very first verse of the Letter of Jude, St. Jude, also known as Thaddeus, was the brother of St. John, the beloved disciple and author of the fourth Gospel. Jude is also mentioned in the Gospels as a relative of Jesus (see Matthew 13:55 and Mark 6:3). In those passages he was called Judas. Likely his name was changed later so it was not associated with Judas Iscariot, the betrayer of Jesus.

Jude is quoted one time in the Gospels. At the Last Supper, he is the Apostle who asks Jesus: "Master, [then] what happens that you will reveal yourself to us and not to the world?" (Jn 14:22). Jesus's answer is that "whoever loves me will keep my word, and my Father will love him, and we will come and make a dwelling in him" (Jn 14:23). Jude took these words to heart. After Jesus's Death, Resurrection, and Ascension, Church tradition affirms that Jude traveled extensively in the Middle East and into part of North Africa, evangelizing the people there for more than thirty years. Tradition also holds that St. Jude was martyred in AD 65 at Beirut (which was in the

Catholics gather in Mexico City for a festival in honor of St. Jude Thaddeus.

Roman province of Syria) along with the Apostle St. Simon the Zealot. The two have been associated with each other ever since. Images and icons of St. Jude often show him holding an axe, symbolizing the way he was killed. St. Jude is especially venerated in the Eastern Church and in India. His feast day in the Roman Church is October 28, and June 19 in the East.

The Letter of Jude is the shortest book in the New Testament and is the second to last book of the canon, right before the Book of Revelation. Whether St. Jude was the actual author of the letter is debatable. The vocabulary of the letter indicates that the author was a Jewish Christian who was well versed in Hebrew, yet also acquainted with koine Greek. There are thirteen words found in the Letter of Jude that are not found anywhere else in the New Testament; for example, "holy ones" (Jude 1:3) refers to members of the Church, and "love feasts" (Jude 1:12) is another name for the celebration of Eucharist.

The letter is hard-hitting; it speaks of those who have come into the Church and who are upsetting faithful Christians by deviating from the apostolic faith and engaging in various acts of immorality, probably sexual in nature. The essential message of the letter for Christians of every generation is that no one is entitled to tamper with the core and eternal truths of the faith.

St. Jude is the patron of desperate situations and hopeless causes. This designation is rooted in the Letter of Jude, which stresses that Christians should persevere in harsh and difficult circumstances, just as the Apostles had.

Comprehension

1. Why was Jude's name likely "changed" in the Gospels?
2. How did Jude respond in action to Jesus's answer to the question he asked?
3. Why are St. Jude and St. Simon the Zealot often associated with each other?
4. What is unique about the Letter of Jude?
5. How did the Letter of Jude contribute to St. Jude becoming the patron saint of desperate situations and hopeless causes?

Reflection

When have you recently felt hopeless? How did your faith help you to persevere?

Prayer

The Prayer to Saint Michael is a prayer to strengthen us in spiritual battle spoken of in Ephesians 6:10–11: "Draw your strength from the Lord and from his mighty power. Put on the armor of God so that you may be able to stand firm against the tactics of the devil." From 1886 to 1964 the prayer was recited after **Low Mass** on Sundays. Recently, it is again said at Mass, usually just before dismissal in many parishes. Pope John Paul II said of the Prayer to Saint Michael: "I ask everyone not to forget it and to recite it to obtain help in the battle against the forces of darkness and against the spirits of the world."[7]

Prayer to St. Michael

> St. Michael the Archangel, defend us in battle. Be our protection against the wickedness and snares of the devil. May God rebuke him, we humbly pray, and do thou, O Prince of heavenly host, by the power of God, thrust into hell Satan, and all evil spirits, who prowl the world seeking the ruin of souls. Amen.

Low Mass Prior to the reforms of the liturgy after the Second Vatican Council, a Low Mass was the name to differentiate it from a High Mass. In a Low Mass, the priest spoke rather than chanted the prayers that were assigned to him.

5

Jesus and God's Kingdom Seen through the Synoptic Gospels

Cathedral of Brasília

➤ *Oscar Niemeyer*

One of the most unique renderings of the four evangelists in art are four bronze sculptures of Matthew, Mark, Luke, and John that are set in the outside square in front of the entrance to the Cathedral of Brasília in Brazil. The cathedral itself is an architectural marvel. It was formally dedicated in 1970, and just recently it underwent a significant update and repair of its infrastructure. The cathedral is a hyperboloid structure, meaning it curves inward rather than outward or with straight beams. The Cathedral of Brasília was constructed with sixteen concrete columns weighing ninety tons each.

A Brazilian architect, Oscar Niemeyer, designed the cathedral. In his thirties, Niemeyer had designed Brazil's exhibit in the 1932 World's Fair in New York. He was famous for his use of abstract forms and curves. He wrote in his memoirs: "I am not attracted to straight angles or to the straight line, hard and inflexible, created by man. I am attracted to free-flowing, sensual curves. The curves that I find in the mountains of my country, in the sinuousness of its rivers, in the waves of the ocean, and on the body of the beloved woman. Curves make up the entire universe, the curved universe of Einstein." In fact, the columns on the outside of the cathedral are meant to represent hands moving upward to heaven.

The four bronze sculptures of the evangelists are each nearly ten feet in height. Niemeyer commissioned two sculptors, Alfredo Ceschiatti with the collaboration of Dante Croce, for the project. The sculptures were completed just before the dedication of the cathedral.

As with many building projects in Brazil in the mid-to-late twentieth century, the cathedral's completion was delayed for several years. The cornerstone was laid in 1958, and the structure itself was completed in 1960. Brazilian president Juscelino Kubitschek had hoped the cathedral would be state-run and ecumenical for all faiths, but when he was ousted from office, taxpayer funding dried up and the project was eventually turned over to the Catholic Church. Besides the four statues of the evangelists, the Cathedral of Brasília's altar was donated by Pope Paul VI. Inside the cathedral over the nave are three angels, suspended by cables. The largest of the angels is nearly fourteen feet long and weighs 660 pounds.

Focus Question

When seen together, how do the Gospels of Matthew, Mark, and Luke help me to know more about Jesus and God's Kingdom?

Chapter Overview

Introduction

UNDERSTANDING MATTHEW, MARK, AND LUKE

The Gospels of Matthew, Mark, and Luke share quite a bit in common when compared to the fourth Gospel, the Gospel of John. For this reason, they are known as *synoptic Gospels*, because they can be "seen together" and offer a "shared view" of Jesus's life (see the subsection "Who Were the Authors of the Bible?" in Chapter 2, Section 2). When lined up in parallel columns, the synoptic Gospels contain many similarities. For example, note the following similarities (and subtle differences) among the three Gospels' versions of Jesus's parable of the mustard seed.

MATTHEW 13:31-32	**MARK** 4:30-32	**LUKE** 13:18-19
He proposed another parable to them. "The kingdom of heaven is like a mustard seed that a person sowed in the field. It is the smallest of all seeds, yet when full grown it is the largest of plants. It becomes a large bush and the 'birds of the sky come and dwell in its branches.'"	He said, "To what shall we compare the kingdom of God, or what parable can we use for it? It is like a mustard seed that, when it is sown in the ground, is the smallest of all the seeds on earth. But once it is sown, it springs up and becomes the largest of plants and puts forth large branches so that the birds of the sky can dwell in its shade."	Then he said, "What is the kingdom of God like? To what can I compare it? It is like a mustard seed that a person took and planted in the garden. When it was fully grown, it became a large bush and 'the birds of the sky dwelt in its branches.'"

Of the 661 verses in Mark's Gospel, 80 percent of these appear in Matthew's Gospel, and 65 percent occur in Luke's Gospel. Matthew's (1,068 verses) and Luke's (1,149) Gospels are considerably longer than Mark's Gospel, but they follow the general outline of Mark in reporting the events of Jesus's life. At least that is the commonly accepted contemporary opinion. Another perspective is that it is Mark's Gospel that follows the outline of Matthew and Luke, as a condensed version.

Which Synoptic Gospel Was Written First?

This is a question that always accompanies the question of why the material in the synoptic Gospels is so similar. Which synoptic Gospel came first? Is it an important one?

Traditionally, soon after the New Testament canon was established by the Church, the writings of Church Fathers and others directly associated with the Apostles asserted that the Gospel of Matthew had primacy. Early witnesses stated that there was an Aramaic edition of the Gospel of Matthew that was later translated to Greek. According to this understanding, the Gospel of Mark then drew from the Greek translation of Matthew's Gospel. Similarly, another early view was that the oral tradition of the Gospel was so well-known and standardized in capturing the body of Jesus's words and actions that it in itself was the source used to create each of the synoptic Gospels. From this perspective, it was also held that Matthew's Gospel came first.

Why? Because only the Gospel of Matthew is named for an Apostle among the three synoptics, it was hard to imagine an Apostle/eyewitness having to draw on another written source (Mark or Luke) to compose his Gospel. For example, St. Clement of Rome, who was a contemporary of St. Peter and the fourth pope, spoke of a hierarchical sharing of the Gospel, beginning with the preaching of Christ and extending down to the Apostles, and then to the ordained bishops. In his *Epistle to the Corinthians* (not to be confused with St. Paul's Letter to the Corinthians) he wrote: "The apostles have preached the gospel to us from the Lord Jesus Christ; Jesus Christ [has done so] from God. Christ therefore was sent forth by God, and the apostles by Christ. Both these appointments, then, were made in an orderly way, according to the will of God. . . . And thus, preaching through countries and cities, they appointed the first fruits [of their labors], having first proved them by the Spirit, to be bishops and deacons of those who should afterwards believe" (*Epistle to the*

St. Clement of Rome is listed as the fourth pope, though another source indicates he may have been the third pope. St. Clement was a follower of St. Peter and perhaps St. Paul as well. His name is included in Philippians 4:2. According to the historian Tertullian, St. Clement succeeded St. Peter directly in governing the Church in Rome. There was a schism at Corinth during Clement's pontificate, requiring his letter to the Corinthians, which is preserved to this day.

Corinthians, 42). While St. Clement does not explicitly state that the Apostle Matthew was the first to share a written Gospel, the epistle does allude to a chain of command in which an Apostle's words had primacy over those who were not eyewitnesses to Jesus and his ministry.

Though recognizing how the Gospels are ordered in the New Testament canon, the Church does not officially declare that this is the order that the synoptics were written. There are many other hypotheses for the ordering of the synoptics and for what sources they used. In fact, one website dedicated to the synoptic problem listed 1,488 different potential answers!

Since the advent of advanced biblical scholarship near the beginning of the twentieth century, the most common theory is the "two-source hypothesis." According to this hypothesis, Mark's Gospel was written first, and then Matthew and Luke used it independently of each other as a source. This hypothesis explains why Matthew and Luke share common material from Mark, but not why they have certain material not found in Mark in common with each other. In fact, there are 235 verses that appear in both Matthew and Luke that are not found in Mark. Scholars have proposed a second source, which they have named "Q" from the German word *Quelle*, which means "source," hence the name "two-source hypothesis." While this remains the most common current explanation for the similarities among the synoptic Gospels, it remains just a theory. The Church encourages further study of this question.

You might not be overly concerned about which Gospel came first. Perhaps you may even surmise that the three synoptic Gospels were written independently of one another. (This isn't likely, however, given the many common verses!) In any case, awareness of the "synoptic problem" is important as you study the Bible. Understanding how Jesus fits into history by stripping away layers of added tradition is a worthwhile exercise in coming to understand how Jesus is much more than a person of history, but the divine Son of God who appeared in a *particular time in history*. For that reason, a common examination of the synoptic Gospels—Mathew, Mark, and Luke—is necessary and helpful for you to learn more about him and to be convincing when you share your faith with others who may have doubts.

SECTION *Assessment*

Comprehension

1. Why are the Gospels of Matthew, Mark, and Luke called synoptic Gospels?
2. Name one difference in the three versions of the parable of the mustard seed.
3. How does St. Clement of Rome imply that the Gospel of Matthew was the first written?
4. What are the two sources of the "two-source hypothesis"?
5. What does "Q" stand for?

Reflection

6. Why do you think it is essential to sample and read all three synoptic Gospels rather than reading only one of them?
7. Which hypothesis of the "synoptic problem" resonates most with you? Why?

Section 1

INDIVIDUAL CHARACTERISTICS OF THE SYNOPTIC GOSPELS

If Matthew's Gospel was written first, it is difficult to explain why Mark, whose Gospel is much shorter, would have eliminated so much of Matthew. Much of the missing material would seem to be essential, including the Sermon on the Mount (Mt 5:1–7:29) and Jesus's instructions for how to pray the Our Father (Mt 9:5–15). For the purposes of our study—and to be most in line with biblical scholarship over the last century—we will continue under the premise that Matthew added material to Mark, rather than Mark deleted it from Matthew. In doing so, we can date the authorship of Mark's Gospel between AD 67 and 73, either shortly before or after the destruction of the Jewish Temple by the Romans in AD 70. Sometime in the following years, Matthew and Luke wrote their Gospels and used three sources: Mark, Q, and their own unique sources (sometimes known as "M" for Matthew and "L" for Luke).

To support this premise, also consider a point first proposed by linguists who studied the Greek editions of the synoptics. They pointed out that Matthew's and Luke's use of grammar is better than Mark's, which is rough at very best. The follow-up question is why Mark deliberately turned their good grammar into something less polished. The more likely conclusion is that Matthew and Luke *corrected* the grammar in Mark's Gospel.

In addition, the narrative sequences of events between Matthew and Mark are different. Whenever Matthew and Mark differ, Luke's sequence of events always agrees with the order in Mark's Gospel. When Luke does change the sequence, Matthew and Mark always agree. It makes the most sense to hold that Mark contained the original order that, on occasion, Matthew or Luke independently chose to alter.

Each of these Gospels had a unique way of presenting the mystery of salvation, as it came to a climax in the Divine Person of Jesus Christ. Each had different perspectives, much of which was built around the audiences for whom they were writing. The next subsections look more closely at each of the synoptic Gospels.

Overview of Mark's Gospel

Recall that the author of Mark's Gospel is not known with certainty (see the subsection "Who Were the Authors of the Bible?" in Chapter 2, Section 2). The early Church's connection of the Gospel with John Mark, a disciple of Peter, was due to the resemblance of the Gospel to themes of Peter's preaching. The Gospel highlights Jesus's deeds more than his words and presents a vivid, human, and down-to-earth portrait of Jesus.

Remember also that the real-life situations of the early Christian communities—years after Jesus's Death—influenced the focus and content of the Gospels. Mark likely wrote his Gospel for a Gentile-Christian audience that was undergoing persecution, perhaps in Rome. He chose to focus on this central theme: following Jesus often means suffering as Jesus did. Theologically, Mark emphasized Jesus Christ's role as a Suffering Messiah for Christians to imitate.

A Direct Style

In the Gospel's very first verse, Mark clearly tells readers who Jesus is: "Jesus Christ [the Son of God]" (Mk 1:1). Interestingly, the disciples portrayed in the Gospel struggle to reach the same conclusion that the readers hear in this very first verse. Mark also stressed Jesus's humanity throughout his Gospel, even if this meant presenting a more direct or blunt view of Jesus than the other synoptic Gospels or the Gospel of John:

- Mark described Jesus feeling a very human emotion: "Looking around at them *with anger* and grieved at their hardness of heart . . ." (Mk 3:5, italics added). In their versions of the story, Matthew and Luke do not mention that Jesus was angry.
- Mark minced no words when he reported that Jesus's family said, "He is out of his mind" (Mk 3:21). Matthew and Luke do not include this quote in their accounts.

While it is impossible to know the exact intentions of the evangelists regarding their presentation of Jesus, it is appropriate to assume that Matthew and

Luke nuanced their accounts in contrast to Mark's way to present a different, if not softer view of Jesus.

Titles for Jesus in Mark

Mark used several titles for Jesus. This central passage from Mark 8:27–34 offers two titles and hints at a third. Try to identify these three titles as you read.

> Now Jesus and his disciples set out for the villages of Caesarea Philippi. Along the way he asked his disciples, "Who do people say that I am?" They said in reply, "John the Baptist, others Elijah, still others one of the prophets." And he asked them, "But who do you say that I am?" Peter said to him in reply, "You are the Messiah." Then he warned them not to tell anyone about him.
>
> He began to teach them that the Son of Man must suffer greatly and be rejected by the elders, the chief priests, and the scribes, and be killed, and rise after three days. He spoke this openly. Then Peter took him aside and began to rebuke him. At this he turned around and, looking at his disciples, rebuked Peter and said, "Get behind me, Satan. You are thinking not as God does, but as human beings do."
>
> He summoned the crowd with his disciples and said to them, "Whoever wishes to come after me must deny himself, take up his cross, and follow me."

In this passage, we find that Jesus accepted the title *Christ*∞ that Peter gave him, but then immediately began to use the title *Son of Man*≈ to describe himself. Though Jesus does not use the term here, he also alludes to himself as a *Suffering Servant*+ for his people.

All three titles fit Jesus because Jesus, the Son of Man, is the Messiah who will come in glory, but only after he has suffered and sacrificed his life for his people. Peter had difficulty accepting Jesus's understanding of the Messiah as the Suffering Servant. Peter was judging Jesus by the human standards of his time, not by God's standards as being communicated by Jesus. Not until the Resurrection and Ascension of Jesus would the early Church begin to understand that Jesus's way was the Way of the Cross.

Mark's Gospel shows that to follow Jesus is to pick up our own cross daily. God does not want us to suffer unnecessarily, but offering up our suffering for and with Christ leads to our salvation and our participation in his glorious Resurrection.

∞ Note

Christ comes from the Greek word *Christos* and is the English translation of the Hebrew word *Messiah*, meaning "anointed one." Various groups within Judaism at the time of Jesus had different ideas of who the Messiah would be: an earthly king, a religious leader, a priest, a revolutionary. After Jesus accepted Peter's proclamation about his identity as the Messiah, he warned Peter not to tell anyone; he was reluctant to let many people know his identity, perhaps because his understanding of the "anointed one" was radically differed from that of the people and of his disciples. His approach here is sometimes referred to as the **messianic secret**.

≈ Note

The title *Son of Man* comes from a prophecy in the Old Testament Book of Daniel in which the author calls the glorious Messiah the "Son of Man" (Dn 7:14). Throughout the Gospels, Jesus referred to himself this way.

+ Note

Jesus understood the titles *Messiah* and *Son of Man* in light of the prophecies in Isaiah 42–53 that call the Messiah a *Suffering Servant*.

Overview of Matthew's Gospel

The author of Matthew's Gospel most likely wrote sometime after Mark's Gospel was in circulation, maybe in the AD 80s. Whether he was the Apostle himself or a Jewish scribe associated with the Apostle is uncertain. In either case, Matthew's Gospel emphasizes the link between Judaism and Christianity.

Matthew wrote to at least two different groups: Jews who followed Jesus and Gentiles who followed Jesus. Matthew's Gospel emphasized to Jewish-Christian readers, as well as to new Gentile converts, that Jesus Christ—*Emmanuel*—is indeed the Messiah prophesied in the Old Testament. Matthew did this in several ways, explained in the following section.

Connections between Jesus and the Old Testament

Matthew's Gospel makes several connections between Moses and Jesus, portraying Jesus as the "New Moses":

- Moses made the Sinai Covenant on behalf of the Chosen People. Jesus made a New Covenant with all people.
- Moses presented the Ten Commandments to the Israelites from a mountain. Jesus offered his primary moral teaching, the Beatitudes, in the Sermon on the Mount.
- The Gospel is divided into five sections between the infancy and the Passion narratives. This five-book arrangement, centered on five important sermons of Jesus, parallels the five books of the Pentateuch that present the Old Testament Law.

---

messianic secret Several passages in the Gospel of Mark (e.g., 1:21–28; 1:32–34; 1:40–45; 3:7–12; 5:21–43; 7:31–37; and 8:22–23) indicate that Jesus directed even his own disciples to keep quiet about his identity. These passages have been termed the "messianic secret."

Matthew also ties Judaism with Jesus in other ways. The Gospel quotes many Old Testament prophecies to proclaim Jesus's identity as the promised Messiah. For example:

MATTHEW REFERENCE	EVENT	OLD TESTAMENT REFERENCE
1:22–23	Born of a virgin	Isaiah 7:14
2:5–6	Born in Bethlehem	Micah 5:1
2:15	Flight into Egypt	Hosea 11:1
2:18	Slaughter of the Innocents	Jeremiah 31:15
4:15–16	Ministry in Galilee	Isaiah 8:23–9:1
12:18–21	Serving by leading	Isaiah 42:1–4
13:14–15	Spiritual blindness	Isaiah 6:9–10
13:35	Teaching in parables	Psalm 78:2
21:5	Entry into Jerusalem on a donkey	Isaiah 62:11; Zechariah 9:9
27:9–10	Judas betrays Jesus	Zechariah 11:12–13

Matthew used the title *Son of David*, a Jewish title, more than any other evangelist. His Gospel attempts to show that Jesus Christ fulfilled all of God's promises to the Chosen People and, through them, to all people. At the end of the Gospel, Jesus instructed his disciples to go to the ends of the earth to preach the Good News and make disciples of all the nations.

Overview of Luke's Gospel

Traditionally, the author of Luke's Gospel is identified as a Gentile Christian. The same author also wrote the Acts of the Apostles; he thus wrote about one-fourth of the New Testament. A second-century Church Father, St. Irenaeus, believed that Luke was a doctor and a traveling companion and friend of St. Paul.

Luke wrote to a largely Gentile-Christian audience about AD 75–90, perhaps around 85. His writing style was highly polished. He featured the city of Jerusalem as an important symbol in both of his works. His Gospel emphasizes that the Messianic age began in Jerusalem and that the second part of Jesus's ministry centers on his journey to this Holy City where the drama of salvation unfolded. The Acts of the Apostles tells of the Apostles' journeys, also beginning in Jerusalem, where they received the Holy Spirit to take the message of Jesus Christ to the ends of the world. Luke emphasizes that Jesus is a universal Savior who brings salvation to Jew and Gentile alike.

A Universal Savior: Jesus Is for Everyone

Luke's Gospel stresses Jesus's practice of looking out for everyone: Jew and Gentile, rich and poor, women and men. Jesus sought out those whom society considered lowly or "outcasts," including the following:

Common People

Jesus appealed to the simple Jews who were open to his message of conversion, repentance, and salvation. These were Jews who tried to follow the Law, pray, and participate in the synagogue services. Some of the Pharisees thought that the common people's ignorance kept them from holiness. Some Pharisees attributed ignorance to Jesus and his disciples because they did not strictly follow the Law in regard to fasting (see Luke 5:33) and washing (see Matthew 15:2).

Lepers

Leprosy was a serious and contagious skin disease, and those who suffered from it were avoided by everyone else. Jesus embraced lepers and cured them.

"And when he saw them, he said, 'Go show yourselves to the priests.' As they were going they were cleansed. And one of them, realizing he had been healed, returned, glorifying God in a loud voice; and he fell at the feet of Jesus and thanked him. He was a Samaritan" (Lk 17:14–16).

He praised a Samaritan leper for returning to thank him for his cure when nine others did not (see Luke 17:11–19).

Samaritans

Samaritans descended from foreigners who intermarried with Israelite tribes at the time of the Assyrian conquest of the northern kingdom. Though Jews and Samaritans recognized Abraham as the founding father of their faith, Jews viewed Samaritans as foreigners and just a notch above Gentiles. Jesus made a point to praise Samaritans by making one the hero of a parable (see Luke 10:25–37).

Tax Collectors

Jews who collected taxes for the Romans were generally despised by their fellow Jews. Some tax collectors were further corrupt, in that they charged people more than the prescribed tax and kept the extra money. Jesus associated with tax collectors, accepted dinner invitations from them, and called one, Levi, to follow him (see Luke 5:27–32 and the feature "Faithful Disciple: St. Matthew the Apostle and Evangelist" in the Chapter 5 Review).

Women

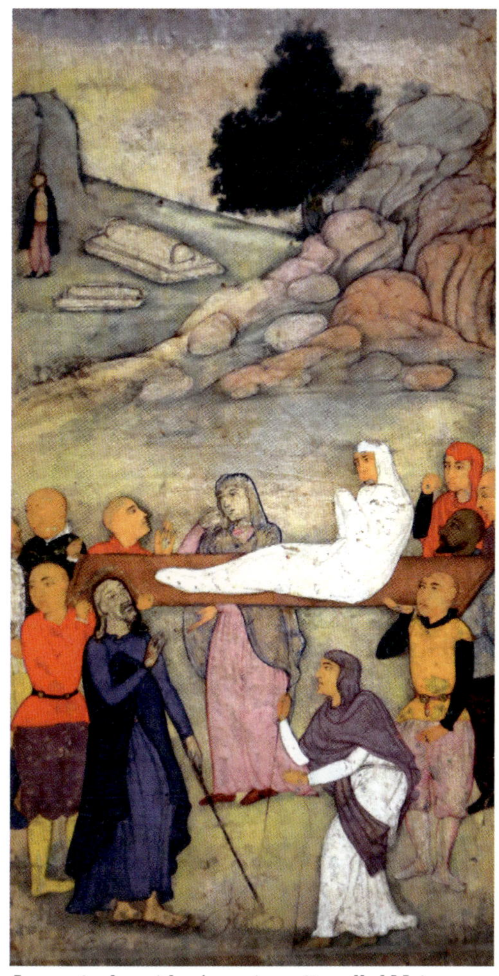
Jesus raised a widow's son in a city called Nain.

Luke's Gospel also highlights Jesus's revolutionary approach to women in his culture. Luke's infancy narrative is focused on the perspective of Mary, and Luke 1:39–56 contains the words of Mary spoken in a canticle known as the **Magnificat**.

Luke's focus on women does not end with Mary. Jesus ministered directly with women. For example, he brought back to life the only son of a desperate widow in the city of Nain (see Luke 7:11–15). Jesus also had close friends who were women. Martha and Mary shared a friendly intimacy with Jesus that allowed Mary to sit at Jesus's feet in the role of a disciple that was usually reserved for men and Martha to chide Jesus for not encouraging Mary to get up off the ground to help her with hospitality (see Luke 10:38–42).

Luke also seemed to balance bringing both women and men into important moments in the Gospel. For example, in the Presentation of Jesus in the Temple, Jesus was greeted and recognized both by a holy man, Simeon (see Luke 2:25–35), and also by the prophetess Anna (see Luke 2:36–38).

Magnificat A Latin term for "magnifies" that comes from the first word of the Canticle of Mary in Luke 1:46-55. A canticle is a song, and the Magnificat is likely the first song of Mary. There are four canticles in the Gospel of Luke. The other three are spoken by Zechariah (Lk 1:67-69), angels at Jesus's birth (Lk 2:13-14), and Simeon at the Presentation of the Lord (Lk 2:28-32).

Most significantly, it is women who witness Jesus's Death on the Cross (see Luke 23:46–49), see the tomb where Jesus is laid (see Luke 23:55), and discover it empty (see Luke 24:1). These women were the first to proclaim Jesus's Resurrection to the Apostles and other disciples, though initially, they were not believed (see Luke 24:8–9).

Jesus said to the good thief, "Amen, I say to you, today you will be with me in Paradise" (Lk 23:43).

Thieves

Jesus's compassion is evident throughout the Gospel, even in his dying moments. With his last ounce of energy, he spoke to the good thief hanging in misery next to him, promising him paradise (see Luke 23:39–43).

Executioners

While he was being crucified, taunted, and tormented by his executioners, Jesus said, "Father, forgive them, they know not what they do" (Lk 23:34).

In summary, in Luke's Gospel, Jesus is *everyone's* compassionate Savior. His love has no limits.

SECTION *Assessment*

Comprehension

1. Identify the primary audience for each of the synoptic Gospels.
2. In Mark's Gospel, why did Peter have trouble identifying Jesus as the Suffering Servant?
3. What does the Gospel of Matthew mean when it refers to Jesus as the "Son of David" and suggests that he is the "New Moses"?
4. What are two major themes highlighted in the Gospel of Luke?

Vocabulary

5. What is the meaning of the term *Magnificat*?

Reflection

6. Choose one theme from each synoptic Gospel, and link the themes to your life today.
7. What is your understanding of the message that "Jesus is for everyone"?

Section 2

THE TIME BEFORE JESUS'S PUBLIC MINISTRY IN THE SYNOPTIC GOSPELS

The synoptic Gospels each open in a different way. Recall that Matthew's Gospel begins with the genealogy or family tree of Jesus, linking him to Abraham, the patriarch of Israel (see, for example, the subsection "The Stages of Divine Revelation" in Chapter 1, Section 3, and the sub-subsection "Jacob's Deception" in Chapter 4, Section 2). The long list of unfamiliar names from Matthew 1:1–17 is usually read at the Christmas vigil Mass.

There are several important lessons to learn from the genealogy. It mentions every Israelite king from King David on. It further cements Jesus's connection with David by dividing the genealogy into three parts of fourteen verses each. Fourteen is the numerical value of the Hebrew spelling of David. Interestingly, this genealogy, intending to show that Jesus is part of the Davidic line, traces to Jesus's foster father, Joseph, who is not a relative by blood. The first Jewish-Christian readers of Matthew's Gospel would have had no issue with this connection between Jesus and Joseph. Adopted children had all the same legal rights as natural children in Jewish society. And because first-century Jews lived in a patriarchal society, it would have been more unsettling if a connection had been forged with Jesus's mother. Matthew's genealogy of Jesus *does* refer to four women: Tamar, Rahab, Ruth, and Bathsheba. None of these women were perfect; the story of Bathsheba's indiscretions with David is the most well-known of these examples (see 2 Samuel 11). Their inclusion was intended to show that all people—men, women, righteous, and sinners—are part of and welcomed into God's family.

---

infancy narratives The Gospel accounts of the birth and early life of Jesus found in Matthew 1:1–2:23 and Luke 1:5–2:52. The Gospels of Mark and John do not contain infancy narratives.

After presenting the genealogy of Jesus, Matthew's Gospel goes on to give details leading up to Jesus's birth. Luke's Gospel begins with the **infancy narratives**, extending them uniquely through his mention of the finding of Jesus in the Temple (see Luke 2:41–52) up to the time of Jesus's baptism (see Luke 3:21–22) and his threefold temptation in the desert (see Luke 4:1–13). It is at that point that Luke begins to detail the beginning of Jesus's Galilean ministry.

Mark's Gospel opens with Jesus already an adult. Mark offers his readers only a little information about Jesus's origins: that he was from Nazareth in Galilee (see Mark 1:9), had been a carpenter, was the son of Mary, and was a relative ("brother") of James, Joses, Judas, and Simon (see Mark 6:3). Jesus's baptism and temptation are covered briefly in the first thirteen verses of chapter 1. Mark begins details of Jesus's public ministry in verse 14.

Infancy Narratives in Matthew and Luke

Matthew and Luke both provide details leading up to Jesus's birth. They agree on a number of key points:

- The infancy narratives begin when Mary and Joseph were legally engaged or, perhaps, married, but neither living together nor sexually involved with each other (see Matthew 1:18; Luke 1:27, 34).
- Joseph was a descendant of King David (see Matthew 1:16, 20; Luke 1:27, 32; 2:4).
- An angel announced the coming birth of a baby named Jesus (see Matthew 1:20–23; Luke 2:11).
- The baby would be the Savior (see Matthew 1:21; Luke 2:11).
- Mary conceived, not through sexual relations with Joseph, but by the Holy Spirit (see Matthew 1:18–24; Luke 1:34–35).
- Jesus was born after Mary and Joseph lived together as a family (see Matthew 1:24–25; Luke 2:5–6).
- Jesus was born in the town of Bethlehem (see Matthew 2:1; Luke 2:4–6).
- Jesus was born while Herod the Great was still king (see Matthew 2:1; Luke 1:5).
- Jesus grew up in Nazareth (see Matthew 2:23; Luke 2:39).

According to the Gospels, what is inaccurate from this Peruvian Nativity scene from the twentieth century?

It is worth noting that in Matthew's and Luke's infancy narratives there are no descriptions of any animals present. Luke is the only Gospel to mention a manger (see Luke 2:7, 12, 16). Scholars have speculated that the Nativity reference to animals and a manger might have originated from a verse in the Book of Isaiah: "An ox knows its owner, and an ass, its master's manger" (Is 1:3), in which the people of Israel themselves were associated with the Messiah.

The infancy narratives in Matthew and Luke also have some striking differences. For example, in Luke, the angel Gabriel only speaks to Mary (see Luke 1:26–38). In Matthew, an unnamed angel speaks only to Joseph (see Matthew 1:20, 24; 2:13, 19). In Matthew's Gospel, there is no mention of the angelic choirs and shepherds found in Luke 2:8–18. In Luke's Gospel, there is no visit or gifts from the magi (see Matthew 2:1–13).

While these differences could be simply omissions on the part of one or the other evangelist, some differences are irreconcilable. For example, in Luke, Joseph's original home is in Nazareth, and Jesus only ended up being born in Bethlehem because of a census (see Luke 2:1–7). In Matthew, however, Joseph appears to live in Bethlehem, and it would seem that Jesus was born at home (again, no mention of a manger) where magi visit him (see Matthew 2:9–11). Matthew also adds a story, missing from Luke, in which Joseph takes Mary and Jesus to Egypt to escape Herod's attempt to slay the infant. After Herod's death, they don't return to their "home" in Bethlehem, but go to live in Nazareth because they want to live far from Herod's son, Archelaus (see Matthew 2:13–23). So, while in both stories Jesus is born in the same town, Bethlehem, and grows up in the same village, Nazareth, the explanations as to how this happened are quite different in each Gospel.

Speaking from a strictly historical perspective, *both* Luke and Matthew cannot be accurate. Joseph's home can't originally have been in Nazareth and Bethlehem at the same time. The Church is content to understand these narratives, not so much as history, even though they certainly contain historical details. Rather, it would seem, each Gospel writer, as inspired by the Holy Spirit, took those details known to them and popularly shared about Jesus's early years (perhaps including some of the shared common material as given above) and fleshed them out into creative introductions. They used these "forewords" to their Gospels not so much as sources for history, but to lay out for us important themes that would echo throughout Jesus's life and ministry in their distinctive Gospels.

Baptism of Jesus

To understand Jesus's baptism, it is helpful to understand the origins of *baptizo* (the Greek word for "baptism") as it is used in the New Testament. Thirty of the 116 times it occurs it has something to do with Christian initiation. Many other times it is associated with John the Baptist. The original meaning of the word is likened to "plunge" or to "dip, sink, and plunge into liquid." Often this had to do with "plunging" cloth or utensils into water in order to clean them. What would cleansing have to do with Jesus, especially in connection with John the Baptist preaching repentance of sins? Jesus, obviously, had no need for cleansing himself of sin, which is an effect of the Sacrament of Baptism today.

The "criterion of embarrassment" (see the feature "The Gospels Are Ancient Biographies" in Chapter 4, Section 3) is one way scholars cite the historical accuracy of a biblical text. In summary, if something is written that would embarrass the author or subject of a passage, it is likely to be historically accurate because there would have been no other reason to include it unless it

The Jordan River near Jericho today. This is the place traditionally believed to be where the Israelites crossed into the Holy Land and where Jesus was baptized.

was a well-known event and really happened. It could be that the baptism of Jesus falls under the criterion of embarrassment. To have each of the synoptic Gospels and the Gospel of John include mention of his baptism is a clue to the very strong likelihood that it occurred. Imagine the early Christians having to explain to those new to the faith why Jesus, who was without sin, had to be baptized. Unless it really happened, why would evangelists have bothered including this event in their Gospels?

There are only subtle differences among the synoptic Gospels in the account of Jesus's baptism. Mark prefaces Jesus's baptism by mentioning that "one mightier than I is coming after me" (Mk 1:7). Jesus appears on the scene as a traveler from Nazareth in Galilee in both Mark's and Matthew's Gospels. Luke has a much more detailed introduction to Jesus's baptism, setting the stage for the coming of the Messiah by pointing out that people were questioning whether or not John the Baptist was himself the Messiah (see Luke 3:15).

All of the Gospels (including John's) emphasize the significance of Jesus's baptism in the following ways:

- The opening of the sky shows that God has come to his people and Jesus's ministry is about to begin.
- The descending dove—representative of the Holy Spirit—suggests the dawn of a new age under the Holy Spirit's direction.
- The voice proclaiming, "You are my beloved Son" (Mk 1:11; Lk 4:22), calls to mind Psalm 2:6–7, which promised the coming of the anointed king, and Isaiah 53:4, which addressed the Messiah as a Suffering Servant.

Likewise, the Church, in her reflection, has understood theological reasons for why Jesus allowed John to baptize him. It showed his perfect submission to his Father's will. His baptism foreshadowed his Death for the remission of our sins. By being baptized himself, Jesus left us a prototype for our own Baptism.

Temptations of Jesus

Immediately after Jesus's baptism, each of the synoptic Gospels reports that Jesus went out into "the desert" where "he was among wild beasts" (Mk 1:13). In the desert, Jesus faced a threefold temptation from Satan. While these temptations have symbolic meaning, the Church teaches that they really happened. Hence, it's important to keep in mind Jesus's actual journey to the desert and his forty-day stay there. St. Thomas Aquinas even addressed Christ's temptation—including the place and time of its occurrence—in the *Summa Theologiae*.∞

The presence of wild beasts brings up differing symbolic images. It might reflect the harmony of creation described in Isaiah 11:6 when the wolf, lamb, leopard, goat, calf, and lion all live peacefully together, or beasts could conjure

∞ Note

In *Summa Theologiae*, III, q. 41, a. 3, Aquinas asks whether Christ's temptation should have taken place after a forty-day fast when Jesus was likely weaker due to hunger. He points out that Christ did so, first, to give us an example to follow. "He teaches us the need of fasting in order to equip us against temptation." A second lesson is also important: Satan attacks even those who fast and do other good works.

The desert wilderness where Jesus underwent his temptations from Satan is a desolate area located near Jericho and the Dead Sea.

up something more foreboding such as the desert being the home of demons. Literally, at the time of Jesus, the wilderness of Judea was populated by many types of wild animals, including lions, oxen, bears, and antelope.

Mark's Gospel does not give particular details of the temptations; Matthew's and Luke's Gospels do (Mt 4:1–11; Lk 4:1–13), although Luke reverses Matthew's order of the second and third temptations: Satan's asking Jesus to jump from the parapet of the Temple so his angels can save him and Satan's offer of worldly power if Jesus will worship him. The first temptation in both Gospels was Satan's challenging Jesus to use his power to satisfy his own

---

concupiscence Disordered human desires resulting from Original Sin that produce an inclination to sin, also expressed as "the rebellion of the 'flesh' against the 'spirit'" (*CCC*, 2515). Concupiscence remains even after a person has been baptized.

physical hunger by commanding a stone to become bread. Jesus responded by quoting Deuteronomy 8:3: "One does not live by bread alone, but by every word that comes forth from the mouth of God" (Mt 4:4; cf. Lk 4:4).

As human beings, we know about being tempted. Like Jesus, we, too, can be tempted by outward forces—possessions, media, other people, and Satan himself. We can also face **concupiscence**, which Jesus, as the sinless Son of God, did not face. Satan attacks us through inward temptations, hence the petition in the Our Father to "lead us not into temptation and to deliver us from evil" or, in other words, the "evil one." Another word for "temptation" is *test*.

The Letter to the Hebrews explains that Jesus underwent testing so that he might sympathize with human weaknesses (see Hebrews 4:14–15). He also underwent many other tests in his life but never sinned.

The temptations in the desert serve as a vivid contrast to the way that Adam and Eve responded to temptation. When the serpent told them about a way to become like God, they disobeyed God. In Genesis, the man and woman sinned to become like God, whereas Jesus *is* God and accepted the human condition in order to redeem humanity. The *Catechism of the Catholic Church* expands on the meaning of this mysterious event: "Jesus is the new Adam who remained faithful just where the first Adam had given in to temptation. . . . Jesus's victory over the tempter in the desert anticipates his victory at the Passion, the supreme act of his filial love for the Father" (*CCC*, 539).

As we subscribe to the Church's long-standing belief that Jesus's temptations in the desert really happened, another question to ponder is why the evangelists each positioned their accounts of the temptations immediately after his baptism and directly before the start of his public ministry. The forty days Jesus spent fasting were similar to the forty days Moses spent fasting with God on Mount Zion before the giving of the Law (see Exodus 34:28) and the forty years the Israelites spent in the desert in preparation for entering the Promised Land (see Numbers 14:34). At his baptism, the Holy Spirit—that is, divine intervention—is a type of anointing, pointing to Jesus's mission to redeem the world. It was in the desert, through being tested, that Jesus acknowledged his acceptance of this mission given to him by the Spirit.

SECTION *Assessment*

Comprehension

1. How does Jesus's genealogy in the Gospel of Matthew connect him with the Davidic line of kings?
2. What lesson does Matthew's inclusion of four women in the genealogy teach?
3. How does Mark's Gospel begin?
4. How is the criterion of embarrassment evidence that Jesus was baptized?
5. Name two similarities of Jesus's baptism accounts in the Gospels.
6. What did St. Thomas Aquinas teach was a reason for why Jesus was tempted in the desert?
7. What is the difference between how Adam handled temptation and how Jesus handled temptation?
8. Why did the evangelists place the account of Jesus's temptations after his baptism and before the beginning of his public ministry?

Vocabulary

9. How does *concupiscence* factor into our temptations but not into how Jesus was tempted?

Reflection

10. Which of Jesus's temptations in the desert do you think was most difficult for him? Why?
11. How can resisting temptation strengthen you?

Section 3

JESUS'S TEACHINGS, PRONOUNCEMENTS, AND MIRACLES IN THE SYNOPTIC GOSPELS

Jesus's first words in the Gospel of Mark announce why he is in the world: "This is the time of fulfillment. The kingdom of God is at hand. Repent and believe in the Gospel" (Mk 1:14). Similar words were spoken by John the Baptist in introducing the coming of Jesus in the Gospel of Matthew: "Repent, for the kingdom of heaven is at hand" (Mt 3:2). Out of respect for his Jewish-Christian audience, which refrained from saying the name of God, Matthew substituted in the word *heaven*.

The Kingdom of God or Kingdom of Heaven is not a *place* like an earthly nation. This was a difficult concept for some Jews at the time of Jesus to understand. While they anticipated the coming of a Messiah, or "Anointed One," some had the notion that he would be a ruler who would establish a political, earthly kingdom. The kingdom John the Baptist and Jesus announced in the openings of Mark's and Matthew's Gospels was one that was being established in stages—beginning with the announcement that it was present on earth in the here and now, but it was at the same time not culminating until the Parousia at some point in the future.

Two other things were clear about the Kingdom of God from the openings of both Mark's and Matthew's Gospels. First, Jesus ushered in its beginning by following the will of the Father. Second, our participation in the Kingdom of God requires the initial step of *repentance* and *belief*. What was less clear is what the Kingdom of God really is like. Jesus used parables to help people understand. Also, his teachings and pronouncements provided details of how we are to live in God's Kingdom. And his miracles verified the supernatural aspect of the Kingdom, that it extends beyond this world.

Use of Parables

The synoptic Gospels contain thirty-three parables, though the number rises when some of the proverbial expressions used by Jesus are included in the total. Three of the parables (the sower, the mustard seed, and the tenants) are in all three synoptic Gospels. One parable, the seed that grows itself, is unique to Mark's Gospel (see Mark 4:26–29). There are two unique parables in the Gospel of Matthew and eighteen in the Gospel of Luke. There are no parables in the Gospel of John.

Recall that a *parable* is defined simply as "a short story that illustrates a moral or spiritual lesson" and that the lesson is usually made at the very end of the parable and is often surprising or out of the ordinary. Matthew seems to divide his parables into two groups; the first four were particularly addressed to Jesus's closest disciples, the others to the larger audience of listeners. When Jesus's disciples asked him why he spoke to the crowds in parables,

Return of the Prodigal Son *by Georgi Skripnichenko.*

he replied, "Because knowledge of the mysteries of the kingdom of heaven has been granted to you, but to them it has not been granted" (Mt 13:11). Parables require reflection in order for us to understand them.

There are two central lessons about the Kingdom of God that Jesus taught using parables:

- *The Kingdom of God is for all.* The parable of the mustard seed (Lk 13:18–19) teaches that though the Kingdom of God may have a small beginning like a seed, it can grow into a very large bush to provide a home for everyone.
- *Sinners are welcome in the Kingdom of God.* The parable of the prodigal son (Lk 15:11–32) is probably Jesus's most famous parable. It is about a compassionate father and his two sons. The prodigal (carelessly spending) younger son foolishly wastes his inheritance and ends up taking care of swine, the most demeaning of jobs for a Jew because of the uncleanliness of the animal. The father forgives him and welcomes him home with a celebration. The older son (who, like the Pharisees in the preface to this parable, complains about God's generosity) is likewise treated compassionately by his father: "You are here with me always; everything I have is yours" (Lk 15:31).

Though all are invited and welcome in the Kingdom of God, acceptance of the offer comes with a duty on our part. We are required to make a personal choice to accept Jesus and our place in the Kingdom, and that choice must be made today, not tomorrow. The parable of the rich fool (see Luke 12:16–21) points out that tomorrow might be too late.

Pronouncement Stories and Independent Sayings

If you do an internet search today for quotations of famous people, many will appear. For example, there are over five hundred quotations of Abraham Lincoln listed on one website. However, usually the quotations are listed randomly and not in any order, nor are they set in the overall context of the person's life. Now imagine the well-known pronouncements and sayings of Jesus that were shared over thirty years of the oral tradition. What would the Gospel authors do with these pronouncements and sayings once they began to construct their written Gospels? They did not simply list everything that Jesus said and taught in a numbered or bulleted list. Instead, in slightly different ways among the synoptic Gospels, they provided a narrative and context to his teachings and placed them within his movements over the course of his public ministry, a time of about three years.∞

Jesus was a memorable teacher. Consider a thumbnail sketch of his accomplishments: He gathered twelve common Jewish men to his inner circle and taught them that the Law of Moses was fulfilled in his coming. He taught them about the Holy Trinity, with a loving Father who was the Almighty Creator of heaven and earth and the Third Divine Person, the Holy Spirit, who would come to support them and their own teaching after he had left them. Through his actions, he initiated them in the sacraments (e.g., he was baptized, he forgave, he healed, etc.). And especially through the use of short pronouncements and sayings, he stressed how they were to live—in other words, moral teachings.

A pronouncement story captures a teaching of Jesus in a particular form. Though contained in the narrative of the Gospel, there is usually no explicit connection to the material that precedes it or follows it. It's easy to imagine that a pronouncement story was once told in the oral tradition as a separate, independent unit. Pronouncement stories (see the feature "How Were Early Christians Able to Tell and Retell the Gospel?" in Chapter 2, Section 1 for an example) are vague in details. Exact locations are not given, nor are the actual names of the people in the story. General information surrounds the important part of the story: Jesus making a pronouncement or declaration that often centers on his call for repentance and the necessity of faith in order to enter God's Kingdom.

Not all of Jesus's teachings could be so easily wrapped into a pronouncement story. There were many independent sayings of Jesus that were also part of the oral tradition. The "sayings of the Lord" are grouped by biblical scholars into subcategories as follows:

∞ Note

The verification that Jesus's public ministry took place over the course of three years and that it took place from about his age of thirty to age thirty-three comes from two sources in the Gospels. Luke 3:23 states that when "Jesus began his ministry he was about thirty years of age." John's Gospel cites Jesus celebrating three Passovers during his public ministry.

CATEGORIES	EXAMPLES
Wisdom Sayings *Words of Jesus that reflect the wisdom tradition of the Old Testament*	"The lamp of the body is the eye. If your eye is sound, your whole body will be filled with light; but if your eye is bad, your whole body will be in darkness. And if the light in you is darkness, how great will the darkness be" (Mt 6:23).
Prophetic and Apocalyptic Sayings *Words of Jesus that are similar to the formula of the writing prophets and the apocalyptic literature of the Old Testament*	"But woe to you who are rich, for you have received your consolation" (Lk 6:24). "Do you see these great buildings? There will not be one stone left upon another that will not be thrown down" (Mk 13:2).
Legal Sayings *Rules that require duties and offer guidelines on how Christians should live*	"When you stand to pray, forgive anyone against whom you have a grievance so that your heavenly Father may in turn forgive your transgressions" (Mk 11:25).
"I" Sayings *Sayings of Jesus that point out his special identity or make a demand for himself*	"I have come to set the earth on fire and how I wish it were already blazing! There is a baptism with which I must be baptized, and how great is my anguish until it is accomplished. Do you think that I have come to establish peace on earth? No, I tell you, but rather division" (Lk 12:49–51).

Reading the Gospels as a whole helps us to understand the important theological messages that the Gospel writers were molding from Jesus's teachings. Yet, by understanding the types of stories Jesus told (including parables), we can imagine them as independent units and get a better feel for how Jesus's first disciples and the crowds heard his preaching. The pronouncement stories and independent sayings provide a clear window into the actual words spoken by Jesus.[1]

Miracle Stories

Miracle stories in the synoptic Gospels also follow a set form (see the feature "How Were Early Christians Able to Tell and Retell the Gospel?" in Chapter 2, Section 1). Miracles are defined simply as "signs or wonders that can be attributed to God" or "powerful signs of God's Kingdom worked by Jesus." Miracles recognize the supernatural aspect of the Kingdom of God breaking into our world. They offer divine proof that Jesus is the Messiah. Jesus performed several types of miracles: physical healings, nature miracles, exorcisms, and raisings from the dead.

In today's secular society, skeptics deny the reality of supernatural events. They attempt to debunk Jesus's miracles and miracles that occur today with statements such as these:

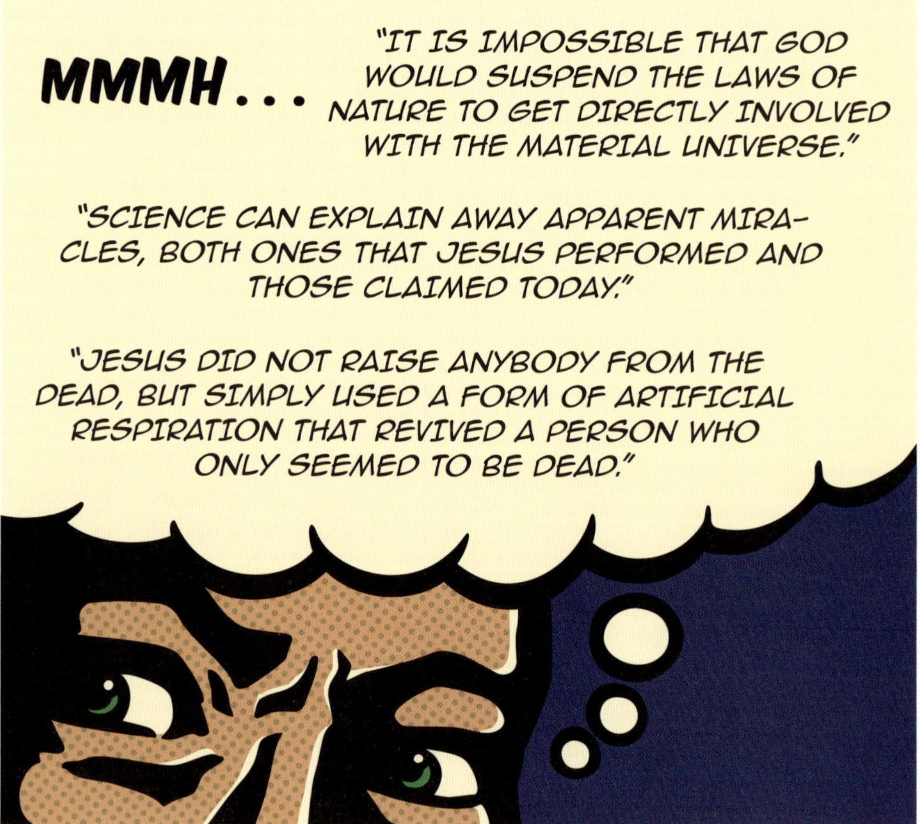

As was then is now: miracles are accompanied by faith. Note how each of these explanations limits God's power. The real basis for some of the disbelief in miracles is the denial of the divinity of Jesus. Those who have accepted that Jesus is the Second Person of the Blessed Trinity, truly God and truly man, and that God's power is unlimited, do not have a problem believing that God is omnipotent.

Physical Healings

Jesus caused blind people to see, deaf people to hear, and lame people to walk. He cured dreaded skin diseases, healed a woman who bled for twelve years, and relieved others' suffering. Jesus performed miracles to confirm that God the Father sent him; he did not perform miracles on demand to satisfy people's curiosity or desire to see something magical.

Faith was indeed a component of Jesus's miracles. He performed them so that the faith of those who witnessed them would be strengthened. Jesus performed miracles when faith was present. The effort some men took to lift a paralytic man on a stretcher down through a thatched roof where Jesus was teaching led to the man being cured and his sins forgiven (see Luke 5:17–26). A woman afflicted with hemorrhages for twelve years encountered Jesus when he was walking through a large crowd. "If I but touch his clothes, I shall be cured," she said. Jesus felt the healing power going out of him, and immediately "her flow of blood dried up" (Mk 5:28–29). Faith also accompanied Jesus's healing of the ten lepers (see Luke 17:11–19). When one Samaritan leper returned to thank Jesus he said to him, "Stand up and go; your faith has saved you" (Lk 17:19).

On the contrary, when faith was absent Jesus performed fewer miracles, as when he encountered people who took offense at him in his hometown of Nazareth. "So he was not able to perform any mighty deed there, apart from curing a few sick people by laying hands on them. He was amazed at their lack of faith" (Mk 6:5–6).

Nature Miracles

Nature miracles are those in which Jesus demonstrated mastery over the elements. For example, he calmed a storm (see Mark 4:35–41; Matthew 8:23–27;

Luke 8:22–25) and walked on water (see Mark 6:45–52; Matthew 14:22–23). He cursed a fig tree that then withered (see Mark 11:12–14; Matthew 21:18–19). Jesus fed five thousand people on the shores of Lake Galilee with five loaves of bread and two fish (see Mark 6:32–44; Matthew 14:13–21; Luke 9:10b–17; and John 6:1–15). Matthew and Luke record a second such miracle as well, the feeding of four thousand people.

Jesus's feeding of the five thousand appears in all four Gospels and is probably very familiar to you. Jesus had gone to the Sea of Galilee to be by himself, but the people followed him there. Their faith moved Jesus, so he healed the sick among them. He also taught them about the Kingdom of God. When evening came, the disciples approached Jesus with a suggestion: "This is a

deserted place and it is already late; dismiss the crowds so that they can go to the villages and buy food for themselves" (Mt 14:15).

Jesus wanted the people to stay, however, so he told his disciples to feed the crowd. This request confused the disciples; the available food for the whole crowd consisted only of five loaves of bread and two fish. Jesus instructed the disciples to bring him the food they had. He took it, looked up to heaven, blessed and broke the loaves, and gave them to the disciples, who in turn distributed them to the crowds. "They all ate and were satisfied, and they picked up the fragments left over—twelve wicker baskets full" (Mt 14:20).

This miracle is meaningful in more than one way. First, notice the use of the number twelve, and think of some other times this number has featured prominently in the Old Testament and New Testament. The twelve baskets bring to mind the twelve tribes of Israel and Jesus's choice of Twelve Apostles. Also, Jesus's actions—blessing, breaking, and giving—point to the Last Supper and Jesus's institution of the Eucharist. This miracle foreshadows the **Sacrament of the Holy Eucharist**, a powerful daily miracle in which ordinary bread and wine are transformed into the Body and Blood of Christ. The Holy Eucharist is the food that sustains us until we reach the messianic banquet in God's Kingdom at the end of time.

Some biblical scholars have tried to dismiss the supernatural nature of the feeding of the thousands with an explanation that "the real miracle was that everybody shared their lunch" with one another. This is a completely false view and, as with other skeptical perspectives, doubts the omnipotence of God. In fact, there is nothing in any of the Gospel accounts of people bringing their own food with them to hear Jesus preach. Likewise, thinking of the miracle of the feeding of the thousands in this way removes any connection it has with the Eucharist. Instead, "the miracles of the multiplication of the loaves, when the Lord says the blessing, breaks and distributes the loaves through the disciples to feed the multitude, prefigure the superabundance of this unique bread of the Eucharist" (*CCC*, 1335).

Sacrament of the Holy Eucharist The liturgical action known as the Holy Sacrifice of the Mass. It "constitutes the principal liturgical celebration of the Paschal Mystery of Christ" (*CCC*, glossary).

Exorcisms

The Gospels describe evil spirits that tormented people and sometimes drove them to insanity. In Mark's Gospel, among Jesus's **exorcisms** was his expulsion of a legion (i.e., multitude) of spirits from a suffering man. These spirits were transferred into a herd of swine that then ran off a cliff (see Mark 5:1–20).

The evil spirits or demons driven out in several of these miracles seemed to recognize Jesus. In Luke 4:31–37, Jesus cured a man possessed by an "unclean spirit" while he was teaching on the Sabbath in a synagogue at Capernaum. The possessed man cried out, "Ha! What have you to do with us, Jesus of Nazareth? Have you come to destroy us? I know who you are—the Holy One of God!" (Lk 4:34). It really isn't surprising that the demons would know Jesus: demons or devils and Satan himself are fallen-away angels, but nevertheless angels who were endowed by God with a superintelligence beyond that of human intelligence. Jesus rebuked—that is, spoke sharply to—the demon and ordered him to be quiet and come out of the man. "Then the demon threw the man down in front of them and came out of him without doing him any harm" (Lk 4:35). The people who observed this were amazed, saying, "What is

exorcism Public and authoritative action of the Church to protect or free a person from the power of Satan (i.e., demonic possession) in the name of Christ.

there about his word? For with authority and power he commands the unclean spirits, and they come out" (Lk 4:36).

As was (and is) common with other aspects of Jesus's life, people misunderstood his exorcisms. In Mark 3:20–27, some scribes accused Jesus of being "possessed by Beelzebul" (that is, by Satan himself) and of doing exorcisms in Satan's name. Jesus pointed out that their logic was flawed and silly. "How can Satan drive out Satan? If a kingdom is divided against itself, that kingdom cannot stand" (Mk 3:23–24). In other words, Satan would not be exorcising his legion of demons from people who were possessed. He would want his demons to remain in them to further his spread of evil.

Raisings from the Dead

There are three examples of Jesus bringing dead people back to life in the Gospels. One of these, the raising of Lazarus, is told only in John 11:1–44. Another, the raising of a widow's son at Nain, is reported only in Luke 7:11–17. The third example, the raising of the daughter of the head of a local synagogue, Jairus, occurs in all three synoptic Gospels (see Mark 5:21–24, 35–43; Matthew 9:18–19, 23–26; Luke 8:40–42, 49–56). Jairus sought Jesus out, fell at his feet, and begged him to come to his house and cure his dying daughter. Before Jesus reached the house, word came that the daughter had died. Jesus told Jairus, "Do not be afraid; just have faith" (Mk 5:36). When Jesus reached the official's house, he found people weeping and wailing over the child's death. Jesus said to them, "Why this commotion and weeping? The child is not dead but asleep" (Mk 5:39).

Sermon on the MOUNT
Sermon on the PLAIN

Focus Question: When seen together, how do the Gospels of Matthew, Mark, and Luke help me to know more about Jesus and God's Kingdom?

On the basis of geography, there is a difference between a key collection of Jesus's teachings in the Gospel of Matthew and those in the Gospel of Luke.

Matthew locates the first of five major discourses of Jesus in his Gospel on a mountain, and this discourse is known as the *Sermon on the Mount* (see Matthew 5:1–7:29). It contains several of the independent sayings of Jesus, many of which are also in Mark's Gospel as well as the speculated Q source. The setting of a mountain fits in well with the organizational structure and intended audience of his Gospel. Recalling that Matthew wrote his Gospel primarily for a Jewish-Christian audience, compare this scene to Moses's deliverance of

the Law from Mount Sinai. Recall also that Matthew's Gospel portrays Jesus as the New Moses, a new lawgiver. Also, that there are five discourses in the Gospel is significant as there are also, similarly, five books in the Jewish Torah.

The Greek word for "plain" (*pedinos*) used to name the *Sermon on the Plain* in Luke 6:20–49 translates literally as "level ground." The description follows Jesus's spending a night on a mountain to pray with his disciples, whom he commissioned as his Twelve Apostles. When they come down the mountain, he is met by a "large number of people from all Judea and Jerusalem and Tyre and Sidon" (Lk 6:17). As Luke's audience was primarily Gentile Christians, the connection with Moses and Mount Sinai was not essential; also, there is symbolism in Jesus *coming down* to be on the same plain as the people to whom he preached. This is literally what the Son of God did in becoming incarnate.

Did Matthew and Luke describe two different events at two different times and places? Certainly, that is possible. Jesus could have repeated the same important sayings more than once, much like a politician today repeats the same campaign speech over and over. There is, in fact, significant overlap in the content of the Sermon on the Mount and the Sermon on the Plain. Among the similarities are these:

- Both versions introduce the sermons by describing large crowds following Jesus seeking his healing for ailments (see Matthew 4:23–25; Luke 6:18).
- Both distinguish between the disciples and the crowds (see Matthew 5:1; Luke 6:20).
- Both start with the Beatitudes∞ (see Matthew 5:2–12; Luke 6:20–23).

∞ Note

The Beatitudes in Matthew present a description of living a full spiritual life. In Luke, the Beatitudes are geared more to respecting economic and social differences. For example, the first Beatitude in Matthew is addressed to the "poor in spirit"; a description of people who recognize their dependence on God for every need, material and spiritual. In Luke the first Beatitude is addressed to people who are simply "poor," reflecting more their economic plight. Also, the four Beatitudes in Luke are followed by four "woes." The woes are addressed to people living a prosperous life with the warning that those enjoying such prosperity in the present will have their roles reversed with those in need, in the future.

- Both versions follow the same order of sayings, though Matthew's version includes much more detail.

The biggest difference between the two is that Luke's version contains less than Matthew's. The more detailed Sermon on the Mount collects in one place Jesus's ethical teachings. Jesus does not abolish the Old Law or even add to it. In fact, the Sermon on the Mount "does not add new external precepts, but proceeds to reform the heart, the root of human acts, where man chooses between the pure and the impure, where faith, hope, and charity are formed and with them the other virtues" (*CCC*, 1968).

Both Matthew's and Luke's versions end with a saying from Jesus about the difference between a person who builds a house with a strong foundation and the one who builds on ground without a foundation (see Matthew 7:24–27; Luke 6:46–49). "Be like a wise man who built his house on rock" (Mt 7:24). In other words, it is not enough for us to speak of our faith; we must back it up with action. These actions create a foundation of faith that nothing can shake.

Further Study and Reflection

- Name and write the verses of the other four discourses of Jesus in the Gospel of Matthew.
- Write a profile of a blessed person. Use at least four references to the Beatitudes (either Matthew's or Luke's version).

People ridiculed his words, but this reaction did not deter Jesus. He took the child's father and mother with him, as well as Peter, James, and John, and entered the child's room. Taking her by the hand, he commanded her to get up (see Mark 5:41). Immediately, the girl got up and started to walk around. This incredible deed of power over death utterly astounded those who witnessed it. As was typical of him, Jesus ordered the witnesses to the miracle not to spread word about it. He did not want people to misunderstand his identity and his mission. He was the Messiah, but not a king intent on earthly power. He was the Suffering Servant who would die to save the people.

This miracle of raising the child from the dead, like all Jesus's miracles that brought people back to life, clearly foreshadowed the resurrected life of Jesus. However, it is also important to understand how this and the other raisings of the dead Jesus performed were different than his own Resurrection. The examples of Lazarus, the widow of Nain's son, and Jairus's daughter were resuscitations of corpses; those raised simply went back to their old life as before. On the contrary, in the words of Pope Benedict XVI:

> Jesus's Resurrection was about breaking out into an entirely new form of life, into a life that is no longer subject to the law of dying and becoming, but lies beyond it—a life that opens up a new dimension of human existence. Therefore, the Resurrection of Jesus is not an isolated event that we could set aside as something limited to the past, but it constitutes an "evolutionary leap" (to draw an analogy, albeit one that is easily misunderstood). In Jesus's Resurrection a new possibility of human existence is attained that affects everyone and that opens up a future, a new kind of future, for mankind.[2]

The synoptic Gospels use the Greek word *dunamis*, which means "act of power," to describe miracles. Jesus's raisings from the dead were certainly "acts of power." *All* of Jesus's miracles demonstrate that Jesus is God; anyone who has God's power—over nature, over sickness and death, over Satan and the forces of evil, over sin itself—must be God himself. His miracles also showed that God's Kingdom is here and Satan's kingdom is ending. Sin, sickness, and death entered the world when Adam sinned. Jesus, the New Adam, has inaugurated God's Kingdom where in the future there will be none of those things.

SECTION Assessment

Comprehension

1. Why did Matthew substitute "heaven" for "God" when addressing the Kingdom?
2. Why did Jesus teach using parables?
3. Rather than simply put the pronouncement stories in a list, how did the Gospel authors arrange them?
4. Name the four categories of "sayings of the Lord."
5. What are four types of Jesus's miracles?
6. Why did Jesus perform fewer miracles in his hometown of Nazareth?
7. How were the raisings from the dead that Jesus performed different from his own Resurrection?

Vocabulary

8. How is the *Sacrament of the Holy Eucharist* evidence of the supernatural dimension of Jesus's feeding of the thousands?
9. When he performed *exorcisms*, why did the demons recognize Jesus?

Reflection

10. Which do you find more difficult in your acceptance of God's Kingdom, repentance or belief? Explain.
11. How would you answer a skeptic who doubts Jesus's miracles?

Section 4

THE PASSION AND RESURRECTION ACCOUNTS IN THE SYNOPTIC GOSPELS

How did such a loving man end up dying on a cross? This question can be answered by reading the Passion narratives—the accounts, found in all four Gospels, of the events leading up to Jesus's Death. The Passion or suffering of Jesus is a response to God's plan foretold in the Old Testament: "Christ died for our sins in accordance with the Scriptures" (1 Cor 15:3). From the time of the **Protoevangelium** immediately after the sin of our first parents, God promised he would not abandon Adam and Eve or their descendants: "I will put enmity between you and the woman, and between your offspring and hers; He will strike at your head while you strike at his heel" (Gn 3:15).

The Passion narratives begin with Jesus's arrival in Jerusalem to celebrate the Passover with his Apostles. They end at his Death and burial. Why call these events "Passion narratives"? You are likely familiar with several meanings of the word *passion*. It can describe a person's intense devotion to a cause or describe the intensity of love. As used in the Passion narratives, however, the word *passion* has the meaning "to suffer," from the Greek *paschō*. Jesus did suffer greatly during the hours leading to his Death.

Narrative is used with *passion* because these events were told and retold as a complete set in the years of the oral tradition. Each of the Passion narratives in the synoptic Gospels quote historically verifiable names, places, and events. All of the Passion narratives in the synoptic Gospels (and the Gospel of John) are very similar, agreeing on most of the major details. Yet, the authors stress different aspects in line with the overall themes of their Gospels and the needs

---

Protoevangelium A Latin term meaning "first gospel" that is the initial sign from Genesis 3:15 of the Good News that God did not abandon humanity's first parents or their descendants after they committed sin. Eve's offspring (Jesus) would someday destroy the snake (sin and death).

of the communities they were writing for. Scripture scholar Fr. Felix Just, SJ, cites the following emphases:

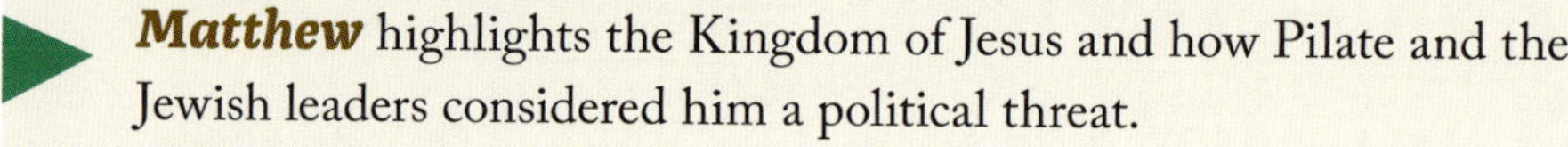

- ***Matthew*** highlights the Kingdom of Jesus and how Pilate and the Jewish leaders considered him a political threat.

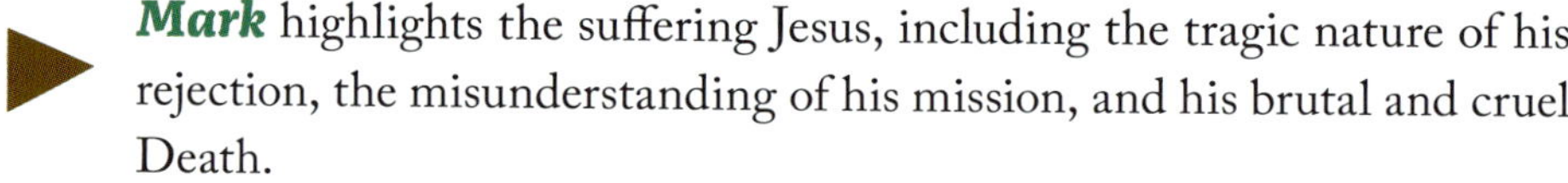

- ***Mark*** highlights the suffering Jesus, including the tragic nature of his rejection, the misunderstanding of his mission, and his brutal and cruel Death.

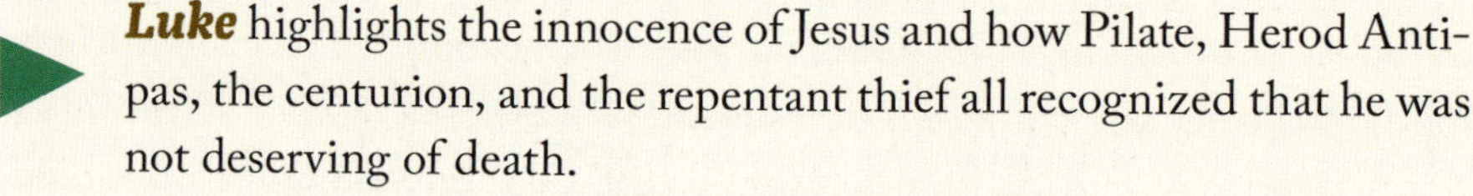

- ***Luke*** highlights the innocence of Jesus and how Pilate, Herod Antipas, the centurion, and the repentant thief all recognized that he was not deserving of death.

- ***John*** highlights the exaltation of Jesus and how he remained in charge and driving of all the action in order to complete his Father's will.[3]

There are some significant differences in the synoptic Gospels' Passion narratives (more on John's Gospel will be covered in Chapter 6). In fact, while Matthew's and Mark's versions are nearly identical, Luke's Passion narrative is more in line with John's. Similarly, each of the Gospels include different accounts of Jesus's Resurrection, with varying details and descriptions of both the empty tomb and of unique appearances of the Risen Lord. The Gospel of Luke and its accompanying Acts of the Apostles provide the fullest account of Jesus's Ascension (see Luke 24:50–52; Acts 1:6–12).

This section examines the synoptic Gospel accounts of the events of the Paschal Mystery, the Passion, Death, Resurrection, and Ascension of Jesus.

The Last Supper (Matthew 26:14–29; Mark 14:10–25; Luke 22:3–23)

According to each of the synoptic Gospels, the Passover meal that Jesus ate with his Apostles was his Last Supper. The synoptics describe the Last Supper as occurring on the "first day of Unleavened Bread"—that is, the first day of Passover when the lambs were sacrificed in the Temple (see Matthew 26:17; Mark 14:12; Luke 11:15). This means that Jesus and his Apostles ate

In a Greek or Roman banquet in Jesus's time, people reclined on couches to eat. The farther away you were from the host during a meal, the less important you were. The Gospels share many scenes of banquets and meals in which the Greek word for "recline" is used to describe the posture of the diners. There is a likelihood the Last Supper was shared using this configuration.

a Passover meal on the evening of the Day of Preparation—that is, the day before the onset of ***Shabbat***, which begins on Friday at sundown. There is seemingly a contradiction in John's Gospel that has caused some confusion among biblical scholars. John's Gospel states that the day Jesus was *crucified* "was preparation day for the Passover, and it was about noon" (Jn 19:14). One possible explanation to support the synoptics is that the Last Supper was celebrated as a Passover meal, but a day early. Another explanation is that when John writes of a "day of preparation" it could have referred to Friday itself as a preparation for *Shabbat* occurring later that evening.

Either way, it is essential to our understanding to connect the Last Supper with the Passover. Just as Exodus 12 tells how the Israelites ate a Passover meal prior to their liberation from slavery in Egypt, so too Jesus celebrated the memorial of this Exodus event before he liberated humanity from sin and death. The central part of the Last Supper was the institution of the Sacrament

---

Shabbat A Hebrew word for "Sabbath." *Shabbat* essentially means "rest" or "cessation." The Jewish Sabbath is celebrated from sunset Friday until sunset Saturday. *Shabbat* is a reminder to Jews that God rested from the work of creation on the seventh day and that they should rest too.

of the Holy Eucharist, in which Jesus spoke prayers of blessing and said that the bread and wine are his own Body and Blood (see Matthew 26:26–29; Mark 14:22–25; Luke 22:15–20; also 1 Corinthians 11:23–25).

Also, in each synoptic Gospel account of the Last Supper, Jesus lets his Apostles know that "one of you will betray me." Only in Matthew's Gospel does Judas come forward and question Jesus: "Surely, it is not I, Rabbi?" Jesus responds, "You have said so" (Mt 26:25).

The Beginning of the Passion of Christ (Matthew 26:30–27:31; Mark 14:26–15:20; Luke 22:39–23:25)

The actual Passion of Christ—that is, the sufferings he endured on our behalf for our redemption—begins with his agony in the garden, though it is not explicitly called a "garden" in any of the synoptic Gospels. (John 18:1 identifies a garden where Jesus went to pray.) After the Passover meal, Jesus and his disciples go out to the Mount of Olives (see Mark 14:26; Matthew 26:30; Luke 22:39). The place where Jesus prays is said to be Gethsemane in Mark 14:32 and Matthew 26:36. Gethsemane derives from an Aramaic word meaning "oil press." It is believed that there was a garden in which oil was pressed from the olives of the trees at the foot of the Mount of Olives.

Jesus withdraws to pray on his own. Each of the synoptic Gospels record that Jesus was sorrowful and despondent, even to the point of asking the Father to remove him from the suffering that he knew he would endure. Nevertheless, he prays, "But not what I will but what you will" (Mk 14:36). Matthew and Mark report that Jesus returned to his disciples three times, finding them asleep each time. Luke shortens much of the account of Jesus at prayer and only mentions that he returns one time

to find the disciples asleep. Jesus then tells them to "get up and pray that you may not undergo the test" (Lk 22:46).

Jesus is betrayed and arrested where he is at prayer. Judas, one of the Apostles, identifies Jesus for the chief priest and elders who come with a crowd armed with swords and clubs, according to both Matthew's and Mark's accounts. One of those with Jesus draws a sword and strikes the slave of the high priest, cutting off his ear. Only Luke identifies it as "his right ear" (Lk 22:50). Also, it is only in Luke that Jesus "touched the servant's ear and healed him" (Lk 22:51).

When Jesus is arrested, all of his followers flee. There is a unique addition in Mark's Gospel that mentions a young man that followed Jesus "wearing nothing but a linen cloth about his body." When he was seized "he left the cloth behind and ran off naked" (Mk 14:51–52).∞

Jesus faces a night trial before the **Sanhedrin**. According to Jewish law codified in approximately the third century AD, authorities were not permitted to hold trials for capital crimes at night or on the eve of a feast day. If witnesses contradicted one another (as in Jesus's trial), they were to receive the penalty the accused would have suffered. Furthermore, a person was not guilty of **blasphemy** unless he expressly pronounced the divine name (something Jesus

---

Sanhedrin The seventy-one-member supreme legislative and judicial body of the Jewish people during Jesus's time. Many of its members were members of the Sadducee sect of Judaism.

blasphemy Hateful, defiant, reproachful thoughts, words, or acts against God or the act of claiming oneself to be God. For Catholics, blasphemy applies in these types of actions against Jesus, the Church, and saints.

∞ Note

Who was the young man who ran off naked? Common speculation is that it was Mark himself, who would have been just a boy at the time of Jesus's Passion and Death. He may have been employing a technique that some filmmakers use today of allowing themselves to make a brief appearance in their films (e.g., the famous director Alfred Hitchcock did this; director Ron Howard allows his brother Clint to make cameo appearances in his films). Perhaps the unidentified man was a follower of Jesus (but not one of the Apostles) who was wanted for another crime. When the authorities spotted him, they tried to apprehend him. These are only two of many theories of who this young man was.

did not do). It is unclear, however, if any of these laws were in place at the time of Jesus's trial. Biblical scholars are in agreement on two things: first, the Sanhedrin had a session where they discussed Jesus, and second, the high priest or elders interrogated him sometime not long before the Roman execution. Jesus does not defend himself in this legal proceeding. However, in Mark's Gospel he forcefully and without hesitation acknowledges that he is "the Messiah, the son of the Blessed One" (Mk 14:61). He predicts that the Son of Man will come in glory. This statement outrages the leaders. To them, this *is* blasphemy, which was punishable by death under Jewish law. At this point, they accuse Jesus of this crime, spit on him, strike him, and ridicule him.

Pontius Pilate was the Roman prefect or governor (i.e., "ruler") of Judea from AD 26 to 36. Though his name is used fifty-five times in the New Testament, his full name is only used by Luke twice (see Luke 3:1 and Acts 4:27) and once in the First Letter to Timothy (6:13). Luke's Gospel describes the charges against Jesus in the greatest detail (see Luke 23:2, 5, 14). Mark's Gospel points out six different times that Jesus is accused of calling himself "King of the Jews" (see Mark 15:2, 9, 12, 18, 26, 32). This leads to Roman soldiers mocking him with symbols of royal power, including a scarlet (or purple) cloak, a crown made of thorns, and a reed to parody a king's scepter.

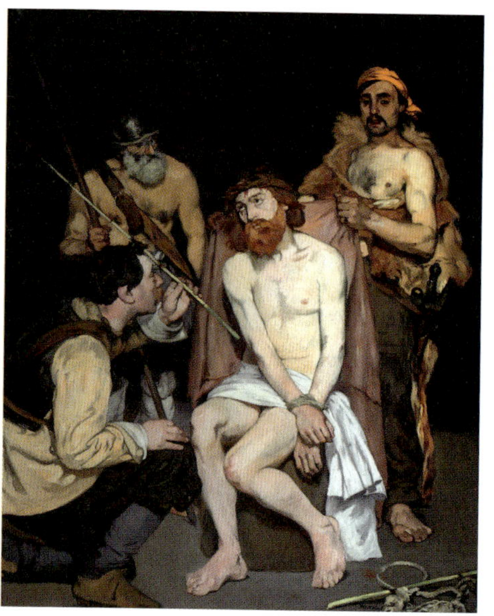

In one way or another, all the Gospels agree that Pilate knows that Jesus is innocent, that "he knew that it was out of envy that the chief priests had handed him over" (Mk 15:10). In Luke's Gospel (and in John's), Pilate interrupts the trial to send Jesus to Herod Antipas, the tetrarch, who was governor of one of the four regions of the Roman Empire that included Galilee. During the trial, Pilate had heard that Jesus was from Galilee and under Herod's jurisdiction (see Luke 23:5–17).

In the Roman Empire, the death penalty could only be carried out with the approval of the Roman governor. After Pilate gives in to the demands of the Jewish authorities and the shouts of the crowds, he hands him over to Roman soldiers to be crucified (see Mark 15:15–16; Matthew 26:26–27). In Luke's Gospel, Jesus is handed over to Jewish authorities (see Luke 23:24 and also John 19:16) by Pilate.

The Way of the Cross and the Crucifixion (Matthew 27:32–61; Mark 15:21–47; Luke 23:26–45)

Crucifixion was typical of Roman executions of Jesus's day. Crucifixion not only prolonged the sentenced person's agony, but it also allowed other citizens to watch and learn what would happen to them if they broke Roman law. Executions took place at Golgotha, the "Place of the Skull" (see Mark 15:22). Golgotha was probably an abandoned stone quarry just outside the walled city of Jerusalem. However, after Jesus's Death the boundaries of the city were expanded. Since the late fourth century, Golgotha has been inside the Jerusalem city walls, and it is the site of the Church of the Holy Sepulchre, also built in the fourth century.

After being condemned, Jesus was forced to carry the horizontal beam of his Cross to Golgotha. The horizontal beam weighed anywhere from 75

The site of the Church of the Holy Sepulchre in Jerusalem is identified as the place of both the crucifixion and the tomb of Jesus of Nazareth. It is one of the holiest sites in all of Christianity.

to 125 pounds. The path from the **praetorium** to Golgotha was about one-third of a mile. Jesus was already so weak that Simon of Cyrene was forced to assist him (see Matthew 27:32). The vertical beam was already in the ground at Golgotha. When the horizontal beam was attached, crosses at Golgotha were usually "t" shaped, the shape with which we are most familiar, though sometimes they were in an "x" shape.

A Roman centurion accompanied by other soldiers would lead the procession of the condemned. A *titulus* (Latin for "inscription") with the person's name and crime listed, carried by a soldier, was later attached to the cross. Jesus's inscription read: "This is Jesus, the King of the Jews" (Mt 27:37).

Upon reaching the execution site, Roman law mandated that the victim be given a bitter drink of wine mixed with myrrh (gall) as an analgesic for pain relief (see Matthew 27:34). Jesus chose to not accept this drink. Typical to this time, crucifixion consisted of stretching a person's extremities on the crossbeam and nailing or tying them to the wood. Only John's Gospel mentions "nails" and "nail marks" (see John 20:15 and also Colossians 2:14). When nails were used, archaeological evidence shows them to be tapered iron spikes approximately seven inches in length with a square shaft of about 3/8 of an inch in diameter. The nails were driven through the wrists between the radius and ulna in order to support the person's weight. The crossbeam was connected with the vertical beam, and the person's feet were tied or nailed directly to it or to a small footrest known as the *suppedaneum*. It is also possible that Jesus's Cross had a support seat for his buttocks, though that is not for certain. The purpose for either of these supports was to keep the victim breathing and thus prolong the agony. Ultimately, crucifixion resulted in a horrible death, usually by dehydration, loss of blood, shock, or respiratory arrest due to suffocation.

---

praetorium A Greek word that means "common hall." In this reference it refers to the governor's house, which belonged to Pontius Pilate.

With all of this pain, it is not surprising that Jesus did not speak much while on the Cross. A traditional Catholic devotion often commemorated on Good Friday known as the "Seven Last Words of Christ" can be considered a misnomer in that the devotion reflects on seven *phrases* Christ spoke while on the Cross, not *words*. None of the Gospels contain all of these seven phrases:

1 "Father, forgive them, they know not what they do" (directed toward those crucifying him; Lk 23:33).

2 "Woman, behold your son" (to his mother) and "Behold, your mother" (to the beloved disciple, John; Jn 19:26–27).

3 "Amen, I say to you, today you will be with me in Paradise" (to the repentant thief; Lk 23:43).

4 "*Eloi, Eloi, lema sabachthani*?" which is translated, "My God, my God, why have you forsaken me?" (Mk 15:34; Mt 27:46).

5 "I thirst" (to fulfill Scripture, perhaps Psalm 22:16 or 69:22; Jn 19:28).

6 "It is finished" (after a sponge soaked in wine on a sprig of hyssop, or vinegar, was placed up to his mouth; Jn 19:30).

7 "Father, into your hands I commend my spirit" (as he was dying; Lk 23:46).

According to Matthew's and Mark's Gospels, at the moment of Jesus's Death "the veil of the sanctuary was torn from top to bottom" (see Matthew 27:51; Mark 15:38). Luke puts this event immediately before the Death of Jesus (see Luke 23:45). There were two veils in the tabernacle that was in the Temple. The inner veil was before the **Holy of Holies**, and only the high priest

---

Holy of Holies A room in the ancient Jewish Temple that housed the Ark of the Covenant, the portable shrine that held the tablets on which Moses wrote the Law. This was a place where YHWH was believed to be present. Only the high priest could enter this room on Yom Kippur, the Day of Atonement.

could pass through it on the **Day of Atonement**. This was likely the veil that was torn. As the Church came to understand it, this signified that now all people have access to the presence of God and that the Old Law has given way to the New Law. The tearing of the veil was also a prediction that the Temple would soon be destroyed, which in fact it was in AD 70 by the Romans.

There were many witnesses to all the events around Jesus's crucifixion, as the Romans intended. There were women who had followed Jesus from Galilee and who were looking from afar (see Mark 15:40; Matthew 27:55; Luke 23:49). Mark names three women: Mary Magdalene, Mary, the mother of James and Joses, and Salome. Matthew names the same women slightly differently: Mary Magdalene, Mary the mother of James and Joseph, and the mother of the sons of Zebedee. In Luke, the women are anonymous at the time of Jesus's Death but not at his empty tomb (see Luke 24:12). Fittingly, as Jesus's disciples had trouble understanding his identity as Messiah in Mark's Gospel (see the sub-subsection "Titles for Jesus in Mark" in Chapter 5, Section 1), it is left to an outsider, a Roman centurion, to be the one who finally correctly identifies Jesus: "Truly this man was the Son of God!" (Mk 15:39; also Mt 27:54–56; Lk 23:47–49). This is also ironic in another way, because readers of Mark's Gospel were aware of Jesus's identity as Son of God from the very first verse (see Mark 1:1).

Empty Tomb and Resurrection Appearances (Matthew 28:1–20; Mark 16:1–20; Luke 24:1–49)

As with other parts of the synoptic Gospels (and John's Gospel too!), the evangelists had freedom to record the testimonies and events around the Resurrection of Jesus as they chose. The fact that there are some differences in details and not verbatim agreement is not only similar to the way other parts of the Gospels compare, but the differences also are evidence that the Resurrection accounts were truly historical. Each evangelist relied on his own eyewitnesses and testimonies to present his own account, rather than simply copying and reusing the earliest reports. The last verse in John's Gospel points

---

Day of Atonement The name in English for Yom Kippur, the holiest day of the year for Jews. It is a day when Jewish people ask for forgiveness for both personal and communal sins. A person goes directly to the person he or she has offended, if possible, asking for forgiveness.

out that "there are so many other things that Jesus did, but if these were to be described individually, I do not think the whole world would contain the books that would be written" (Jn 21:25).

Also, none of the Gospels were the earliest written record of the Resurrection in the New Testament. The First Letter to the Corinthians was written about a decade before the first Gospel, and it contains a long exposition of the resurrection of the dead, including the teaching that "Christ has been raised from the dead, the first fruits of those who have fallen asleep" (1 Cor 15:20). A few verses earlier, St. Paul wrote of the necessity of belief in the historicity of Christ's Resurrection: "And if Christ has not been raised, then empty [too] is our preaching; empty too your faith" (1 Cor 15:14).

The Gospels all agree that it was after the Sabbath, on the first day of the week, when Jesus's tomb was discovered empty. Matthew says the "first day of the week was dawning" (Mt 28:1). Mark reports that it was "very early when the sun had risen, on the first day of the week" (Mk 16:2). Luke writes that it was "at daybreak on the first day of the week" (Lk 24:10). John's Gospel describes the time as being "early in the morning, while it was still dark" (Jn 20:1). John's statement doesn't mean that it was completely dark, just not fully light yet. All four evangelists mention that women were the ones who first came to the tomb to anoint Jesus's body with spices and prepare it for burial. As with the arrangement and naming of the women around Jesus's Death, there are slight differences in how the women are described. All four Gospels name Mary Magdalene as being among the women (see Matthew 28:1; Mark 16:1; Luke 24:10; John 20:1).

The empty tomb was the first step toward belief that Jesus had been raised. The stone had been removed from the tomb according to all four Gospels, though they differ slightly on how it happened. In Mark 16:4, Luke 24:2, and John 20:1, the women find that it has already been rolled back on their arrival. Matthew's Gospel has a significant difference in that there was an earthquake and "an angel of the Lord descended from heaven, approached, and rolled back the stone, and sat upon it" (Mt 28:2). This happened while the women were on their way to the tomb. If, in fact, Matthew was writing after Mark, he could have added this fact to explain *how* the stone was rolled away to make it clearer for the readers. Someone had to roll it away!

At the empty tomb, the women encounter angels or messengers. Matthew reports one angel. Mark describes the messenger as "a young man sitting on the right side, clothed in a robe" (Mk 16:5). Luke tells of "two men in dazzling garments" (Lk 24:4). In Matthew, the angel told the women that "Jesus is risen," instructing them to go to Galilee to meet the other Apostles. In Luke's Gospel, after the women told the Apostles the news, the Apostles did not believe them. Peter, however, ran to the tomb to see for himself and was amazed when he found the tomb open and only the burial cloths inside.

More details of the Resurrection are included in all four Gospels and in other places in the New Testament. Face-to-face meetings with the Risen

Lord transformed the frightened and disillusioned disciples into bold eyewitnesses who spread the Good News of Jesus Christ far and wide. Jesus appeared to his disciples several times after the Resurrection prior to his Ascension to heaven. These visits are known as "post-Resurrection appearances." Besides Jesus's appearances to Mary Magdalene, to two followers on the road to Emmaus (see Chapter 4, Section 4, "Surveying the New Testament"), and to Peter on the shores of the Sea of Galilee (see the sub-subsection "Jesus Questions Simon Peter" in Chapter 4, Section 4), he appeared twice to the Apostles behind locked doors in a room presumed to be the same place where the Last Supper was held (see John 10:19–29). In the First Letter to the Corinthians, St. Paul lists various people to whom Jesus appeared. These people include Peter, the Twelve Apostles, five hundred other disciples (some of whom were still living when Paul wrote his letter), James, and all the Apostles yet again. Finally, Jesus appeared to Paul himself, when he went by the name Saul and was a Pharisee known for persecuting Christians. After this experience, Saul became St. Paul (see 1 Corinthians 15:1–11).

This section has emphasized the historical nature of Christ's Resurrection. It is also a transcendent event. *Transcendent* means that it goes beyond time and space, despite it being a real historical occurrence. Christ's Resurrection is a central mystery of the Christian faith. The *Catechism of the Catholic Church* teaches:

> Although the Resurrection was an historical event that could be verified by the sign of the empty tomb and the reality of the Apostles' encounters with the risen Christ, still it remains at the very heart of the mystery of faith as something that transcends and surpasses history. That is why the risen Christ does not reveal himself to the world, but to his disciples, "to those who came up with him from Galilee to Jerusalem, who are now his witnesses to his people." (*CCC*, 647, quoting Acts 13:31; cf. Jn 14:22)

Ascension of Jesus

Just like the Resurrection, the Ascension of Jesus to heaven is a mystery of faith. The Ascension of Jesus is the transfer of his risen, glorious body to heaven. It is mentioned briefly in Mark's Gospel: "So then the Lord Jesus, after he spoke to them, was taken up into heaven and took his seat at the right hand of God" (Mk 16:19). This passage is influenced by Psalm 110: "The Lord says to my lord: 'Sit at my right hand, while I make your enemies your footstool'" (Ps 110:1). This was a familiar image to the first disciples from their own society in which rulers were surrounded by ministers, with the most prominent of these sitting at the ruler's right hand.

Mark, Luke, and John present Jesus's Ascension as occurring on the same day as his Resurrection. The Resurrection and Ascension are part of the same event. It is Luke who provides the most details of the Ascension. He uses the Ascension as a bridge between the final verses of his Gospel and the first verses of the Acts of the Apostles, mentioning it in both places. In the Gospel, Luke dates the Ascension of Jesus on Easter Sunday night, the night of the Resurrection. In Acts, he presents the Risen Jesus alive with his disciples for "forty days" (Acts 1:3) before "he was lifted up, and a cloud took him from their sight" (Acts 1:9). The number "forty" in Scripture is symbolic (e.g., the Israelite's forty years in the desert; Jesus's forty days in the desert), signifying a full period of time. It does not necessarily mean forty days on the calendar.

What is significant is the heavenly glorification of Christ after his Resurrection. The Ascension marks Jesus's final appearance to his Apostles before he returns to heaven and the presence of his Father.

SECTION *Assessment*

Comprehension

1. Share two ways that the Last Supper is associated with the Passover.
2. Why can the "Seven Last Words of Christ" be considered a misnomer?
3. Who do all four Gospels agree were present at the empty tomb?
4. Name one "post-Resurrection appearance" of Jesus.
5. What does it mean to say that the Resurrection of Jesus was both a historical event and a transcendent event?
6. Which Gospel has the most details about the Ascension of Jesus?

Vocabulary

7. How did the Sanhedrin connect Jesus with the crime of *blasphemy*?
8. Explain how the *Holy of Holies* and *Day of Atonement* relate to what happened at the moment of Jesus's death.

Reflection

9. Why do you think it was important for Luke to add the detail that Jesus healed the servant's ear that had been cut off?

Section Reviews

Focus Question

When seen together, how do the Gospels of Matthew, Mark, and Luke help me to know more about Jesus and God's Kingdom?

Complete one of the following:

- Locate a passage you find difficult to understand from one of the synoptic Gospels. Consult two biblical commentaries. Then, write a three-paragraph explanation of what you learned about the meaning of the passage.
- Write a sentence to describe each synoptic Gospel. Use two of the following words in each sentence based on which of the synoptic Gospels they are most associated with: *tradition, joy, spirit, discipleship, secret, law.*
- Cross-reference a passage (minimum three verses) from each of the three synoptic Gospels. Transcribe each selection in a chart as on the table in sub-subsection "Connections between Jesus and the Old Testament" in Chapter 5, Section 1. Write a paragraph explaining how the three passages are both similar and different. Answer the question, What might be a reason for the differences?

Introduction

Understanding Matthew, Mark, and Luke

Review Points

- The Gospels of Matthew, Mark, and Luke are called synoptic Gospels because they share quite a bit of the same information. About 80 percent of the verses in Mark's Gospel appear in Matthew and about 65 percent appear in Luke. The word *synoptic* means "seen together."
- While Matthew's Gospel is ordered first in the New Testament canon, most recent biblical scholarship holds that Mark's Gospel was written first. The answer to the question of primacy remains an open one.

Assignment

Using the percentages listed above or in the introduction to Chapter 5, create two pie graphs for the approximate percentages to represent the sources of Matthew's and Luke's Gospels (e.g., Mark, Q, unique verses).

Section 1
Individual Characteristics of the Synoptic Gospels

Review Points

- It is most likely, according to modern biblical scholarship, that Matthew and Luke used Mark's Gospel, "Q," and their own unique sources to create their own Gospel accounts.
- The synoptic Gospels offer unique glimpses of the life and message of Jesus. Mark presents a vivid, human, and down-to-earth portrait of Jesus, focusing on Jesus's suffering as a means of encouraging suffering Christians. Matthew emphasizes the connection between Judaism and Christianity by creating a parallel between Moses and Jesus, quoting Old Testament prophecies and calling Jesus the "Son of David." Luke's Gospel emphasizes that Jesus is the universal Savior and that this is a cause for celebration.

Assignment

Explain in writing how you understand the meaning of the following quotation from the introduction to the New Testament of the *New American Bible, revised edition*: "While the New Testament contains four writings called 'Gospels,' there is really only one Gospel running through all the Christian Scriptures, the Gospel of and about Jesus Christ."

Section 2
The Time before Jesus's Public Ministry in the Synoptic Gospels

Review Points

- Each of the synoptic Gospels opens in a different way. Matthew begins with a genealogy of Jesus in which his ancestry is traced from King David through his foster father, Joseph. Luke's Gospel begins with an infancy narrative, tracing Jesus's birth especially through the eyes of his mother. Mark's Gospel opens with Jesus already an adult, just before his baptism.

- All three synoptic Gospels detail Jesus's baptism. Because of this, and the fact that Jesus was sinless and did not need any sins washed away, there is strong likelihood, through the criterion of embarrassment, that this event occurred. There would have been no reason for the early Church to explain why the sinless Jesus needed to be baptized unless it really happened.
- Likewise, all three synoptics mention the temptations of Jesus in the desert. The Church has always understood this as a historical event that occurred over forty days, likely in the wilderness of Judea.

Assignment

How would the events in Matthew's and Luke's infancy narratives have connected with their original primary audience? Share references from each Gospel to support your answer.

Section 3

Jesus's Teachings, Pronouncements, and Miracles in the Synoptic Gospels

Review Points

- Jesus, the Revelation of the Father, came to deliver the essential message that the Kingdom of God is at hand. He ushered in the Kingdom by following the will of the Father. Our participation in God's Kingdom requires the initial step of repentance and belief.
- Jesus used parables, pronouncement stories, and independent sayings to help people understand the Kingdom of God. These elements were arranged by the four evangelists into narratives.
- Miracle stories showcased the divine, supernatural aspect of the Kingdom. Physical healings, nature miracles, exorcisms, and raisings from the dead are various types of miracles performed by Jesus.
- Matthew and Luke highlight essential teachings—including moral teachings—in discourses. Matthew sets a primary discourse on a mountain, Luke on a plain.

Assignment

Read one of the following sermons in Matthew's Gospel: Matthew 10 or Matthew 18. Write a profile of Christian leadership based on what Jesus taught in these sermons.

Section 4

The Passion and Resurrection Accounts in the Synoptic Gospels

Review Points

- The Passion and Resurrection narratives describe the most significant events that are important to our salvation.
- Jesus freely went to Jerusalem, knowing what was coming. He celebrated the Passover with his Apostles, instituting the Eucharist to commemorate his loving sacrifice. After his arrest, Jewish authorities accused Jesus of blasphemy and handed him over to the Romans. He was sentenced to death. The Romans scourged and crucified Jesus.
- Women close to Jesus found his tomb empty and shared this news with the Apostles. The empty tomb was the first evidence leading to belief in Jesus's Resurrection. The Gospels also share many post-Resurrection appearances of Jesus before he ascended to heaven and returned to his Father.

Assignment

Put the following events that Jesus experienced in the order in which they occurred: Death, Last Supper, entry into Jerusalem, Resurrection, agony in the garden, going before the Sanhedrin, Ascension, Pilate's condemnation, carrying the Cross, burial.

Chapter Projects

Choose and complete at least one of the following projects to assess your understanding of the material in this chapter.

1. Design a Hyperboloid Model of a Church

A hyperboloid structure, such as the Cathedral of Brasília, is supported by inwardly curved beams. In effect, the structural strength of the inward beams is able to support the highest reaches of the church itself. There are several other hyperboloid-designed churches around the world as well as other buildings and towers. The Sydney Tower in Australia, completed in 1981, is one example. The first hyperboloid structures were built by Vladimir Shukhov (1853–1939), a Russian engineer.

Draw your own design of the exterior of a church using this style, making sure to show the use of inward supports. In addition, use wood skewers to piece together an equilateral triangle that is able to support itself. There are several directions online for making an equilateral triangle using skewers.

You will need:

- Several six-inch skewers
- Glue
- Marking pen

2. Write and Illustrate Your Own Parable

Do one of the following activities on the parables:

- Write an original parable to exemplify one theme in the teaching of Jesus. Create your own artwork to illustrate your story.
- Rewrite the parable of the good Samaritan (Lk 10:25–37) in a modern urban setting.
- After choosing one of the parables from the synoptic Gospels, research at least two biblical commentaries to discover more about its meaning. Write a two-page report using appropriate footnotes. Conclude the paper with your own interpretation of the parable.

- With several other students, enact a skit of the parable of the prodigal son (Lk 15:11–32) or the good Samaritan (Lk 10:25–37). Set the skit in a contemporary setting.

3. Share Personal Reflections on the Stations of the Cross

Learn the Stations of the Cross, and use creative media to share your deeper reflection on the Stations. For example, you could do one of the following:

- Retell the Passion story from the point of view of one of the Apostles.
- Write your own short reflections and prayers for each station.
- Create a multimedia or other visual presentation of the Stations.
- Make a detailed sketch of a station that particularly strikes you.
- Compose a song or create a playlist that connects to the Stations.

4. Write a Summary of the Resurrection Appearances

Listed below are the Resurrection appearances of Jesus recorded in the New Testament. Read and summarize at least six of these references. Then imagine yourself to be one of the persons to whom Jesus appeared. Write three to five paragraphs describing the following: what you feel about Jesus being alive, what he looks like, and what he says to you.

- Disciples on the road to Emmaus (Lk 24:13–35)
- Women (Mt 28:9–10)
- Mary Magdalene (Jn 20:11–18)
- Peter (Lk 24:34; 1 Cor 15:5)
- Four separate appearances to the Eleven and some other disciples (Jn 20:19–23; Jn 20:24–29; Mt 28:16–20; Acts 1:6–9)
- Seven disciples (Jn 21:1–14)
- More than five hundred brethren (1 Cor 15:6)
- James (1 Cor 15:7)
- Paul (Acts 9:3–8)

5. *Research and Report on Post-Biblical Miracles*

When the Vatican beatifies people or canonizes them, the committee needs to associate one miracle with the person for each step toward becoming a saint. Following are a few people whose healings have been considered miraculous and have been used in recent canonization processes. Research and report on two of the three people below. Find and report on another example of a person whose miraculous healing has contributed to a beatification or canonization.

- Jake Finkbonner (St. Kateri Tekakwitha)
- María Isabel Gomes de Melo (St. Carmen Sallés y Barangueras)
- Floribeth Mora (St. John Paul II)

Faithful Disciple
St. Matthew the Apostle and Evangelist

St. Matthew's two titles—Apostle and evangelist—each merit explanation.

As Apostle, Matthew appears in the lists of the Twelve Apostles in each of the synoptic Gospels (see Matthew 10:25; Mark 3:16–19; Luke 6:13–16). When he is introduced in his own Gospel, he is "Matthew" (Mt 9:9), but Mark (2:13–14) and Luke (5:27–28) address him as Levi, and specifically the "son of Alpheus" in their accounts of his call by Jesus. The connection between Matthew and Levi as the same person is made by the common description of the Apostle's occupation: he is a tax collector in all three Gospels.

From your studies, you are probably already very familiar with why Matthew goes by two names. Many biblical people (e.g., Abram/Abraham, Sarai/Sarah; Simon/Peter) often take a new name after a religious conversion. Also, many Jews of the first century who lived and worked among Gentiles had both a Hebrew and a Greek name—for example, Saul (Hebrew) and Paul (Greek). Matthew's case is unusual as both versions of his name are Hebrew in origin.

As evangelist, the words "according to Matthew" were placed on the Gospel in the fourth century. Eusebius, a fourth-century Christian historian, referenced a quotation from Papias, a second-century bishop of Hieropolis in modern-day Turkey, in which he wrote: "Matthew collected the *logia* ["words of Jesus"] in the Hebrew language and everyone interpreted them as he could."[4] However, Papias was likely not referring to the Gospel

St. Matthew the Apostle

of Matthew, since it was written in Greek by an author who used other Greek documents (e.g., the Gospel of Mark and Q) as sources for the Gospel.

What happened to Matthew, the tax collector-turned-Apostle, after Jesus's Resurrection? He was present at the Ascension of Jesus and in the upper room afterward (see Acts 1:13). The rest of St. Matthew's life is based mostly on legend. St. Irenaeus said Matthew preached the Gospel among the Jews in Palestine, which matches up with the intended audience of the Gospel of Matthew. St. Clement of Alexandria said that he spent fifteen years doing this. Other legends associated with Matthew have him traveling to many other places to witness to Jesus, including Persia, the kingdom of the Parthians, Macedonia, and Syria. Nearly all the sources mention that he evangelized in Ethiopia to the south of the Caspian Sea (not Ethiopia in Africa).

Matthew, like the other Apostles, was martyred, though the place and kind of martyrdom he suffered are unknown. He may have been burned, stoned, or beheaded. St. Matthew has two feast days. The Roman Church celebrates St. Matthew on September 21, the Eastern Church on November 16.

Comprehension

1. How do we know that Matthew and Levi of the Gospels are the same person?
2. Why did Matthew likely go by two names?
3. What was Matthew's occupation before following Jesus?
4. When did the Gospel become associated with Matthew?
5. What did St. Clement of Alexandra say that Matthew did after Jesus rose from the dead?
6. According to a majority of sources, where did Matthew most likely evangelize?

Reflection

When Jesus first encountered Matthew he said, "Those who are well do not need a physician, but the sick do. Go and learn the meaning of the words, 'I desire mercy, not sacrifice.' I did not come to call the righteous but sinners" (Mt 9:12–13). How did these words apply to St. Matthew? How do they apply to your life?

Prayer

Before studying Scripture, pray that you come to know Jesus better so that you might share his Gospel with others who have never heard it. St. Thomas Aquinas, the great theologian of the Church, offers this prayer before study.

Prayer before Study

Creator of all things,
true source of light and wisdom, lofty origin of all being,
graciously let a ray of your brilliance
penetrate into the darkness of my understanding
and take from me the double darkness in which I have been born,
an obscurity of both sin and ignorance.
Give me a sharp sense of understanding,
a retentive memory,
and the ability to grasp things correctly and fundamentally.
Grant me the talent of being exact in my explanations,
and the ability to express myself with thoroughness and charm.
Point out the beginning, direct the progress,
and help in the completion;
through Christ our Lord.
Amen.

Christology in the Gospel of John

Wedding at Cana

➤ *Jacob Tintoretto*

The canvas for the painting of sixteenth century artist Jacob Tintoretto—the *Wedding at Cana*—is colossal in size—14.3 feet by 19.3 feet—especially considering that it originally hung in the dining room of a convent in Venice, Italy. It was completed in 1561.

Tintoretto himself had a huge reputation among Renaissance artists. The name Tintoretto is actually a nickname meaning "the little dyer." His father made his living dying clothes. One of the legends of Tinoretto's life is that he originally began painting on the walls of his father's business. Rather than punish him, his father sent him off to an art studio to see if he could be trained as a painter. The intuition paid off; Tintoretto was one of the most innovative painters of the period. He was known for using flowing colors, including muscular figures in his paintings and dramatic contrasts of light and dark, known as "chiaroscuro effects ." Tintoretto was muscular and fit himself. He was able to complete paintings in rapid time. The speed of his brushwork was both admired and criticized by other artists. One of his nicknames was *Ill Furioso*, "the Madman."

The marriage at Cana was a popular subject of Renaissance artists, depicting Jesus's first miracle as requested by his Mother. It was a popular subject because artists could show off their own financial success by dressing the guests at the wedding in clothing that resembled their own status. Tintoertto's version is different in a couple of different ways. First, our eyes are drawn to Christ who is seated at the end of the table on the back of the room. Also, it is the architectural elements of the furniture in the painting that draws more attention than the wedding guests.

Today, the *Wedding at Cana* is housed in Santa Maria della Salute, the basilica in Venice. The painting is contained in a smaller moon-shaped corridor that is part of the larger sacristy. Interestingly another version of this painting with only slight variations to the original was done by Greek artist Michael Damaskinos at the end of the sixteenth century and is kept in the Venice Art Museum—giving visitors to the city a chance to closely examine both versions.

Focus Question

In what ways is the Gospel of John different from the synoptic Gospels?

Chapter Overview

Introduction

The Uniqueness of the Fourth Gospel

Section 1

Formation of John's Gospel

Section 2

What Do the Seven Signs in the Gospel of John Reveal about Jesus?

Section 3

Jesus Preaches in Long Discourses

Section 4

How John Presents Jesus's Passion, Death, and Resurrection

Introduction

THE UNIQUENESS OF THE FOURTH GOSPEL

The Gospel of John differs in many ways from the synoptic Gospels. New characters are introduced, such as Nicodemus, Lazarus, a man born blind, and a Samaritan woman. These characters are historical, but each also represents symbolically a particular kind of disciple. They seem to fulfill a role as determined by how they respond to Jesus. For example, the Samaritan woman at the well (see John 4:3–26) represents a person who grows beyond her past sinfulness. She is someone who undergoes change from the words of Jesus, leading her to reach out to her neighbors and share news of him. Likewise, the man born blind (see John 9:1–38) represents others who have been ignored or harassed throughout their lives only to be healed and converted by Jesus to be people of strength.

Stylistically, the Gospel of John is very poetic, using literary techniques such as irony (where opponents often say things about Jesus that have opposite, unintended meanings than they realize), plays on words, figurative language to help clarify many misunderstandings people have of Jesus, and metaphors that illustrate complicated comparisons. Some of the implied metaphors Jesus uses for himself help one to a better understanding of **Christology**—that is, the study of Christ's identity as the Second Divine Person of the Holy Trinity and his relationship with God the Father. Note also the play on words with the use of "I am" in each metaphor. Jewish listeners especially would have understood this, as "I am" translates to YHWH in Hebrew and is the name for himself that God gave to Moses. For example:

Christology A branch of theology that studies the meaning of the Divine Person of Jesus Christ.

- "I am the bread of life" (Jn 6:35).
- "I am the light of the world" (Jn 8:12).
- "I am the gate for sheep" (Jn 10:7).
- "I am the good shepherd" (Jn 10:11).
- "I am the resurrection and the life" (Jn 11:25).
- "I am the way and the truth and the life" (Jn 14:6).
- "I am the true vine, and my Father is the vine grower" (Jn 15:1).

The Light of the World *by William Henry Simmons.*

The framing of time is also more definite in John's Gospel. John's Gospel does mention three Passovers that take place during Jesus's ministry (see John 1:13, 6:4, and 12:1, and the subsection "Pronouncement Stories and Independent Sayings" in Chapter 5, Section 3). This timeframe seems more plausible, especially since the synoptic Gospels detail how Jesus attracted certain fame, drawing interested crowds from Tyre and Sidon in the north, Jerusalem in the south, and beyond the Jordan River to the east (see Mark 3:8, Luke 6:17, and Matthew 4:25). A longer public ministry makes it easier to understand how people from such distant places would have heard of Jesus and been willing to journey long distances, almost exclusively by foot, to be with him. As far as location, John's Gospel is confined mainly to events that took place in Judea and Jerusalem, rather than a broader mention of activity throughout Galilee that occurs in the synoptics.

Other Unique Elements of John's Gospel

The organization of John's Gospel into two books, the Book of Signs (Jn 1:19–12:50) and the Book of Glory (Jn 13:1–20:31), is a distinct feature. The Book of Signs is organized around seven miracles. In contrast to the synoptic Gospels, which describe miracles as "acts of power" (*dunamis* in Greek), John uses either the word *ergon* ("work") or *semeion* ("sign") to describe Jesus's miracles. Similarly, the Old Testament referred to the *works* of God that brought Israel out of Egypt at the time of the Exodus and the *signs* of God performed through Moses. Interestingly, however, John's Gospel has few direct references to the Old Testament in comparison to the synoptic Gospels.

The Book of Glory, the second major part of John's Gospel, consists of two main sections: the Last Supper discourses (Jn 13–17) and Jesus's Death and Resurrection (Jn 18–20). In the Last Supper discourses, Jesus offers a priestly prayer that prepares the Apostles for his hour of glory (the Passion), promises them the Holy Spirit, and instructs them how they are to live after his Resurrection. John's Gospel significantly omits from the account of the Last Supper Jesus's blessing of bread and wine and words of consecration of the first Eucharist. Uniquely, John's Gospel includes Jesus's washing of the disciples' feet at the Last Supper (see John 13:1–20). Also, John's Gospel goes to much greater depth than the synoptic Gospels do in explaining the significance and purpose of Jesus's Body and Blood being real food and drink (see John 6:26–59).

An epilogue follows the Book of Glory in John 21. Biblical scholars have speculated that John's Gospel originally ended at chapter 20. Chapter 21 contains Jesus's appearance to the Apostles in Galilee. There he helped the disciples catch fish, symbolic of their future roles as "fishers" of new disciples. He also recommissioned Peter, who had earlier denied him three times, with a threefold promise of Peter's love (see John 21:15–19 and the sub-subsection "Jesus Questions Simon Peter" in Chapter 4, Section 4).

This chapter explores in greater depth how each part of John's Gospel reveals more about Christ's divine nature as God's only-begotten Son.

SECTION Assessment

Comprehension

1. Who might the man born blind represent symbolically as disciples?
2. Why is it logical that Jesus's public ministry took place over three years?
3. How is the Book of Signs organized?
4. What are the two main sections of the Book of Glory?
5. How does John's Gospel differ from the synoptic Gospels in its coverage of the Last Supper?

Vocabulary

6. What is the meaning of *Christology*?

Reflection

7. Which "I am" metaphor stands out most for you in describing Jesus's relationship with God the Father? Explain why.

Section 1

FORMATION OF JOHN'S GOSPEL

Why did God choose to become human? The famous passage from John 3:16 provides an answer: "For God so loved the world that he gave his only Son, so that everyone who believes in him might not perish but might have eternal life." St. Irenaeus, the second-century Church Father, stated it this way: "For this is why the Word became man, and the Son of God became the Son of Man: so that man, by entering into communion with the Word and thus receiving divine sonship, might become a son of God" (*Adversus Haereses*, quoted in *CCC*, 460). St. Irenaeus was also the first to attribute the fourth Gospel to the Apostle John, who is associated in the Gospel text itself with the "beloved disciple" of the Lord and with the son of Zebedee (see the subsection "Who Were the Authors of the Bible?" in Chapter 2, Section 2). Further study of the Gospel reveals that several writers and editors other than the Apostle may have contributed to its formation. For example, some material appears twice with only slight changes in the wording (see John 6:35–50; 6:51–58). This is in addition to John 21, which reads like an appendix that someone other than the original author added to the end of the Gospel.

The author of John's Gospel was certainly an eyewitness to Jesus's public life: "It is this disciple who testifies to these things and has written them, and we know that his testimony is true" (Jn 21:24). Using the statements of St. Irenaeus, who was a disciple of St. Polycarp who learned the faith from John the Apostle, as well as the testimony of other Church Fathers, such as St. Justin Martyr, St. Clement of Alexandria, and Tertullian, there is nearly unanimous evidence that it was the Apostle himself, an eyewitness to Jesus, who authored the Gospel. Further, solid tradition places the Apostle John in Ephesus (in present-day Turkey) after Jesus returned to heaven, where he likely gathered around him a community of believers. Papias, a Church bishop, described meeting one of these followers, a certain priest called Presbyter John. This John was a close associate of the Apostle John (and may have been the author of the Second and Third Letters of John). It is possible that disciples such as Presbyter John took the Apostle's testimony, prayed about his words, and later produced, in stages, a Gospel that addressed the concerns of their own Christian community.

The First Letter of John (besides the Second and Third Letters) and the Book of Revelation have also been associated with the author of the Gospel. The prologue to the First Letter of John is very similar to the prologue of the Gospel, which could link the two authors. The author of Revelation is identified as a prophet named John who was exiled to the island of Patmos off the coast of Greece. It is unclear if John of Patmos is the same person as the author of the Gospel of John.

Composition of the Gospel

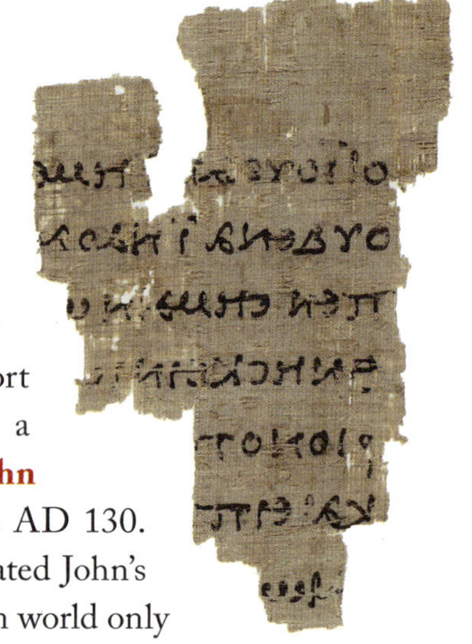

John's Gospel describes many of the same events as the synoptic Gospels, but in a different way, suggesting that the author possessed a unique source or sources. The Gospel of John was likely composed between AD 90 and 100. The earliest fragment of any New Testament writing found to date is a short piece of papyrus discovered in Egypt with a verse from John's Gospel. Known as the **John Rylands Greek papyrus**, it dates to around AD 130. This finding indicates that Christians circulated John's Gospel widely throughout the Mediterranean world only a few decades after its composition.

Who was this Gospel's audience? John wrote for Christians who may have needed to differentiate themselves from other groups—such as the followers of John the Baptist, the Jews who had expelled Jewish Christians from

John Rylands Greek papyrus Part of the collection of thousands of fragments of papyrus, mainly from North Africa and Egypt, housed in the John Rylands University library in Manchester, England. The John Rylands Greek papyrus (Rylands Greek Papyrus 457) is a 2.5-by-3.5-inch piece of papyrus from the earliest surviving edition of John's Gospel, likely between AD 150 and 200.

the synagogues, Samaritan converts, Gentile Christians, and other Christians who may have separated themselves from the Church over the topic of Jesus's divinity.

The Gospel may have challenged certain followers of John the Baptist who, even as late as the last decade of the first century, wrongly believed that John the Baptist was the Messiah. In contrast, the Gospel of John insists that Jesus is superior to John the Baptist, who proclaimed that there was one coming "whose sandal strap I am not worthy to untie" (Jn 1:27).

The Gospel of John is also more *mystical* than any of the synoptic Gospels. Recall that *mystery* is a word that points to something hidden as well as to the plan of God's saving action in human history—that is, "the mystery of salvation." To describe John's Gospel as mystical highlights both aspects of this definition: the God who is mystery and his plan of salvation that comes together in Jesus Christ.

Christology in John's Gospel

All of the Gospels are interested in Christology—that is, the study of Jesus Christ's identity—but John's Gospel stresses more strongly than the synoptics Christ's heavenly origins, his fundamental identity as the Son of God, and his preexistence as the Word of God. This latter point is expressed in the Nicene Creed, which states, Jesus Christ was "begotten not made."∞ The prologue to John's Gospel opens with this very teaching in a poem in which Jesus is identified as the "Word," always present with God, and always God:

∞ Note

In *Mere Christianity*, C. S. Lewis explains that "to beget is to become the father of: to create is to make. And the difference is this. When you beget, you beget something the same kind as yourself. A man begets human babies, a beaver begets little beavers, and a bird begets eggs which turn into little birds. But when you make, you make something of a different kind from yourself. A bird makes a nest, a beaver builds a dam, a man makes a wireless set. . . . If he is a clever enough carver he may make a statue which is very like a man indeed. But, of course, it is not a real man; it only looks like one. It cannot breathe or think. It is not alive. Now that is the first thing to get clear. What God begets is God; just as what man begets is man. What God creates is not God, just as what man makes is not man." Lewis, *Mere Christianity* (New York: Collier Books, 1960), 138.

In the beginning was the Word,
and the Word was with God,
    and the Word was God.
He was in the beginning with God.
All things came to be through him,
    and without him nothing came to be.
What came to be through him was life,
    and this life was the light of the human race;
the light shines in the darkness,
    and the darkness has not overcome it. (Jn 1:1–5)

This passage speaks of the difference between the way God *thinks* and the way that human beings think. Human thoughts are incomplete and imprecise, no matter how much a person concentrates. When God thinks, his thoughts are so complete that they come into existence. All God has to do is think, "Let there be light," and, by virtue of him thinking that, "there is light" (Gn 1:13). Connect this to what happens when God thinks about himself. God's thought of himself is so complete, and so perfect, that it is more than a mirror *image* of God. His thought of himself is as complete as the original.

God's *thought* is the "Word" in the prologue of John's Gospel. In Greek, the language in which the Gospel was composed, the term for "word" is *logos*. Logos implies much more than what *word* means in English. *Logos* can mean "message," "teaching," "extended speech," or "self-expression." The term *logos* is used specifically in the prologue as *self-expression*. The "Word" in the prologue is not a *different* God. It is the very same God, complete in every way, including complete enough to be conscious. This complete self-expression of God is called "God the Son."

God the Son is the complete and eternal self-expression of God the Father (*CCC*, 102). As Father and Son contemplate each other, they are united in an endless love so great that the love takes on an identity all its own—that is, God the Holy Spirit.[1] As their love is essentially self-love, it is not something or someone new. God the Son has always existed, since God the Father has always been aware of himself and always had a complete understanding of himself. God the Holy Spirit has always existed, as God the Father and God the Son have always loved each other. This is why Jesus says, when asked how he could speak so authoritatively about the Jewish patriarch Abraham, as though he and Abraham were contemporaries, "Amen, amen, I say to you, before Abraham came to be, I AM" (Jn 8:58). Jesus was teaching that not only is he God in the present, but he has always been God, even before he became incarnate as a human being, since he has always existed. This is also why, in the Nicene Creed, we state that "through him [Jesus] all things were made"—because he (the Son) and the Father are one.

The Gospel of John emphasizes that Jesus Christ is the One who mediates between God and humanity, because he is true God and true man, in the unity of the Divine Person.∞

The Incarnation in John's Gospel

The first eighteen verses of John's Gospel are a beautiful poetic expression of Jesus Christ as the preexistent Word, his participation in creation, and his role in guiding human beings, who often reject divine wisdom. All of these teachings contained in the prologue culminate in the Incarnation, God's becoming a human being. Recall that the Incarnation of Jesus Christ is an essential dogma of faith. Because the Word of God took on human flesh from his mother Mary by the power of the Holy Spirit, Jesus is fully God and fully human. The prologue (Jn 1:1–18) provides more scriptural evidence of the Church's belief in the Incarnation.

In John 1:14, the evangelist uses a word that you could use to describe yourself—*flesh*—in order to make it clear that the *Logos* or Word of God became a real human being. *Incarnation* literally means "enfleshment." John

---

hypostatic union The doctrine of faith that recognizes two natures (one human and one divine) in the One Divine Person of Jesus Christ.

∞ Note

Pope John Paul II wrote of Jesus in *Crossing the Threshold of Hope*: "If he were only a wise man like Socrates, if he were a 'prophet' like Muhammad, if he were 'enlightened' like Buddha, without any doubt he would not be what he is. He is *the one mediator between God and humanity*. He is mediator because he is both God and man." John Paul II, *Crossing the Threshold of Hope* (New York: Alfred A. Knopf, 1994), 42–43. Jesus is not "part man, part God," nor is he some mixture of the two. He became truly man while remaining truly God. The union of the divine and human natures in One Divine Person, Jesus Christ, is called the **hypostatic union**.

Theotokos derives from the Greek terms: Theos *("God") and* tiktein *("to give birth"). Mary is the Theotokos, the one who gave birth to God. Theotokos sums up the meaning of St. Elizabeth's words to Mary: "How does this happen to me, that the mother of my Lord should come to me?" (Lk 1:43).*

likely chose the word *flesh* to counteract a first-century heresy known as **Docetism**. Docetists did not believe that the almighty God would become human, so they taught that Jesus only *seemed* to be a man.

Docetism was heretical because if Jesus Christ only seemed to be human, then he could not have *really* died and risen from the dead. The Paschal Mystery would not have taken place, so Jesus would not have saved humanity. The Gospel of John counteracts this heresy by emphasizing the truth that Jesus was *really* human and *really* divine.

Through the Incarnation, Jesus reveals God the Father. In his book *Jesus of Nazareth*, Pope Benedict XVI stressed that only the Son of God can reveal God the Father perfectly. Moses spoke to God one-on-one but was never able to see God's face. The last verse of John's prologue addresses this truth: "No one has ever seen God. The only Son, God, who is at the Father's side, has revealed him" (Jn 1:18). Pope Benedict wrote: "Jesus's teaching is not the product of human learning, of whatever kind. It originates from immediate contact with the Father, from 'face-to-face' dialogue—from the vision of one who rests close to the Father's heart. It is from the Son's word. . . . Jesus is only able to speak about the Father in the way he does because he is the Son."[2]

The significant lesson of the Incarnation for us is that by becoming human, the Word of God made it possible for you to share in God's nature.

Docetism An early heresy associated with Gnosticism that taught that Jesus had no human body and only appeared to die on the Cross. The word *Docetism* has Greek origins and literally means "illusion."

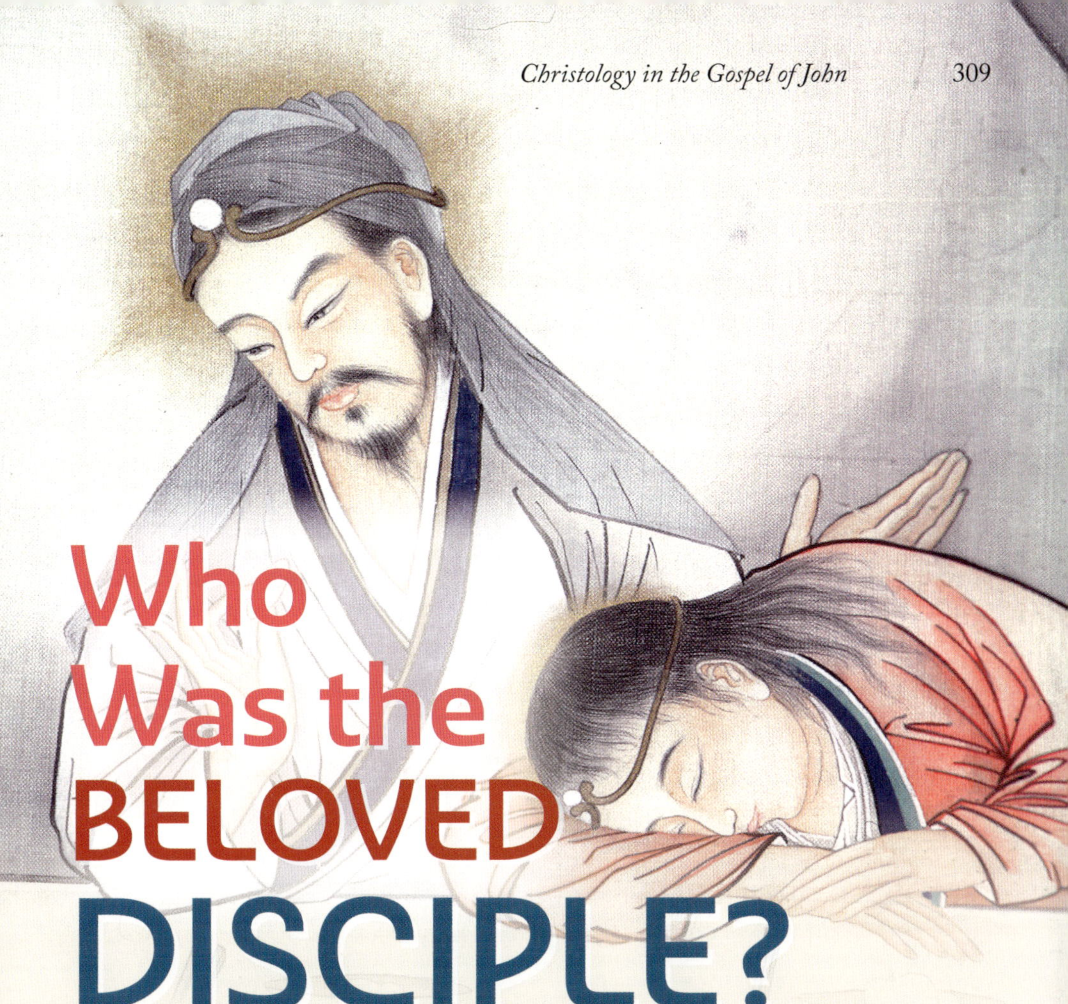

Who Was the BELOVED DISCIPLE?

Focus Question: In what ways is the Gospel of John different from the synoptic Gospels?

The Gospel of John is popularly attributed to John, called the evangelist, the brother of James, both sons of Zebedee (Mk 1:19; Jn 21:2). The Gospel, however, while never mentioning the name of its author, credits its composition to a certain disciple whom Jesus loved: "It is this disciple who testifies to these things and has written them, and we know that his testimony is true" (Jn 21:20–24). Just because the verse says that the disciple "has written them" does not necessarily mean that he wrote them with his own hand.

This "beloved disciple" appears in at least four places in the Gospel. He is first identified as such at the Last Supper, where he was reclining on the same couch as, and just in front of, Jesus, as was common in feasts of that time (see John 13:23–25). His closeness to Jesus indicated a position of high favor, according to the customs of the first century, where up to five people could recline on the same couch to eat.

He next appeared at the foot of the Cross at the crucifixion. He was the only one of Jesus's male disciples with the courage to be present. Jesus's great trust in this disciple was evident in his decision to give the care of his own mother into the beloved disciple's hands: "Then he said to the disciple [whom he loved], 'Behold, your mother'" (Jn 19:25–27).

The beloved disciple surfaces seventeen verses later in Peter's company, when Mary of Magdala reported that Jesus's body had been removed from the tomb. Both Peter and this disciple ran to the tomb to verify her report. The disciple arrived at the empty tomb first, where he saw the head cloth and believed (Jn 20:1–9). Finally, in the last of his appearances, Peter asked Jesus what would become of the disciple Jesus loved (21:20–24). Jesus cautioned Peter, in response, to focus on following Jesus, and not on the affairs of the disciple. This last passage indicates that the Gospel was later edited to explain the beloved disciple's death for those who believed he would live until the Lord's return.∞

It should be noted that this beloved disciple is *never* named "John" in any of these passages. Whoever the beloved disciple was, he was clearly both a disciple and an eyewitness to Jesus, as well as the founder of a community that had taken his message of the Good News to heart. He passed on his memories of Jesus to this community. This disciple probably did not refer to himself as Jesus's "beloved disciple." It seems more likely that the community he had brought to faith by his evangelism referred to him that way, in essence, because *they* loved him. He must have been a very special person. They were convinced that Jesus must have loved their founder with as much enthusiasm as they did. If this is true, he was able to engender this love from others, all the while never making the message center on himself; it was always about Jesus.

Further Study and Reflection

- Read the following passages about John, the "beloved disciple": John 13:23; 19:26; 20:2; 21:7, 20–23. Answer the following questions in writing: How did Jesus especially favor this disciple? How can imitating the beloved disciple help you to be a better evangelist?
- Jesus entrusted his mother, Mary, to the care of the beloved disciple (see John 19:25–27). Most Catholic churches have at least one statue of Mary, usually on the left side of the sanctuary. Read *Ad Diem Illum Laetissimum*, an encyclical by Pope Pius X on the Immaculate Conception. What does this encyclical say about why a statue of Mary is placed on the left side of the sanctuary?

∞ Note

John's Gospel sets up an interesting contrast between the beloved disciple and Peter. For example, at the Last Supper, the beloved disciple is in closer proximity to Jesus than Peter (Jn 13:23); at the empty tomb the beloved disciple came to belief while Peter's faith remained in doubt (Jn 20:8). At the post-Resurrection appearance at the Sea of Tiberias, Peter was questioned three times on his love for Jesus, clearly a chance for him to repent of his three denials of Jesus in the high priest's courtyard (Jn 18:16–18, 25–27). At that same time, Jesus also chided Peter for asking impertinent questions of the beloved disciple (Jn 21:15–23). Also, at the foot of the Cross, when the beloved disciple was given the care of Jesus's mother, Peter was very conspicuously absent (Jn 19:25–26). What is clear from the mention of Peter in the Gospel in so many key places, including with Jesus after the Resurrection, is that the Johannine community was aware of Peter's primacy in the Church. The contrast of Peter with the beloved disciple also shows how John's community relished the opportunity to portray their own teacher in a positive light. These kinds of subtle differences between the Gospels highlight the rich diversity that always has been present in the Church, even as she earnestly pursued unity in belief and practice.

As the prologue states, “But to those who did accept him he gave the power to become children of God” (Jn 1:12). John speaks to this gift in other places in his Gospel, connecting belief in Jesus to being saved (see John 2:23). Also, the evangelist concludes a conversation between Jesus and Nicodemus, a Pharisee, who was called “a ruler of the Jews” (Jn 3:1), with one of the most famous passages in Scriptures: “For God so loved the world that he gave his only Son, so that everyone who believes in him might not perish but might have eternal life. For God did not send his son into the world to condemn the world, but that the world might be saved through him” (Jn 3:16–17). Add to this the Gospel’s mention of Judas accompanied by those who seized Jesus (see John 18:1–14) and Jesus being questioned by Pilate who then “handed him over” (Jn 19:16) to be crucified. In light of all these passages, John 3:16–17—and particularly the words “he gave his only Son”—is definitely a further reference to the saving actions of Christ in the Paschal Mystery.

SECTION *Assessment*

Comprehension

1. Differentiate between speculation on the Apostle John, the Presbyter John, and John of Patmos.
2. How are the Gospel of John and the First Letter of John similar?
3. How did the Gospel of John address followers of John the Baptist?
4. What is the difference between the way God thinks and the way human beings think?

Vocabulary

5. What is significant about the discovery of the *John Rylands Greek papyrus*?
6. What was heretical about *Docetism*?

Reflection

7. Explain the difference between "to beget" and "to make" in your own words.
8. How does the prologue to the Gospel of John help you to understand how God is Three Divine Persons in one?
9. What does it mean for you to be able to share in God's nature?

Section 2

WHAT DO THE SEVEN SIGNS IN THE GOSPEL OF JOHN REVEAL ABOUT JESUS?

The preexistent Word of God represented in the prologue does not disappear in the rest of John's Gospel. The seven signs performed by Jesus in chapters 2–11 continue to emphasize a *Logos* who is not limited by time, nor by race, culture, or space. The Word of God acts in these areas much differently from how God acts in the Old Testament.

For example, in the Old Testament the presence of God was limited to certain times and spaces as *when* the Jews returned from exile and *where* they rebuilt the Temple. There were restrictions for worship on the Day of Atonement after the Ark of the Covenant was lost during the Babylonian Captivity. Prior to the to the time of captivity, on the Day of Atonement the high priest would enter the inner sanctuary and sprinkle blood of sacrificed goats on the Mercy Seat—that is, the lid of the Ark of the Covenant. Without the Ark's presence, the Day of Atonement ritual could not be completed, though the high priest continued to sprinkle blood where the Ark would have sat.

In John's Gospel, however, Jesus performs signs anywhere and everywhere. He is not limited by space or time. The signs were performed in a variety of places (e.g., a wedding, a healing pool, in homes), and not just in a designated sacred place such as the Temple or a synagogue. Likewise, the signs communicated a transcendent dimension of time. For example, Jesus's first sign was the changing of water into wine at a wedding in Cana of Galilee on a particular day. Whereas Jesus performed this miracle at his mother's request, Mary's concern was only for the particular event itself: "They have no wine" (Jn 2:3). Jesus was concerned that his "hour has not yet come" (Jn 2:4). Jesus was thinking ahead to a day and hour that would have more significance: the hour of his Passion, Death, Resurrection, and Ascension. He performed the miracle at Cana on that day, but he did so as a symbol of the greater miracle that would occur at a future

This is a model of the Second Temple, the Temple rebuilt after the exile. In Second Temple times it is likely that Passover was marked as a seven-day festival which began with the slaughtering of lambs in the Temple. The meat was then consumed by families during a meal that included unleavened bread (matzah) and bitter herbs.

time. The water Jesus turned into wine at the wedding at Cana represents both the wine he would change into his Blood at the Last Supper and his corruptible body that would be changed to an incorruptible one at his Resurrection.

In the synoptic Gospels, Jesus does miracles when his identity as the Son of God is tested. Recall that faith among the people involved was usually a prerequisite in order for Jesus to be able to perform a miracle (see the sub-subsection "Physical Healings" in Chapter 5, Section 3). In John's Gospel, it is just the opposite. The signs Jesus performed are done "in order to bring people to believe in him." The signs are intended to cause people with no faith to believe. "If people do not come to believe despite having seen the signs, then the signs did not fulfill their purpose."[3] It follows that various people in John's Gospel are classified by their belief, partial belief, and unbelief related to Jesus's signs. For example:

- Those who come to believe in him and are recognized as his disciples, such as the Samaritans (see John 4:41–42) and the man born blind (see John 9:35–38).
- Those who come to believe in him but are afraid to acknowledge their faith publicly, such as the parents of the man born blind (see John 9:18–23).

- Those who come to believe in him even without seeing any signs, such as Martha before Lazarus is raised (see John 11:27) and believers down through today, who as mentioned to Thomas (see John 20:19–29) are likewise counted among the faithful.[4]

The seven signs in the Book of Signs (specifically John 1:19–12:50) reveal Jesus's identity, explain his reason for coming to earth, display his heavenly glory, and illuminate his relation to God the Father.

Faith in the Seven Signs

Jesus's miracles in the Gospel of John are meant to elicit belief for those who witness them. This reaction, while intended, is not fulfilled completely in each example. In this section, you will read each of the seven signs directly from the Gospel, focusing especially on the faith responses of those who were present. Follow this format:

- First, read the opening question.
- Second, read the information in this text for contextual background on the sign.
- Third, and more importantly, undertake a thoughtful and careful reading of each passage directly from your Bible. Ask yourself: How would I have responded if I witnessed this miracle? What is the meaning of this miracle for my life today?
- Finally, go back to the opening question and make sure you can answer it.

First Sign: The Wedding at Cana (John 2:1–12)

What was Jesus's desired effect of this first miracle? How did he achieve it?

As mentioned, this miracle is different from those in the synoptic Gospels in that Jesus does not change water to wine to fulfill a test of his divinity. In fact, at first, he does not want to do it at all. The "mother of Jesus" (not named Mary in any place in John's Gospel) is the one who brings the issue of the wine running short to Jesus. His response is at first a rebuke: "Woman, how does your concern affect me? My hour has not yet come" (Jn 2:4). Mary's persistence and confidence that her son will act—she says to the servers, "Do whatever he tells you" (Jn 2:5)—is a model of her unwavering faith in him.

Jesus's disciples, whom he had just chosen (see John 1:35–51), are present at the wedding. The miracle, done after the faithful request of his mother, also had Jesus's desired effect on them: it "revealed his glory, and his disciples began to believe in him" (Jn 2:11).

The changing of water to wine is a nature miracle; Jesus is able to change one natural substance to another. Remember, it also alludes to the changing of table wine into his own Blood at the Last Supper, details that are covered in each of the synoptic Gospels. John significantly places this miracle after the call of the first disciples and just before his conversation with the Pharisee leader Nicodemus in John 3:1–15. John's arrangement points out that Jesus has power not only over nature, changing one natural substance to another, but also over human beings, changing minds from unbelief to belief.

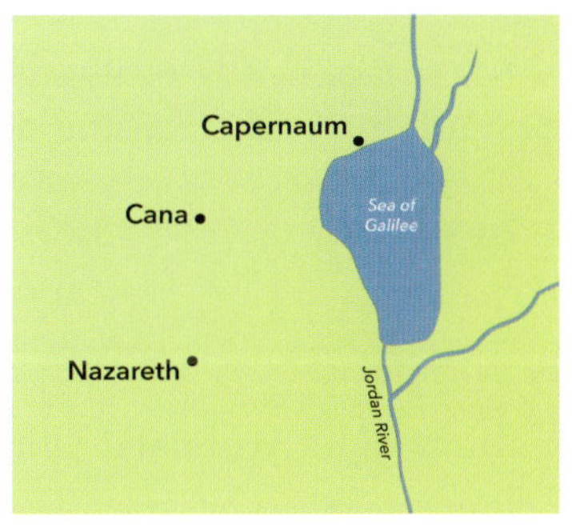

Second Sign: Cure of the Official's Son (John 4:46–54)

What was significant about the boy being healed at one in the afternoon?

Jesus's second sign is linked to the first sign because of location. Like the changing of water to wine, this second miracle also takes place at Cana. But was it really his second miracle, or just his second miracle at Cana? Earlier, while he was in Jerusalem for the Feast of Passover, the Gospel states that "many came to believe in his name when they saw the signs he was doing" (Jn 3:23). John 4:45 also reiterates that "the Galileans welcomed him, since they had seen all he had done in Jerusalem at the feast."

The cure of a royal official's son suggests that Jesus already carried the reputation of a healer and that he had performed other healing miracles after changing water to wine. The labeling of this cure as Jesus's second sign likely is because of its connection to Cana where the first sign took place.

The man seeking out Jesus for a miracle was from Capernaum, a town on the shores of the Sea of Galilee, about twenty-five miles from Cana. The man was an unnamed official, perhaps a steward of King Herod, who had obviously heard about the power of Jesus as a healer. The man's son was ill, on the brink of death. He asked Jesus to travel to Capernaum in order to heal the son. Jesus answered abruptly, "Unless you people see signs and wonders, you will not believe" (Jn 4:48). The man believed—at first—that Jesus could not heal unless he was physically present next to the boy.

Something changed when Jesus reassured him: "You may go; your son will live" (Jn 4:50). The man did believe what Jesus said and left. But did he remain in Cana overnight, or did he return home right away? Given the distance, the assumption is that he left right away, though it is obvious by the message he receives from his slaves who meet him on the way back that the boy was healed on the day Jesus spoke to the man and that it was the following day that he returned home. The man's slaves told him that the fever had left the boy "yesterday, about one in the afternoon" (Jn 4:52).

There are also similarities between this miracle as recorded in John and the cure of the centurion's son in Matthew 8:5–13 or the servant in Luke 7:1–10. It also connects with the seventh sign in John's Gospel, the raising of Lazarus from the dead (see the sub-subsection "Seventh Sign: The Raising of Lazarus" later in this section).

Third Sign: Cure on a Sabbath (John 5:1–47)

What are three ways Jesus claimed equality with God?

Jesus encountered a man who had been lame for thirty-eight years and who waited to immerse himself in a pool that was thought to bring healing. The pool is identified as Bethesda in John 5:2 and located at the Sheep Gate in Jerusalem. In the original translation of the Scripture the noun "gate" is not included with "sheep," but the Book of Nehemiah (e.g., 3:1, 32; 12:9) does mention a Sheep Gate. This was a place near the northeast wall of Jerusalem where sheep and other animals were brought in to be sacrificed in the Temple.

There is a second pool—the Pool of Siloam—mentioned in John's Gospel that was the site of Jesus's sixth sign, the healing of a man born blind (see the sub-subsection "Sixth Sign: The Cure of the Man Born Blind" later in this section). These pools have been identified as *mikveh*, Jewish ritual baths, where healings were believed to have taken place. John 5:7 mentions water that is

Ruins of the Pool of Bethesda.

"stirred up," indicating the influx of water from a hidden spring. The Pool of Bethesda was discovered and excavated in the late nineteenth century. It did reveal a rectangular pool with two basins separated by a wall and five porticos, or columns, as mentioned in the Gospel. Why the two basins? The northern basin acted as a reservoir to continually refresh the *mikveh* in the southern basin with fresh water flowing through a dam between them.

The Gospel describes "a large number of ill, blind, lame, and crippled" at the Pool of Bethesda waiting to be healed. It was believed that the first person who was able to enter the pool when the spring water was released from the northern basin to the southern basin would be healed. The man who had been lame for thirty-eight years was never able to lift himself in order to get into the pool in time. Although he only asked for help getting to the pool, Jesus ordered him to rise, take his mat, and walk.

Some "Jews" told the man that he should not be carrying his mat because it was the Sabbath. The Jews asked who was the man who told him he should walk with his mat, and they began to persecute Jesus because he had done this cure on the Sabbath. Jesus sided with some rabbis who believed that God does not rest from all things on the Sabbath, using the logic that, after all, people die and are born on the Sabbath: "My Father is at work until now, so I am at work" (Jn 5:17). Jesus's statement making him equal with God irritated his adversaries even more than did his work on the Sabbath. His clear claim of divine authority enraged his opponents: "For this reason the Jews tried all the more to kill him, because he not only broke the Sabbath but he also called God his own father, making himself equal to God" (Jn 5:18).

Note that in describing this sign, the evangelist uses the expression "the Jews" in a negative way. Several times throughout John's Gospel the antagonism between Jesus and "the Jews" is so intense that it appears that Jesus is *anti-Semitic*—that is, prejudiced against Jewish people. Remember, though, that Jesus and all his early disciples were Jews also. John wrote for a largely Jewish-Christian community. In John's Gospel, a mention of "the Jews" does not refer to all those who practice Judaism. Instead, it represents those who persisted in not accepting Jesus while at the same time persecuting Jewish Christians.

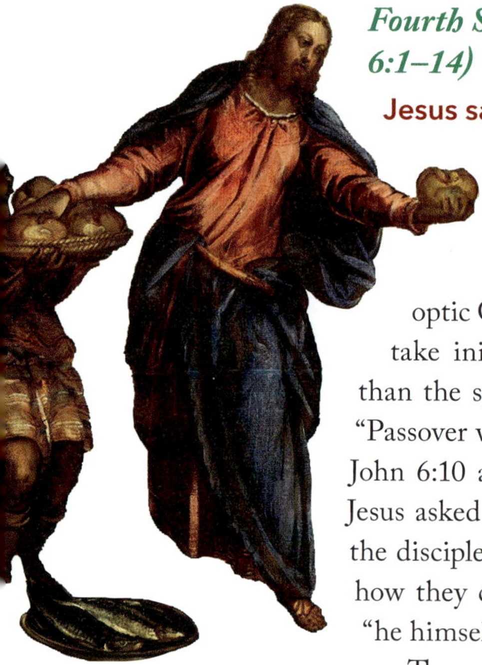

Fourth Sign: Multiplication of Loaves (John 6:1–14)

Jesus says he wanted to test his disciples. What was the subject of the test?

The multiplication of loaves is the only miracle story that is found in all four Gospels. In John's Gospel, unlike the synoptic Gospels, it is Jesus and not the disciples who take initiative to feed the hungry. Also different than the synoptic accounts, John points out that the "Passover was near" (Jn 6:4). (The mention of grass in John 6:10 also is an indication that it is springtime.) Jesus asked Phillip, rather than taking a request from the disciples as the synoptic Gospels document, about how they could provide food for the crowds because "he himself knew what he was going to do" (Jn 5:6).

The specific identification of the loaves being "barley" loaves (unique among the four Gospels) also has meaning. The prophet Elisha multiplied twenty barley loaves to feed a hundred people, and they, too, had some left over. Barley was also much less expensive than wheat (see, e.g., 2 Kings 7:1). The Book of Revelation adds further that "a ration of wheat costs a day's pay, and three rations of barley cost a day's pay" (Rv 6:6). Barley was clearly the food of the poor.

As with the other signs, Jesus's miracle had a desired effect among those who witnessed it: "When the people saw the sign he had done, they said, 'This is truly the Prophet, the one who is to come into the world'" (Jn 6:14). Jesus feared that they would make him a king at that point, so he went off to a mountain alone, setting up the occasion of the fifth sign.

Fifth Sign: Walking on Water (John 6:16–24)

Knowing what we know about the distance to the other shore and where the disciples' boat was when Jesus walked toward them on water, what is odd about the information shared in John 6:21?

The beach of Capernaum on the Sea of Galilee.

While Jesus went up a mountain to be alone and to pray, the disciples went to the shore of the Sea of Galilee to cross by boat to Capernaum on the other side. The distance across from the presumed location (see Luke 9:10–11) was between six and seven miles. The Gospel says "it had already grown dark" and that "it was evening" (Jn 6:16, 17), so it might have been between seven and eight o'clock. Remember from the multiplication of loaves account, we know that it was springtime.

About halfway across the lake ("three or four miles") Jesus came near the boat "walking on the sea" (Jn 6:19). The Greek translation for "on the sea" could literally mean "on the seashore" or "by the sea," but the verification in

Mark 14:25 makes it clear that Jesus was really walking to them on the water. The disciples were afraid. Jesus said to them, "It is I. Do not be afraid." The translation of "It is I" is literally "I am." Jesus was again pointing to his divine identity by using this term. The "I am" statement also is a significant connection with the "Bread of Life" discourse (see the sub-subsection "Bread of Life Discourse" in Section 3 of this chapter) that follows in the Gospel and is an explanation of Jesus's multiplication of loaves miracle.

Sixth Sign: The Cure of the Man Born Blind (John 9:1–41)

What is the meaning of Jesus's statement to the Pharisees in John 9:41?

There is a wealth of characters mentioned in the sixth sign recorded by John, which is Jesus's cure of a man who was blind from birth. The miracle, recall, is offensive to the Pharisees and other Jewish leaders because it is performed on the Sabbath. The action of Jesus himself—using his own spit and kneading clay to put on the man's eyes—was work on the Sabbath that was in opposition to Jewish law. Jesus also told him to wash in the Pool of Siloam, a Jewish *mikveh* (see the sub-subsection "Third Sign: Cure on a Sabbath" earlier in this section). The Gospel account then goes on to describe other characters and tensions.

First, there are neighbors who recognize the man as a beggar whom they had seen earlier (see John 9:8). There is no rejoicing among them for the man's new eyesight. Instead they question him abruptly and then bring him to the Pharisees. The Pharisees hear the man recount his story of how Jesus healed him and are angry that this took place on the Sabbath. They also ask about Jesus: "How can a sinful man do such signs?" (Jn 9:16). The next characters are "the Jews" who did not believe that the man had really been born blind or regained his sight. This group questions the man's parents about whether or not their son was blind from birth. The Gospel says the parents "were afraid of the Jews," probably reflecting the experience of the time when the Gospel was written. Jews who confessed their belief in Jesus were being expelled from worshipping in the synagogue.

The blind man's physical cure brought growth in his own faith. Responding to the Pharisees' questions, he first referred to Jesus as "the man called Jesus" (Jn 9:11); then he called him a "prophet" (Jn 9:17); next he testified that he believed Jesus was the Son of Man, and he worshipped Jesus (see John 9:35–39). The message of his healing is that Jesus is the "light of the world," as he previously proclaimed in John 8:12. This miracle is evidence of that claim.

Some of the Pharisees, in contrast to the blind man, were people with physical sight but spiritual blindness. In this account, they called Jesus "a sinner" (Jn 9:24). This narrow interpretation of the Law blinded some Pharisees to God's presence in their midst. Jesus taught that spiritual blindness is worse than physical blindness (see John 9:41).

Seventh Sign: The Raising of Lazarus (John 11:1–44)

What caused Jesus to weep?

This is Jesus's greatest sign, the raising of a dead man to new life. Be assured that the Gospel takes pains to make sure that the readers understand that Lazarus was really dead and not just in a coma. This passage establishes

∞ Note

The Lazarus in this story is sometimes associated with the Lazarus of the parable of the rich man and Lazarus in Luke 16:19–31. However, there is no evidence to support this. In fact, it is possible that later editors of Luke's Gospel may have added the name Lazarus to the parable after John's Gospel was in circulation in order to connect the character in the parable with the man who had been raised from the dead.

Resurrection of Lazarus *by Mexican artist José Clemente Orozco.*

enough time from when Jesus heard the news that Lazarus was ill (see John 11:3) to the time he reaches the sisters of Lazarus,∞ Martha and Mary, in their home of Bethany. Jesus remained where he was for two days before he set off to Judea to answer their request. By the time he arrived, Lazarus had already been in the tomb for four days. This timeframe was such that Lazarus would have been declared dead by the rabbinic authorities. His soul would have left his body. Decay would have set in.

The raising of Lazarus is the longest continuous narrative in John's Gospel besides the Passion account. It not only prefigures Jesus's own Death and Resurrection; it is the cause of his Death. The ensuing session of the Sanhedrin (see John 11:45–54) occurred because some of the witnesses to the raising of Lazarus went to the Pharisees and told them what Jesus had done. Caiaphas, the high priest, commented, "It is better for you that one man should die instead of the people, so that the whole nation may not perish" (Jn 11:50). From that time on there was a plan in place to kill Jesus (see John 11:53).

The Gospels mention other "raisings from the dead" (see the sub-subsection "Raisings from the Dead" in Chapter 5, Section 3), but this occasion was the greatest show of Jesus's divinity. At the tomb of Lazarus, Jesus stated: "I am the resurrection and the life; whoever believes in me, even if he dies, will live, and everyone who lives and believes in me will never die" (Jn 11:25–26). When Jesus asked her if she believed this, Martha replied that she did believe that Jesus was the Messiah, the Son of God (see the feature "Faithful Disciple: St. Martha of Bethany" in the Chapter 6 Review).

The seventh sign sums up all the other signs and pulls together the important theological themes in the Gospel of John:

- Jesus is the way to life.
- He is the Resurrection.
- He is light of the world.
- He is God ("I AM").

For us, the lesson of all seven signs—and the seventh sign in particular—is that faith in Jesus is essential to gain eternal life in union with him, God the Father, and God the Holy Spirit.

SECTION *Assessment*

Comprehension

1. What was different about the signs in John's Gospel and the miracles in the synoptic Gospels?
2. What was a *mikveh*?

Reflection

3. Why might Jesus have wanted these signs to be public?
4. What might you name as a common theme for all seven signs?
5. Choose one of Jesus's signs and explain its meaning in your own words.

Section 3

JESUS PREACHES IN LONG DISCOURSES

A *discourse* is defined as "an extended expression of ideas." It can be given in written form, as in a doctoral discourse prepared by a graduate student being tested to receive a degree. A discourse can also be spoken orally. This was the style of discourse given by Socrates, the great philosopher. His discourses, often organized as debates, were later recorded in writing by his student, Plato. Jesus also taught in discourses; five of his discourses were recorded in the Gospel of Matthew (see, for example, the feature "Sermon on the Mount Sermon on the Plain" in Chapter 5, Section 3). However, most of Jesus's teachings in the synoptic Gospels can be broken up and viewed as short sayings. The Gospel of John includes extended discourses that do not have the same fragmented structure that can be identified with short sayings; rather, they are long speeches on specific topics, such as Jesus as the "Bread of Life" and Jesus as the "Good Shepherd." He also shares a series of discourses at the Last Supper—recorded in John 14–17—in which Jesus makes clearer his identity.

A question must be asked about how the evangelist was able to remember and record such long, extended speeches. John's Gospel, though composed later than the synoptic Gospels, was still from an era when eyewitnesses would have been alive who had heard Jesus speak. The oral tradition remained strong at this time. First-century Christians, especially those who grew up as Jews, were adept at remembering long oratories. Also, while written notes were not often taken at the time, they were not completely absent. For example, Quintilian, a famous Roman teacher of rhetoric of the same era, attested that the notes his students took of his lectures were fairly accurate. Some of his students even attempted to publish their notes of his lectures: "I appreciate their kindness," wrote Quintilian, "but they showed an excess of enthusiasm and a certain lack of discretion in doing my utterances the honor of publication."[5]

There is a possibility that there were at least partial notes summarizing Jesus's longer discourses that the evangelist was able to craft and include in the narrative of his Gospel.

Whether through the likely preservation of Jesus's words from the oral tradition or the less likely possible availability of written notes, it can be stated that John's Gospel provides an accurate portrait of Jesus's discourses that cover some main elements of his essential teachings.

Bread of Life Discourse (John 6:25–70)

The verses in John 6:25–40 transition Jesus to the shores of Capernaum where he gives a key address, first to the larger crowds who have followed him there, and eventually moving inside a synagogue where he explains the meaning of his words to a smaller group of disciples. The actual discourse, in John 6:35–59, forms essential and irrefutable evidence of a key Catholic teaching on the **Real Presence**: that Jesus is the "bread of life" and that his Body replaces the manna from the Exodus that must be consumed in order to gain eternal life.

In the main discourse, Jesus repeats six times "I am the bread of life" and adds: "Amen, amen, I say to you, unless you eat the flesh of the Son of Man and drink his blood, you do not have life within you. Whoever eats my flesh and drinks my blood has eternal life, and I will raise him on

---

Real Presence The doctrine that Jesus Christ is truly present in his Body and Blood under the form of bread and wine in the Eucharist. The Bible is clear in declaring this teaching (e.g., 1 Corinthians 10:16-17; 11:23-29; and most definitively in John 6:32-71).

the last day" (Jn 6:53–54). We have the advantage of reading these words in light of the Eucharist, knowing that no one would actually consume Christ in the form of human flesh or blood, but instead under the forms of bread and wine. Nevertheless, from the earliest disciples to the present, many have often failed to acknowledge the clarity of Jesus's words, which command his disciples to "eat and drink" of his flesh and blood. Disciples who followed Jesus into the Capernaum synagogue said: "This saying is hard; who can accept it?" (Jn 6:60). As a result of his words, "many [of] his disciples returned to their former way of life and no longer accompanied him" (Jn 6:66).

The setting for the Bread of Life discourse was not the Last Supper; that fact has been used by Protestants, including Martin Luther, as evidence that Jesus did not intend for his words to mean that his Body and Blood would be *real* food and *real* drink. But this argument has been dismissed because the author of the Gospel, writing years after the synoptic Gospels, was, according to St. Clement of Alexandria, well aware of the synoptic Gospel accounts of Jesus's blessing of the bread and wine at the Last Supper. Jesus's words in this discourse fit in tandem with his words at the Last Supper that were recorded in Matthew, Mark, and Luke. Early Church Fathers, including St. Ignatius of Antioch and St. Justin Martyr, both wrote in support of the doctrine of the Real Presence, using vocabulary similar to that which is used in John's Gospel:

> Take note of those . . . [who] abstain from the Eucharist and from prayer, because they do not confess that the Eucharist is the Flesh of our Savior Jesus Christ. Flesh which suffered for our sins and which the Father, in his goodness raised up again. (Ignatius, *Letter to the Smyrnaeans*)

> We call this food Eucharist; and no one is permitted to partake of it, except one who believes our teaching to be true. . . . The food which has been made into the Eucharist . . . is both the flesh and the blood of that incarnated Jesus. (Justin Martyr, *First Apology*)

Though Jesus's shocking teaching about his Body and Blood did cause some to abandon him, Peter and the Apostles continued to trust him: "Master, to whom shall we go? You have the words of eternal life. We have come to believe and are convinced that you are the Holy One of God" (Jn 5:65–69).

Good Shepherd Discourse (John 10:1–21)

Jesus's discourse about the Good Shepherd continues some of the themes found in John 9 about the man born blind. This appears to be the parallel he is drawing:

- Jesus *is* the Good Shepherd.
- The sheep are the Jewish people who hear Jesus's voice (like the blind man).
- The strangers or hired hands are the Pharisees (as in the story of the blind man).
- Other sheep that do not belong to this fold are possibly the Gentiles or future disciples.

Jesus suggested that the Jewish people who, like the blind man, recognize him by his voice and follow him are like sheep following their shepherd. He then identified himself as the gate for the sheep. In some societies, a sheepfold would not have a gate, because the shepherd would sleep across the fence opening at night to defend the sheep against enemies with his body. In this role, a shepherd might easily have to sacrifice his life trying to protect his herd. Jesus contrasted the role of the Good Shepherd with someone who is simply hired to guard the sheep, a person who will not risk his life for them.

The "other sheep" (Jn 10:16) may refer to Gentiles, followers in the future, or possibly other groups of Christians. Notice that Jesus emphasized that he gives up his life freely, an important truth in the synoptic Gospels as well. The crowd had a mixed response to Jesus's discourse, though most of it was negative. Some thought that Jesus was possessed. Others thought that he had committed blasphemy. Some tried to stone him and arrest him.

This discourse is set at the Feast of the Dedication of the Temple. This is interesting because this isn't one of the three major feasts that Jews are required to attend. By delivering this speech at the Temple, Jesus shows his willingness to preach openly in public. Previously, in John 7:25–31, residents of Jerusalem had wondered that perhaps because Jesus was speaking openly in the Temple area without the authorities arresting him, those same authorities might have "realized that he is the Messiah" (Jn 7:26). Eventually, at that time, the authorities did try to arrest him, but "no one laid a hand upon him, because his hour had not yet come" (Jn 7:30). However, after his Good Shepherd discourse, some did pick up rocks to stone him (see John 10:31). By this point, the hour of his Passion was approaching rapidly.

Last Supper Discourses (John 13:31–17:26)

John wove sayings that Jesus spoke at the Last Supper (and likely on other occasions too) into two farewell discourses and a prayer placed right before the Passion narrative of his Gospel. John 13:31–38 is an introduction to the Last Supper discourses. In these opening eight verses, Jesus predicts that he will be with his disciples for only a short time going forward. He also gives them a "new commandment" to "love one another" (Jn 13:34). The commandment itself is not new; it was stated previously in Leviticus 19:18: "You shall love your neighbor as yourself. I am the Lord." But by restating the commandment, Jesus again clearly puts himself on par with YHWH. Chapter 13 concludes with Jesus predicting Peter's denial of him.

In the discourse in John 14:1–31, Jesus speaks of both his departure from his disciples and his return. John places the same words of Jesus in verses 14 and 27 to break up the text: "Do not let your hearts be troubled." Jesus

---

Paraclete A name for the Holy Spirit that means "Advocate." In John 14:26, Jesus promised to send a helper who would continue to guide, lead, and strengthen the disciples.

encourages his followers to stay close to him. He tells them that he is "the way and the truth and the life" (Jn 14:6). Later in the discourse, he promises that he will "ask the Father, and he will give you another Advocate to be with you always" (Jn 14:16). This **Paraclete**, or Holy Spirit, will be the judge of truth after Jesus leaves. John 16:4b–33 is a paraphrase of the first Last Supper discourse, containing the same message about Jesus's departure and return.

The Last Supper *by Vladimir Odinokow.*

The longest of the Last Supper discourses is recorded in John 15:1–16:4. It fits the definition of a monologue as Jesus shifts focus from what will occur in the future to speak about his union with the disciples in the present. In John 15:1–17, Jesus uses a vine and branches to illustrate how necessary it is for his followers to remain attached to him. In fact, this description resembles a parable; Israel is also spoken of as a vineyard in Isaiah 5:1–7. Remember, John's account of the Last Supper does not include Jesus's institution of the Eucharist in the blessing of the bread and wine. However, Jesus's connection of himself with the "true vine" (Jn 15:1) does contain Eucharistic symbolism.

The Last Supper ends with the *High Priestly Prayer* of Jesus. It is called that because Jesus prayed these words directly to his Father on behalf of his people, just as the Jewish high priest prayed in the Temple on behalf of the Jewish people. Jesus asks the Father to protect his people and bring them to be with him. The High Priestly Prayer marked a transition in the way that the disciples related to Jesus. Up to this point, they had followed him in the physical world, but through the words of this prayer, Jesus spoke about connecting with him and the Father in a spiritual way. He also extended the prayer to include people in the future who would believe in him through the word of the disciples "so that they may all be one, as you Father, are in me, and I in you, that they also may be in us, that the world may believe that you sent me" (Jn 17:21).

SECTION *Assessment*

Comprehension

1. How are Jesus's discourses in John's Gospel different from those in the synoptic Gospels?
2. How might the evangelist have been able to remember and record long discourses?
3. Why did so many of Jesus's followers leave him after the Bread of Life discourse?
4. What are the parallel meanings of Jesus, sheep, strangers, and other sheep in the Good Shepherd Discourse?

5. What is the subject of Jesus's longest discourse in John's Gospel?
6. Why is Jesus's prayer at the Last Supper called the "High Priestly Prayer"?

Vocabulary

7. What is a Protestant argument for not allowing the Bread of Life discourse to be evidence for the doctrine of the *Real Presence*? What is the response of the Church Fathers?

Reflection

8. Explain in your own words how Jesus is the Good Shepherd.

Section 4

HOW JOHN PRESENTS JESUS'S PASSION, DEATH, AND RESURRECTION

The Passion, Death, and Resurrection of Jesus are consistent with the evangelist's overall presentation of Christology in which he focuses on Jesus's heavenly origins and divinity (see the subsection "Christology in John's Gospel" in Section 1 of this chapter.). This is sometimes called "Christology from above" or "descending Christology." Whereas the synoptic Gospels stress the humanity of Jesus, the divinity of Jesus ("descending from above") shines forth in almost every verse of John's Gospel from beginning to end. In John's Passion, Death, and Resurrection accounts, Jesus—not his accusers, judge, or executioners—continues to drive all of the action by completing the will of his Father.

The discourses of Jesus in John 13–17 serve as the prologue to the traditional narratives of the Passion, Death, and Resurrection in John 18–20. In the Resurrection account, Jesus reveals his glory and confesses the need for his disciples to give testimony that he is risen from the dead.

Jesus Remains in Control through His Passion and Death

After praying the High Priestly Prayer, the Gospel says that Jesus "went out across the Kidron valley to where there was a garden, into which he and his disciples entered" (Jn 18:1). There is no mention of his going off to pray with Peter, James, and John or that Jesus was anguished while in the garden. The Gospel only uses the garden as the setting for Jesus's arrest. When Judas and a band of soldiers appear, Jesus remains in control as he is apprehended. The soldiers turn away from him and fall to the ground when he identifies himself as "I am" (YHWH), similar to the way someone would prostrate themselves before a human king (see John 18:6). After Peter comes to Jesus's defense by attacking one of the servants of the high priest, Jesus admonishes Peter: "Put

A view of the Mount of Olives from the Kidron Valley.

your sword into its scabbard. Shall I not drink the cup that the Father gave me?" (Jn 18:11).

Only in John's Gospel is Jesus interrogated by Annas, the father-in-law of Caiaphas, the high priest. This interrogation by Annas is likely not the same trial as the one with Caiaphas mentioned in the synoptic Gospels, because it occurs at night right after Jesus was arrested. (We know it is nighttime from John 18:3, which details that the soldiers came with "lanterns and torches.") A meeting with Caiaphas does follow, but it is not described; we, as readers, are left to infer that the meeting with Caiaphas went poorly because Jesus is bound and brought before Pilate.

During his meeting with Pilate, Jesus remains in control. Jesus and Pilate converse about his royal identity, the meaning of truth, and the source of Pilate's power. Pilate says that he cannot find Jesus guilty and gives responsibility for his Death to the Jewish crowd, appealing to the custom of releasing one prisoner to the people. The people choose Barabbas, a revolutionary. The crowd cries that they oppose any king but Caesar and that they want Jesus crucified. Ironically, the Jewish crowd acclaims, "We have no king but Caesar" (Jn 19:15).

Jesus carries his own Cross to Golgotha. John does not mention Simon, the Cyrenian, being called to help him. Again, this fits with John's focus on Jesus's divinity. Why would there be need for another person to help the Son of God fulfill his mission of doing his Father's will?

Jesus's mother, Mary, is there to witness her Son's crucifixion, just as she had been present at his first sign at Cana. From the Cross, Jesus addresses her the same way he did at the wedding at Cana, calling her "woman" and telling her to "behold her son," the beloved disciple who is nearby. Recall that Jesus had told his mother at Cana that "my hour has not yet come" (Jn 2:4). The hour has now certainly arrived.

When he is aware that "everything was now finished, in order that Scripture might be fulfilled," Jesus says, "I thirst" (Jn 19:28). He is given common wine (not drugged wine) on a sprig of hyssop, a loose evergreen plant that would have likely folded over and not been effective in being a receptacle for the wine. There was symbolic meaning, if not practicality. Hyssop was used to dab the blood of the paschal lamb on the doorposts of the Hebrew slaves as they left Egypt (see Exodus 12:22).

The hyssop plant would not have been effective in absorbing the wine given to Jesus.

John's Gospel also highlights the Old Testament prophecies concerning the crucifixion. Jesus is the persecuted "just man" of Psalms 22 and 69, and the soldiers gamble for his seamless tunic (see Psalm 22:18). Treating Jesus like the Paschal Lamb of Exodus 12:46, the soldiers do not break his legs. Finally, Jesus's last words on the Cross are unique to John's Gospel: "It is finished." It is he, not his executioners, who decided when he would die. The Gospel continues sharing that "bowing his head, he handed over his spirit" (Jn 19:30). Jesus had previously referred to the "Spirit that those who came to believe in him were to receive," but was not yet present "because [he] had not been glorified" (Jn 7:39). Also, when he appears to his disciples after he had risen from the dead, Jesus breathes on them and says to them, "Receive the holy spirit" (Jn 20:22). The Gospel has reached its penultimate scene.

Jesus's Resurrection (John 20–21)

The Resurrection is the central event of human salvation and an indication of the glory of the Father and the Son. In John's Gospel, Jesus appears first to a woman, Mary Magdalene, who stays at the tomb, weeping. At first, she does not recognize the transformed, glorified Lord (she thought he was a gardener), but when he calls her by name, Mary knows it is the Lord. Mary Magdalene runs to Simon Peter and the beloved disciple. Unlike in the synoptic Gospels, she does this on her own; no angel or young man directs her. John 20:3 indicates that both Peter and the beloved disciple go to the tomb to verify what Mary had told them. This is different from Luke 24:12, which only reports that Peter went to the tomb. However, the disciples on the way to Emmaus in Luke 24:24 say that "some" of the disciples did go to the empty tomb.

Jesus also appears to the Apostles in a locked room. The Risen Jesus, not bound by the laws of ordinary physics, suddenly is in their midst. The Apostles "rejoiced when they saw the Lord" (Jn 20:20). The Lord wishes them peace and commissions them to continue his work. This is the occasion that he breathed on them, signifying the descent of the Holy Spirit, and he instructs them to forgive sins in his name.

The Risen Jesus's next appearance came eight days later, to Thomas the Apostle, who was absent when Jesus first appeared to the others. Thomas acknowledges Jesus's divinity, saying, "My Lord and my God!" (Jn 20:28). In answer to Thomas, Jesus blesses all people who believe without seeing him. This, of course, includes believers living today.

Biblical scholars believe that John's Gospel originally ended with chapter 20. Chapter 21 is written similarly to Luke's Greek style (see, for example, the call of Simon in Luke 5:1–11), though it has several parallels to other parts of John's Gospel as well. It is possible that chapter 21 was originally preserved by other members of John's community apart from the rest of the Gospel and then added later. Chapter 21 *was* included in the Gospel by the time the canon of the Bible was established. It is in this chapter that Jesus elicits from Peter a threefold promise of his love (see John 21:15–19 and the sub-subsection "Jesus Questions Simon Peter" in Chapter 4, Section 4).

SECTION *Assessment*

Comprehension

1. What is meant by "descending Christology" or "Christology from above"?
2. Explain how John carried the focus on Jesus's divinity into his Passion narrative.
3. How do we know that Jesus's arrest took place at night?

4. Who was Annas?
5. Who was the first person to look into the empty tomb in John's Gospel?
6. Why do biblical scholars believe that John 21 may have been added to the Gospel at a later date?

Reflection

7. With whom among the following characters mentioned in the Passion and Resurrection narratives in John's Gospel do you most identify: Pilate, Peter, John, Mary Magdalene, Mary the mother of Jesus, or Thomas? Explain why.

Section Reviews

Focus Question

In what ways is the Gospel of John different from the synoptic Gospels?

Complete one of the following:

- Read the "I am" titles Jesus uses for himself (see the introduction to this chapter). Write a prayer to Jesus using your favorite title.
- Write a short report on how the image of light is used in the Gospel of John. Refer to at least two of the following passages from John: 3:19–21; 8:12; 11:9–10; 12:35–36, 46.
- Answer this question in writing: Does the fact that John's Gospel contrasts dramatically with the synoptic Gospels diminish or increase the believability of its content for you? Explain your answer.

Introduction

The Uniqueness of the Fourth Gospel

Review Points

- John's Gospel is organized into two books, the Book of Signs and the Book of Glory. The Book of Signs contains seven miracles, which John describes either as "signs" or "works" rather than acts of power as in the synoptic Gospels. The Book of Glory is made up of the Passion and Resurrection narratives.
- John's Gospel is poetic in nature. Some of the implied metaphors that Jesus uses for himself ("I am") help us to a deeper understanding of Christology and to appreciate Jesus's relationship with God the Father.

Assignment

Illustrate with an example how you understand the different emphases of Christology between John's Gospel and the synoptic Gospels.

Section 1
Formation of John's Gospel

Review Points

- The fourth Gospel is attributed to John, the "beloved disciple" of Jesus. However, the Gospel may have been written in several stages with John providing its foundation. It is certain that an eyewitness to Jesus and his ministry is connected to the Gospel's authorship.
- The prologue of the Gospel serves as an introduction to the major themes of the entire Gospel, including the Incarnation and ways to understand Christology.
- To describe the Gospel of John as *mystical* highlights both that God is mystery and that God's plan of salvation is fulfilled in Jesus Christ.

Assignment

Ephesus, in modern-day Turkey, includes tours of sites connected with St. John the Apostle. Look up tours in Ephesus to find out what you could learn about St. John if you went there. Report on your findings.

Section 2
What Do the Seven Signs in the Gospel of John Reveal about Jesus?

Review Points

- The seven miracles in the Book of Signs are meant to bring people to faith. Oppositely, in the synoptic Gospels faith was a prerequisite for Jesus to be able to perform miracles.
- The seven signs in John's Gospel reveal Jesus's identity, his reason for coming into the world, his heavenly glory, and his relationship to the Father.
- Jesus's raising of Lazarus from the dead was his final and greatest sign. It prefigured his own Death and Resurrection, and his performance of this miracle led to him being arrested, charged, and put to death.

Assignment

In the first sign, Jesus changed the water in six large jars into wine. The jars were used for washing, and each contained about twenty-five gallons of water. Suppose a cup held four ounces of wine, and each wedding guest had one cup of wine. How many people could toast the bride and groom at this wedding?

Section 3
Jesus Preaches in Long Discourses

Review Points

- John's Gospel includes extended speeches of Jesus, called discourses. These are different than discourses in the synoptic Gospels because they are not simply short sayings that are gathered in one place. The discourses in John's Gospel are focused on specific topics (e.g., Jesus as the Bread of Life or the Good Shepherd).
- The Last Supper discourses, which preface the Passion, Death, and Resurrection accounts, change Jesus's focus on what will occur to him in the future to his present relationship with his disciples. The Last Supper discourses end with the High Priestly Prayer of Jesus.

Assignment

Read John 15:13–14. Answer these questions in writing: What are some demands of being a good friend? How do friends figuratively and literally lay down their lives for one another? What does it mean to you to be a friend of Jesus?

Section 4
How John Presents Jesus's Passion, Death, and Resurrection

Review Points

- Reflecting a Christology that focuses on Jesus's heavenly origins and divinity, in John's Gospel Jesus remains in control of the events surrounding his Passion and Death. The Passion narratives also highlight the fulfillment of Old Testament prophecies concerning the crucifixion of Jesus.

- There are some differences between the Resurrection account in the Gospel of John and those in the synoptic Gospels. For example, in John's Gospel, both Peter *and* John run to the tomb.

Assignment

"Blessed are those who have not seen and have believed" (Jn 20:29). These words of Jesus are directed at you. What does Jesus's Resurrection mean to you?

Chapter Projects

Choose and complete at least one of the following projects to assess your understanding of the material in this chapter.

1. Create a Notebook of Chinese Catholic Art

Arising from a 1925 major art exhibition to highlight the variety of culture and artistry in the Catholic Church organized by Pope Pius XI, the Vatican Museums now have approximately five thousand items from China from a wide variety of eras. These include items in Catholic art, Buddhist art, and secular art. Research and copy images of the following pieces of Chinese Catholic art into a digital or paper notebook. Write a brief review of each piece including the name of the painting, name of the artist, year created, type of media used, and subject of the painting.

- *Landscape* by Huang Junbi
- *The Virgin and Child* by Chen Yuanda
- *The Flight into Egypt* by Ren Yifang
- One other Chinese Catholic painting of your choice

Below each entry, write your own impression of the painting (e.g., what you like or don't like about it). Include any other interesting facts about the painting or artist you discover in your research.

2. Collate Similarities and Differences among the Four Resurrection Accounts

Make a table similar to the one below. Answer each question according to information in the Gospels. Include Scripture references with each answer. Add to the table at least two more questions of your own about the Resurrection that can be answered from the Gospels. Fill in those details as well.

	MATTHEW	MARK	LUKE	JOHN
When did the Resurrection take place?				
Who discovered the empty tomb?				
Who was at the empty tomb?				
Who went inside the empty tomb?				
To whom did the Risen Jesus appear?				

3. Respond to the Athanasian Creed

Copy into an electronic document the Athanasian Creed (see the feature "Prayer" later in this Chapter Review), a statement of beliefs with origins from the fourth or fifth century. The Athanasian Creed is usually divided into two sections: the first twenty-eight verses have to do with the doctrine of the Trinity; verses 29–44 focus on Christology.

Use the review feature of your electronic document to add at least ten comments to the text of the creed. Your comments should include things such as (but not limited to) background on the history of the Creed, background on the heresies it addressed, its uses in Church history, further information on the doctrines it lists, questions you have about certain verses, and reflections you have on its teachings.

In the document, choose a bold color to highlight what you consider to be three important teachings. In the comment section near the highlighted verses, explain why you think they are important.

4. Illustrate One of the "I Am" Metaphors

Review the "I am" metaphors Jesus uses to describe himself in the introduction to this chapter. Illustrate one of the metaphors of your choice in a drawing, using a medium of your choice. One option is to create a stained-glass window scene. Stained glass is composed of pieces of colored glass held together by lead, arranged to create a window. You might also use black construction paper and colored tissue paper to illustrate the metaphor either literally or symbolically. Write a short reflection about why you chose the metaphor that you did.

5. Reflect on the Seven Signs of Jesus

Listed are Scripture verses from the seven signs of Jesus in the Gospel of John. Print each verse in a journal or notebook that you will hand in to your teacher. After each verse, write your reflection using the prompts that are included with each.

- "Do whatever he tells you" (Jn 2:5).
  Reflect on Mary's confidence in Jesus. Write about your own trust and confidence in Jesus and Mary.
- "Unless you people see signs and wonders, you will not believe" (Jn 4:48).
  Reflect on your need to see in order to believe.
- "Do you want to be well?" (Jn 5:6).
  Reflect on how healing from a physical, emotional, or spiritual wound is often painful.
- "Gather the fragments left over, so that nothing will be wasted" (Jn 6:12).
  Reflect on your and society's natural tendency toward wastefulness and extravagance.
- "It is I. Do not be afraid" (Jn 6:20).
  Reflect on your own fears and how Jesus can quell them.

- "We have to do the works of the one who sent me while it is day. Night is coming when no one can work" (Jn 9:4).
  Reflect on the powers of evil at work in the world.
- "And Jesus wept" (Jn 11:35).
  Reflect on how you are able to express what you feel to others.

Faithful Disciple
St. Martha of Bethany

St. Martha of Bethany, the sister of Mary and Lazarus, appears three times in the Gospels in visits by Jesus. She is known as the meticulous "busy bee" of the siblings, who was "burdened by much of the serving" while her sister sat beside Jesus at his feet listening to him speak. Jesus said to her, "Martha, Martha, you are worried about many things. There is need of only one thing. Mary has the chosen the better part, and it will not be taken from her" (see Luke 10:38–42).

In fact, it was remarkable for a woman to sit at a man's feet in Judaism in the first century, representing Jesus's welcoming attitude toward women. Jesus's words to Martha were encouragement for her to take advantage of *his* hospitality while she was busy trying to offer the same to him.

In John's Gospel, Martha is present when Jesus raises her brother Lazarus from the dead. When Jesus asks her to proclaim her faith in him and what he can do, Martha responds with a strong statement: "Yes, Lord. I have come to believe that you are the Messiah, the Son of God, the one who is coming into the world" (Jn 11:27).

Jesus must have enjoyed going to the home of Martha, Mary, and Lazarus at Bethany, a small village about a mile and a half from Jerusalem. Today,

Bethany is a Palestinian city in the Jerusalem-governed West Bank with a population of more than twenty-two thousand residents, and it goes by the Arabic name of Al-Eizariya, which means "place of Lazarus." Both Christians and Muslims designated a site in the city that they name as the location of Lazarus's tomb, though historically that is not certain. In any case a sanctuary is constructed on top of the tomb, built upon the remains of structures left from the Byzantines and Christian crusaders. This is also believed to be the house of Martha.

What happened to Martha and her siblings after the Death and Resurrection of Jesus? According to legend, they moved to Provence, a city in southeastern France near the current Italian border and the Mediterranean Sea. A further legend is that Martha slayed "La Tarasque," the half-animal, half-fish, man-eating dragon with horns and the tail of a serpent that reportedly traveled by sea from Asia. Armed with a cross and holy water, Martha disposed of the dragon in the nearby Rhone Valley. She is still honored by people of that region today.

A silver pendant molded to represent the monstrous beast La Tarasque.

St. Martha's feast day is July 20. Because of her hospitality and how she took care of Jesus and the poor, she is the patroness of housewives, waiters, waitresses, and cooks.

Comprehension

1. What was unique about Martha's sister, Mary, sitting at the feet of Jesus?
2. What was Jesus's advice to Martha when she complained about her sister?
3. What is Martha's faith statement that she proclaimed about Jesus?
4. What is Bethany like today?
5. How did Martha slay the man-eating dragon?

Reflection

Are you more like Martha or Mary? Is one role better than the other? Explain.

Prayer

St. Athanasius (ca. 296–373), the bishop of Alexandria, was a defender of the Church against Arianism, a fourth-century heresy that denied the divinity of Jesus. In his treatise *On the Incarnation*, Athanasius firmly taught that Christ was "made man that we may be divine" and that if Christ were only a man, and not God, it would be impossible for him to be our Savior. The Athanasian Creed likewise is a statement of beliefs in support of Christ's divinity. Even though it has his name attached, however, St. Athanasius was not the creed's author. Its author is unknown. The Athanasian Creed uses the same terminology as St. Augustine's *On the Trinity*, which was published in the early fifth century. The Athanasian Creed has not been used in the Church's Roman Rite since the introduction of the post–Second Vatican Council liturgical books. It is still found in the Anglican *Book of Common Prayer* and some Lutheran prayer books.

Athanasian Creed

Now the Catholic faith is that we worship One God in Trinity and Trinity in Unity, neither confounding the Persons nor dividing the substance. For there is one Person of the Father, another of the Son, another of the Holy Spirit. But the Godhead of the Father, of the Son, and of the Holy Spirit, is One, the Glory equal, the Majesty coeternal.

Such as the Father is, such is the Son, and such is the Holy Spirit; the Father uncreated, the Son uncreated, and the Holy Spirit uncreated; the Father infinite, the Son infinite, and the Holy Spirit infinite; the Father eternal, the Son eternal, and the Holy Spirit eternal. And yet not three eternals but one eternal, as also not three infinites, nor three uncreated, but one uncreated, and one infinite. So, likewise, the Father is almighty, the Son almighty, and the Holy Spirit almighty; and yet not three almighties but one almighty.

So the Father is God, the Son God, and the Holy Spirit God; and yet not three Gods but one God. So the Father is Lord, the Son Lord, and the Holy Spirit Lord; and yet not three Lords but one Lord. For like as we are compelled by Christian truth to acknowledge every Person by Himself to be both God and Lord; so are we forbidden by the catholic religion to say, there be three Gods or three Lords.

The Father is made of none, neither created nor begotten. The Son is of the Father alone, not made nor created but begotten. The Holy Spirit is of the Father and the Son, not made nor created nor begotten but proceeding. So there is one Father not three Fathers, one Son not three Sons, and one Holy Spirit not three Holy Spirits. And in this Trinity there is nothing before or after, nothing greater or less, but the whole three Persons are coeternal together and coequal.

So that in all things, as is aforesaid, the Trinity in Unity and the Unity in Trinity is to be worshipped. He therefore who wills to be in a state of salvation, let him think thus of the Trinity.

Amen.

The Bible Shares Christ's Mission as Priest, Prophet, and King

The Meeting of Abraham and Melchizedek

➤ *Peter Paul Rubens*

The large figures of Melchizedek and Abraham at the center of the painting symbolize the mystical unity between the Old Testament and the New Testament. *The Meeting of Abraham and Melchizedek* was commissioned in 1625 by Archduchess Isabel Clara Eugenia of the Spanish Netherlands as part of a tapestry series called *The Triumph of the Eucharist* that she wished to give to the Poor Clare nuns of Madrid, Spain. The entire series is a mixture of allegory and advertisement to promote the worship of the Eucharist, which had recently been reemphasized by the Council of Trent as a way to counteract attacks from the Protestant Reformation. As priest, Melchizedek stands a bit above Abraham, just as a Catholic priest might do when saying Mass. Young boys pass out the bread to soldiers, taking up the role of acolytes.

The painting's creator, Flemish artist Peter Paul Rubens (1577–1640), was a well-respected Baroque painter of the seventeenth century, and he also served as a diplomat for the queen and as a court painter for the palace. Rubens recognized the role art had in the Catholic Reformation to be an evangelizing and catechetical agent for the Church. Over his lifetime, Rubens completed over three thousand paintings, woodcuts, and engravings of all kinds. He died in 1640.

Rubens's *The Meeting of Abraham and Melchizedek* is a high-fashioned *modello*, or sketch, meant to prefigure the Eucharist. In the scene Melchizedek the priest and king of Salem (see Chapter 7, Section 1, "Christ Is the New High Priest") offers the gift of bread and wine to Abraham, who gratefully receives the gifts while suited in armor and standing before a group of soldiers. The whole painting is framed between columns and seems to be on a tapestry that is held up by three cherubs.

The series and *The Meeting of Abraham and Melchizedek* itself still hang today at the Descalzas Reales Convent in Madrid.

Focus Question

How are titles and images for Christ linked between the Old Testament and New Testament?

Chapter Overview

Introduction
Christ Is the One Word of Scripture

Section 1
Christ Is the New High Priest

Section 2
Christ Is Prophet

Section 3
Christ Is King

Section 4
Christ Is the Alpha and the Omega

Introduction

CHRIST IS THE ONE WORD OF SCRIPTURE

Though made up of various books and composed over hundreds of years, the Bible clearly shows that God revealed himself to humanity in stages. He spoke to Adam and Eve and made a covenant with them that he would send a Redeemer who would defeat sin and death (recall the Protoevangelium in Genesis 3:15). In the following stages, God spoke to Noah, to Abraham and the patriarchs, and to Moses and made an everlasting covenant with the people of Israel in preparation for fulfilling his promise. All of salvation history leads up to the moment when Christ came into the world as true God and true man. Jesus Christ is the single Word who permeates both the Old Testament and New Testament, every book of the Bible, every chapter, and, in fact, every verse. St. Augustine wrote: "You recall that one and the same Word of God extends throughout Scripture, that it is one and the same Utterance that resounds in the mouths of all the sacred writers, since he who was in the beginning has not need of separate syllables; for he is not subject to time."[1] The *Catechism of the Catholic Church* echoes the words of St. Augustine that "through all the words of Sacred Scripture, God speaks only one single Word, his one Utterance in whom he expresses himself completely" (*CCC*, 102).

Understanding the Threefold Identity and Mission of Christ

The Old Testament is "deliberately so oriented that it should prepare for and declare in prophecy the coming of Christ, redeemer of all" (*Dei Verbum*, 15). Because the Old Covenant has never been revoked, but instead fulfilled in the coming of Christ, it remains essential for Christians to understand its place in both forming and fulfilling the identity and mission of Jesus, so as to better

understand how we, as Christians, are to be formed in him and to serve him by our lives.

Christ's threefold identity and mission as priest, prophet, and king is one that has roots in the Old Testament and was manifested in his life and explained in the New Testament: "Jesus Christ is the one whom the Father anointed with the Holy Spirit and established as priest, prophet, and king. The whole People of God participates in these three offices of Christ and bears the responsibilities for mission and service that flow from them" (*CCC*, 783). As part of the Sacrament of Baptism, the baptized person is brought into the threefold mission of Christ as priest (participating in the Church's worship), prophet (proclaiming God's Word), and king (humbly serving others in Christ's name). It is remarkable to consider that this commissioning is part of our ancestry with the Chosen People of the Old Testament and made possible through Christ's own life, which is described in the New Testament. This chapter explores the history and meaning of these titles from the Bible and how we practice them after Baptism.

The last book of the Bible—the Book of Revelation—refers to Jesus as "the Alpha and the Omega, the one who is and who was and who is to come, the almighty" (Rv 1:8). These first and last letters of the Greek alphabet represent the timelessness of Jesus, though not completely. Remember, Jesus was "begotten not made" and has always existed with the Father before all ages. This reference is meant to indicate not that he has a beginning and end but that he has always existed and will continue to exist for all time. Jesus Christ is the one Word of Scripture. He is the one Word for eternity.

SECTION *Assessment*

Comprehension

1. What are the stages of God's Revelation in the Bible?
2. How do baptized Christians participate in Jesus's mission as priest, prophet, and king?
3. What does the reference to Jesus as "the Alpha and the Omega" represent?
4. How is it a misinterpretation to take "the Alpha and Omega" reference to Jesus to mean that he had a beginning or end?

Reflection

5. How do you understand Jesus as the "one single Word" of Scripture?

Section 1

CHRIST IS THE NEW HIGH PRIEST

Your understanding of priesthood most likely comes from your experience of ordained Catholic priests. These are men you know from presiding at Mass as well as ministering at other sacraments (e.g., Baptism, Penance, Anointing of the Sick). Certainly there is a connection between the priesthood of the Old Testament and the priesthood of Christ referenced in the New Testament, though the connection must be explained. Worship and sacrifice are two elements of priesthood that have remained constant.

In the Old Testament, there are different types of priesthood, though they have one thing in common: each was related to membership in the Israelite tribe or family of Levi. We think of a Catholic priest today being personally called by God to his vocation. For Israelites, to be a priest typically meant being born into that role. The Levitical priesthood was dedicated to the service of offering Temple sacrifice of animals in atonement for sins. Levitical priests also ministered to the members of the other Jewish tribes with efforts of consolation and charity as needed. The high priest likewise came from the tribe of Levi. Moses and his brother Aaron were both Levities. Around the eighth century BC, especially in Jerusalem, a strand of the Levitical priesthood developed around the ancestors of Aaron. These so-called Aaronite priests were mainly responsible for the Temple sacrifices, though they were still considered part of the Levitical priesthood.

Jesus's ancestry did not trace to the tribe of Levi. Through Joseph, Jesus was a descendant of the tribe of Judah. How then does Jesus's own priesthood have roots in the Old Testament? The priesthood of Jesus described in the New Testament has its origins from Melchizedek, "king of Salem" (Gn 14:18). *Salem*, a word that means "peace," is thought to have been Jerusalem, though the kingdom itself was likely symbolic. More certain is that Melchizedek was a Canaanite who brought gifts of bread and wine to Abraham after Abraham had defeated three other Canaanite kings. Abraham and his family would have understood bread and wine not as a pagan offering but as the typical gifts Hebrews offered to the one, true God. Though he was technically a pagan, Melchizedek brought these gifts in the name of the "God Most High" (Gn 14:19).

Melchizedek is connected further with Jesus in a prophetic passage in Psalm 110 in which the kingship of the Messiah is paired with his priesthood: "You are a priest forever in the manner of Melchizedek" (Ps 110:4). The psalm goes on to show how the role of the king is to perform priestly functions. The Letter to the Hebrews expands on the connection between Jesus and Melchizedek.

The Sacrificial Priesthood of Christ

The Letter to the Hebrews makes several comparisons between the Levitical priesthood and the priesthood of Melchizedek, which prefigured the priesthood of Christ. In summary,

Melchizedek

- Neither Melchizedek's nor Jesus's priesthood is based on heredity (as was the Levitical priesthood). Melchizedek was a priest of the unique order created by God for a very special purpose—namely, to foreshadow the priesthood of Jesus, the Son of God
- Abraham, who was the ancestor of the Levi tribe and the Levitical priesthood, recognized Melchizedek by receiving his blessing and giving him tithes. This act of humility showed that the Levitical priesthood would eventually be replaced by a greater priesthood, the royal priesthood of Christ. St. Thomas Aquinas wrote that "it was precisely this pre-eminence of Christ's priesthood in relation to that of the Levites which was foreshadowed by the priesthood of Melchizedek."[2]

- Not being a member of the Chosen People, Melchizedek previewed Jesus's outreach to all people, Jews and Gentiles.
- Melchizedek's offering of bread and wine in thanksgiving to God prefigured what Jesus did at the Last Supper and what occurs at Mass.
- Melchizedek was not a priest of the Old Covenant; "to that same degree has Jesus [also] become the guarantee of an [even] better covenant" (Heb 7:22).

In a reflection on Psalm 110, Pope Benedict XVI pointed out how "royal and priestly power converge in the figure of Melchizedek."[3] The Letter to the Hebrews presents Christ as the High Priest who willingly offered the sacrifice of his life to redeem us from our sins. The sacrificial priesthood of Melchizedek, which Christ emulated and expanded on, was one that did not use animals but instead bread and wine like Melchizedek brought to Abraham. Jesus achieved, once and for all, in the true heavenly Temple where God was present, the reconciliation between humanity and God that the yearly repeated sacrifices with animals in the humanly created Jerusalem Temple could not (see Hebrews 9:11–15). Jesus is the High Priest who not only offered the sacrifice on our behalf; he himself *is* the sacrifice.

Another difference between Jesus and the Levitical priests of the Old Covenant is that Jesus is "holy, innocent, undefiled, separated from sinners, higher than the heavens" (Heb 7:26). Yet his purity and divinity does not separate us from him; in fact, it allows us to draw nearer to Jesus: "because he himself was tested through what he suffered, he is able to help those who are being tested" (Heb 2:18).

Also, Jesus's one sacrifice to "take away the sins of many" (Heb 9:28) removes the need for any other bloody sacrifice, which had not been able to accomplish this objective. The Letter to the Hebrews constructs the words of Psalm 40 as if to come from the mouth of Jesus at the time of his Incarnation: "Sacrifice and offering you did not desire, but a body you prepared for me" (Heb 10:5).

Christ Is Head of the Body of Christ, the Church

Thomas Aquinas wrote: "Only Christ is the true priest, the other being only his ministers."[4] In the ordained minister (especially the bishop and priest), it is

Christ himself who is present to the Church. Through the Sacrament of Holy Orders, the priest acts in the Person of Christ, teaching, sanctifying, and governing the people. It is through the bishops and priests that Christ preaches the Word of God, administers the sacraments, evangelizes new members, and guides the Church to eternal happiness. The ordained ministers are "servants of Christ and dispensers of the mysteries of God."[5]

Through the Sacraments of Baptism and Confirmation, all the faithful come to share in the **common priesthood** of Christ, which is ordered to the **ministerial priesthood** of those who are ordained. The common priesthood allows us to unfold the graces received at Baptism to live "a life of faith, hope, and charity, a life according to the Spirit" (*CCC*, 1557). We participate in Christ's priesthood by taking up our own cross and accepting suffering that comes our way and by worshipping God in the sacraments, especially the Eucharist. These are actions of the priesthood that have been done since the time of Abraham. In the Letter to the Colossians, St. Paul advised that "whatever you do, in word or in deed, do everything in the name of the Lord Jesus, giving thanks to God the Father through him" (Col 3:17).

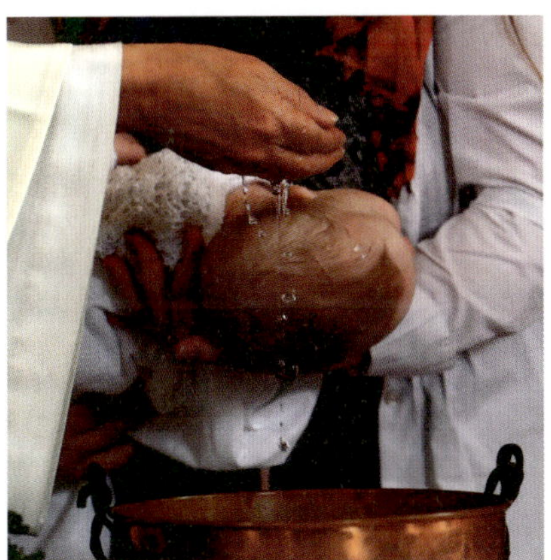

common priesthood The priesthood of the laity. Christ has made the Church a "kingdom of priests" who share his priesthood through the Sacraments of Baptism and Confirmation.

ministerial priesthood A unique sharing in the one priesthood of Christ received in the Sacrament of Holy Orders. By his ordination, a man is configured to Christ by a special gift of the Holy Spirit so that he can act as a representative of Christ, Head of the Church. As a representative of Christ, the ordained man is enabled to serve the common priesthood by building up and guiding the Church.

SECTION Assessment

Comprehension

1. Who was Melchizedek?
2. With what is Salem associated?
3. Name three differences between the Levitical priesthood and the priesthood of Melchizedek.
4. Why does Jesus's sacrifice on the Cross not have to be repeated?

Vocabulary

5. What is the difference between the *ministerial priesthood* and the *common priesthood* in the Church today?

Reflection

6. List five things that you associate with what priests today do.
7. How can you consciously "do everything in the name of Jesus"?

Section 2

CHRIST IS PROPHET

The definition of a *prophet* is "someone who speaks for God." Prophecy doesn't necessarily have to do with foretelling the future; rather, in the cases of Moses and the other Old Testament prophets, especially, it involved urging the people to follow and obey the Torah. Unlike the Levitical priests of the Old Testament, prophets were mainly called and commissioned personally by God. Jesus fits the definition of a prophet.

The Book of Deuteronomy quotes Moses as saying that "a prophet like me will the Lord, your God, raise up for you from your own kindred; that is the one to whom you shall listen" (Dt 18:15). While these words could generally refer to *all* true prophets who would succeed him, they also convey a prediction of the Messiah who is to come. At Jesus's Transfiguration, with Moses and the prophet Elijah present, a voice was heard with a very similar message: "This is my beloved Son, with whom I am well pleased; listen to him" (Mt 17:5).

Moses was not the only Old Testament prophet with similarities to Jesus. The prophet Jeremiah who foretold that the New Covenant would be written, not only on stone tablets, but on people's hearts (see the subsection "The New Covenant Compared to the Old Covenant" in the introduction to Chapter 4), has other direct parallels between his life and the life of Jesus. For example:

BOTH JEREMIAH AND JESUS WERE CHOSEN BY GOD THE FATHER LONG BEFORE THEY WERE CONCEIVED IN THEIR MOTHERS' WOMBS.

Before I formed you in the womb,
I knew you, before you were born
I dedicated you, a prophet to the
nations I appointed you (Jer 1:5).

"Behold, you will conceive in your womb and bear a son, and you shall name him Jesus" (Lk 1:31).

BOTH WEPT OVER JERUSALEM.

Oh, that my head were a spring of water, / my eyes a fountain of tears, / That I might weep day and night / over the slain from the daughter of my people! (Jer 8:23).

As he drew near, he saw the city and wept over it (Lk 19:41).

THEIR FELLOW CITIZENS AND FAMILY MEMBERS REJECTED THEM AND THEIR MESSAGE.

Your kindred and your father's house, even they betray you; they have recruited a force against you. Do not believe them, even when they speak fair words to you (Jer 12:6).

And they took offense against him. Jesus said to them, "A prophet is not without honor except in his native place and among his own kin and in his own house." So he was not able to perform any mighty deed there, apart from curing a few sick people by laying his hands on them. He was amazed by their lack of faith (Mk 6:4–6).

BOTH SPEAK OF THE NEW COVENANT.

I will place my law within them, and write it upon their hearts; I will be their God, and they shall be my people. They will no longer teach their friends and relatives, "Know the Lord!" Everyone, from the least to greatest, shall know me—oracle of the Lord—for I will forgive their iniquity and no longer remember their sin (Jer 31:33–34).

Then he took the bread, said the blessing, broke it, and gave it to them, saying, "This is my body, which will be given for you; do this in memory of me." And likewise the cup after they had eaten, saying, "This cup is the new covenant in my blood, which will be shed for you" (Lk 22:19–20).

Jesus was a prophet, like Moses, in that he was sent by God to share God's Word. But he was also more than Moses and greater than Moses. Jesus taught "as one having authority" (Mt 7:29). His authority was his own as God's only

Son. Jesus's call and the suffering he felt due to being rejected were similar to the life and experiences of Jeremiah. Like Jeremiah, his thoughts and words were based on his human knowledge and experience. But he was also more than Jeremiah and greater than Jeremiah. As a Divine Person, with two natures, a human nature and a divine nature, he also possessed intimate knowledge of God, called **beatific vision**.

The Authority of Jesus

As mentioned, priests of the Old Testament had authority based on their ancestry, and prophets of the Old Testament had authority based on their personal calling from God. Where does authority come from in your own experience? You might associate it with your parents, teachers and staff at school, police officers, or government officials. Mostly authority is earned in these cases. Teachers have specialized college degrees to be in the classroom, police officers go through training at an academy, and government officials campaign for their positions and are elected. Parents have a natural moral authority over their children but also a legal authority as well and can be held responsible by society if they abrogate that responsibility before a child becomes an adult.

Each of the Gospels makes it clear that Jesus had greater authority than any Old Testament priest or prophet. Witnesses to Jesus and his ministry were amazed by what they saw. After Jesus expelled a demonic spirit from a man, people asked one another, "What is this? A new teaching with authority?" (Mk 1:27). Jesus's enemies—the chief priests, scribes, and elders—demanded of Jesus, "By what authority are you doing these things?" (Lk 20:2). They felt trapped by both possible answers, that Jesus's authority was either (1) human in origin, as with other prophets, or (2) from God, in which case others would then question why they didn't believe in him. Jesus would not respond to them directly at the time. Jesus's authority comes from the fact that he is the Word of God made flesh and the "Word was God" (Jn 1:1). In his Last Supper discourse, Jesus answers the question of this authority by directly addressing God the Father: "Give glory to your son, so that your son may glorify you, just as you gave him authority over all people, so that he may give eternal life to all you gave him" (Jn 17:1–2).

---

beatific vision Seeing God face-to-face in heaven, the source of eternal happiness; final union with the Triune God for all eternity.

Leadership takes many different forms. This mural is from Regina Mundi Church, the largest Roman Catholic church in South Africa, located in Rockville, Soweto.

As both true God and true man, Christ had two intellects and wills, divine and human, which cooperated with each other. With his human will and intellect, Jesus developed in completely human ways, and he "advanced in wisdom and age and favor before God and man" (Lk 2:52). Think of Jesus's authority growing as he gained human experience, just as the authority and wisdom of those we know (e.g., grandparents, teachers, priests, business leaders) becomes more pronounced and valued as they get older and can draw on more experiences. In his human will, Jesus had immediate knowledge of the Father and of the secret thoughts of people (see Mark 2:9). Jesus's authority and wisdom also grew because of the union between his two intellects and wills.∞ This is the wisdom of his beatific vision—that is, the intuition he had of God the Father in which he could see God face-to-face. We hope to have the beatific vision someday. "As present we see [God] indistinctly as in a mirror, but then face to face. At present I know partially; then I shall know fully, as I am truly known" (1 Cor 13:12).

∞ Note

The *Catechism of the Catholic Church* reiterates that Christ possesses two wills and two natural operations, divine and human (see *CCC*, 475). The Council of Constantinople taught that Christ's human will "does not resist or oppose but rather submits to his divine and almighty will" (*DS* 556). See the note on the hypostatic union in the subsection "Christology in John's Gospel" in Chapter 6, Section 1.

Even while he developed and grew as a human being, Jesus never lost touch with his divine will and intellect. Jesus's beatific vision applied only to his human nature because the object of his beatific vision was God. In his divine nature, Jesus had no need to see God. Jesus's beatific vision was not faith, even in its highest sense. Rather he had a direct vision of God. This is why Jesus, the Son, was able to know the Father and to make the Father known to his disciples. Jesus said to the Apostle Philip at the Last Supper: "Have I been with you for so long a time and you still do not know me, Philip? Whoever has seen me has seen the Father. How can you say, 'Show us the Father'? Do you not believe that I am in the Father and the Father is in me? The words that I speak to you I do not speak on my own. The Father who dwells in me is doing his works" (Jn 14:9–10).

Jesus is a prophet because he does, indeed, speak for God. He is greater than any other prophet because the words he speaks are the words of God himself as he himself is God. Just as Moses delivered the Israelites from Egypt and gave them God's Law on Mount Sinai, Jesus has delivered us from sin and death in order to place the law of love within our hearts.

"The Wolf Turned Shepherd" from La Fontaine's Fables.

Authentic Prophecy

The mission of a prophet to speak for God has not changed. All Catholics are given this duty based on their anointing at Baptism. "Speaking for God" just as often involves actions as a prophetic example. Whatever authority we are to exercise must be like that of Jesus, done in service to others and with a willingness to suffer on his behalf as necessary. Jesus was clear about this direction in his climactic words on the meaning of discipleship: "Whoever wishes to be great among you will be your servant; whoever wishes to be first among you will be the slave of all" (Mk 10:44).

These directions also help us to reject false prophets. Today, there are many in our midst. Deep polarization of opinion has been prevalent now for many years with no sign of receding. This type of split with each side claiming truth and superiority makes it hard to recognize who is really speaking for God. Take heart; there are clear signs of false prophets—for example:

 False prophets choose an easy course for themselves.

 False prophets preach care for the poor, but live exorbitantly.

 False prophets deny objective truths, including the moral truths taught in the Ten Commandments.

 False prophets ignore the reality of sin.

 False prophets act out of pride and not humility.

There have always been false prophets. The Second Letter of Peter describes false prophets and teachers "who will introduce destructive heresies and even deny the Master who ransomed them" (2 Pt 2:1). The First Letter of John says that "every spirit that does not acknowledge Jesus does not belong to God . . . while anyone who does not belong to God refuses to hear us. This is how we know the spirit of truth and the spirit of deceit" (1 Jn 4:3, 6). One of the easiest ways to test the validity of modern prophets is to examine what they are working for. Are they working to further health, virtue, and life itself, or destruction, vice, and death? Jesus said clearly: "Beware of false prophets, who come to you in sheep's clothing, but underneath are ravenous wolves. By their fruits you will know them" (Mt 7:15–16).

Oppositely, how do we become true prophets as our baptismal anointing demands of us? We bear good fruit. We accept difficult challenges and suffering in the name of Christ. We share our bounty with the poor and live within our means. We acknowledge objective truths, including, foremost, that life is sacred. We acknowledge our sinfulness and ask for forgiveness in the

Sacrament of Penance. We are not boastful and do not seek attention on ourselves as we practice the faith.

Prophecy will also call us to *speak* about Christ and declare our faith in him with words. We are able to do this with more confidence when we know more about what he teaches, especially through reading, studying, and praying with Scripture.

SECTION *Assessment*

Comprehension

1. How were the authority of Jesus and Moses different?
2. What is the mission of a prophet?

Vocabulary

3. Describe the difference between a false prophet and a prophet who preaches with truth.
4. Explain why Jesus's *beatific vision* only applied to his human nature.

Reflection

5. Who is someone in authority that you respect? Why so?
6. What are your thoughts about Jesus's and Jeremiah's vocations originating before they were born?
7. How can you speak for God with your actions and your words?

Section 3

CHRIST IS KING

Born of the tribe of Judah, Jesus was a descendant of King David (see Chapter 5, Section 2, "The Time before Jesus's Public Ministry in the Synoptic Gospels"). Jesus came to the world to establish the Kingdom of God. However, especially in the immediate centuries before Jesus's birth, the Israelites would not have expected a king like Jesus. Hasmonean kings, the descendants of the Maccabees (see the sub-subsection "The Maccabean Revolt and Final Era of Jewish Independence" in Chapter 4, Section 2), were able to set up a puppet kingdom that cooperated with Greek leaders from the mid-second century BC through the establishment of the Roman Empire in 63 BC.∞ The Hasmonean kings attempted to regain the land that Israel possessed at the time of King David, but they also fostered moral decay within Judaism by acting like the political and economic modernists of the Syrian enemies they had defeated when they came to power.

The various Jewish sects of this time reacted to the Hasmonean kings in different ways. The Sadducees, originally a wealthy sect, who believed in the strict letter of the Torah and Temple sacrifices, supported the Hasmonean king Alexander Jannaeus, and Alexander responded with political favors. The Pharisees openly opposed the religious and political policies of Alexander Jannaeus, and they paid a severe price. Alexander had several hundred Pharisees executed by crucifixion. Salome, the wife of Alexander, eventually reconciled with the Pharisees during her rule as queen and allowed the Pharisees to have

∞ Note

The Hasmonean Dynasty was established after the Maccabees ousted the last of the Syrians in 141 BC. John Hyrcanus, the first king of this dynasty, ruled until 104 BC.

a dominant role in establishing local policy. The Pharisees developed much of their identity as described in the Gospels during this period. The Essenes were another Jewish sect of the period. They reacted to the internal bickering among the Pharisees and Sadducees and the overall secularism by withdrawing from Jerusalem completely. They lived in the desert around the Dead Sea, bringing with them copies of most of the books that would become the Hebrew Scriptures (see the sub-subsection "How Did They Compose the Written Copies?" in Chapter 2, Section 2). John the Baptist may have been a member or had a connection with the Essene community.

The period of the Hasmonean kings, the perspectives of the various Jewish sects, and the establishment of the dominant Roman Empire in and around Palestine in the two centuries before Jesus influenced the type of ruler and king the Jewish people anticipated to be their Messiah. A common perception was that a Jewish king would be modeled on the greatest one of the Israelites, King David, and be able to establish a dominant, national, political power while at the same time keeping pure Jewish religious practice.

As we know, Jesus did not come to establish the kingship of a secular ruling nation, but rather to announce the beginning of God's Kingdom on earth that would have its completion in heaven. Recall Jesus's words in the Gospel of Mark as he began his ministry in Galilee: "The kingdom of God is at hand. Repent and believe in the Gospel" (Mk 1:15). St. Paul explained that, in the end, Jesus

Flevit super illam (He Wept Over It) *by Enrique Simonet.*

would hand over the Kingdom to God the Father after he had destroyed all of his enemies, the last enemy being death (see 1 Corinthians 15:27–28).

Whereas Jesus did not present himself as a king, the Jews of his day were able to recognize, on further reflection, that his role as king was clearly laid out in the Old Testament and fulfilled in the New Testament.

Behold the King

Jesus portrayed himself as the Good Shepherd who will lead his flock and lay down his life for his sheep. "All who came [before me] are thieves and robbers, but the sheep did not listen to them. . . . I am the good shepherd, and I know mine and mine know me" (Jn 10:7, 14). Jesus was a new type of king whose coronation came with a crown of thorns, and the acknowledgment of his royalty came from his enemies. Jesus's kingship is made particularly clear in the Gospels beginning from the time he prepares to enter Jerusalem before his Passion and Death.

When Mary, the sister of Martha, rubbed Jesus's feet with costly oil and dried them with her hair six days before the Last Supper at their home in Bethany (see John 12:3; in Matthew 26:6 and Mark 14:3, Jesus's head is anointed), it was a sign of a kingly anointing. Bethany was near the Mount of Olives of which the prophet Zechariah said, "God's feet will stand on the Mount of Olives, which is opposite Jerusalem to the east" (Zec 14:4). Jesus entered Jerusalem on a colt "on which no one has ever sat" (Mk 11:2). Zechariah also prophesized: "Shout for you, O daughter Jerusalem! Behold: your king is coming to you, a just savior is he, humble, and riding on a donkey, a colt, the foal of a donkey" (Zec 9:9). Jesus's request for an unused animal to transport him is also alluded to in other places in the Old Testament; for example, when the Ark of the Covenant was returned to Israel after it had been captured by the Philistines, the stipulation was made that it be brought back by "two milk cows that have not borne the yoke" (1 Sm 6:7).

The spreading of cloaks and branches as Jesus enters the city resembles the treatment sometimes practiced for earthly kings. As close to Jesus's life as 142 BC, Simon Maccabeus, the third son of Mattathias to rule Judea after the Maccabean revolt, entered Jerusalem accompanied by "shouts of praise, the waving of palm branches, the playing of harps and cymbals and lyres, and the singing of hymns and canticles because a great enemy of Israel had been crushed" (1 Mc 14:51). When Jesus enters Jerusalem on the colt, the people shout, "Blessed is he who comes in the name of the Lord," from Psalm 118:26.

Other Old Testament references to Jesus's kingship are confirmed more clearly, and ironically, by accusers, torturers, executioners, and a criminal, as noted in these Gospel passages:

Pilate Questions Jesus's Identity

> Jesus answered, "My kingdom does not belong to this world. If my kingdom did belong to this world, my attendants [would] be fighting to keep me from being handed over to the Jews. But my kingdom is not here." So Pilate said to him, "Then you are a king?" Jesus answered, "You say I am a king." (Jn 18:36–37a)

Soldiers Crown Jesus with Thorns

> Then the soldiers took Jesus inside the praetorium and gathered the whole cohort around him. They stripped off his clothes and threw a scarlet military cloak around him. Weaving a crown out of thorns, they placed it on his head, and a reed in his right hand. And kneeling before him, they mocked him, saying, "Hail, King of the Jews!" (Mt 27:27–29)

Pilate Announces Jesus as King

> [Pilate] brought Jesus out and seated him on the judge's bench in the place called Stone Pavement, in Hebrew, Gabbatha. It was preparation day for Passover, and it was about noon. And he said to the Jews, "Behold, your king!" (Jn 19:13–14)

The Feast of Christ the King

Focus Question: How are titles and images for Christ linked between the Old Testament and New Testament?

The last Sunday of the Church's liturgical calendar—the Sunday before the start of Advent—is marked as the Feast of Christ the King. While the kingship of Christ was prophesized in the Old Testament and described in the New Testament, the Feast of Christ the King itself is barely a century old. Pope Pius XI instituted this feast in 1925 with his encyclical *Quas Primas* (In the First) as a response to the growing secularism and atheism in the world. The Feast of Christ the King was originally celebrated on the Sunday before All Saints Day on November 1. In 1969, Pope St. Paul VI gave the feast its full title—the Solemnity of Our Lord Jesus Christ King of the Universe—and moved it to the last Sunday of the liturgical year.

Much like today, governments of the early twentieth century were highly secular, and often under military rule. Religious freedom and the mere mention of God were being

Several parishes around the world are consecrated and named for Christ the King. The very first parish named for Christ the King is in Cincinnati, Ohio. The first Mass was celebrated at this parish in a room without electricity, even before a church could be built. The parishioners illuminated the makeshift sanctuary by shining the headlamps of their cars through the room's windows.

restricted in places such as Russia and Mexico, where priests were prohibited from wearing clerical clothing in public. Today, modern governments attempt to differentiate between "freedom of religion" and "freedom of worship." The former allows for citizens to practice their faith in the public square and throughout every day and hour of the week. The latter attempts to corral religious practice and contain it to only one day a week (Sunday for Christians) and to one place (on church property). Pope Pius XI recounted:

> The right which the Church has from Christ himself, to teach mankind, to make laws, to govern peoples in all that pertains to their eternal salvation, that right was denied. Then gradually the religion of Christ came to be likened to false religions and to be placed ignominiously on the same level with them. It was then put under the power of the state and tolerated more or less at the whim or princes and rulers. Some went even further, and wished to set up in place of God's religion a natural religion consisting in some instinctive affection of the heart., There were even some nations who thought they could dispense with God, and that their religion should consist in impiety and the neglect of God. The rebellion of individuals and states against the authority of Christ has produced deplorable consequences. (*Quas Primas*, 24)

The Feast of Christ the King counters the argument that Christians must compartmentalize their religion and offer their primary allegiance to the government. When that happens, we risk acknowledging Christ only in our private lives rather than celebrating and living out our faith in public. The Feast of Christ the King reminds us that Jesus is the Lord of the Church and of the entire universe, though those in power may not recognize this fact.

Further Study and Reflection

- The establishment of the Feast of Christ the King also brought with it an annual consecration of the world to the Sacred Heart of Jesus. Research more about this devotion, and explain its connection to the Feast of Christ the King.
- Several Protestant communions also celebrate the Feast of Christ the King. Research and explain two versions of the feast called "the Sunday of Doom" and "Stir-up Sunday."

Good Thief Asks for Entrance into God's Kingdom

> [One criminal said to the other,] "This man has done nothing criminal." Then he said, "Jesus, remember me when you come into your kingdom." (Lk 23:41–42)

Despite the evidence of his kingship, Jesus went to his death with many, including the chief priests and scribes, mocking him and saying: "He saved others; he cannot save himself. Let the Messiah, the King of Israel, come down from the cross that we may see and believe" (Mk 15:31b–32).

We Sanctify the World

For baptized Christians, to share in the kingly mission of Christ means to serve the world as he did. We are to act both as kings and as subjects of Christ the King. This blessing of royal power is likewise nondescript, humbling, and mostly out of the public eye. We will be judged on how well we fulfilled our kingly mission by Jesus himself when he comes again, sits "upon his glorious throne, and all the nations will be assembled before him" (Mt 25:31–32). Using again the image of a shepherd, he will separate the good and evil based on how well or poorly they met the needs of the hungry, naked, thirsty, lonely, and imprisoned (see Matthew 35:31–46).

To share in Christ's kingly mission, we must act in imitation of him. We must embrace his Cross and not run from it. We must keep our minds occupied with the heavenly Kingdom, not with making our kingdom on earth. "Our citizenship is in heaven, and from it we also await a savior, the Lord Jesus Christ. He will change our lowly body to conform with a glorified body by the power that enables him to bring all things into subjection to himself" (Phil 3:20–21).

SECTION Assessment

Comprehension

1. Who were the Hasmonean kings?
2. Explain how Sadducees, Pharisees, and Essenes each responded to the Hasmonean Dynasty.
3. How was Jesus's kingship different than what the world had been used to?
4. How will our lives be judged by Christ when he comes in glory?

Reflection

5. Write a short scenario for how you imagine that Jesus arranged for the colt to be prepared for his entrance into Jerusalem.
6. What do you find most ironic about who confirms Jesus's kingship and how?
7. Write a profile of Jesus's kingship in your own words.

Section 4

CHRIST IS THE ALPHA AND THE OMEGA

Some of the prophetic words and visions in the Book of Revelation are anonymously spoken, but the speaker of the passage in Revelation 22:12–13 is clearly identified as Christ: "Behold, I am coming soon. I bring with me the recompense I will give to each according to his deeds. I am the Alpha and the Omega, the beginning and the end."

The first and last letters of the Greek alphabet would have been understood by a Jewish Christian audience. Jewish rabbis used the Hebrew form of the letters alpha and omega in their preaching to mean wholeness of anything, not just wholeness related to the fullness of the universe or of time. For example, in Hebrew it was said that "Adam violated the *whole* law, from Aleph to Taw whereas Abraham kept the *whole* law from Aleph to Taw."[6] Also, aleph and taw are the first and last letters of the Hebrew word for "truth," *emeth*. The first letter of *truth* in Hebrew teaches that God is the first of all things. The last letter signifies that God is the last of all things. The element of wholeness in *emeth* is that God's truth is plentiful, abundant, and absolute.

Likewise, the Greek words for beginning and end have similar connotations with wholeness. The Greek word for "beginning," *arche*, is associated with coherence to the whole. Christ is not only the origin of our being; he is the One who brings our entire life together in him and, collectively, in his one Body, the Church. The Greek word *telos* for "end" signifies the completion of our whole life. It is God who is the end for which we have been made.

Jesus prefaces his identification of himself as the "Alpha and the Omega" with the declaration that he is "coming soon" (Rv 22:12). Catholics and evangelical Protestants often differ on their understandings of what will occur at this Second Coming of the Lord. Whereas Protestants typically explain the Second Coming as something that will happen *after* the rapture of souls from the earth to heaven, Catholics set the return of Jesus at *the same time* as his judgment of souls. "That is why the Second Coming of the Lord is not only salvation, not only the omega that sets everything right, but also judgment," wrote Joseph Cardinal Ratzinger who later became Pope Benedict XVI.[7]

The Second Coming of Christ

It may also seem that Catholics do not talk about the Second Coming of Christ as much as other Christians. However, if you reconsider what Catholics pray in the liturgy, you will realize that there is plenty of focus on Christ's return. Catholics state in the Nicene Creed that Christ "will come again in glory to judge the living and the dead." During the Eucharistic Prayer, we acclaim, "When we eat this bread and drink this cup, we proclaim your death, O Lord, until you come again." In the Our Father, we pray, "Thy kingdom come," and in the prayer between the two parts of the Our Father at Mass, Catholics say that "we wait in joyful hope for the coming of our Savior, Jesus Christ." The first two weeks of the liturgical season of Advent particularly focus on the Second Coming of Christ.

Differences in how Catholics and some Protestants understand the Second Coming have to do with beliefs about *what* will occur and *when* it will occur. One of the Protestant views is that in the last stages of humanity, some believers will disappear from the earth and be "raptured" into heaven in order to escape a great period of tribulation that will befall those people who will remain. Then, according to this view, Christ will appear at his Second Coming at the end of the tribulation period. The problem with this view is that it is not scriptural. It splits the Second Coming of Christ into different events, which makes three times that Christ comes to the world. Scripture tells of Christ coming to earth only twice: at his Incarnation and at the Parousia (see the sub-subsection "Catholic Letters" in Chapter 4, Section 3). Catholics believe that the Parousia is when all of history and creation will be fulfilled and Christ will judge the living and the dead.

It is important, however, to acknowledge that the term *rapture* does have scriptural roots; the First Letter to the Thessalonians states: "For the Lord

The Last Judgment *by Michelangelo.*

himself, with a word of command, with the voice of an archangel and with the trumpet of God, will come down from heaven, and the dead in Christ will rise first. Then we who are alive, who are left, will be caught up together with them in the clouds to meet the Lord in the air. Thus we shall always be with the Lord" (1 Thes 4:16–17). The Latin root for "caught up" is *rapiemur*, from which comes the word *rapture*. The passage states that believers will be snatched up instantaneously with the "word of a command." Yet, this Scripture also makes it clear that this event is simultaneous with the Second Coming of Christ; it does not precede it in a separate event. Recall what Jesus said of the tribulation and the end of time: "of that day and hour no one knows, neither the angels of heaven, nor the Son, but the Father alone" (Mt 24:36). If there is a separate rapture before the beginning of the tribulation, as some Protestants hold, it would then follow that we would be able to predict the end of time, which Jesus clearly has said we cannot do.

Pope Benedict wrote in his encyclical *Spe Salvi* that hope, and not fear, is the way we should view being taken up by Jesus into eternal life:

> It will be like plunging into the ocean of infinite love, a moment in which time—the before and after—no longer exists. We can only attempt to grasp the idea that such a moment is life in the full sense, a plunging ever anew into the vastness of being, in which we are simply overwhelmed with joy. This is how Jesus expresses it in Saint John's Gospel: "I will see you again and your hearts will rejoice, and no one will take your joy from you" (16:22). We must think along these lines if we want to understand the object of Christian hope, to understand what it is that our faith, our being with Christ, leads us to expect. (*Spe Salvi*, 12)

Living in a world where human beings can destroy the planet by degrading the environment and through the extreme of nuclear destruction, we should work to curtail both types of occurrences and not hasten the end of the world by our own human failings. The proper attitude to take toward Christ's Second Coming is to live in daily hope of Christ's return and to prepare for it by living holy lives.

Other Nonbiblical Titles for Christ

The Bible contains a plethora of titles and images for Jesus Christ. For example, Jesus is the "horn for our salvation" (Lk 1:69), "author of life" (Acts 3:15), "image of the invisible God" (Col 1:5), and "the root and offspring of David, the bright morning star" (Rv 22:16). The early Church also had occasions to use other images for Jesus or Christianity in general that were not directly taken from the Bible. Three of the most popular are listed in the subsections that follow.

Phoenix

Stories and fables of the mythical bird, the phoenix, were part of several cultures prior to the time of Christ. Perhaps its earliest appearance in classical literature was in a mention of the phoenix by Greek poet Hesiod in the seventh or eighth century BC. Later in 8 BC, a Roman poet, Ovid, wrote a poem based on the Greek poem. In the Roman version, the phoenix was linked to the sun and to the goddess of victory. In both the original Greek and Roman poems, the phoenix was seen as a "firebird" who was given new life after dying in flames and then rising from its own ashes. St. Clement of Rome, the fourth pope, provided a Christian interpretation of the phoenix in his *Epistle to the Corinthians*, written around the turn of the first century AD, connecting it with our resurrection at the end of time.

> Let us consider that wonderful sign [of the resurrection] which takes place in Eastern lands, that is, in Arabia and the countries round about. There is a certain bird which is called a phoenix. This is the only one of its kind, and lives five hundred years. And when the time of its dissolution draws near that it must die, it builds itself a nest of frankincense, and myrrh, and other spices, into which, when the time is fulfilled, it enters and dies [then later rises again]. . . . Do we then deem it any great and wonderful thing for the Maker of all things to raise up again those that have piously served Him in the assurance of a good faith, when even by a bird He shows us the mightiness of His power to fulfill His promise? (*Epistle to the Corinthians*, 25, 26)

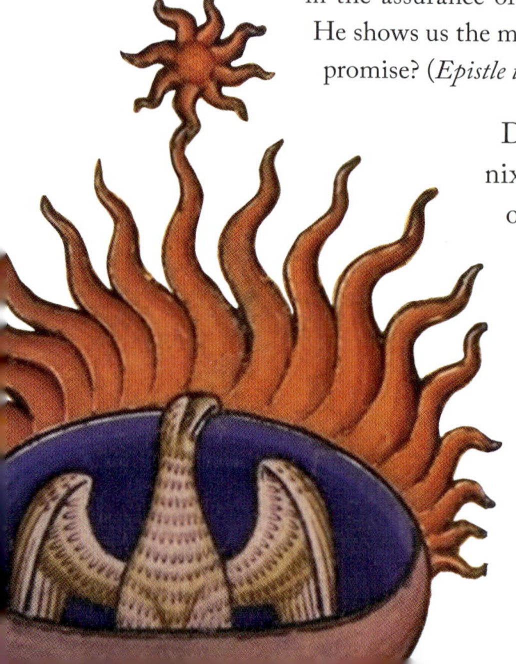

Drawing on St. Clement's words, the phoenix was often depicted in early Christian art on a palm tree, symbolizing the victory of life over death. Later the phoenix became connected to Christ's Resurrection. Why did St. Clement refer to this image at all? Perhaps it showed his willingness to tap into classic myths and foreign cultures that teach Christian truths and to encourage pagans to explore the Gospel of Jesus Christ.

Pelican

As with the phoenix, the pelican found its way into Christianity from an earlier pagan story. As it was originally told, a wounded mother pelican used her own blood to prevent the starvation of her baby pelicans. In doing so, she lost her own life.

A second-century anonymous Christian work called *Physiologus* ("The Naturalist"), which gave animals allegorical interpretations, describes baby pelicans striking at their mother and their mother striking back and killing them. But on the third day the mother pelican uses her beak to peck at her own side, and blood pours out over the dead young pelicans, bringing them back to life. The text in *Physiologus* explicitly connects to a scriptural lesson: "We struck God by serving the creature rather than the Creator. Therefore He deigned to ascend to the cross, and when His side was pierced, blood and water gushed forth into our salvation and eternal life." The *Physiologus* was cited by St. Epiphanius, St. Basil, and St. Peter of Alexandria, and it was often used as a source of symbols for artists in the Middle Ages.

The mother pelican feeding her young is also a symbol rendered in several Catholic churches throughout the world. Durham Cathedral in England has a tabernacle with a pelican that is suspended over its altar.[8] A brown pelican, native to Louisiana, is also on that state's flag.

Fish

The most well-known of the animal Christian symbols in the early Church is the *ichthys*, the Greek word for "fish." Because of the persecution of Christians by the Romans for three centuries, the "sign of the fish" was a secret symbol that allowed Christians to determine if another person or household believed in Jesus.

The *ichthys* was first used in the late second century, and it continued to be prevalent through the fourth century. Christians used it to mark meeting places and tombs. Often when Christians met an approaching stranger, they drew one of the arcs of the fish in the dirt. If the other person completed the drawing of the arc, they would know they were both believers.

The letters of ΙΧΘΥΣ (*ichthys* in Greek) are connected with this Greek phrase: *Iesus Christos Theous hUios Soter*, which means "Jesus Christ, God's Son, Savior." The use of a fish to symbolize Christianity is also a reference to the Holy Eucharist, with which the miracle of Jesus's multiplication of loaves and fishes is connected. St. Peter, the first pope of the Church, and several other Apostles were, of course, originally fishermen.

SECTION *Assessment*

Comprehension

1. Why is Christ associated with the first and last letters of the Greek alphabet, alpha and omega?
2. Explain a difference between a Catholic and an evangelical Protestant understanding of the Second Coming.
3. What do the phoenix, pelican, and *ichthys* represent as Christian symbols?
4. How does the rapture have scriptural roots?

Reflection

5. How do you connect Jesus Christ with wholeness in your own life?
6. If you are present at the Second Coming of Christ, how do you imagine the experience?

Section Reviews

Focus Question

How are titles and images for Christ linked between the Old Testament and New Testament?

Complete one of the following:

- Read the *Catechism of the Catholic Church*, 784–786. Answer all three questions: How do Catholics receive a share of Christ's priesthood? What happens to Catholics who receive the supernatural sense of faith of the Church's prophetic office? What does it mean for a Catholic to reign with Christ in his kingly office?
- Read 2 Timothy 2:1–7. In this passage St. Paul compares the work of a soldier, an athlete, and a farmer to the work of discipleship. Add two of your own examples comparing related work to the work of discipleship.
- Imagine you are an early Christian missionary. Write a short letter to your converts to encourage them to remain strong in their faith in Jesus Christ. Include at least three practices of faith applicable to all generations.

Introduction
Christ Is the One Word of Scripture

Review Points

- All of salvation history leads up to the time that Christ came into the world to fulfill the prophecy of the Old Testament.
- Christ's threefold identity and mission as priest, prophet, and king was predicted in the Old Testament and fulfilled in the New Testament; we are called to participate in this mission by virtue of our Baptism.

Assignment

Identify the difference between the ministerial priesthood and the common priesthood.

Section 1
Christ Is the New High Priest

Review Points

- In the Old Testament, priesthood was hereditary. Priests came from the tribe of Levi. The origins of the priesthood of Jesus trace to Melchizedek, a priest and king from Salem, who presented bread and wine on a visit to Abraham.
- The Letter to the Hebrews outlines several similarities between the priesthood of Melchizedek and the priesthood of Jesus. Hebrews also presents Christ as the High Priest whose one sacrifice on the Cross brought about our salvation.
- At Baptism, all Catholics participate in the common priesthood of Christ that allows us to take up our own cross and live a life of faith, hope, and charity according to the Holy Spirit.

Assignment

Following Jesus's example is a characteristic of discipleship. How might you imitate Jesus by expanding your group of friends to include a greater variety of different people?

Section 2
Christ Is Prophet

Review Points

- A prophet is "someone who speaks for God." Jesus fits the definition of prophet, though he is much more. He has similarities with Old Testament prophets, especially Moses and Jeremiah.
- A prophet speaks with wisdom and authority. Human wisdom and authority come with age and experience. The human wisdom and authority of Jesus was furthered because he is a Divine Person, with two natures, a human nature and a divine nature, and so he possessed intimate knowledge of God.

- Jesus is greater than any other prophet because the words he speaks are the words of God because he is God.

Assignment

- Read John 6:14. What does the Scripture note in the *New American Bible, revised edition,* say is the meaning of "prophet" in this verse?

Section 3
Christ Is King

Review Points

- The Jews expected a king who would establish a dominant political nation while at the same time promoting Jewish religious teachings and practice. Jesus did not enter the world to establish a worldly kingdom.
- Jesus modeled his kingship as the Good Shepherd who cares for all of his sheep. As shepherd, Jesus will also be a judge who determines our eternal destiny based on our actions in this world.
- We are called to share in Jesus's kingly mission by acting humbly and, especially, by taking up our own cross in imitation of him.

Assignment

What precedence is there for Jesus's mother, Mary, to be queen? See 1 Kings 2:19–20.

Section 4
Christ Is the Alpha and the Omega

Review Points

- The first and last letters of the Greek alphabet, alpha and omega, describe the wholeness of Christ in all things. He is the origin of our being, and also he is the One who brings our entire life together in his Body, the Church.

- The Second Coming will also mark the time of judgment in which the Good Shepherd, Jesus, will determine our eternal destiny based on our good and bad actions.
- Three nonbiblical titles for Christ and Christianity used in the early centuries of the Church are animals or mythical animals: phoenix, pelican, and fish.

Assignment

Draw one arc of the *ichthys*. Ask a classmate to draw the other. Then repeat the process with your classmate going first. Finally, do both steps again so that you each have two drawings to turn in to your teacher.

Chapter Projects

Choose and complete at least one of the following projects to assess your understanding of the material in this chapter.

1. Paint a Tapestry of an Early Christian Image

Peter Paul Rubens designed tapestries for his series *The Triumph of the Eucharist*. As with *The Meeting between Abraham and Melchizedek*, the other four subjects of Rubens's series were allegorical illustrations of important Church doctrine. *The Triumph of the Church* is the central work of the series with the most complex themes and composition.

For this project, create your own tapestry of one of the following nonbiblical Christian images described in this chapter: the phoenix, pelican, or *ichthys*. You will need supplies such as the following: canvas or burlap (suggested size: 1 foot by 3 feet), painter's tape, fabric paint, paintbrush, template, iron, hot glue or fabric glue, dowels, eye hooks, and twine or rope to hang.

Search online for instructions on how to transfer your drawing onto the canvas or burlap as well as the other necessary steps for painting a tapestry.

2. Create a Word Cloud Chart for the Letter to the Hebrews

A word cloud chart is a representation of the frequency of words that occur in a document. The more a word occurs, the larger and more brightly colored it appears. There are several online applications for making your own word cloud. For this project, make a word cloud for the Letter to the Hebrews. You can copy and paste the text of the Letter to the Hebrews from the *New American Bible, revised edition*, located at the United States Conference of Catholic Bishops website (www.usccb.org).

After you have created the word cloud, complete the following items in writing:

- What five words are used the most?
- Write one sentence using two of the five most-used words.
- What is a word with a frequency of use that surprised you? Why?

- Pretend you never heard of the Letter to the Hebrews. Using only the word cloud, write one paragraph explaining what it is about.

3. Make a Chart with Symbols from the Book of Revelation

Research the origins and meanings of the symbols from the Book of Revelation named below. List each symbol in column one of a chart. In column two, list the Scripture references where the symbol appears in the Book of Revelation. In column three, give the Judeo-Christian meaning of each symbol.

- *Numbers*: 7, 6, 12, 1,000, 144,000
- *Colors*: black, red, white
- *Names and Figures*: Babylon, dragon, Four Horses of the Apocalypse, horn

4. Write a Biography of a Modern-Day Prophet

Identify a person you know personally or have heard about recently who you think possesses prophet qualities. This person must be living now or have died within the last ten years. Include the following material in a biographical essay:

- a definition of what makes a prophet
- a short narration of the person's life
- a connection of the person's prophetic actions to how Jesus lived his prophetic mission
- a short reflection about why this person inspires you

5. Summarize the Role of the Laity from Lumen Gentium

Recite aloud chapter 4, "The Laity" (paragraphs 30–38), from the Second Vatican Council document *Lumen Gentium* (www.vatican.va) on video. After each numbered paragraph (not the individual paragraphs within the numbered sections), offer your own commentary on (1) the meaning of what you read and (2) how you can apply what you read to your own life as a lay Catholic. Practice the reading before recording it. Also, have written notes prepared for your commentary to use for the actual recording. Turn in the completed video to your teacher.

Faithful Disciples
The Archangels

There are a number of angels and archangels mentioned in the Bible, but only three of them are named and called saints: St. Michael is the archangel who fights against Satan and all evil spirits. St. Gabriel is the archangel who announced the births of both Jesus and John the Baptist. St. Raphael is the archangel who took care of Tobias from the Old Testament on his journey. Archangels are a special category of angels whose name refers to their chief rank among the angels. There are nine choirs or classes of angels, which are, in ascending order, (1) angels, (2) archangels, (3) principalities, (4) powers, (5) virtues, (6) dominations, (7) thrones, (8) cherubim, and (9) seraphim.

Prior to the Second Vatican Council, each of the archangels had its own feast day on the liturgical calendar: St. Michael on September 29, St. Gabriel on March 24, and St. Raphael on October 24. Today the three archangels share September 29 as one feast day. More information on each archangel and their place in Scripture follows.

St. Michael the Archangel

The name *Michael* in Hebrew means "Who is like God?" Note the question mark. This name is meant to signify that neither Michael nor any other angel has the same power and capacities as God. However, Michael *is* known as the "prince of the heavenly host." His mission is to defeat Satan. Pope John Paul II said of Michael: "The battle against the devil is his principal task."

St. Michael is mentioned in three books of Sacred Scripture. A prophetic passage from the Book of Daniel says that in a time of distress "there shall arise Michael, the great prince, guardian of your people" (Dn 12:1). The archangel is also mentioned in the New Testament. The Letter to Jude portrays Michael battling with evil and points out that Michael had fought with the devil over the body of Moses (see Jude 1:9). In the Book of Revelation, when a woman in labor (thought to be Mary) "clothed with the sun, with the moon under her feet, and on her head a crown of twelve stars" (Rv 12:1), is poised to be devoured by a dragon, Michael and other angels battle the dragon, who is thrown down to earth with the evil angels.

St. Michael's role to preserve the world and individuals from evil is ongoing. St. Bernard of Clairvaux said that whenever any temptation or sorrow oppresses us, we should "cry out to Michael, and say, 'Lord, save us, lest we perish.'" The Church traditionally holds that St. Michael is one of the angels present at our **particular judgment** who advocates for our admittance into heaven. Many Catholic cemeteries are dedicated to St. Michael. In 1886, Pope Leo XIII introduced the Prayer to St. Michael (see the section "Prayers" in the Appendix) to be recited as part of the Eucharistic liturgy. This is a tradition that is returning in many places today. Pope John Paul II urged Catholics to pray the Prayer to St. Michael "to obtain help in the battle against the forces of darkness and against the spirit of this world."[9]

---

particular judgment The individual's judgment immediately after death, when Christ will rule on one's eternal destiny to be spent in heaven (after purification in Purgatory, if needed) or in hell.

St. Gabriel the Archangel

The archangel Gabriel is mentioned three times in Sacred Scripture. In the Old Testament, Gabriel is called on to explain to Daniel the meaning of a messianic figure (see Daniel 8:16; 9:21). We quote Gabriel each time we recite a Hail Mary. The archangel's words to her, "Hail Mary, full of grace," not only foretold Mary's experience in becoming God's Mother, but they also are accurate for all time as Mary remains full of grace, which she freely shares with the world. St. Gabriel also visited Zechariah, the father of John the Baptist, instructing him on what to name his son, even though John was not a family ancestral name (see Luke 1:12–25).

St. Raphael the Archangel

St. Raphael, whose name means "God has healed," appears in the Book of Tobit. Tobit was an Israelite who had been captured and taken to Nineveh in the land of the Assyrians. While he was sleeping outside, bird droppings fell on his eyes and blinded him, for which there was no cure. He prayed for death.

Meanwhile, in a different town, a woman named Sarah had been given in marriage to seven husbands who all died by the hand of a demon, Admodeus, before they could spend their wedding night with her. She, too, prayed for death.

God heard both of their prayers and sent Raphael to heal them. Tobit told his son Tobiah about some money that he had left with a trusted kinsman in Media, the place where Sarah lived. Tobiah went to retrieve it, and the archangel Raphael was his companion on the journey. Along the way, while Tobiah bathed in the Tigris River, a fish attacked Tobiah and tried to swallow his foot. Raphael told Tobiah to capture the fish and keep its insides for medicine. In Media, Tobiah met Sarah and asked for her hand in marriage.

On Tobiah and Sarah's wedding night, Tobiah smoked the fish's liver and heart to repulse the demons and drive them away. Later, when he returned to Nineveh, Tobiah applied the fish to his father's eyes and cured the blindness. After this second miracle, Raphael revealed his identity, saying, "I am Raphael, one of the seven angels before the glory of the Lord" (Tb 12:15).

Comprehension

1. What is the meaning of the term *archangel*?
2. What is St. Michael's role at the time of our death?
3. Why is it important to read the meaning of St. Michael's name with a question mark?
4. What is the occasion of St. Gabriel's appearance in the Book of Daniel?
5. What two problems did St. Raphael address in the Book of Tobit?

Reflection

Angels, who were created by God, are spiritual creatures who surpass in perfection human beings. Yet, God became incarnate as a human being. He did not become an angel. What does this fact tell you about how God esteems human beings?

Prayer

If the celebration of Confirmation does not follow immediately after Baptism (as in adult Baptism), the celebrant anoints each newly baptized (called the neophyte) on the crown of the head with consecrated oil known as *sacred chrism*, perfumed oil that is consecrated by the bishop and used for anointing in the Sacraments of Baptism, Confirmation, and Holy Orders. This anointing symbolizes the coming of the Holy Spirit to the newly baptized. It signifies that a new character, or identity, has been given to the person. This person now officially belongs to Christ and may be called a Christian. The anointing also brings the baptized person into union with the threefold mission of Christ as priest, prophet, and king.

Prayer for the Anointed from the Rite of Baptism

> God the Father of our Lord Jesus Christ has freed you from sin, given you a new birth by water and the Holy Spirit, and welcomed you into his holy people. He now anoints you with the chrism of salvation. As Christ was anointed Priest, Prophet, and King, so may you live always as a member of his body, sharing everlasting life. Amen.

The Bible in the Life of the Church

Santa Teresa de Jesús

José Alcázar Tejedor

St. Teresa of Avila, a Spanish Carmelite nun who lived in the sixteenth century, spent much of her life contemplating Jesus and trying to keep him close to her heart. "I tried as hard as I could to keep Jesus Christ present within me," she said. "My imagination is so dull I had no talent for imagining or coming up with great theological thoughts."

The convent St. Teresa lived in was not a particularly pious place. Many poor women used it as a refuge from poverty. Once there, several excesses were present. There were parties with a stream of visitors, including men. Teresa became frustrated by her life there and went years without praying. In her early forties, at the encouragement of a priest, she returned to a devoted prayer life. She was eventually able to put her mental prayer into words: "In my opinion, mental prayer is nothing else but an intimate sharing between friends; it means taking time frequently to be alone with him who we know loves us."

The painting *Santa Teresa de Jesús* was composed by Spanish artist José Alcázar Tejedor (1850–1907) in 1884. Alcázar Tejedor studied at the Academy of Fine Arts of San Fernando in his hometown of Madrid and later in Paris, thanks to a donation from his town's provincial council. There he entered, and won, many competitions; and his paintings were displayed at several exhibitions in Paris. He won a second-prize medal at a national exhibition for a painting of his parents. Alcáraz Tejedor was known to paint "genre scenes," a style known for portraying common people in ordinary situations.

Santa Teresa de Jesús shows the anguish of mental prayer. With sacred reading at her side, St. Teresa is worn out by the exercise of prayer. She is completely dedicated to seeking God in her life. Mental prayer became, in her later years, the primary exercise of her life. "I think that if I had understood then as I do now that this great King really dwells in a little palace of my soul, I should not have left him alone so often and never allowed his dwelling place to get so dirty," St. Teresa of Avila reflected.

Focus Question

How is the Bible used in communal and personal prayer?

Chapter Overview

Introduction

THE BIBLE AND PRAYER

Even when undertaking biblical studies, you should be open to the inspiration of the Holy Spirit and read the Bible with the desire that its message will help you to become more holy and faithful. In fact, apart from any requirement, Catholics should make reading and praying with the Bible a daily event. The United States Conference of Catholic Bishops taught: "Reading these inspired words, people grow deeper in their relationship with God and come to understand their place in the community God has called them to in himself."[1]

Of course the Bible has always been important in the Church, but individual Catholics using it for reading and prayer has not always been easy or encouraged. For one thing, until the invention of the printing press, individuals could not have a personal copy of the Bible, and even when printed editions of the Bible were available, most people couldn't afford their own copies. Also, after the Council of Trent responded to Martin Luther's *sola scriptura* ("Scripture alone") by reiterating the two sources of Divine Revelation—Sacred Scripture and Sacred Tradition—and making the Latin Vulgate the only approved edition of the Bible, the Church still had some hesitancy about encouraging private reading of Scripture. Building on Trent, the Second Vatican Council emphasized the unity of Sacred Scripture and Sacred Tradition and that both sources flow from the one "divine wellspring, and in a certain way come together in a single current toward the same end" (*Dei Verbum*, 9). The Second Vatican Council encouraged Catholics to listen attentively to Scripture when it is shared in liturgy, and also read the Bible regularly and reflectively. Since the Second Vatican Council, there has been an increase in such prayerful reading known as *lectio divina*, which means "divinely inspired reading."

Keeping God's Word Alive

The Bible is central to the Church's life. The Bible enables you to hear God speak to you personally. The words of Scripture also strengthen the Church as a whole. Just about any document or teaching over the entire history of the Church quotes from Sacred Scripture. As you have learned, the Bible is made up of many types of literature. Because it is a *library* of books, there is history, poetry, laws, and letters. That said, the Bible is primarily a source of prayer. Reading the Bible is not like reading a history book or a novel. No matter which book of the Bible you are reading, you should do so prayerfully.

Familiarity with the Bible grew initially after the Second Vatican Council because the Mass began to be celebrated in the vernacular. This included the Scripture readings that were heard completely in the language of the people, after previously being only partially so in combination with Latin. Also, the council document *Sacrosanctum Concilium* (Sacred Council) led to the Church adopting a greater sample of readings from the Bible for Sunday Mass so that a majority of the Bible would be read over the course of the three-year liturgical cycle. The **homily** became more essential as an accompaniment to the Scripture readings: "By means of the homily the mysteries of the faith and the guiding principles of the Christian life are expounded from the sacred text" (*Sacrosanctum Concilium*, 52). Previously, the homily was more often a sermon preached on a particular Church teaching and not necessarily applicable to the Scripture readings.

The Bible is also meant to be used for both personal prayer and communal prayer of other kinds. Lectio divina is one meditative approach to Scripture, and there are others. Many parishes foster Scripture study and prayer groups, and both offerings are available online. Scripture is also at the heart of the Liturgy of the Hours, or Divine Office, which is the public prayer of the Church that praises God and sanctifies the day and is prayed from morning to night. Another reform from the Second Vatican Council was to open up praying of the Liturgy of the Hours to the laity, and not just to the ordained.

In this course, you have completed a thorough study of Sacred Scripture—how it was created, its contents, and much of its subject matter. But studying and reading the Bible are not enough. The Bible must be prayed. St. Ambrose

---

homily A reflection given by a bishop, priest, or deacon based on the Scripture read at Mass or a sacramental celebration. The homily helps us to apply God's Word to our own lives.

(339–397), the bishop of Milan, explained the Bible's purpose and practice in this way: "We speak to God when we pray; we hear God when we read the divine sayings."[2] Only through a prayerful and reflective reading of Scripture are we able to discover that the "word of God is living and effective, sharper than a two-edged sword, penetrating even between the soul and spirit, joints and marrow, and able to discern reflections and thoughts of the heart" (Heb 4:12).

SECTION *Assessment*

Comprehension

1. What are two ways that the Council of Trent responded to Martin Luther's claim of *sola scriptura*?
2. After the Second Vatican Council, what was a way that Catholics first began a new appreciation of the Bible?
3. What is meant by *lectio divina*?

Vocabulary

4. What is the difference between a *homily* and a sermon?

Reflection

5. How do you currently pray with the Bible?

Section 1

COMMON BIBLICAL PRAYERS

From the Bible comes the exact wording of many prayers of both Christians and Jews. The central Christian prayer, spoken and taught by Jesus to his disciples, is recorded in all three synoptic Gospels. The Our Father, or Lord's Prayer, is found in Matthew 6:9–13, in Luke 11:2–4, and in an abbreviated form in Mark 11:25: "When you stand to pray, forgive anyone against whom you have a grievance, so that your heavenly Father may in turn forgive your transgressions." Besides the Our Father, the Bible also contains the words of other prayers from Mass—for example, the Gospel acclamation, prayer over the gifts, Lamb of God, and more.

The most important Jewish prayer in the Bible is the ***Sh'ma***, which is composed of a combination of verses from Deuteronomy 6:4–9; 11:13–21 and Numbers 15:37–41. The name *Sh'ma* comes from the first word of the prayer in Hebrew, meaning "hear" or "listen." The first two verses contain the Great Commandment and the basic principle of Mosaic Law, that the Lord alone is God who must be loved with an undivided heart: "Hear, O Israel! The Lord is our God, the Lord alone! Therefore, you shall love the Lord, your God, with your whole heart, and with your whole being, and with your whole strength" (Dt 6:4–5). Jesus cites these words when he is asked what is the greatest and first commandment. Each of the synoptic Gospels record his response (see Matthew 23:37–39; Mark 12:29–30; Luke 10:27). He would have also prayed these words himself along with the addition of the full *Sh'ma*, which includes dietary and liturgical laws that Christians are no longer obligated to follow.

Sh'ma The *Sh'ma Israel* or *Shema Yisrael* is considered the most important part of Jewish prayer. It is recited twice daily by observant Jews as a *mitzva*—that is, a religious commandment. In the Catholic Liturgy of the Hours, the *Sh'ma* is recited as part of Night Prayer (Compline) every Saturday.

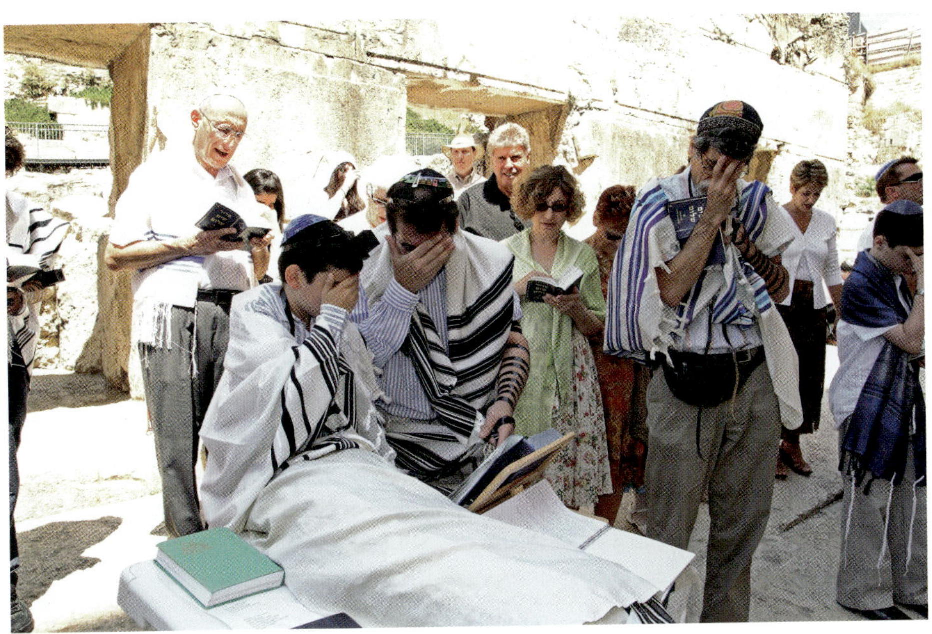

Jews praying the Sh'ma.

Jews today continue to recite the *Sh'ma* as part of synagogue services and include reflections on a series of blessings. Individually, Jews also recite the *Sh'ma* when they first wake in the morning and before going to sleep at night. For Jewish people, this is regarded as an essential biblical commandment.

The Psalms

Judaism and Christianity also share a love for the psalms as a form of prayer. Another regular prayer at Mass comes from the Book of Psalms. At Sunday Mass, a psalm is read or sung between the first and second readings. (Daily Mass also includes a psalm, but no second reading.) The cantor sings the body of the psalm, while the congregation sings the refrain. The psalms are reflective in nature and are able to capture senses of anxiety, joy, frustration, and gratitude.

The term *psalm* derives from a Greek word connected with the name of a stringed instrument called a *psaltery*, a kind of harp. Accordingly, the psalms are songs that were intended to be sung with a harp. King David is associated with the authorship of the psalms because he was also known as a gifted poet and musician. There are references to David in the first dozen psalms; however, Psalm 137 mentions the Babylonian Exile, which occurred hundreds of years *after* the time of David. Popularly, David is believed to be the author of the psalms at least through Psalm 72, which states, "The end of the psalms of David, son of Jesse." The other two-thirds of the Book of Psalms come from the period of the **Second Temple**—that is, after 520 BC but before 333 BC.

Biblical scholars have noted that the Book of Psalms may have originally been five "books of psalms," perhaps coinciding with the five books of the Pentateuch. The five books of the psalms were divided in this way:

Book 1: Psalms 1–41

Book 2: Psalms 42–72

Book 3: Psalms 73–89

Book 4: Psalms 90–106

Book 5: Psalms 107–150

The evidence that the Book of Psalms was originally made up of five separate books is twofold. First, the final psalms of each book (e.g., 41, 72, 89, 106, and 150) include a **doxology** usually ending with a double "Amen." This would have been a conclusion at the end of each separate book. Second, there is one doublet, or repeated passage, in the Book of Psalms. Psalms 14 and 53 are the same. In other biblical research, doubles are evidence that at least two text versions have been brought together, creating some duplication of material.

Second Temple The Second Temple replaced the First Temple, Solomon's Temple, that was destroyed in the capture of Jerusalem in 587–586 BC by the Babylonians. The Second Temple was destroyed by the Romans in AD 70 except for the Western Wall or Wailing Wall. Modern Israel recaptured the Western Wall from the Palestinians in 1967 after it was out of Israel's control for nineteen years.

doxology A hymn or liturgical formula that offers praise to God. The doxology dividing the sections of the Book of Psalms is a form of "Blessed be the Lord, the God of Israel."

Scotland's oldest surviving book is a pocket-size Book of Psalms from the eleventh century.

Many kinds of psalms make up the entire 150-psalm collection. They seem to have been written for different occasions or purposes. As with the inclusion of psalms in Catholic liturgy, Jews of biblical times prayed psalms as part of Temple celebrations. There is no description in the Bible of *how* the psalms were sung in the Temple services, but it is presumed they were sung in a dialogue structure by two choirs or by a cantor with the congregation responding. For example, Psalm 15 was perhaps sung when a Jew requested entrance into the Temple. Psalm 24 may have been sung while traveling to the Temple. Besides use in liturgy, psalms were also written to pray communally or individually in times of sorrow (e.g., Psalms 3, 10, 38, 44), to offer praise and thanksgiving (e.g., Psalms 19, 33), and for instruction or retelling significant portions of the history of the Chosen People (e.g., Psalms 1, 104, 105, 106).

The psalms have been called "Jesus's prayer book." He prays from Psalm 22 while he is on the Cross: "My God, my God, why have you forsaken me?" (Mt 27:46). St. Augustine, who spent twenty-six years writing homilies on each of the 150 psalms, believed the psalms to be the principal food of Christian prayer (see *CCC*, 2762). From this supposition, St. Augustine also concluded that the psalms flow together in the petitions of the Our Father: "I do not think you will find anything in them that is not included in the Lord's Prayer."[3]

Our Father

Because the Our Father is included in both Matthew's and Luke's Gospels, it is worth examining the settings and occasions in each when Jesus taught his disciples this prayer. In Matthew's Gospel, the scene is the Sermon on the Mount. Large crowds are present. This is the part of the Gospel that includes the Beatitudes and instructions on law, anger, adultery, divorce, and more. In Matthew 6, Jesus begins an instruction on how to pray. He says to "not be like hypocrites, who love to stand and pray in the synagogues and street corners so that others may see them" (Mt 6:5). He tells them to "not babble like the pagans, who think they will be heard because of their many words" (Mt 6:7). At this point, Jesus introduces the Our Father by simply saying, "This is how you are to pray." He doesn't specifically say "pray these words" or "memorize this prayer." His presentation of the Our Father is consistent with how Jews prayed. Even with using the words of the Our Father, it seems that Jesus is reminding his disciples that their prayer should be spontaneous and from the heart as Jewish people were used to doing.

Luke's Gospel introduces the Our Father even more simply. Jesus was praying alone in a "certain place, and when he had finished one of his disciples

said to him, 'Lord, teach us to pray just as John taught his disciples'" (Lk 11:1). Jesus then gives his disciples the prayer in a manner similar to other teaching rabbis of his day. Arranged next in the Gospel, Jesus shares the parable of the friend who comes at midnight to ask for bread for an unexpected visitor (see Luke 11:5–8). The message of the parable (and the teaching that follows in Luke 11:6–13) is that we should be persistent in our prayer. Jesus's point again is that we should have the proper attitude of prayer, not just be reciting words.

The individual parts of the Our Father (shared below) are themselves profound and not meant to be "babble" in any way. Rather, they are intended to lead to the persistence of the knocking neighbor and the action of the man who got out of bed at midnight to answer a need.

➤ The Address of God as Father

"Our Father in heaven,
hallowed be your name"

Jesus's address of God as "Father" is something found previously in Judaism and documented in the Old Testament (see Deuteronomy 32:5; Malachi 2:10; Psalms 68:6; 89:27; 103:13; Jeremiah 3:4; 31:9). The use of "Father" for God was also in many Jewish prayers after the time of Jesus. Jesus's use of the pronoun "our" supports his words in the Last Supper discourse in John's Gospel that "I am in my Father and you are in me and I in you" (Jn 14:20).

Asking God's name to be "hallowed" or "blessed" was common in prayers of ancient Judaism. First Chronicles quotes King David blessing the Lord in sight of the whole assembly (see 1 Chronicles 29:10). When Daniel received a vision of God in a dream, he offered this blessing: "Blessed be the name of God forever and ever, for wisdom and power are his" (Dn 2:20).

➤ Petitioning for the Coming of God's Kingdom

"your kingdom come,
your will be done,
on earth as it is in heaven"

This petition sets the tone for the entire prayer. God's Kingdom, which is established in heaven, will now be implemented on earth. How would Jesus's Jewish disciples have understood this petition? The longing for the coming of God's Kingdom was always part of the tradition of Judaism. Since the destruction of Jerusalem and the Temple during the time of the Assyrian captivity in the eighth century BC, Jews had looked for a restoration of God's Kingdom as it had been in the prosperous times of the kings. The Old Testament has examples of Jews praying for God's Kingdom to arrive. For example: "Treat Zion kindly according to your good will, build up the walls of Jerusalem" (Ps 51:20) and "Afterward all of them will return from their captivity, and they will rebuild Jerusalem with good honor" (Tb 14:5).

Jesus's understanding of the coming of God's Kingdom differed from the Jewish understanding. While he inaugurated the Kingdom in his life, Death, and Resurrection, it is only in his return that God's Kingdom will come in perfect righteousness, peace, and joy. The petition in the Our Father indicates that all people have a responsibility for bringing God's Kingdom to its ultimate fruition.

➤ Petitioning for Our Daily Needs

"Give us today our daily bread"

Interestingly, the Greek word for "daily" is *epiousion*, which occurs in only two places in all of Greek literature: in the two versions of the Our Father found in the Gospels of Matthew and Luke. What this means is that there is no other context for understanding the word's meaning. How, then, did the Church come to associate this Greek term with "daily"? When St. Jerome translated the New Testament into Latin, he used two different words for *epiousion*. In Matthew's Gospel he invented a Latin word, *supersubstantialem*, which means "supersubstantial." However, when *epiousion* occurs in Luke's Gospel, he used another Latin word, *quotidianus*, meaning "daily." Finally, in a commentary on Matthew's Gospel, Jerome uses a third Latin word, *crastinum*, which means "tomorrow." The meaning of *epiousion* as "daily" became most used because earlier Syriac translations of the New Testament connected it with that definition.

Also, Jesus spoke of "daily needs" in some of his other teachings. He told parables that urge us not to store up treasures on earth (see Luke 12:20–21) and not to worry about what we are to eat or wear (see Matthew 6:25–31). Jesus intends that in praying for our "daily bread" we are to trust in God to provide for our needs. Additionally, this petition challenges us to remember the needs of others, especially our obligation to share with poor people. And the petition has a future dimension in that we pray for the fullness of God's spiritual blessings that will be ours in heaven.

➤ The Request for Forgiveness of Sins

"and forgive us our debts,
as we forgive our debtors"

"Debts" is used in Matthew's version of the Our Father metaphorically as debts we owe to God. This means that our forgiveness is conditional. God will have mercy on us as we have mercy on others. Think of the parable of Lazarus and the rich man (see Luke 16:19–31). The rich man who showed no mercy to the poor man Lazarus in this life will not receive mercy from God in the next.

The understanding that the forgiveness of our sins by God depends on our forgiveness of those who sin against us is also found in the Old Testament: "Forgive your neighbor the wrong done to you; then when you pray, your own sins will be forgiven" (Sir 28:2).

➤ Begging for Deliverance from the Evil One

"and do not subject us to the final test,
but deliver us from the evil one"

There were several nonbiblical Jewish apocalyptic writings from around 100 BC through Jesus's time that spoke of severe trials called "messianic woes," meaning that people would suffer and be persecuted before the end of time. The "evil one" refers to Satan himself. In one of these apocalyptic writings, the *Book of Jubilees*, there are prayers asking God to guide people through temptation and preserve them from evil. In one prayer, Noah asks God to protect his sons: "Let your grace be lifted up upon my sons, and do not let the evil spirits rule over them. . . . And let them not rule over the spirits of the living . . . and do not let them have power over the children of the righteous."

The Old Testament also has several examples that connect with the idea of asking God's protection from evil. For example, Psalm 5 states: "You will protect them, and those will rejoice in you who live your name" (Ps 5:12). The Book of Sirach has a similar statement: "No evil can harm the one who fears the Lord; through trials, again and again he is there" (Sir 33:1).[4]

The Lord's Prayer contains, in the form of petitions, everything that Christ came into the world to teach the human race about God, his gift of

SAYINGS YOU *Might Not Know* ARE FROM THE BIBLE

Focus Question: How is the Bible used in communal and personal prayer?

In ages before the printing press and when most people could not read, Christians could still recite many biblical passages. Typically, the Bible was read to them, and eventually certain passages took hold and became part of their lexicon. These days, biblical phrases have continued to make their way into popular culture. For example, many musicians have created lyrical melodies and refrains from the Bible, whether or not they knew the words they had chosen were biblical in origin. For example, "The Prophet's Song" by Queen was composed by the band's guitarist Brian May after he had a dream of a great flood as in the time of Noah. One of the refrains references Noah's invitation of pairs of animals onto his saving ark: "Ah-ah-ah-ah / And two by two, my human zoo / They'll be running for to come." More recently, Kelly Clarkson wrote a song, "Be Still," with Aben Eubanks inspired by Psalm 46:1: "Be still and know that I am God!"

Kelly Clarkson and Brian May

There are also many biblical passages that people speak in common parlance and, perhaps, without a clue that they come from Sacred Scripture. Here are a few along with their meanings:

A little birdie told me.

Used when you heard some information about someone else:

"*A little birdie told me* that tomorrow is your birthday."

For the birds of the air may carry your voice, a winged creature may tell what you say (Eccl 10:20).

As old as Methuselah.

Someone or something that is very old.

"My neighbor knows the history of this town better than anyone. He is *as old as Methuselah*."

The whole lifetime of Methuselah was nine hundred and sixty nine years; then he died (Gn 6:27).

No rest for the wicked.

Evil doers will never prosper and their work will never end.

"I've got so much to do, but I guess there *is no rest for the wicked*."

There is no peace for the wicked! says my God (Is 57:21).

Straight and narrow.

To behave in a proper or virtuous way.

"My husband and I never stay out too late and always stay on the *straight and narrow*."

How narrow the gate and constricted the road that leads to life (Mt 7:14).

Fight the good fight.

Persist in doing what is right despite any difficulties and challenges.

"She may not get the promotion, but she knows she will *fight the good fight* in making her case with the boss."

Compete well for the faith (1 Tim 6:12).

The Bible is ingrained in our culture and, despite any efforts of atheists and those who insist on its separation from our secular life, the Good News it presents is irreplaceable.

Further Study and Reflection

- Find and list three other passages from the Bible, like the ones above, that have been incorporated into secular sayings. Write a definition of the saying, use it in a sentence, and write the biblical passage and reference from where it originated.
- Memorize a biblical passage of your choice (minimum five verses). Share the passage by memory with your teacher either live or via a video recording.

salvation, and our response to that gift. For that reason, Church Father Tertullian said that the Our Father "is truly the summary of the whole Gospel."[5] Because the Our Father is used in liturgy, it is essentially a communal prayer: "[The Lord] teaches us to make prayer in common for all our brethren. For he did not say 'my Father' who art in heaven, but 'our' Father, offering petitions for the common Body."[6]

SECTION *Assessment*

Comprehension

1. How were the psalms originally intended to be sung?
2. What is twofold evidence that the Book of Psalms was originally five separate books?
3. What is the context for Jesus's introduction of the Our Father in Matthew's and Luke's Gospels?
4. What is unusual about the Greek source for the word *daily* in the Lord's Prayer?

5. Who is the "evil one" referred to in the Our Father?

Vocabulary

6. What are ways Jews pray the *Sh'ma*?
7. Explain the dating of the psalms related to the time of King David and the period of the *Second Temple*.

Reflection

8. Reflect on the words of the Our Father. What is something from your heart that comes to mind from the words of this prayer?
9. When is a time besides Mass that you regularly pray the Our Father? Why is this so?

Section 2

THE LITURGY OF THE HOURS

The Mass is the "source and summit of the Christian life" (*CCC*, 1324), a sacrament in which we are nourished with Christ's Body and Blood and also assisted in avoiding mortal sin. The effects of Christ's presence in the Eucharist linger in us even after Mass. Additionally, **Eucharistic Adoration** is one way that the Church is able to extend even more the graces of the Mass. You may be familiar with and have participated in Eucharistic Adoration, in which you sit and pray in Christ's Real Presence of the Blessed Sacrament apart from Mass.

Another connection with the Sacrament of the Holy Eucharist is the Liturgy of the Hours, or Divine Office. This public prayer of the Church praises God and sanctifies each day. Its connection with the Mass is primarily made through the inclusion of Sacred Scripture. The Liturgy of the Hours most commonly consists of the following:

- a time of Scripture readings (Office of Readings)
- Morning Prayer (Lauds)
- Midday Prayer
- Evening Prayer (Vespers)
- a short Night Prayer (Compline)

Each day follows a separate pattern of prayer with themes closely tied in with the liturgical year and the lives of the saints. The psalms, especially, are at the heart of the Liturgy of the Hours.

Eucharistic Adoration Eucharistic Adoration refers to any prayer before the Blessed Sacrament, where Jesus is present in the consecrated host. At certain times, the Eucharist is exposed in a monstrance and placed on the altar. This practice allows people to sit and pray in front of the Real Presence of Jesus.

Like the Mass, the Liturgy of the Hours is a prayer of praise and thanksgiving. The Greek word *Eucharist* is translated as "thanksgiving." The word *liturgy* is defined as "work of the people." The Liturgy of the Hours extends our gratitude and praise at all hours of the day. Both the Eucharist and the Divine Office bring Christ's presence into the world. The Second Vatican Council put it this way: "Christ is present when the Church prays and sings, for he promised 'Where two or three are gathered together for my sake, there am I in the midst of them.'"[7]

Who is to pray the Liturgy of the Hours? Priests are "called to remain diligent in prayer and the service of the word" by praying the Liturgy of the Hours. Religious, on the basis of their consecrated vows, are to pray the Divine Office as much as possible. Likewise, and at the instruction of the Second Vatican Council, the "laity, too, are encouraged to recite the Divine Office, either with the priests, among themselves, or even individually."[8]

Priests and religious pray the Divine Office regularly, typically, from the *breviary*, the name of an abbreviated or abridged form of the prayers of the Liturgy of the Hours. When a breviary was approved for use at the Council of Trent, it came to be used more popularly by priests. The Code of Canon Law to this day specifies the obligation of bishops, priests, and deacons to pray the Liturgy of the Hours daily if possible. Perhaps you have noticed a priest walking around the parish grounds by himself while carrying a black book at some point during the day. There is a likelihood that he is praying the Divine Office.

Fr. John De Guzman

Yet, in recent years, despite the opening of Liturgy of the Hours to all in the Church—including the laity—its practice has waned. When Fr. John De Guzman of the Diocese of Raleigh, North Carolina, was in the seminary in 2019, he happened upon a new way to promote the praying of the Liturgy of the Hours. "When I first starting praying the breviary, I was overwhelmed at the amounts of times and hours that were required of me to pray," he recalled. Beginning slowly by praying only Morning Prayer and Evening Prayer, by his fifth year in the seminary, he was able to grow into the discipline of incorporating the entire Liturgy of the Hours into his day.

And then something out of the ordinary happened. Seminarian De Guzman posted a picture of himself praying the daytime prayer one afternoon in a park in

Pinehurst, North Carolina. A friend of his suggested a hashtag to go along with the photo, so he added #BreviaryView with the "thought it might be cool to see where people who do use the breviary pray with it." The response was surprising and overwhelming as the ordained, religious, and laypeople began to add photos under the hashtag of themselves praying with the breviary in unique places. Today, the hashtag continues to have thousands of daily views on social media.

Fr. De Guzman has a couple of recommendations for those who want to start this practice themselves. First, he suggests starting slowly as he did, choosing one or two parts, called hours, of the Liturgy of the Hours to begin. He also advises using a physical book rather than a digital app, though there is nothing wrong with using an app either. Personally, he lists the Office of Readings as his favorite part of the Liturgy of the Hours. This part incorporates Scripture readings and readings from the Church Fathers, saints, and Church documents. "As they say nowadays, they are 'straight fire,'" Fr. De Guzman added.[9]

Brief History of the Liturgy of the Hours

Public prayer and worship began in Old Testament times. The Book of Genesis details that after Adam and Eve had another son, Seth, who in turn had a son Enosh, "people began to invoke the Lord by name" (Gn 4:26). The name *Enosh* translates as "human being." Regular and communal prayer using God's name (well before the time of Moses) was the start of formalized religion.∞ Later in history, King Josiah worked to reform religious practice and center it again on the Law of Moses. Prayers were standardized under Josiah, prefiguring the Divine Office. By the time of Jesus, Jews prayed regularly from Sacred Scripture, with most of the prayers coming from the Pentateuch and a **psalter**. Jewish men were required to recite the prayers daily, either publicly in a synagogue or privately in a special sacred designed place in the home. Jesus himself prayed in this fashion, participating in public prayer in synagogues.

Likewise, in the early Church, Christians developed a routine for daily prayer, which was often prayed in secret, in the catacombs, as Christianity

∞ Note

Recall that the Yahwist sources used in the formulation of the Book of Genesis employed the name YHWH well before the time of Moses (see the sub-subsection "Pentateuch" in Chapter 4, Section 1). It was Moses who was the first to use YHWH as the proper name for the God of Israel.

A priest reads a breviary after a Sunday Mass.

was illegal and punishable by death in the Roman Empire. In these surroundings Christians began to designate the third hour after dawn (9 a.m.), the sixth hour (noon), and the ninth hour (3 p.m.) as times for private prayer. By the fourth century, with Christianity legalized and part of the mainstream culture, monastic communities began to adopt the practice of reciting prayers throughout the day and into the night. There was no uniformity to the Divine Office prior to the eighth century, and even then, a complete recitation was difficult as several sources needed to be on hand: a psalter, the Book of the Prophets, the Book of the Law (Pentateuch), an Antiphonary (book of chants), the Responsorial and Hymnal, a Passional that contained the Acts of the Martyrs (later called the Martyrology), and the Sanctoral (calendar of saints). It was at this point of great need that the *breviarium*, or breviary, was developed to act as a concise summary of all of the material.

The breviary of the Council Trent was promulgated by a **papal bull** on July 9, 1560. It kept the tradition of offering the entire psalter—that is, the

---

psalter A prayer book that includes the Book of Psalms and other readings that accompany the Liturgy of the Hours. The term *psalter* derives from the Latin *psalterium,* which is the name of the Book of Psalms.

papal bull The name for an official letter written by the pope. The term *bull* comes from the Latin name for the leaden seal that was used to authenticate it.

Book of Psalms—over the course of one week; and it restored the balance between the **temporal cycle** (seasons and Sundays of the liturgical year) and the **sanctoral cycle** (feasts of saints). Over the years the feasts of the saints had increased—from 136 in 1568 to 266 in 1911—which had led to many of the psalms connected with the original feast days of saints being repeated because they were also connected with the feast days of the new saints. St. Pius X completely restored the psalter by distributing the psalms differently and reformed the feasts of the saints by combining certain feast days, eliminating others, and reclassifying even more to a commemoration instead of a feast.

The breviary was modified several more times after St. Pius X, leading up to, during, and after the Second Vatican Council. Part of this modification was due to the revisions and a new English translation of the Roman Missal in 2011. At that time, the United States Conference of Catholic Bishops determined that it would be a priority to revise the Liturgy of the Hours as there was overlap between some of the various prayers of the breviary and the Roman Missal; to keep the overlap, the breviary had to be revised when the Roman Missal was revised. The new translation of the breviary will also further the connection between the Liturgy of the Hours, the Mass, and other sacraments as well as allow for easier use by all, including the laity.

Praying the Liturgy of the Hours

You can never go wrong with praying throughout the day. St. Paul's instruction to the Thessalonians has stood the test of time: "Rejoice always. Pray without ceasing" (1 Thes 5:16). The Liturgy of the Hours is meant for everyone and offers a formula for keeping Catholics on track with their prayer and connecting them with the psalter, the Scripture readings of the day, and the words of the saints and Church Fathers. Still, the process can be confusing and discouraging if you do not approach it with a plan. Remember Fr. De Guzman's suggestion to start slowly. He chose to pray only two hours of the Liturgy of the Hours at first, usually Morning Prayer and Evening Prayer. That is one way to do it. Others have suggested praying three times a day, but doing fewer prayers and readings for those hours of the day. In whatever way you choose,

---

temporal cycle Refers to the "Prayer of Time" and is based on the liturgical year.

sanctoral cycle Meaning "holy cycle," it includes the feast days and memorials of saints as they occur throughout the temporal cycle.

a first step is to familiarize yourself with the principal parts of the Liturgy of the Hours according to the times of the day.

Office of Readings (Matins)

The Office of Readings is made up of two long readings. One of the readings is from Sacred Scripture, and the other is from the Church Fathers or saints. You can read these readings at any time during the day, but they are typically read immediately before Morning Prayer. The Latin name for this hour of the Divine Office is *Matins*, which means "relating to early in the morning." Monks often do these readings between midnight and 4 a.m.

The Office of Readings consists of three psalms or one psalm broken into three sections. Next is a reading from the Old Testament or New Testament. A person who prays with the Office of Readings for an entire year will read a majority of the Bible. The readings from the Church Fathers or saints are based on the liturgical season or the particular feast day of the saint.

Morning Prayer (Lauds)

St. Basil the Great wrote that Moring Prayer "is said in the morning in order that the first stirrings of our mind and will may be consecrated to God and that we may take nothing in hand until we have been gladdened by the thought of God."[10] Nevertheless, you do not have to set your alarm to pray Morning Prayer at daybreak or 6 a.m. This prayer can be prayed whenever you wake up.

Chinese Catholic worshippers pray during an early morning Mass at a village's Catholic church.

Lauds means "praise" or "acclaim." If this is the first hour you are praying, you begin Morning Prayer by saying, "Lord, open my lips, and my mouth will proclaim your praise." You also recite an antiphon, such as "Come, let us give thanks to the Lord, for his great love is without end," with an invitatory psalm, usually Psalm 95. Following the format and directions in a breviary (printed or digital), you then pray a hymn, three psalms, a passage from Scripture, and a response. Next, you pray the Canticle of Zechariah (based on Luke 1:68–79), intercessions, the Our Father, and a closing prayer. The hour ends with "May the Lord bless us, protect us from all evil and bring us to everlasting life. Amen."

Evening Prayer (Vespers)

Evening Prayer or *Vespers* (literally, "evening star") is prayed at the conclusion of the day, usually around 6 p.m. The prayer is spent in gratitude "for what has been given us or what we have done well, during the day."[11] Like Morning Prayer, Vespers is one of the major hours of the Divine Office. It starts by saying, "God, come to my assistance. Lord, make haste to help me," and the Glory Be. After that the format follows the same prescription as Morning Prayer, but with different psalms and readings, all located in the breviary. For Vespers, you recite the Canticle of Mary (the Magnificat, based on Luke 1:46–55), instead of the Canticle of Zechariah. Typically, praying Morning Prayer and Evening Prayer each takes about thirty minutes to complete (less if prayed by yourself).

Priests officiate a Vespers Mass inside the Notre-Dame de Paris cathedral in Paris.

Besides being a prayer of thanksgiving, Vespers recalls the sacrifice Christ previewed in the evening at his Last Supper and enacted the next day on Good Friday. In Evening Prayer, "we also recall the redemption through the prayer we send up 'like incense in the Lord's sight' and in which 'the raising up of our hands' becomes 'an evening sacrifice.'"[12]

In the Liturgy of the Hours, Lauds and Vespers are called "the hinge" as they are the most important hours.[13] If you are choosing to pray two hours of the Divine Office each day, these should be the two. While you may pray each hour by yourself, it is also appropriate for both Morning Prayer and Evening Prayer to be prayed in common, perhaps as part of a parish service. Vespers, especially, is "celebrated in common in church on Sundays and on the more solemn feasts" (*CCC*, 1175).

Prayers during the Day

Three other prayer times are shorter than Morning Prayer and Evening Prayer; these are known as the "prayers during the day" or sometimes the "little hours" or "daytime hours." They are intended for midmorning (*Terce* or "third"), midday (*Sext* or "sixth"), and afternoon (*None* or "ninth")—that is, 9 a.m., noon, and 3 p.m. The little hours developed in the early monastic age and are still prayed by monks today, mostly in private.

Midday Prayer is part of the Liturgy of the Hours.

All of the prayers during the day follow a similar format. The opening verses are the same as used in Morning Prayer and Evening Prayer. You start by saying, "God [make the Sign of the Cross], come to my assistance. Lord, make haste to help me." You then follow by reciting the Glory Be, bowing your head as you say, "the Father and the Son and the Holy Spirit." Then there are three psalms with antiphons, a Bible reading, and a closing prayer. Each of the three hours ends with "Let us praise the Lord. And give him thanks."

Night Prayer (Compline)

Compline (Latin for "complete") is a short prayer, the last prayer of the day said before going to sleep. It can be prayed while you are in bed. Like the prayers during the day, it is short and simple and considered one of the little hours. Compline is also used as an occasion for an **examination of conscience**. After the opening call to prayer and Glory Be, you review your day looking for sins and omissions, or you say the Penitential Act from Mass ("I confess to almighty God . . .). Compline then continues with a simple formula of a hymn, one or two psalms, a Gospel reading, the Canticle of Simeon (Lk 2:29–32), and a concluding prayer. Compline ends with an antiphon to the Blessed Virgin Mary, usually the Salve Regina ("Hail, holy Queen . . ."), or the Regina Caeli ("O Queen of heaven rejoice . . .) during Easter, though a Hail Mary is certainly appropriate.

---

examination of conscience An honest self-assessment of how well you have lived God's covenant of love, leading you to accept responsibility for your sins and to realize God's merciful forgiveness.

The primary purpose of exploring the Liturgy of the Hours and using it as a framework for prayer is that it extends the mysteries of Christ's Incarnation and Paschal Mystery into daily life, widening his presence from Holy Eucharist. Celebrated using an approved form, the Liturgy of the Hours "is truly the voice of the Bride herself addressed to the Bridegroom. It is the very prayer which Christ himself together with his Body addresses to the Father."[14]

SECTION *Assessment*

Comprehension

1. What Scripture is at the heart of the Liturgy of the Hours?
2. What are the two main hours of the Liturgy of the Hours?
3. Why was it important to revise the breviary after the revision of the Roman Missal?
4. What makes up the Office of Readings?
5. What hour of the Liturgy of the Hours is commonly prayed in church on Sunday evenings?

Vocabulary

6. What is contained in a *psalter*?
7. What hour of the Liturgy of the Hours is often used as an occasion for an *examination of conscience*? Why?
8. How do the *temporal cycle* and *sanctoral cycle* of the Divine Office differ?

Reflection

9. How do you understand the purpose of praying the Liturgy of the Hours?
10. What strategy would you employ to begin praying the Liturgy of the Hours?

Section 3
USING SCRIPTURE FOR MEDITATION

Besides being a source for both individual prayer and liturgical prayer, the Bible is a source of *meditation* in which "the mind seeks to understand the why and how of the Christian life, in order to adhere and respond to what the Lord is asking" (*CCC*, 2705). One goal of meditation is to see how God is revealed in everyday life, from the biggest events and experiences right down to the smallest of details. Such revelations can be found in several places: through the writings of spiritual fathers, works of spirituality, liturgical texts, historical texts, and particularly in the living Word of God in Sacred Scripture. The Bible is the prime source for Christian meditation.

Meditation using the Bible is known as *lectio divina* ("sacred reading" or "divine reading"). It was originally celebrated in early monastic communities by monks as they both prepared for Eucharist and prayed the Liturgy of the Hours. Lectio divina also relies heavily on the psalms as a source of prayer; however, other Scripture readings, including the Gospels, are well-suited for this practice. Oftentimes, Catholics use the Gospel readings from an upcoming or recently passed Sunday. Or you may choose a familiar passage or one you discover by paging through the Bible. St. Augustine once randomly opened the pages of the Bible to a passage from Romans 13:12, where he read it was time to "throw off the works of darkness and put on the armor of light." This experience was the catapult for Augustine to reform his life and seek Baptism. The method of lectio divina follows four steps: *lectio* (reading), *meditatio* (meditation), *contemplatio* (contemplation), and *oratio* (prayer).

Scripture is also used in combination with another traditional prayer, the Rosary. Praying a "scriptural Rosary" incorporates lectio divina. In a scriptural Rosary, you read a verse (*lectio*) before saying a Hail Mary (*oratio*), meditate on its connection to the overall mystery (*meditatio*), and further contemplate (*contemplatio*) its place in the entire life of Christ and in God's plan for our salvation.

As suggested in the steps of lectio divina, meditation leads to contemplation. Contemplation is more passive than meditation; in contemplation a person simply becomes aware of God's presence and rests in it, basking in God's love. Again, Scripture is a primary source for this form of prayer.

Praying a Scriptural Rosary

In considering a scriptural Rosary, it's helpful to first understand the history of the Rosary itself. The origins of the Rosary are connected with monks praying the complete psalter of 150 psalms. Laypeople had a desire to pray in this way, yet because for the most part they could not read and the psalms are too long to memorize, they could not develop this practice. At the turn of the ninth century, Irish monks suggested that laypeople might pray 150 Our Fathers instead of 150 psalms. This practice took off and became popular. At first, the people carried around 150 pebbles in their pockets to count the Our Fathers; then they began to use rope tied with fifty knots, and finally strings with fifty small pieces of threaded wood.

In 1072, St. Peter Damian mentioned another way to recite repetitive prayer, which became known as the *Angelic Salutations*. "Angelic" refers to the words that the angel Gabriel spoke to Mary at her Annunciation, which make up the first part of the Hail Mary. Some people continued to recite 150 Our Fathers, while others adopted the Angelic Salutations. In the thirteenth century yet another form of repetitive prayer developed. Theologians constructed 150 "praises" to honor Jesus that were based on the 150 psalms. This meant that during this era there were four psalters: 150 Psalms, 150 Our Fathers, 150 Angelic Salutations, and 150 praises of Jesus! In 1365, Henry of Kalbar, a theologian associated with the Carthusian order, divided the 150 Angelic Salutations into decades and inserted the Our Father before each one. For the first time, the Our Father and Hail Mary were combined into one devotion. In 1509, another Carthusian, Dominic the Prussian, attached a series of scriptural meditations on the life of Jesus to a Rosary of fifty Hail Marys. Nonetheless, there is a long-standing tradition in the

St. Dominic de Guzman

Church that in the early thirteenth century the Blessed Virgin Mary gave the Rosary with the three sets of mysteries to St. Dominic de Guzman, the founder of the Order of Preachers (Dominicans). In 2002, Pope John Paul II added the Luminous Mysteries on the life and ministry of Christ in his apostolic letter *Rosarium Virginis Mariae.*

Recent popes have reminded the Church of Scripture references connected with the Rosary and its four sets of mysteries, Joyful, Luminous, Sorrowful, and Glorious, that cover the life of Christ and Mary's participation in her Son's work of salvation. St. Pope Paul VI wrote: "The Rosary considers in harmonious succession the principal salvific events accomplished in Christ, from His virginal conception and the mysteries of His childhood to the culminating moments of the Passover—the blessed Passion and the glorious Resurrection—and to the effects of this on the infant Church on the day of Pentecost, and on the Virgin Mary when at the end of her earthly life she was assumed body and soul into her heavenly home" (*Marialis Cultus*, 45).

A scriptural Rosary is prayed the same as any recitation of the Rosary, but with each decade of a mystery focused on a particular event in the life of Christ. Before saying a Hail Mary on each bead, you read and reflect on a Gospel passage connected with that mystery. For example, the following ten Gospel passages are connected with the Third Joyful Mystery, the Nativity:

...... *Our Father* ....

...... *Hail Mary* ....

While Mary and Joseph were in Bethlehem, the time came for her to have her child. (Lk 2:6)

...... *Hail Mary* ....

She gave birth to her firstborn son and she wrapped him in swaddling clothes. (Lk 2:7)

...... Hail Mary ....

And she laid him in a manger because there was no room for them in the inn. (Lk 2:7)

...... Hail Mary ....

The Word became flesh and made his dwelling among us. (Jn 1:14)

...... Hail Mary ....

Now there were shepherds in that region living in the fields and keeping the night watch over the flock. The angel of the Lord appeared to them and the glory of the Lord shone around them, and they were struck with great fear. (Lk 2:8–9)

...... Hail Mary ....

The angel said to them, "Do not be afraid; for behold, I proclaim to you good news of great joy that will be for all people." (Lk 2:10)

...... Hail Mary ....

For today in the city of David a savior has been born for you who is Messiah and Lord. (Lk 2:11)

...... Hail Mary ....

And this will be a sign for you; you will find an infant wrapped in swaddling clothes and lying in a manger. (Lk 2:12)

......Hail Mary ....

And suddenly there was a multitude of the heavenly host with the angel, praising God and saying: "Glory to God in the highest and on earth peace to those on whom his favor rests." (Lk 2:13–14)

...... *Hail Mary* ....

So the shepherds went in haste and found Mary and Joseph, and the infant lying in the manger. When they saw this, they made known the message that had been told them about this child. And Mary kept all these things, reflecting on them in her heart. (Lk 2:16–17, 19)

...... *Glory Be* ....

...... *Fatima Prayer* ......

From the announcement of Christ's birth, to his Ascension to heaven and the Assumption of his mother, Mary, and her crowing as Queen of Heaven and Earth, "the prayer of the Rosary is," according to Pope Francis, "in many ways, the synthesis of the history of God's mercy, which becomes a history of salvation for all who let themselves be shaped by grace. . . . Through prayer and meditation on the life of Jesus Christ, we see once more his merciful countenance, which he shows to everyone in all the many needs of life."[15]

Meditation to Contemplation

St. John Vianney

Contemplation is, in one way, a more passive form of meditation. Rather than reciting rote prayers, in contemplation we often sit in silence. Think of contemplation as two people who share a deep friendship. There are times when they can simply *be* with each other. They are silent together, enjoying each other's company, whether sitting in the same room, taking a walk, or riding together in a car on a long drive. This kind of comfortable "being together" usually comes only after the friends have spent considerable time sharing and growing closer. Contemplative prayer can be compared to this special human experience.

Contemplative prayer is sometimes called passive because we don't have to do anything except be ourselves and put ourselves in God's presence. St. John Vianney, pastor of a small parish in Ars, France, in the nineteenth century, knew of an old peasant who spent hours and hours sitting motionless in the chapel, apparently doing nothing. When the saint asked him what he was doing all those hours, the old peasant said, "I look at God, he looks at me, and we are happy."

Lectio divina is a form of contemplation. The purpose of sacred reading of God's Word is not necessarily to cover a lot of territory or to use study aids or notes. Its purpose is simply to meet God through the written word and allow the Holy Spirit to lead you into a deeper union with him. Therefore, it is best to take a short Scripture passage, read it slowly and attentively, and let your imagination, emotions, memory, desires, and thoughts engage the written text.

SECTION *Assessment*

Comprehension

1. What are the four steps of lectio divina?
2. What is the difference between meditation and contemplation?
3. Briefly explain how praying a "scriptural Rosary" developed.
4. What did Pope Francis say about praying the Rosary?

Vocabulary

5. What does the Annunciation have to do with the Angelic Salutations?

Reflection

6. What is a favorite Scripture passage that you would like to meditate on? Why?
7. Use a metaphor to describe the meaning of contemplation.

Section 4

WHAT'S NEXT FOR YOU AND THE BIBLE?

You've spent this semester studying about the Bible—how it was created and formed, how it is organized, and how it should be understood and read. You may want to continue with Bible study outside of a classroom setting but wonder how to do it. Bible study should never be undertaken completely alone all of the time. Serious Bible study belongs in the Church as part of our common life together as the People of God. It is in Bible study groups that you have the ability to share your insights, your questions, and your wonderings. The good news is that most parishes sponsor Bible study as part of adult education, which you either qualify for on the basis of your participation in this course or are just on the verge of qualifying for based on your age. Many parishes also offer Bible study as part of their youth ministry programs. If your parish does not have any type of Bible study available, you and your peers could be catalysts for approaching parish leadership to begin one.

The United States Conference of Catholic Bishops offers some basic principles about how to start and sustain a parish Bible study group. Here are three general points:

1. Define your purpose.

Is your Bible study group's purpose to learn *about* the Bible, with classroom-style exegesis, similar to what has taken place in this course? If so, it will require a trained catechist to lead. The group's purpose, in this case, will be to study particular passages, read what Church Fathers and others have written about the passages, and likely comment on the passages with the group in a discussion format with light facilitation. On the other hand, if your Bible study group might function more as a prayer group, then no regular facilitator is needed. Each participant may take turns researching and preparing a prayer service around a particular long Bible reading or short passage.

2. Recruit leaders.

Once the purpose of the Bible study is determined, the type of leader needed will naturally follow. For example, if the purpose of the Bible study group is to connect with the weekly readings from Sunday Mass, the pastor or another parish priest who is also a homilist would be a natural leader. If the purpose is a deeper exegetical study, the leader should be someone trained in biblical scholarship. It is very likely that this person might come from outside of the parish and be designated to lead the group in consultation with the pastor. For a simpler prayer reading around the Bible, any person with the assistance of training by parish catechists (who will also provide Catholic source materials) can lead a Bible study. For a Bible study group focused on prayer and reflection, it may even be held in someone's home.

3. Establish the format of the session.

Whether exegetical or not in format, all Bible study groups should include prayer, direct proclamations from the Bible, and "regular reminders that we gather to encounter a living dynamic Word."[16]

Bible study groups can form without a leader, if necessary, as long as the group relies on Church-approved workbooks, guides, and suggestions for format and discussion. However, caution is needed. The Bible study program chosen should be Catholic-based.[17] Many Protestant programs interpret Scripture from a fundamentalist perspective and without reliance on how a Bible passage or book has been interpreted by apostolic tradition. In whatever form, Bible study should always be open to questions and dialogue.

While group Bible study is helpful and enriching, you should also be a regular and active Bible reader on your own. That said, many people have no idea where to begin and how to develop a regular routine for reading Sacred Scripture.

Eight Steps to Becoming a Bible Reader

Reading the Bible on your own is a gigantic and daunting assignment. Where do you begin? From cover to cover beginning with Genesis and ending with the Book of Revelation? Or with the Gospels while simultaneously checking the margin references to Old Testament passages and brushing up on those as you go? Maybe, like St. Augustine once did (see Section 3 in this chapter, "Using Scripture for Meditation"), you open the Bible randomly and choose a passage or two from the page you turned to. Other Bible readers follow the liturgical-year calendar and focus especially on the Sunday readings week by week. Mark Hart, a Catholic who goes by the nickname "Bible Geek," encounters many Catholics who want to start reading the Bible or develop a more consistent habit of doing so, but simply do not know where to begin. To help, he came up with eight steps to become a Bible reader—or a better Bible reader:[18]

Step 1: Pick a Time, but Not Just Any Time

While it's important to pick a consistent daily time to read the Bible, the time needs to work for you. For example, don't commit to reading the Bible early in the morning if you are not a morning person. Choose a time when you are most awake, focused, and able to give your full attention.

Step 2: Gather Extra Resources

Read commentaries on the Bible passages or biblical book you will study on a particular day. Introductory essays at the start of a book of the Bible are helpful. Also, margin notes at the bottom of a page provide excellent context. You may also invest in a separate Catholic printed or digital commentary to assist you in understanding what you are reading.

Step 3: Pray, and Then Pray Some More

Before you begin reading the Bible, call on the Holy Spirit to be present. Ask God, through the power of the Holy Spirit, to open your mind and heart to what he is communicating to you in the words you will read.

Step 4: Have a Plan

You should have a particular plan for how you will read the Bible. However, at first, don't try to read the Bible from cover to cover. Remember, the Bible is a library of books, not a novel. It's better to choose particular books and passages to focus on. One suggestion is to begin with the Gospel of Mark, the shortest of the four Gospels. It is a direct account of the life of Jesus. Also, see the sample Bible reading plans in the section "Deposit of Faith" in the Appendix.

Step 5: Get the Background

This step is connected with Step 2 and the resources you have collected. This is the time to use the resources to learn about the author and the basic themes, purpose, and context of the biblical book you will read from. When you know the background of a writing, the words will make much more sense to you.

Step 6: Remember That Sometimes Less Is More

Take your time when you read the Bible. Don't read until you get tired! Take plenty of breaks in your reading so that you can reflect and pray over what you have read. Use the periods at the end of a sentence as reminders to slow down. Also, use your imagination as you read. Put yourself in the story. Picture the setting. Place yourself in the scene.

Step 7: Write in a Journal

Make journaling part of your Bible reading. Consider these options in journaling: (1) Underline passages that are confusing to you or words you don't understand. Go back later to research the meanings rather than stopping in the middle to answer your questions. (2) Write your own reflections or prayers in response to passages that you find meaningful. (3) Write out a Scripture passage that is significant to you in the margin of your journal. This will help you to remember this occasion of prayer and call up the importance of this passage to you in the future.

Step 8: Put the Bible Down

Or, in other words, put the Bible down and share its contents with others. The Bible is the living Word of God, and it is meant to be shared with others through your words and actions. Also, invite others to learn about the Bible and the Good News that it offers through whatever help and encouragement that you can provide.

The Bible is a book for everyone. You don't need an advanced degree in biblical studies or theology to read and understand it. Jesus Christ, the one Word of Scripture, was a traveling preacher who walked around the environs of first-century Palestine. His primary audience was people who were poor and in need of repentance. His closest followers were mostly fishermen. They certainly were not great theologians, at least not by modern standards. The Bible is completely accessible. It is to be picked up and read. And it is to be shared with others.

Graces from Reading the Bible

There's an old saying that goes something like "your life may be the only Bible some people will ever read." French novelist François Mauriac took this a step further when he stated that "people don't criticize Christ. They criticize Christians because they do not resemble him." These insights underscore the necessity for having a personal, intentional response to Jesus's question "Who do you say that I am?" (Mk 8:29). We are not left without a resource to answer this question. We possess the knowledge base to arrive at an answer that includes the writings of early Church Fathers, the words of the saints throughout the Church's history, teachings from encyclicals, and passages from the *Catechism of the Catholic Church*. Primarily, however, it is through the Bible, and particularly the Gospels, that we are able to *learn about* Jesus, but more importantly *really know* Jesus.

Pope Benedict XVI gave an impassioned address to the World Youth Day audience in 2006 about the importance of the Bible in the life of the Christian. He said, in part:

> My dear young friends, I urge you to become familiar with the Bible, and to have it at hand so that it can be your compass pointing out the road to follow. By reading it, you will learn to know Christ. Note what Saint Jerome said in this regard: "Ignorance of the Scriptures is ignorance of Christ." A time-honored way to study and savor the Word of God is lectio divina which constitutes a real and veritable spiritual journey marked out in stages. After the *lectio*, which consists of reading and rereading a passage from Sacred Scripture and taking in the main elements, we proceed to *meditatio*. This is a moment of interior reflection in which the soul turns to God and tries to understand what his word is saying to us today. Then comes *oratio* in which we linger to talk with God directly. Finally we come to *contemplatio*. This helps us to keep our hearts attentive to the presence of Christ whose word is "a lamp shining in a dark place, until the day dawns and the morning star rises in your hearts" (2 Pet 1:19). Reading, study, and meditation of the Word should then flow into a life of consistent fidelity to Christ and his teachings.

St. James tells us: "Be doers of the word, and not merely hearers who deceive themselves. For if any are hearers of the word and not doers, they are like those who look at themselves in a mirror; for they look at themselves and, on going away, immediately forget what they were like. But those who look into the perfect law, the law of liberty, and persevere, being not hearers who forget but doers who act—they will be blessed in their doing." Those who listen to the Word of God and refer to it always, are constructing their existence on solid foundations. "Everyone then who hears these words of mine and acts on them," Jesus said, "will be like a wise man who built his house on rock" (Mt 7:24). It will not collapse when bad weather comes.

To build your life on Christ, to accept the word with joy and put its teachings into practice: this, young people of the third millennium, should be your program! There is an urgent need for the emergence of a new generation of apostles anchored firmly in the word of Christ, capable of responding to the challenges of our times and prepared to spread the Gospel far and wide. It is this that the Lord asks of you, it is to this that the Church invites you, and it is this that the world—even though it may not be aware of it—expects of you! If Jesus calls you, do not be afraid to respond to him with generosity, especially when he asks you to follow him in the consecrated life or in the priesthood. Do not be afraid; trust in him and you will not be disappointed.[19]

Pope Francis holds Holy Mass for World Youth Day 2023.

As a Catholic, reading the Bible will help you to be a participant in the words of Scripture. For example, as someone who is baptized you will be able to experience creation from the waters at the beginning of time, survive the waters of the Great Flood, cross the Red Sea with the Israelites, and sink into and rise from the waters of the Jordan River with Jesus as he is baptized. Likewise, when you receive the Eucharist, you will share in the fruit from the tree of life in the Garden of Eden, the manna in the desert with the Israelites, the great feasts of David and his successors as king, and the last Passover meal celebrated by Jesus and his Apostles. When this happens, you will make the story of God's People from the Bible your own story.[20]

SECTION *Assessment*

Comprehension

1. What type of leader is needed for a Bible study group that focuses on exegesis?
2. What type of assistance is needed for a leader of a Bible study group that focuses on prayer?
3. What is the best time to read the Bible?
4. Why is it not recommended that you read the Bible from cover to cover?

Reflection

5. What type of Bible study group would you prefer to be part of? Why?
6. What are two practical ways you can share your love for the Bible with another person?

Section Reviews

Focus Question

How is the Bible used in communal and personal prayer?

Complete one of the following:

- Look up today's Scripture readings for Mass. Write two or three sentences that either explain one of the readings or apply a lesson from a reading to your life today.
- Read James 1:21–24. Write two or three sentences explaining the meaning of this passage and how you might live its lesson.
- Outline the next three days of a Bible reading plan, listing the Scripture you will read. As you complete each day, write a one-paragraph reflection for each Scripture reading.

Introduction

The Bible and Prayer

Review Points

- The Bible is a primary source of prayer. Since the Second Vatican Council, all Catholics have been encouraged to use the Bible in meditative prayer known as lectio divina.
- Prayers from the Bible are used in the liturgy. At Mass, Scripture readings are heard over a three-year liturgical cycle. The homily explains the meaning and common themes of the readings.

Assignment

Find and list Scripture references for the following prayers prayed at Mass: Penitential Rite (Kyrie Eleison); Gloria; Holy, Holy, Holy (Sanctus); any of the Memorial Acclamations; and Lamb of God (Agnus Dei).

Section 1
Common Biblical Prayers

Review Points

- The preeminent Jewish prayer, the *Sh'ma*, comes from the Bible (Dt 6:5). Jesus prayed this prayer and cited its words when he was asked to name the first and greatest commandment.
- Jews and Christians share a love for the psalms as a form of prayer. The psalms are songs of praise that represent a variety of human emotions. Jews may have sung the psalms in Temple services. A psalm and a response is recited or sung after the first reading at Mass.
- The Our Father, or Lord's Prayer, is the prayer that Jesus taught to his disciples. Each of its petitions has references to other words or teachings of Jesus and to other Old Testament passages. Jesus taught the Our Father in a spontaneous way, indicating that prayer should likewise remain spontaneous and not a rote recitation of words.

Assignment

Print one example of a doxology and one example of a doublet from the Book of Psalms that indicate that there originally may have been five "books of psalms."

Section 2
The Liturgy of the Hours

Review Points

- The Liturgy of the Hours, or Divine Office, is the public prayer of the Church. It is a prayer that is prayed throughout the day, and it is for priests, religious, and laity.
- A routine for daily prayer has been a practice of both Jews and Christians throughout their histories. The breviary of the Council of Trent restored the balance between the temporal cycle (readings based on the liturgical year) and the sanctoral cycle (readings based on the feasts of the saints).

- The Liturgy of the Hours is made up of the Office of Readings, Morning Prayer (Lauds), Evening Prayer (Vespers), and other little hours throughout the day.

Assignment

Read the *Catechism of the Catholic Church*, 1174–1178. Copy one sentence in these paragraphs that is meaningful to you. Write an explanation of why this is so.

Section 3
Using Scripture for Meditation

Review Points

- The Bible is the primary source for meditative prayer. Using Scripture, the method of lectio divina (reading, meditation, contemplation, and prayer) is a way to forge a deeper connection with God.
- Praying the Rosary, and in particular a "scriptural Rosary," is another form of meditation that also incorporates reading, contemplation, and prayer.
- Contemplation is a more passive form of meditation. It slows down meditation so that we can simply be one-on-one in the presence of God.

Assignment

Research the history of the Angelus, a devotion prayed three times a day. How is the Angelus related to the Liturgy of the Hours?

Section 4
What's Next for You and the Bible?

Review Points

- Bible study groups are typically organized through parishes and have various purposes—for example, for exegetical study or for prayer and reflection.

- It is also important to do Bible reading on your own. While the process can be daunting, there are several suggestions to begin and reading plans to keep the process going.

Assignment

Examine the Sunday bulletins from five local parishes. In a chart, list the names of the parishes in one column and the types of Bible study groups or Scripture courses they offer in a second column. If the parish does not offer either, print "none" in the second column.

Chapter Projects

Choose and complete at least one of the following projects to assess your understanding of the material in this chapter.

1. Draw the Mansions of the Interior Castle of St. Teresa of Avila

The Interior Castle was written by St. Teresa of Avila in 1577. It is one of the greatest books on mysticism ever written. In it, St. Teresa begins with a vision of the soul as a "castle made of a single diamond . . . in which there are many rooms, just as in heaven there are many mansions." In the book, she details seven rooms or mansions, which she interpreted as an ascending journey of faith ending with a final union with God.

In an art medium of your choice, illustrate seven rooms of a castle that lead to God. Before beginning, research the description of St. Teresa's seven mansions. Incorporate her mansions into your "castle," and also be original in depicting seven stages that lead to God.

2. Create a Chart with Five Types of Prayer from the Bible

Five types of prayer present in the Bible are (1) blessing and adoration, (2) petition, (3) intercession, (4) thanksgiving, and (5) prayer. Do the following: Write a definition for each type of prayer. Next, find two examples of each type of prayer from the Bible. Copy the text and the verse. Arrange the definitions and examples into a chart.

3. Display Photos from Your Life to Accompany a Scriptural Rosary

There are five decades for each of the four mysteries of the Rosary: Joyful, Luminous, Sorrowful, and Glorious. Your task is to arrange a digital photo display of each decade using photos from your own life. For example, a photo of you as a newborn could represent the third Joyful Mystery, the Nativity of Jesus. A photo of you engaging in a strenuous activity, such as running a race, could represent the fourth Sorrowful Mystery, Jesus's carrying of the Cross.

A photo of you in Easter clothes might represent the first Glorious Mystery, the Resurrection. Alternatively, photos can indicate a virtue represented by the particular mystery. For example, a photo of your grandparent could signify someone who exhibited patience in suffering; a photo of you on vacation in a beautiful natural scene could represent hope in eternal life. Arrange the twenty photos in a digital presentation. Include the title of each mystery and a Scripture verse to describe the mystery with each photo. Make sure that your presentation is in a format approved by your teacher.

4. Paraphrase Scripture as a Meditation

One way to increase your understanding of Scripture is to paraphrase Scripture verses in your own words. This can be done by personalizing verses or rewriting verses that include concrete examples for your own life. Here are two examples:

> Blessed are the poor in spirit
> For theirs is the kingdom of heaven. (Mt 5:3)
> *My joy is in God alone on whom I am dependent. May I serve him forever.*
>
> Give us today our daily bread.
> *Lord, provide for my needs today and always.*

Paraphrase the Beatitudes (Mt 5:3–12), the Our Father (Mt 6:9–15), and one psalm of your choice in your own words.

5. Analyze and Perform a Christian Hymn

Philippians 2:5–11 is recognized as an early Christian hymn. Write a reflection on the hymn that includes its origins, authorship, and meaning. Include your own reflection about how the hymn applies to your own life. Next, research several traditional and contemporary Catholic musicians. Choose one favorite song, copy one verse and its refrain, and include it with your reflection paper. Finally, sing or play an instrumental version of the hymn on audio or video recording. Turn in the written reflection and the recording to your teacher.

Faithful Disciple
St. Benedict of Nursia

St. Benedict of Nursia

St. Benedict was born at Nursia, a town in Umbria in north central Italy, in 480. He was a monk who founded the Benedictine order and is known as the father of Western **monasticism**. Around 520, St. Benedict founded the monastery of Monte Cassino, about eighty miles southeast of Rome. From this community, St. Benedict wrote a famous *rule*, or standard, for monks that would influence the monastic rule for the entire Western Church. The Rule of St. Benedict is still practiced in monastic life today; it also serves as a model for the prayer and spiritual lives of all Christians.

The history of Monte Cassino and monasticism has roots in the fourth century, in the period after Christianity was legalized by the Roman emperor Constantine and Christians were no longer persecuted and martyred for their faith under Roman law. During that time, Christians began to seek out other intense ways to practice their faith. In every age, there have been Christians who have felt drawn to single-minded devotion to God in prayer, solitude, and communal living. In the early centuries of legal Christianity, some men and women withdrew from everyday life to go to the desert to be alone with God. There they prayed, fasted, read and meditated on the Scriptures, and performed other works of penance and sacrifice. They were known as *hermits*.

---

monasticism Religious life in which men or women leave the world and enter a monastery or convent to devote themselves to solitary prayer, contemplation, and self-denial.

Monte Cassino Abbey, Italy.

Before long, hermits saw advantages in gathering with others to live the same type of lifestyle in community. Monasteries were formed so that these men and women could share the burden of providing for food, shelter, and protection and could then devote more time to prayer.

Benedict attempted to seek a balance among three things: (1) public prayer at set times throughout the day; (2) regular reading and meditation on the Bible; and (3) manual work for the physical support of the whole monastery. Benedict's motto was *Ora et Labora*, "Pray and Work." In chapter 40 of *The Rule of St. Benedict*, he instructs, "Idleness is the enemy of the soul; and therefore the community ought to be employed in manual labor at certain times, at others, in divine reading." While the monks worked, they often combined their work with prayer by meditating on Scripture using lectio divina. Work and prayer remain the practice of the Benedictines today.

By following their rule faithfully, those who live a monastic life grow in deeper union with God. Monastic life also provides a strong statement about God's Kingdom. The witness that monks and nuns offer to the world is their dedication to the coming of God's Kingdom without being attached to the passing things of this world. This lifestyle—codified by St. Benedict—is intended to inspire all people to look seriously at their own level of commitment to God and prayer.

Comprehension

1. What is a name for people who withdrew to the desert to pray and fast?
2. Why were monasteries formed?
3. How did St. Benedict's Rule reflect his motto *Ora et Labora*?

Reflection

What are three ways you can combine prayer with your activities throughout the day (e.g., in the car, while exercising, etc.)?

Prayer

Meditation is an active turning to God using all the faculties of the mind, including the imagination. Meditate on Jesus's words on the Last Judgment. Follow these steps:

1. Assume a comfortable position. Relax and get ready for your time with Jesus.
2. Become aware of the Lord's presence. Focus on his love for you.
3. Slowly, meditatively read Matthew 25:31–46. Put yourself into the scene. Engage all of your senses. The Lord is separating the sheep from the goats. Listen carefully once again to his words.
4. Reflect by reviewing your life right now. What if you were to meet the Lord tonight at midnight? What would you say to him?
5. Let your thoughts wind down around this passage. Thank the Lord for his time with you.

Matthew 25:31–46

When the Son of Man comes in glory, and all the angels with him, he will sit upon his glorious throne, and all the nations will be assembled before him. And he will separate them one from another, as a shepherd separates the sheep from goats. He will place the sheep on his right hand and the goats on his left. Then the king will say to those on his right, "Come, you who are blessed by my Father. Inherit the kingdom prepared for you from the foundation of the world. For I was hungry and you gave me food, I was thirsty and you gave me drink, a stranger and you welcomed me, naked and you clothed me, ill and you cared for me, in prison and you visited me." Then the righteous will answer him and say, "Lord, when did we see you hungry and feed you, or thirsty and give you drink? When did we see you a stranger and welcome you, or naked and clothe you. When did we see you ill or in prison, and visit you?" And the king will say to them in reply, "Amen, I say to you, whatever you did for one of these least brothers of mine, you did for me." Then he will say to those on the left, "Depart from me, you accursed, into the eternal fire prepared for the devil and his angels. For I was hungry and you gave me no food,

I was thirsty and you gave me no drink, a stranger and you gave me no welcome, naked and you gave me no clothing, ill and in prison, and you did not care for me." Then they will answer and say, "Lord, when did we see you hungry or thirsty or a stranger or naked or ill or in prison, and not minister to your needs?" He will answer them, "Amen, I say to you, what you did not do for one of these least ones, you did not do for me." And these will go off to eternal punishment, but the righteous to eternal life.

Appendix

BELIEFS

From the beginning, the Church expressed and handed on her faith in brief formulas accessible to all. There are early formulas of belief in the New Testament, especially in 1 Corinthians 15. Early Christians continued to develop their understanding of the God who saves in Jesus Christ and in the Church, and they formed professions of faith to pass on for generations. These professions of faith are called creeds because their first word in Latin, credo, *means "I believe." The following three creeds have special importance in the Church. The Apostles' Creed is an early summary of the Apostles' faith. The Nicene Creed expresses the Church's faith in the Trinitarian God who saves in Jesus Christ. It was developed from the Councils of Nicaea (325) and Constantinople (381) and remains the common profession of faith between the Churches of the East and West; it is typically recited at Mass on Sundays. The Chalcedonian Creed (also known as the Symbol of Chalcedon or the Chalcedonian Definition) was issued by the Council of Chalcedon (451). This creed summarized the Church's understanding of the Person of Jesus Christ, rejecting the view that we can no longer distinguish Jesus's divinity from his humanity because they became commingled into one (the notion of a single nature in Christ).*

Apostles' Creed

I believe in God,
the Father almighty,
Creator of heaven and earth,
and in Jesus Christ, his only Son, our Lord,
who was conceived by the Holy Spirit,
born of the Virgin Mary,
suffered under Pontius Pilate,
was crucified, died, and was buried;
he descended into hell;
on the third day he rose again from the dead;
he ascended into heaven,
and is seated at the right hand of God the Father Almighty;
from there he will come to judge the living and the dead.

I believe in the Holy Spirit,
the holy catholic Church,
the communion of saints,

the forgiveness of sins,
the resurrection of the body,
and life everlasting. Amen.

Nicene Creed

I believe in one God,
the Father almighty,
maker of heaven and earth,
of all things visible and invisible.

I believe in one Lord Jesus Christ,
the Only Begotten Son of God,
born of the Father before all ages.
God from God, Light from Light,
true God from true God,
begotten, not made, consubstantial with the Father;
through him all things were made.
For us men and for our salvation
he came down from heaven,
and by the Holy Spirit was incarnate of the Virgin Mary,
and became man.

For our sake he was crucified under Pontius Pilate,
he suffered death and was buried,
and rose again on the third day
in accordance with the Scriptures.
He ascended into heaven
and is seated at the right hand of the Father.
He will come again in glory
to judge the living and the dead
and his kingdom will have no end.

I believe in the Holy Spirit, the Lord, the giver of life,
who proceeds from the Father and the Son,
who with the Father and the Son is adored and glorified,
who has spoken through the prophets.

I believe in one, holy, catholic, and apostolic Church.
I confess one baptism for the forgiveness of sins

and I look forward to the resurrection of the dead
and the life of the world to come. Amen.

Chalcedonian Creed

Following therefore the holy Fathers, we unanimously teach and confess one and the same Son, our Lord Jesus Christ, the same perfect in divinity and perfect in humanity, the same truly God and truly man composed of rational soul and body, the same one in being [*homoousios*] with the Father as to the divinity and one in being with us as to the humanity, like unto us in all things but sin (cf. Heb 4:15). The same was begotten from the Father before the ages as to the divinity and in the later days for us and our salvation was born as to his humanity from Mary the Virgin Mother of God.

We confess that one and the same Lord Jesus Christ, the only-begotten Son, must be acknowledged in two natures, without confusion or change, without division or separation. The distinction between the natures was never abolished by their union but rather the character proper to each of the two natures was preserved as they came together in one person [*prosopon*] and one hypostasis. He is not split or divided into two persons, but he is one and the same only-begotten, God the Word, the Lord Jesus Christ, as formerly the prophets and later Jesus Christ himself have taught us about him and has been handed down to us by the Symbol of the Fathers.

DEPOSIT OF FAITH

Deposit of Faith *refers to both Sacred Tradition and Sacred Scripture handed on from the time of the Apostles, from which the Church draws all that she proposes is revealed by God.*

Relationship between Sacred Scripture and Sacred Tradition

The Church does not derive the revealed truths of God from the Holy Scriptures alone. Sacred Tradition hands on God's Word, first given to the Apostles by the Lord and the Holy Spirit, to the successors of the Apostles (the bishops and the pope). Enlightened by the Holy Spirit, these successors faithfully preserve, explain, and spread it to the ends of the earth. The Second Vatican Council Fathers explained the relationship between Sacred Scripture and Sacred Tradition:

> It is clear therefore that, in the supremely wise arrangement of God, Sacred Tradition, Sacred Scripture, and the Magisterium of the Church are so connected and associated that one of them cannot stand without the others. Working together, each in its own way, under the action of the one Holy Spirit, they all contribute effectively to the salvation of souls. (*Dei Verbum*, 10)

Canon of the Bible

There are seventy-three books in the canon of the Bible—that is, the official list of books that the Church accepts as divinely inspired: forty-six Old Testament books and twenty-seven New Testament books.

THE OLD TESTAMENT	
THE PENTATEUCH	
Genesis	Gn
Exodus	Ex
Leviticus	Lv
Numbers	Nm
Deuteronomy	Dt
THE HISTORICAL BOOKS	
Joshua	Jos
Judges	Jgs
Ruth	Ru
1 Samuel	1 Sm
2 Samuel	2 Sm
1 Kings	1 Kgs
2 Kings	2 Kgs
1 Chronicles	1 Chr
2 Chronicles	2 Chr
Ezra	Ezr
Nehemiah	Neh
Tobit	Tb
Judith	Jdt
Esther	Est
1 Maccabees	1 Mc
2 Maccabees	2 Mc
THE WISDOM BOOKS	
Job	Jb
Psalms	Ps(s)
Proverbs	Prv
Ecclesiastes	Eccl
Song of Songs	Sg
Wisdom	Ws
Sirach	Sir
THE PROPHETIC BOOKS	
Isaiah	Is
Jeremiah	Jer
Lamentations	Lam
Baruch	Bar
Ezekiel	Ez
Daniel	Dn
Hosea	Hos
Joel	Jl
Amos	Am
Obadiah	Ob
Jonah	Jon
Micah	Mi
Nahum	Na
Habakkuk	Hb
Zephaniah	Zep
Haggai	Hg
Zechariah	Zec
Malachi	Mal

THE NEW TESTAMENT	
THE GOSPELS	
Matthew	Mt
Mark	Mk
Luke	Lk
John	Jn
Acts of the Apostles	Acts
THE NEW TESTAMENT LETTERS	
Romans	Rom
1 Corinthians	1 Cor
2 Corinthians	2 Cor
Galatians	Gal
Ephesians	Eph
Philippians	Phil
Colossians	Col
1 Thessalonians	1 Thes
2 Thessalonians	2 Thes
1 Timothy	1 Tm
2 Timothy	2 Tm
Titus	Ti
Philemon	Phlm
Hebrews	Heb
THE CATHOLIC LETTERS	
James	Jas
1 Peter	1 Pt
2 Peter	2 Pt
1 John	1 Jn
2 John	2 Jn
3 John	3 Jn
Jude	Jude
Revelation	Rv

How to Locate a Scripture Passage

Example: 2 Tm 3:16–17

1. Determine the name of the book.

   The abbreviation "2 Tm" stands for the Second Letter of St. Paul to Timothy.

2. Determine whether the book is in the Old Testament or New Testament.

   Second Timothy is one of the New Testament Letters.

3. Locate the chapter where the passage occurs.

   The first number before the colon—"3"—indicates the chapter. Chapters in the Bible are set off by the larger numbers that divide a book.

4. Locate the verses of the passage.

   The numbers after the colon indicate the verses referred to. In this case, verses 16 and 17 of chapter 3.

5. Read the passage.

   For example: "All Scripture is inspired by God and is useful for teaching, for refutation, for correction, and for training in righteousness, so that one who belongs to God may be competent, equipped for every good work."

Bible Reading Plans

There are many Bible reading plans available, both in print and online. There are plans to fit any goal you have for Bible reading: academic study, personal prayer, spiritual formation, group discussions, and so on. Likewise, there are reading plans to fit various approaches for reading the entire Bible. Among the approaches are the following:

Liturgical Year

Read the daily or Sunday Mass readings. All are available at the United States Conference of Catholic Bishops website (www.usccb.org).

Christological Approach

Focus all of your Bible reading on Jesus. Begin with the Gospel of Mark, then read the other Gospels and the New Testament Letters. Even when moving into the Old Testament, look for Jesus, the one Word of Scripture, in the readings that he studied or that prophesized his coming.

Thematic Approach

Choose a theme (e.g., social justice, Mary, discipleship, resurrection, suffering, anxiety, gratitude), and search (online) for readings that correspond to the theme. List them and read them in increments.

Individual Book Approach

Study an individual book of the Bible accompanied by a good commentary. Read the book from beginning to end while going back and forth to the commentary in order to get the background on chapters and passages.

Cover-to-Cover Approach

While not the best method for beginners (because the Old Testament is so long), many Bible reading plans today use this approach, with helpful and interesting commentary to keep you engaged.

Whatever plan you choose, make a commitment to read and pray with the Bible at least ten minutes a day. Lectio divina is a well-proven method to help you to keep this promise.

Lectio Divina

Pray with the Bible using lectio divina. Select your Scripture readings using one of the approaches suggested under "Bible Reading Plans" in the previous subsection. Then follow these steps:

1. *Read (lectio).* Select a short Bible passage. Read it slowly. Pay attention to each word. If a word or phrase catches your attention, read it to yourself several times.
2. *Think (meditatio).* Savor the passage. Read it again. Reflect on it. This time feel any emotions that may surface. Picture the images that arise

from your imagination. Pay attention to any thoughts or memories the passage might call forth from you.

3. *Pray (oratio).* Reflect on what the Lord might be saying to you in this passage. Talk to him as you would to a friend. Ask him to show you how to respond to his Word. How can you connect this passage to your daily life? How does it relate to the people you encounter every day? Might there be a special message in this Scripture selection just *for* you? Pay attention to any insights the Holy Spirit might send you.
4. *Contemplate (contemplatio).* Sit in the presence of the Lord. Imagine him looking on you with great love in his heart. Rest quietly in his presence. There is no need to think here, just enjoy your time with him as two friends would who quietly sit on a park bench gazing together at a sunset.
5. *Resolution.* Take an insight that you gained from your sacred reading, and resolve to apply it to your life. Perhaps it is simply a matter of saying a short prayer of thanks. Perhaps it is to be more patient with someone in your life. Let the word that the Holy Spirit spoke to you come alive in your life.

MORAL TEACHING

Morality refers to the goodness or evil of human actions. Listed below are several helps the Church offers for making good and moral decisions.

The Ten Commandments

The Ten Commandments are a main source for Christian morality. The Ten Commandments were revealed by God to Moses. Jesus himself acknowledged them. He told the rich young man, "If you wish to enter into life, keep the commandments" (Mt 19:17). Since the time of St. Augustine (fourth century), the Ten Commandments have been used as a source for teaching baptismal candidates.

I. I am the Lord, your God: you shall not have strange gods before me.
II. You shall not take the name of the Lord your God in vain.
III. Remember to keep holy the Lord's day.
IV. Honor your father and your mother.
V. You shall not kill.
VI. You shall not commit adultery.
VII. You shall not steal.
VIII. You shall not bear false witness against your neighbor.
IX. You shall not covet your neighbor's wife.
X. You shall not covet your neighbor's goods.

The Beatitudes

The word *beatitude* means "happiness." Jesus preached the Beatitudes in his Sermon on the Mount (see Matthew 5–7). They are as follows:

Blessed are the poor in spirit, for theirs is the kingdom of heaven.
Blessed are they who mourn, for they will be comforted.
Blessed are the meek, for they will inherit the land.
Blessed are they who hunger and thirst for righteousness, for they will be satisfied.
Blessed are the merciful, for they will be shown mercy.
Blessed are the clean of heart, for they will see God.
Blessed are the peacemakers, for they will be called children of God.

> Blessed are they who are persecuted for the sake of righteousness, for theirs is the kingdom of heaven. (Mt 5:3–12)

Cardinal Virtues

Virtues (habits that help in leading a moral life) that are acquired by human effort are known as moral or human virtues. Four of these are known as the cardinal virtues, as they form the hinge (*cardinal* comes from the Latin word for "hinge") that connects all the others:

- prudence
- justice
- fortitude
- temperance

Theological Virtues

The theological virtues are the foundation for a moral life. They are gifts infused into our souls by God:

- faith
- hope
- charity (love)

Works of Mercy

The works of mercy are charitable actions that remind you how to come to the aid of a neighbor and fulfill his or her bodily and spiritual needs.

Corporal Works of Mercy

1. Feed the hungry.
2. Give drink to the thirsty.
3. Clothe the naked.
4. Visit the imprisoned.
5. Shelter the homeless.

6. Visit the sick.
7. Bury the dead.

Spiritual Works of Mercy

1. Counsel the doubtful.
2. Instruct the ignorant.
3. Admonish sinners.
4. Comfort the afflicted.
5. Forgive offenses.
6. Bear wrongs patiently.
7. Pray for the living and the dead.

Precepts of the Church

The precepts of the Church are basic obligations for all Catholics decreed by laws of the Church. They are intended to guarantee to Catholics the minimum in prayer and moral effort to facilitate their growth in love for God and neighbor.

1. You shall attend Mass on Sundays and on Holy Days of Obligation and rest from servile labor.
2. You shall confess your sins at least once a year.
3. You shall receive the Sacrament of the Eucharist at least during the Easter season.
4. You shall observe the days of fasting and abstinence established by the Church.
5. You shall help to provide for the needs of the Church.

Understanding Sin

Being a moral person entails avoiding sin. Sin is an offense against God.

Mortal sin is the most serious kind of sin. Mortal sin destroys or kills a person's relationship with God. For a sin to be mortal, three conditions must exist:

1. The moral object must be of grave or serious matter. Grave matter is specified in the Ten Commandments (e.g., do not kill, do not commit adultery, do not steal, etc.).
2. The person must have full knowledge of the gravity of the sinful action.
3. The person must deliberately consent to the action. It must be a personal choice.

Venial sin is less serious sin. Examples of venial sins are petty jealousy, disobedience, or "borrowing" a small amount of money without the intention of repaying it. Venial sins, when not repented, can lead a person to commit mortal sins.

Vices are bad habits linked to sins. Vices come from particular sins, especially the seven *capital sins:* pride, avarice, envy, wrath, lust, gluttony, and sloth.

Steps for Celebrating the Sacrament of Penance

- Spend some time examining your conscience. Consider your actions and attitudes in each area of your life (e.g., faith, family, school, work, social relationships). Ask yourself: Is this area of my life pleasing to God? What needs to be reconciled with God? With others? With myself?
- Sincerely tell God that you are sorry for your sins. Ask God for forgiveness and for the grace you will need to change what needs changing in your life. Promise God that you will try to live according to his will for you.
- Approach the area for confession. Wait at an appropriate distance until it is your turn.
- Make the Sign of the Cross with the priest. He may say: "May God, who has enlightened every heart, help you to know your sins and trust in his mercy." You reply: "Amen."
- Confess your sins to the priest. Simply and directly talk to him about the areas of sin in your life that need God's healing touch.

- The priest may talk to you about your life and encourage you to be more faithful to God in the future, and he will impose on you a penance for your sin. The penance corresponds as far as possible with the gravity and nature of the sins committed. It can consist of prayer, offerings, works of mercy, service to neighbor, voluntary self-denial, sacrifices, and patient acceptance of the crosses you must bear. You should continue in acts of penance, prayer, charity, and bearing sufferings of all kinds for the removal of the remaining temporal punishment for sin.
- The priest will ask you to express your contrition or sorrow and to pray an Act of Contrition. Pray an Act of Contrition you have committed to memory. See the section "Prayers" later in the Appendix for an example.
- The priest will then extend his hands over your head and pray a prayer of absolution for your sins. You respond: "Amen."
- The priest will wish you peace. Thank him and leave.
- Go to a quiet place in the church and pray your prayer of penance. Then spend some time quietly thanking God for the gift of forgiveness.

PRAYERS

Some common Catholic prayers are listed below. The Latin translation for four of the prayers is included. Latin is the official language of the Church. There are occasions when you may pray in Latin (for example, at a World Youth Day when you are with young people who speak many different languages).

Sign of the Cross

In the name of the Father,
and of the Son,
and of the Holy Spirit. Amen.

In nómine Patris,
et Filii,
et Spíritus Sancti.
Amen.

Our Father

Our Father
who art in heaven,
hallowed be thy name.
Thy kingdom come;
thy will be done on earth as it is in heaven.
Give us this day our daily bread
and forgive us our trespasses
as we forgive those who trespass against us.
And lead us not into temptation,
but deliver us from evil. Amen.

Pater Noster qui es in caelis:
sanctificétur Nomen Tuum;
advéniat Regnum Tuum;
fiat volúntas Tua, sicut in caelo, et in terra.
Panem nostrum quotidiánum da nobis hódie;
et dimítte nobis débita nostra,
sicut et nos dimíttimus debitóribus nostris;
Et ne nos inducas in tentatiónem,
sed libera nos a malo.
Amen.

Glory Be

Glory be to the Father
and to the Son
and to the Holy Spirit,
as it was in the beginning,
is now, and ever shall be,
world without end.
Amen.

Glória Patri
et Fílio
et Spirítui Sancto.
Sicut érat in princípio,
et nunc et semper,
et in saécula saeculórum.
Amen.

Hail Mary

Hail Mary, full of grace,
the Lord is with thee.
Blessed art thou among women
and blessed is the fruit of thy womb, Jesus.
Holy Mary, Mother of God,
pray for us sinners
now and at the hour of our death.
Amen.

Ave, María, grátia plena,
Dóminus tecum.
Benedícta tu in muliéribus,
et benedíctus fructus ventris tui, Iesus.
Sancta María, Mater Dei,
ora pro nobis peccatóribus
nunc et in hora mortis nostrae.
Amen.

Memorare

Remember, O most gracious Virgin Mary,
that never was it known
that anyone who fled to thy protection,
implored thy help,
or sought thy intercession was left unaided.
Inspired by this confidence I fly unto thee,
O virgin of virgins, my Mother,
To thee do I come, before thee I stand,
sinful and sorrowful.
O Mother of the Word Incarnate,
despise not my petitions,
but in thy mercy hear and answer me. Amen.

Fatima Prayer

O my Jesus, forgive us our sins, save us from the fires of hell; lead all souls to heaven, especially those in most need of your mercy.

The Angelus

V. The Angel of the Lord declared unto Mary.
R. And she conceived of the Holy Spirit.

Hail Mary . . .

V. Behold the handmaid of the Lord.
R. Be it done unto me according to thy word.

Hail Mary . . .

V. And the Word was made flesh.
R. And dwelt among us.

Hail Mary . . .

V. Pray for us, O holy Mother of God,
R. That we may be made worthy of the promises of Christ.
Let us pray: Pour forth, we beseech you, O Lord, thy grace into our hearts; that we, to whom the Incarnation of Christ thy Son was made known by the message of an angel, may by his Passion

and Cross be brought to the glory of his Resurrection. Through the same Christ our Lord. Amen.

Grace at Meals

Before Meals

Bless us, O Lord,
and these thy gifts,
which we are about to receive from thy bounty,
through Christ our Lord. Amen.

After Meals

We give you thanks, almighty God,
for these and all the gifts
which we have received
from your goodness
through Christ our Lord. Amen.

Guardian Angel Prayer

Angel of God, my guardian dear,
to whom God's love commits me here,
ever this day be at my side,
to light and guard, to rule and guide. Amen.

Prayer to St. Michael the Archangel

St. Michael the Archangel,
defend us in battle,
Be our defense against the wickedness and snares of the Devil.
May God rebuke him, we humbly pray,
and do thou,
O Prince of the heavenly hosts,
by the power of God,
thrust into hell Satan,
and all the evil spirits,
who prowl around the world
seeking the ruin of souls.
Amen.

Prayer for the Faithful Departed

Eternal rest grant unto them, O Lord,
and let perpetual light shine upon them.
May they rest in peace. Amen.

Morning Offering

O Jesus, through the Immaculate Heart of Mary, I offer you my prayers, works, joys, and sufferings of this day in union with the holy sacrifice of the Mass throughout the world. I offer them for all the intentions of your Sacred Heart: the salvation of souls, reparation for sin, and the reunion of all Christians. I offer them for the intentions of our bishops and all Apostles of Prayer and in particular for those recommended by our Holy Father this month. Amen.

Act of Faith

O my God, I firmly believe that you are one God in Three Divine Persons, Father, Son, and Holy Spirit. I believe that your divine Son became man and died for our sins and that he will come to judge the living and the dead. I believe these and all the truths which the Holy Catholic Church teaches because you have revealed them who are eternal truth and wisdom, who can neither deceive nor be deceived. In this faith I intend to live and die. Amen.

Act of Hope

O Lord God, I hope by your grace for the pardon of all my sins and after life here to gain eternal happiness because you have promised it who are infinitely powerful, faithful, kind, and merciful. In this hope I intend to live and die. Amen.

Act of Love

O Lord God, I love you above all things and I love my neighbor for your sake because you are the highest, infinite, and perfect good, worthy of all my love. In this love I intend to live and die. Amen.

Act of Contrition

O my God, I am heartily sorry for having offended Thee, and I detest all my sins because of thy just punishment, but most of all because they offend Thee, my God, who art all good and deserving of all my love. I firmly resolve with the help of Thy grace to sin no more and to avoid the near occasion of sin. Amen.

DEVOTIONS

Devotions are external acts of holiness that are not part of the Church's official liturgy but are popular spiritual practices of Catholics through history and today. Catholics have also expressed their piety around the Church's sacramental life through practices such as the veneration of relics, visits to churches, pilgrimages, processions, the Stations of the Cross, religious dances, the Rosary, praying the Chaplet of Divine Mercy, wearing religious medals, and many more. Some popular Catholic devotions are included in this subsection.

The Mysteries of the Rosary

The Joyful Mysteries

1. The Annunciation
2. The Visitation
3. The Nativity
4. The Presentation
5. The Finding in the Temple

The Mysteries of Light

1. The Baptism of Jesus
2. The Wedding Feast of Cana
3. The Proclamation of the Kingdom, with the Call to Conversion
4. The Transfiguration
5. The Institution of the Eucharist

The Sorrowful Mysteries

1. The Agony in the Garden
2. The Scourging at the Pillar
3. The Crowning with Thorns
4. The Carrying of the Cross
5. The Crucifixion

The Glorious Mysteries

1. The Resurrection
2. The Ascension
3. The Descent of the Holy Spirit
4. The Assumption of Mary
5. The Coronation of Mary Queen of Heaven and Earth

How to Pray the Rosary

Opening

1. Begin on the crucifix and pray the Apostles' Creed.
2. On the first bead, pray the Our Father.
3. On each of the next three beads, pray the Hail Mary. (Some people meditate on the theological virtues of faith, hope, and charity on these beads.)
4. On the fifth bead, pray the Glory Be.

The Body

Each decade (set of ten beads) is organized as follows:

1. On the larger bead that comes before each set of ten, announce the mystery to be prayed (see above), and pray one Our Father.
2. On each of the ten smaller beads, pray one Hail Mary while meditating on the mystery.
3. Pray one Glory Be at the end of the decade. (There is no bead for the Glory Be.)

4. Pray the Fatima Prayer.

Repeat from step 1 with each of the mysteries.

Conclusion

Pray the following prayers at the end of the Rosary:

> Hail, holy Queen, Mother of Mercy,
> our life, our sweetness, and our hope.
> To thee do we cry,
> poor banished children of Eve.
> To thee do we send up our sighs,
> mourning and weeping in this valley of tears.
> Turn then, most gracious advocate,
> thine eyes of mercy toward us,
> and after this our exile,
> show unto us the blessed fruit of thy womb, Jesus.
> O clement, O loving, O sweet Virgin Mary.
>
> V. Pray for us, O holy Mother of God,
> R. That we may be made worthy of the promises of Christ.
> Amen.
>
> O, God, whose only-begotten Son, by His life, death, and resurrection, has purchased for us the rewards of eternal life; grant, we beseech Thee, that, meditating upon these mysteries of the Most Holy Rosary of the Blessed Virgin Mary, we may imitate what they contain and obtain what they promise, through the same Christ our Lord. Amen.

The Stations of the Cross

The Stations of the Cross is a meditative prayer based on the Passion of Christ. This devotion developed in the Middle Ages, as a way to allow the faithful to retrace the last steps of Jesus on his way to Calvary without making the journey to the Holy Land. Most Catholic churches have images or symbols of the Stations depicted on side walls to help Catholics imagine the sufferings of Jesus and focus on the meaning of the Paschal Mystery. Praying the Stations means meditating on each of the following scenes:

1. Jesus is condemned to death.

2. Jesus takes up his Cross.
3. Jesus falls the first time.
4. Jesus meets his mother.
5. Simon of Cyrene helps Jesus carry his Cross.
6. Veronica wipes the face of Jesus.
7. Jesus falls the second time.
8. Jesus consoles the women of Jerusalem.
9. Jesus falls the third time.
10. Jesus is stripped of his garments.
11. Jesus is nailed to the Cross.
12. Jesus dies on the Cross.
13. Jesus is taken down from the Cross.
14. Jesus is laid in the tomb.

Some churches also include a fifteenth station, the Resurrection of the Lord.

How to Pray the Divine Mercy Chaplet

You can use Rosary beads or special Divine Mercy Chaplet beads to pray the Divine Mercy Chaplet.

Opening

1. Make the Sign of the Cross.
2. Pray an optional opening prayer.

St. Faustina's Prayer for Sinners

> O Jesus, eternal Truth, our Life, I call upon you and I beg your mercy for poor sinners. O sweetest Heart of my Lord, full of pity and unfathomable mercy, I plead with you for poor sinners. O Most Sacred Heart, Fount of Mercy from which gush forth rays of inconceivable graces upon the entire human race, I beg of you light for poor sinners. O Jesus, be mindful of your own bitter Passion and do not permit the loss of souls redeemed at so dear a price of your most precious Blood. O Jesus, when I consider the great price of

your Blood, I rejoice at its immensity, for one drop alone would have been enough for the salvation of all sinners. Although sin is an abyss of wickedness and ingratitude, the price paid for us can never be equaled. Therefore, let every soul trust in the Passion of the Lord, and place its hope in His mercy. God will not deny his mercy to anyone. Heaven and earth may change, but God's mercy will never be exhausted. Oh, what immense joy burns in my heart when I contemplate your incomprehensible goodness, O Jesus! I desire to bring all sinners to your feet that they may glorify your mercy throughout endless ages (*Diary of Saint Maria Faustina Kowalska*, 72).

You expired, Jesus, but the source of life gushed forth for souls, and the ocean of mercy opened up for the whole world. O Fount of Life, unfathomable Divine Mercy, envelop the whole world and empty yourself out upon us.

O Blood and Water, which gushed forth from the Heart of Jesus as a fount of mercy for us, I trust in you! *(Repeat three times.)*

3. Pray the Our Father.
4. Pray the Hail Mary.
5. Pray the Apostles' Creed.

Body

6. On a large bead pray the Eternal Father.

   Eternal Father, I offer you the Body and Blood, Soul and Divinity of your Dearly Beloved Son, Our Lord, Jesus Christ, in atonement for our sins and those of the whole world.

7. On the ten small beads of each decade say:

   For the sake of His sorrowful Passion, have mercy on us and on the whole world. *(Repeat steps 6 and 7 for the remaining four decades.)*

Concluding Prayer

8. Pray the Holy God.

   Holy God, Holy Mighty One, Holy Immortal One, have mercy on us and on the whole world. *(Repeat three times.)*

9. Pray the closing prayers.

    Eternal God, in whom mercy is endless and the treasury of compassion inexhaustible, look kindly upon us and increase your mercy in us, that in difficult moments we might not despair nor become despondent, but with great confidence submit ourselves to your holy will, which is Love and Mercy itself.

    O Greatly Merciful God, Infinite Goodness, today all mankind calls out from the abyss of its misery to your mercy—to your compassion, O God; and it is with its mighty voice of misery that it cries out. Gracious God, do not reject the prayer of this earth's exiles! O Lord, Goodness beyond our understanding, Who are acquainted with our misery through and through, and know that by our own power we cannot ascend to you, we implore you: anticipate us with your grace and keep on increasing your mercy in us, that we may faithfully do your holy will all through our life and at death's hour. Let the omnipotence of your mercy shield us from the darts of our salvation's enemies, that we may with confidence, as your children, await your [Son's] final coming—that day known to you alone. And we expect to obtain everything promised us by Jesus in spite of all our wretchedness. For Jesus is our Hope: through his merciful Heart, as through an open gate, we pass through to heaven (*Diary of Saint Maria Faustina Kowalska*, 1570).

GLOSSARY

analogy of faith The analogy of faith holds that God's Revelation in Sacred Scripture is never contradictory. In other words, truth cannot contradict truth.

anthropomorphism Refers to instances in the Bible when God is described using human characteristics; for example, there are several instances when God "stretches out his hand" over the people (see Exodus 7:5; Isaiah 23:11).

apocalyptic From a word meaning "revelation" or "unveiling." Apocalyptic literature is a highly symbolic style of writing in which hidden truths are revealed within a narrative framework. These writings were usually written in time of crisis and used symbolic language to bolster faith by reassuring believers that the current age, subject to the forces of evil, will end when God intervenes and establishes a divine rule of goodness and peace.

apologist The name for a "defender of the faith." A Catholic who works to dispel false rumors about Catholicism and Christianity and who makes the faith appear more reasonable and acceptable to non-Christians.

apparition An appearance of a heavenly being—Christ, Mary, an angel, or a saint.

Ark of the Covenant The most important symbol of the Jewish faith. It served as the only physical manifestation of God on earth. The Ark was built while the Israelites wandered in the desert and was used until the building of the First Temple.

ascetic Characterized by the practice of severe discipline and abstinence for religious reasons.

Baal The Canaanite god of fertility, associated with storms and rain. He was the most prominent of the Canaanite gods and the one most often worshipped falsely by the Israelites.

beatific vision Seeing God face-to-face in heaven, the source of eternal happiness; final union with the Triune God for all eternity.

biblical criticism A general term that describes several ways to understand biblical texts in their original setting, for discovering the intention of the original author, and for examining their literary style. It includes form criticism, historical criticism, source criticism, and redaction criticism.

blasphemy Hateful, defiant, reproachful thoughts, words, or acts against God or the act of claiming oneself to be God. For Catholics, blasphemy applies in these types of actions against Jesus, the Church, and saints.

catechesis A term that describes a process of "education in the faith" for young people and adults with the view of making them disciples of Jesus Christ.

Chosen People A name to describe the descendants of Abraham who made a series of covenants with the one true God. The Sinai Covenant made through Moses solidified them as God's chosen ones. Other names used for the Chosen People in the Old Testament are Israelites, Hebrews, and Jews.

Christological Refers to the study of Jesus Christ; the academic effort to understand who he is.

Christology A branch of theology that studies the meaning of the Divine Person of Jesus Christ.

codex The name for an ancient book that used papyrus or parchment stacked together and bound rather than strung together on a scroll. The term comes from a Latin word that means "trunk of a tree" or "block of wood."

common priesthood The priesthood of the laity. Christ has made the Church a "kingdom of priests" who share his priesthood through the Sacraments of Baptism and Confirmation.

concupiscence Disordered human desires resulting from Original Sin that produce an inclination to sin, also expressed as "the rebellion of the 'flesh' against the 'spirit'" (*CCC*, 2515). Concupiscence remains even after a person has been baptized.

covenant A binding and solemn agreement between human beings or between God and people, holding each other to a particular course of action.

Day of Atonement The name in English for Yom Kippur, the holiest day of the year for Jews. It is a day when Jewish people ask for forgiveness for both personal and communal sins. A person goes directly to the person he or she has offended, if possible, asking for forgiveness.

deist One who believes in God based only on natural reason, not on any specific Divine Revelation or teachings of a religion.

Deposit of Faith "The heritage of faith contained in Sacred Scripture and Sacred Tradition, handed down in the Church from the time of the Apostles, from which the Magisterium draws all that it proposes for belief as being divinely revealed" (*CCC*, glossary).

Desert Father The name for Christians of about the fourth century who withdrew to the desert to live an ascetic life of prayer, fasting, and abstinence. Their teachings had a profound impact on the theology and spirituality of the Church and the development of monasticism.

deuterocanonical The term for the writings that are in the Catholic Old Testament but not in the Hebrew Scriptures. It means "second canon."

Diaspora A group migration or flight away from the homeland into one or more other countries. The word can also refer to people who have maintained their separate identity (often religious but occasionally ethnic, racial, or cultural) while living in those countries after their migration. The Jewish Diaspora began with the exile of the Jews from the Kingdoms of Israel and Judah and is considered to continue to this day for Jews not living in the State of Israel.

Divine Revelation The way God communicates knowledge of himself to humankind, a self-communication realized by his actions and words over time and most fully realized by the sending of his divine Son, Jesus Christ.

Docetism An early heresy associated with Gnosticism that taught that Jesus had no human body and only appeared to die on the Cross. The word *Docetism* has Greek origins and literally means "illusion."

Doctor of the Church A Church writer of great learning and holiness whose works the Church has highly recommended for studying and living the faith.

doxology A hymn or liturgical formula that offers praise to God. The doxology dividing the sections of the Book of Psalms is a form of "Blessed be the Lord, the God of Israel."

eschaton The final age and the end of human history, including the Last Judgment, the defeat of evil, and the creation of a new heaven and earth. *Eschaton* is the Latin form of a Greek word that literally means "last" or "most remote."

Eucharistic Adoration Eucharistic Adoration refers to any prayer before the Blessed Sacrament, where Jesus is present in the consecrated host. At certain times, the Eucharist is exposed in a monstrance and placed on the altar. This practice allows people to sit and pray in front of the Real Presence of Jesus.

evangelist The name for one who proclaims in word and deed the Good News of Jesus Christ. The "four evangelists" refers to the authors of the four Gospels: Matthew, Mark, Luke, and John.

examination of conscience An honest self-assessment of how well you have lived God's covenant of love, leading you to accept responsibility for your sins and to realize God's merciful forgiveness.

Exodus A foundational event in the history of the Chosen People that occurred when Moses led the Hebrews out of Egypt and slavery.

exorcism Public and authoritative action of the Church to protect or free a person from the power of Satan (i.e., demonic possession) in the name of Christ.

Fertile Crescent Also known as the "cradle of civilization" because it was the place where farming became prevalent, the Fertile Crescent is a crescent-shaped portion of the Middle East. Today, it is made up of Iraq, Syria, Lebanon, Israel, Jordan, Northern Egypt, the northern region of Kuwait, the southeastern region of Turkey, and the western portion of Iran.

Gentile A term for one who is not Jewish.

grace The name for God's gifts to us that are free and undeserved and that assist us in responding to his call to be his adopted children.

Gutenberg Printing Press The name for the first printing press to use movable type. It was created by goldsmith Johannes Gutenberg in Germany in 1440. It produced up to 3,600 pages per day in comparison to about forty hand-copied pages per day.

Hellenize A term with Greek origins that literally means "to make into Greek" in both form and culture.

hieroglyphic writing An Egyptian term that literally means "sacred carvings." This type of writing was first used exclusively for inscriptions on the walls of tombs or temple walls.

Holy of Holies A room in the ancient Jewish Temple that housed the Ark of the Covenant, the portable shrine that held the tablets on which Moses wrote the Law. This was a place where YHWH was believed to be present. Only the high priest could enter this room on Yom Kippur, the Day of Atonement.

homily A reflection given by a bishop, priest, or deacon based on the Scripture read at Mass or a sacramental celebration. The homily helps us to apply God's Word to our own lives.

hypostatic union The doctrine of faith that recognizes two natures (one human and one divine) in the One Divine Person of Jesus Christ.

Incarnation The assuming of a human nature by Jesus Christ, God's eternal Son, who became man in order to save humankind from sin. The term literally means "being made flesh."

inerrancy Refers to the belief that the Bible is infallible or without error.

infancy narratives The Gospel accounts of the birth and early life of Jesus found in Matthew 1:1–2:23 and Luke 1:5–2:52. The Gospels of Mark and John do not contain infancy narratives.

John Rylands Greek Papyrus Part of the collection of thousands of fragments of papyrus, mainly from North Africa and Egypt, housed in the John Rylands University library in Manchester, England. The John Rylands Greek Papyrus (Rylands Greek Papyrus 457) is a 2.5-by-3.5-inch piece of papyrus from the earliest surviving edition of John's Gospel, likely between AD 150 and 200.

Low Mass Prior to the reforms of the liturgy after the Second Vatican Council, a Low Mass was the name to differentiate it from a High Mass. In a Low Mass, the priest spoke rather than chanted the prayers that were assigned to him.

Magisterium The official teaching authority of the Church. Christ bestowed the right and power to teach in his name on St. Peter and the Apostles and their successors. The Magisterium is the bishops in communion with the successor of Peter, the bishop of Rome (the pope).

Magnificat A Latin term for "magnifies" that comes from the first word of the Canticle of Mary in Luke 1:46–55. A canticle is a song, and the Magnificat is likely the first song of Mary. There are four canticles in the Gospel of Luke. The other three are spoken by Zechariah (Lk 1:67–69), angels at Jesus's birth (Lk 2:13–14), and Simeon at the Presentation of the Lord (Lk 2:28–32).

messianic secret Several passages in the Gospel of Mark (e.g., 1:21–28; 1:32–34; 1:40–45; 3:7–12; 5:21–43; 7:31–37; and 8:22–23) indicate that Jesus directed even his own disciples to keep quiet about his identity. These passages have been termed the "messianic secret."

mezuzah A Hebrew word that means "doorpost." Practically, it consists of a small scroll parchment on which one of two passages is written: Deuteronomy 6:4–9 or Deuteronomy 11:13–21. The parchment is placed on the front and back doorposts of a Jewish home and on every door in the home except for the bathroom. The practice is taken from Deuteronomy 6:9: "Write them on the doorposts of your houses and your gates."

ministerial priesthood A unique sharing in the one priesthood of Christ received in the Sacrament of Holy Orders. By his ordination, a man is configured to Christ by a special gift of the Holy Spirit so that he can act as a representative of Christ, Head of the Church. As a representative of Christ, the ordained man is enabled to serve the common priesthood by building up and guiding the Church.

modernism A movement of the late nineteenth and early twentieth centuries that attempted to reduce Church teaching to modern advances in history, science, and biblical research.

monasticism Religious life in which men or women leave the world and enter a monastery or convent to devote themselves to solitary prayer, contemplation, and self-denial.

Mystical Body of Christ A truth that all of the Church—in heaven, in Purgatory, and on earth—is bound up and directed by Christ the Head. *Mystical* refers to the supernatural life we share with Christ, especially bound up while on earth through the sacraments.

natural revelation The knowledge of the existence of God and his basic attributes that can be derived by human reason while reflecting on created order.

New Jerusalem A symbol of the Church that is present both in heaven and on earth through the Communion of Saints. At the Last Judgment, the New Jerusalem will exist in the world transformed by Christ's Resurrection.

omnipotent An attribute of God that he is everywhere, unlimited, and all-powerful.

oral tradition The process of sharing stories and other important pieces of information by word of mouth.

papal bull The name for an official letter written by the pope. The term *bull* comes from the Latin name for the leaden seal that was used to authenticate it.

Paraclete A name for the Holy Spirit that means "Advocate." In John 14:26, Jesus promised to send a helper who would continue to guide, lead, and strengthen the disciples.

Parousia A Greek word for "presence." It refers to the Second Coming of Christ, which will usher in the presence of God's Kingdom on earth as it is in heaven.

particular judgment The individual's judgment immediately after death, when Christ will rule on one's eternal destiny to be spent in heaven (after purification in Purgatory, if needed) or in hell.

Paschal Mystery Christ's work of redemption, accomplished principally by his Passion, Death, Resurrection, and glorious Ascension. This mystery is commemorated and made present in the sacraments, especially the Eucharist.

pastoral letters Three epistles of the New Testament—the First and Second Letters to Timothy and the Letter to Titus—that are specifically addressed to individual pastors in the Church.

Pentateuch In Greek it means "five books." The term refers to the first five books of the Bible: Genesis, Exodus, Leviticus, Numbers, and Deuteronomy.

praetorium A Greek word that means "common hall." In this reference it refers to the governor's house, which belonged to Pontius Pilate.

Protoevangelium A Latin term meaning "first gospel" that is the initial sign from Genesis 3:15 of the Good News that God did not abandon humanity's first parents or their descendants after they committed sin. Eve's offspring (Jesus) would someday destroy the snake (sin and death).

psalter A prayer book that includes the Book of Psalms and other readings that accompany the Liturgy of the Hours. The term *psalter* derives from the Latin *psalterium*, which is the name of the Book of Psalms.

pseudonymous A work written under a name that is not the name of the person doing the actual writing. It was a common and accepted practice for disciples and admirers of great teachers to write works under their names to extend their legacies.

Real Presence The doctrine that Jesus Christ is truly present in his Body and Blood under the form of bread and wine in the Eucharist. The Bible is clear in declaring this teaching (e.g., 1 Corinthians 10:16–17; 11:23–29; and most definitively in John 6:32–71).

Rosetta Stone An ancient Egyptian stone that contained writings in several different ancient languages and led to the understanding of hieroglyphics. It was discovered in 1799.

Sacrament of the Holy Eucharist The liturgical action known as the Holy Sacrifice of the Mass. It "constitutes the principal liturgical celebration of the Paschal Mystery of Christ" (*CCC*, glossary).

Sacred Scripture The *written* transmission of the Church's Gospel message found in the Church's teaching, life, and worship. It is faithfully preserved, handed down, and interpreted by the Church's Magisterium.

Sacred Tradition The *living* transmission of the Church's Gospel message found in the Church's teaching, life, and worship. It is faithfully preserved, handed down, and interpreted by the Church's Magisterium.

salvation history The term used to describe God's presence and work throughout all of human history.

sanctoral cycle Meaning "holy cycle," it includes the feast days and memorials of saints as they occur throughout the temporal cycle.

Sanhedrin The seventy-one-member supreme legislative and judicial body of the Jewish people during Jesus's time. Many of its members were members of the Sadducee sect of Judaism.

scientism The belief that only knowledge obtained from scientific research is valid.

scribe Ancient Jewish record keeper who was trained in the earliest forms of writing before literacy was widespread.

Second Temple The Second Temple replaced the First Temple, Solomon's Temple, that was destroyed in the capture of Jerusalem in 587–586 BC by the Babylonians. The Second Temple was destroyed by the Romans in AD 70 except for the Western Wall or Wailing Wall. Modern Israel recaptured the Western Wall from the Palestinians in 1967 after it was out of Israel's control for nineteen years.

self-esteem A sense of happiness and contentment about who you are as a human being. People with self-esteem consciously appreciate their own worth and importance.

Shabbat A Hebrew word for "Sabbath." *Shabbat* essentially means "rest" or "cessation." The Jewish *Shabbat* is celebrated from sunset Friday until sunset Saturday. *Shabbat* is a reminder to Jews that God rested from the work of creation on the seventh day and that they should rest too.

Sh'ma The *Sh'ma Israel* or *Shema Yisrael* is considered the most important part of Jewish prayer. It is recited twice daily by observant Jews as a *mitzva*—that is, a religious commandment. In the Catholic Liturgy of the Hours, the *Sh'ma* is recited as part of Night Prayer (Compline) every Saturday.

temporal cycle Refers to the "Prayer of Time" and is based on the liturgical year.

theological virtues Three important virtues bestowed on us at Baptism that relate us to God: *faith* (belief in and personal knowledge of God), *hope* (trust in God's salvation and his gift of the graces needed to attain it), and *charity* (love of God and love of neighbor).

theory of evolution The belief that in the progression of a series of events living organisms accumulate changes over successive generations due to genetic inheritance and adaptive variation.

Torah A Hebrew term that, in the broadest sense, reflects the totality of God's Revelation. However, *Torah* most commonly refers to the first five books of the Old Testament, also called the "Law" or, in Greek, the "Pentateuch."

typology A form of biblical exegesis in which Old Testament people and events (types) are seen as preceding or foreshadowing New Testament people and events.

wisdom literature Collections of wise sayings, proverbs, and short stories that offer insights into the proper way to live. Hebrew wisdom literature began to be collected during the Babylonian Exile and the post-exilic periods.

NOTES

1. God Wants to Be Known

1. "U.S. Teens Take After Their Parents Religiously, Attend Services Together and Enjoy Family Rituals," Pew Research study, September 10, 2020, https://www.pewresearch.org/religion/2020/09/10/u-s-teens-take-after-their-parents-religiously-attend-services-together-and-enjoy-family-rituals/.

2. International Theological Commission, "Theology Today: Perspectives, Principles and Criteria" (November 29, 2011), https://www.vatican.va/roman_curia/congregations/cfaith/cti_documents/rc_cti_doc_20111129_teologia-oggi_en.html, 7, quoting Benedict XVI, *Verbum Domini*, 7; cf. *Catechism of the Catholic Church* (*CCC*), 108.

3. International Theological Commission, "Theology Today," 30, quoting Second Vatican Council, *Dei Verbum*, 9; cf. *CCC*, 81.

4. Second Vatican Council, *Dei Verbum*, 44, quoted in *CCC*, 82.

5. Pope Benedict addressed "The Mysterious Desire for God" in a general audience on November 7, 2012, https://www.vatican.va/content/benedict-xvi/en/audiences/2012/documents/hf_ben-xvi_aud_20121107.html.

6. Fr. Spitzer's teaching about "unfulfilled yearnings" is from Steven Hemler, "Five Human Desires That Point to God," *Strange Notions* (blog), May 29, 2015, https://strangenotions.com/5-human-desires-that-point-to-god/.

7. Peter S. Williams, "A Change of Mind for Antony Flew," bethinking.org, March 2005, https://www.bethinking.org/does-god-exist/a-change-of-mind-for-antony-flew.

8. Information on the premise of Dr. Avi Loeb quoted in Stacy Trasancos, "So Aliens Created Humanity in a Lab," *Catholic Answers*, January 18, 2022, https://www.catholic.com/magazine/online-edition/so-aliens-created-humanity-in-a-lab.

9. The "five ways" can be found in Thomas Aquinas, *Summa Theologiae*, I, q. 2, a. 3.

10. Second Vatican Council, *Dei Verbum*, 4, quoted in *CCC*, 66. See also 1 Timothy 6:14, Titus 2:13.

11. Quoted in Francis Mershman, "St. Hildegard," in *The Catholic Encyclopedia*, vol. 7 (New York: Robert Appleton Company, 1910), New Advent, https://www.newadvent.org/cathen/07351a.htm.

12. Quoted in Barbara Newman, "Hildegard of Bingen: Visions and Validation," *Church History* 54, no. 2 (1985).

2. How the Bible Came to Be

1. Brant Pitre, *The Case for Jesus: The Biblical and Historical Evidence for Christ* (New York: Image, 2016), 101.

2. John Burger, "What Is the Best Edition of the Bible for Catholics?," *Aleteia*, June 23, 2020.

3. Jerome, "Letter 108: To Eustochium," trans. W. H. Fremantle, G. Lewis, and W. G. Martley, in *Nicene and Post-Nicene Fathers*, Second Series, vol. 6, ed. Philip Schaff and Henry Wace (Buffalo, NY: Christian Literature, 1893), ed. Kevin Knight, http://www.newadvent.org/fathers/3001108.htm.

3. How to Understand the Bible

1. Peter Kreeft, "Fundamentalists," *National Catholic Register*, October 1988.

2. Pontifical Biblical Commission, *The Interpretation of the Bible in the Church* (1993), III.

3. Benedict XVI, "To the Participants in the International Congress Organized to Commemorate the 40th Anniversary of the Dogmatic Constitution on Divine Revelation 'Dei Verbum,'" September 16, 2005.

4. Citing Second Vatican Council, *Dei Verbum*, 32–33.

5. Joseph T. Lienhard, SJ, "Pope Benedict XVI: Theologian of the Bible," *Homiletic & Pastoral Review* (September 1, 2011). Cf. Second Vatican Council, *Dei Verbum*, 97.

6. John Henry Newman, *The Idea of a University*, 2.8.4.

7. Quotations are from Peter M. J. Hess and Paul L. Allen, *Catholicism and Science* (Westport, CT: Greenwood Press, 2008), 76, 175.

8. Adapted from Henry Karlson, "Truth Does Not Contradict Truth," *A Little Bit of Nothing* (blog), May 12, 2020, https://www.patheos.com/blogs/henrykarlson/2020/05/truth-does-not-contradict-truth/.

9. Much of this section is adapted from an interview with Hesemann in Paul Senz, "Archaeology and the Historical Truth of the Gospels," *Catholic World Report*, March 8, 2021.

10. This material, including the mnemonic device, is included in William L. Burton, OFM, *Abba Isn't Daddy and Other Biblical Surprises: What Catholics Really Need to Know about Scripture Study* (Notre Dame, IN: Ave Maria Press, 2019).

11. Quoted in Hannah Brockhaus, "Pope Francis Recalls Powerful Message from Pius XII 70 Years Later," *Catholic News Agency*, February 10, 2022, https://www.catholicnewsagency.com/news/250343/pope-francis-recalls-powerful-message-from-pius-xii-70-years-later.

4. What Is in the Bible

1. This information is paraphrased from Joel Schorn, "What Is the Relationship between the Old and New Testaments?" *U.S. Catholic* 79, no. 2 (February 2014).

2. Brant Pitre lists five traits of how the Gospels meet the criteria of an ancient biography in *The Case for Jesus: The Biblical and Historical Evidence for Christ* (New York: Image, 2016). Brandon Vogt summarizes those points and offers additional reasons in *What to Say and How to Say It* (Notre Dame, IN: Ave Maria Press, 2020).

3. Pitre, *The Case for Jesus*, 76–77.

4. Vogt, *What to Say*, 83.

5. Quoted in Joseph Pronechen, "Archbishop Sheen Makes a Superman and Christmas Connection," *National Catholic Register* blog, December 29, 2019, partial transcript from Sheen's television show *The Fulton Sheen Program*, episode 13, "Superman and Christmas," which aired in the 1960s.

6. Ibid.

7. John Paul II, Regina Caeli address, April 24, 1994.

5. Jesus and God's Kingdom Seen through the Synoptic Gospels

1. The classification of Jesus's teachings used in this subsection comes from Keith F. Nickle, *The Synoptic Gospels: An Introduction* (Atlanta: John Knox Press, 1980).

2. Benedict XVI, *Jesus of Nazareth: Holy Week—From the Entrance into Jerusalem to the Resurrection* (San Francisco: Ignatius Press, 2011), 244.

3. Felix Just, SJ, "The Passion and Death of Jesus," Catholic Resources, March 26, 2022, https://catholic-resources.org/Bible/Passion.htm.

4. Eusebius, *Ecclesiastical History*, 3.39.16.

6. Christology in the Gospel of John

1. See Thomas Aquinas, *Summa Theologiae*, I, q. 37, a. 1

2. Benedict XVI, *Jesus of Nazareth: From the Baptism in the Jordan to the Transfiguration*, trans. Adrian J. Walker (New York: Doubleday, 2007), 7.

3. Felix Just, SJ, "'Signs' in the Fourth Gospel," Catholic Resources, March 26, 2022, https://catholic-resources.org/John/Themes-Signs.htm.

4. Information is summarized from Felix Just, SJ, "'Believing' in the Fourth Gospel," July 8, 2013, https://catholic-resources.org/John/Themes-Believe.htm.

5. Quintilian, *Institutio Oratoria*, book 1, preface, 7 (LCL 1:8–9).

7. The Bible Shares Christ's Mission as Priest, Prophet, and King

1. Augustine, *Enarrationes in Psalmos*, 103, 4, 1: PL 37, 1378; cf. Ps 104; Jn 1; quoted in *CCC*, 102.

2. Thomas Aquinas, *Summa Theologiae*, III, q. 22, a. 6; see Marcus Benedict Peter, "Christ, Melchizedek, and the Eucharistic Sacrifice," *Homiletic & Pastoral Review*, September 2, 2018, https://www.hprweb.com/2018/09/christ-melchizedek-and-the-eucharistic-sacrifice/#fnref-22045-6.

3. John Paul II, general audience, November 16, 2011.

4. Thomas Aquinas, *In ad Hebraeos*, 8, 4, quoted in *CCC*, 1545.

5. Second Vatican Council, *Lumen Gentium*, 21, citing 1 Corinthians 4:1.

6. Stephen Beal, "Why Christ Is the Alpha and the Omega," October 17, 2016, *Catholic Exchange*, https://catholicexchange.com/christ-alpha-and-the-omega/.

7. Joseph Ratzinger, *Introduction to Christianity*, trans. J. R. Foster (San Francisco: Ignatius Press, 1990), 247.

8. Information on the pelican as a Christian symbol drawn from Fr. William Saunders, "The Symbolism of the Pelican," *Arlington Catholic Herald*, November 20, 2003.

9. John Paul II, Regina Caeli, April 24, 1994.

8. The Bible in the Life of the Church

1. United States Conference of Catholic Bishops, "Understanding the Bible," USCCB, 2023, https://www.usccb.org/bible/understanding-the-bible.

2. Ambrose, "On the Duties of Ministers," quoted in Second Vatican Council, *Dei Verbum*, 25.

3. Augustine, *Epistulae* 130, 12, 22: PL 33, 503, quoted in *CCC*, 2762.

4. The section on the Our Father was adapted from William L. Burton, OFM, *Abba Isn't Daddy and Other Biblical Surprises: What Catholics Really Need to Know about Scripture Study* (Notre Dame, IN: Ave Maria Press, 2019).

5. Tertullian, *De oratione*, 1: PL 1, 1155, quoted in *CCC*, 2761.

6. John Chrysostom, *Homiliae in Mattaeum* 19, 4: PG 57, 278, quoted in *CCC*, 2768.

7. Second Vatican Council, *Sacrosanctum Concilium*, 7, quoting Matthew 18:20.

8. Both quotations are from Second Vatican Council, *Sacrosanctum Concilium*, 100, quoted in *CCC*, 1175.

9. Quotations are from Fr. Edward Looney, "The Seminarian and Story behind a Viral Catholic Hashtag, #BreviaryViews," July, 2, 2019, *Aleteia*, https://aleteia.org/2019/07/02/the-seminarian-and-story-behind-a-viral-catholic-hashtag-breviaryviews/.

10. Basil the Great, *Regulae fusius tractatae*, Resp. 37, 3: PG 31, 1014, quoted in Congregation for Divine Worship, *General Instruction on the Liturgy of the Hours*, 38.

11. Ibid., 39.

12. Basil the Great, *Regulae fusius tractatae*, resp. 37, 3: PG 31, 1015; and see Psalm 141:2, quoted in Congregation for Divine Worship, *General Instruction on the Liturgy of the Hours*, 39.

13. Congregation for Divine Worship, *General Instruction on the Liturgy of the Hours*, 29.

14. Second Vatican Council, *Sacrosanctum Concilium*, 84, quoted in *CCC*, 1174.

15. Pope Francis, meditation at the Marian vigil for the Extraordinary Jubilee of Mercy, October 8, 2016.

16. This quotation and the organization of this section is taken from United States Conference of Catholic Bishops, "How to Start and Sustain Parish Bible Study," USCCB, 2015, https://www.usccb.org/bible/national-bible-week/upload/bible-study-groups.pdf.

17. A Catholic-based Bible study ought to be familiar with the statement by the Pontifical Biblical Commission, "The Interpretation of the Bible in the Church," to Pope John Paul II on April 23, 1993.

18. From Mark Hart, "Eight Steps to Becoming a Bible Reader," *The Ave Catholic Notetaking Bible* (Notre Dame, IN: Ave Maria Press, 2021).

19. Benedict XVI, message to the youth of the world on the occasion of the 21st World Youth Day, April 9, 2006.

20. The benefits of Bible reading are adapted from John Bergsma, *Bible Basics for Catholics: A New Picture of Salvation History* (Notre Dame, IN: Ave Maria Press, 2015).

SUBJECT INDEX

PRIMARY SOURCE INDEX

CATECHISM OF THE CATHOLIC CHURCH (CCC) INDEX

SCRIPTURE INDEX

Old Testament

New Testament

PHOTO CREDITS

Alamy
pages 2, 6, 26, 80, 94, 125, 162, 170, 228, 244, 254, 279, 291, 315, 322, 331, 337, 348, 356, 358, 400

BibleMapper.com
page 250

Bridgeman Images
pages 309, 310, 311, 329

Cathopic
page 35

Getty
pages 2, 4, 5, 8, 10, 13, 16, 22, 24, 25, 27, 28, 29, 34, 36, 37, 39, 48, 54, 56, 57, 60, 63, 65, 66, 73, 75, 77, 83, 84, 86, 87, 89, 90, 104, 110, 112, 113, 114, 118, 121, 122, 123, 124, 129, 130, 134, 138, 140, 141, 142, 145, 146, 156, 164, 165, 166, 167, 171, 172, 173, 175, 177, 178, 180, 181, 183, 185, 186, 188, 190, 191, 192, 193, 194, 196, 197, 201, 204, 206, 207, 211, 222, 226, 229, 231, 235, 237, 238, 239, 240, 241, 242, 246, 248, 250, 253, 258, 259, 260, 262, 263, 264, 266, 269, 271, 272, 274, 275, 276, 280, 281, 282, 296, 298, 299, 300, 303, 308, 310, 314, 316, 319, 320, 321, 326, 327, 334, 335, 336, 338, 349, 350, 354, 357, 360, 361, 363, 365, 368, 369, 372, 380, 381, 382, 384, 385, 394, 395, 396, 397, 402, 403, 405, 406, 407, 409, 410, 414, 418, 421, 423, 424, 425, 426, 428, 429, 430, 434, 435, 439, 440, 448, 449, 474

Granger
pages 79, 233

Shutterstock
page 17

Superstock
pages 128, 209, 324, 374